Becoming a

Whole
Man

❧———❧

Principles and Archetypes

David Matheson, m.s.

CONTENTS

Acknowledgments

I wish to thank the many men who have allowed me to observe their lives in a very personal way. It is they, most of all, who have inspired what is written here. Especially I want to thank those who participated in the groups where I experimented with early versions of the material that has grown into this book.

I must acknowledge the pioneers of the modern "gathering of men"—Robert Moore, Douglas Gillette, and Robert Bly. Their interpretations of the philosophies of Carl Jung, as well as their own research and personal wisdom, laid the foundation on which much of my thinking is based.

Thanks to Peggy and to our children Katherine, Grant, and Jon for lending me to this cause—not just during the writing of this book but over many years as I've feverishly labored on so many projects. And thanks to Susan Christiansen for her tireless work and to Michael and Sarah for supporting her obsession with helping me.

And I most humbly acknowledge the Higher Power who is the source of all good things that are created. I am the weak conduit attempting to bring more of his light into this world.

INTRODUCTION

didn't want to write a book on how to *not* be gay. Being well over twenty years into my own journey with same–sex attraction at the time of this writing—and with the advantage of more than fifteen years experience as a therapist working with hundreds of other men on that same journey—I've developed some very strong beliefs about what it takes to successfully resolve unwanted same–sex attraction. Among the most core of those beliefs is that we are most successful in that process when we feel whole as men. So rather than writing another book that laments the problems people face related to homosexuality, I've written a book about masculine wholeness. We have enough of the former and precious few of the latter.

The idea that masculine wholeness is the surest help for those who want to resolve their unwanted same–sex attraction could raise a few questions in some people's minds. If I've done my job right, those questions will be answered by reading the book. But, for the sake of the skeptic or critic, a few basic questions should be answered right up front before you invest in a thorough reading.

First of all, you might ask, "What exactly do you mean by masculinity?" Masculinity is a concept that is as mysterious as it is mundane. Masculinity is around us all the time and yet we are hard–pressed to define it. On the simplest level, masculinity may be described as the expressions of maleness—that which men spontaneously manifest when they are connected to their manhood. We can understand it best by watching how men express it. When men are disconnected from their maleness, they appear to be "unmasculine"—they don't reflect maleness. When they are connected to their maleness, masculinity is their natural expression of self. When men are living from their "shadow" side, we see their masculinity as dark and ugly. But when they're whole, they reflect a masculinity that seems full of power and grace. The manifestations of maleness are diverse, appearing in literally billions of unique forms around the world. Indeed, every male reflects aspects of masculinity.

A second question you might ask is, "What do you mean by wholeness?" Wholeness implies balance, moderation, and integration of all our parts and potentials. For men, it means that all of our essential male traits are online and active, integrated into a functioning, unified Self.

This may beg the question, "Are you saying that wholeness will cure homosexuality?" No, I'm not. I haven't found anything that "cures" homosexuality. Cure implies getting rid of a disease. Homosexuality is not a disease. Nor is it, in my experience, something one simply gets rid of. But it is something one can diminish, give different meaning to, and move to the sidelines in one's life. This is why I use the term "resolve" when I speak of journeying with unwanted same–sex attraction. "Resolve" can imply clearing something up, reaching a decision, or creating consonance out of dissonance. That's a good way to think of the kinds of changes that wholeness can bring to your journey. It's vital, though, that we view resolving same–sex attraction as an imperfect and ongoing process—not as a short path leading to a final conclusion. In this way it's much like many other character traits a person might want to change.

"So then, how does wholeness help resolve same–sex attraction?" A very good question—and I don't fully know the answer. I know it decreases shame, isolation, and anxiety while increasing resilience, contentment, and peacefulness. In turn, this seems to diminish the intensity and compulsiveness of sexual desires for other men. I know wholeness intensifies feelings of masculinity and maximizes a sense of belonging among other men, which tend to enhance one's male identity and fulfill normal needs for male–male connection. And I know wholeness brings greater focus to the natural distinctions between males and females, which heightens awareness of gender.

Why, how, and whether these effects bring about shifts in sexual feelings is as speculative as it is individual. Some men experience a dramatic drop in homosexual desires. Some feel the emergence or intensification of attractions to women. And some experience only moderate, or even minimal, shifts in their sexual disposition. A better understanding of these phenomena awaits agenda–free, bipartisan scientific study.

Next you might ask, "So if wholeness helps resolve homosexuality, do you assume that straight men are whole and gay men aren't?" No, I don't. Masculine wholeness is in short supply these days among all men, regardless of which team they bat for. While I make no secret of my belief that, for most men with same–sex attraction, homosexuality emerges out of gender disruption (which is a lack of wholeness), that doesn't mean straight guys don't experience disruptions to their wholeness. Though I believe we're all born whole, no one makes it through childhood unscathed.

"Hmm," you might ponder. "So you think homosexuality is caused by issues in childhood?" Yes, I do. And so is heterosexuality. I believe our hardwiring disposes us to develop a sexual propensity of some kind. But the specific target of our sexual and romantic desires is, I believe, developed largely through childhood experiences. In terms of outcome, the clear norm for this biological/developmental process is heterosexual, as evidenced by statistics showing that over 96 percent of the population identify as heterosexual. But for a wide variety of reasons, this process can also lead to homosexuality or bisexuality, and does so for 3.5 percent of the population.[1] And a certain number of individuals develop some other type of sexuality, including asexuality. More and better scientific research could disprove the theories I believe in. But such research wouldn't change the lived experience of those of us who have felt changes in our sexuality.

"So if homosexuality is a minority occurrence, is caused by stuff in childhood, and can change, does that justify prejudice against gays or efforts to make them change?" No, why would it? If we are going to call ourselves a civilized society, we must defend the right of individuals to respond to their sexual feelings in any way they please—regardless of the cause—so long as the individual doesn't compromise the rights of others. The right to life, liberty, and the pursuit of happiness is foundational to our society. Sexual self–determination is included within our inalienable rights.

Hopefully I have addressed the main questions a skeptic or critic might have. Though we may not agree, perhaps we can disagree with understanding and tolerance.

So now, back to the seeker after masculine wholeness. To facilitate the grand purpose of helping you deepen your understanding of whole masculinity, I've combined ideas from many sources. The foundation of this book is what I consider to be the four basic principles of growth into wholeness—masculinity, authenticity, need fulfillment, and surrender. These principles are explained and clarified using the four masculine archetypes as described in the works of Robert Moore and Douglas Gillette: the King, the Warrior, the Magian, and the Lover.[2] And I've included some material on gender wholeness theory, which I began developing in 2005.

I've also included a chapter on some of the major challenges that many men with same–sex attraction face, including shame, anxiety, addiction and compulsions, and a variety of other psychological issues. Another chapter delves into the most common factors that I believe dispose men to develop sexual attractions toward other men, including gender shame, gender double binds, gender incongruity, and same–sex disaffiliation. All of this is intended to help you identify and free yourself from problems you may have in those areas.

I wanted to make this book a very substantial tool for you. As a result, it's *not* light reading. It contains profound principles from many sources that have finally been gathered into one place. I wanted to provide these resources for you because I believe that ignorance condemns a man to an impoverished life. If we want to grow to our full potential as men, we must acquire knowledge and integrate it in our daily lives so that, through experience, it becomes wisdom.

Throughout the book, you will notice a handwriting symbol ( ) followed by a set of numbers. The numbers refer to specific journaling opportunities contained in the journal that accompanies this book, titled *Becoming a Whole Man—Journal*. If you didn't purchase the journal together with the book and are interested in acquiring it, you can do so through Amazon.com.

You may find that the concepts captured in this book warrant more than a single reading. The nature of the principles contained here is that they all interrelate—to understand one principle you must understand the others. Learning such principles is rather tricky since you have to understand principle *B* in order to understand principle *A*, but you must grasp principle *A* before principle *B* will really make sense. I've provided many explanations to help you along, but a second reading of key chapters will likely shed greater light on the whole picture.

In order to help you really understand and internalize these concepts, I have also created some valuable online resources. The *Becoming a Whole Man* website and blog (http://becomingawholeman.com) were created to foster discussion specific to each chapter of the book. Contributors include myself and staff from the Center for Gender Wholeness, all of whom have expertise on these topics. We'll share insights we gain over time about topics in the various chapters, and we look forward to your questions and comments. We'll also post our thoughts on movies and books related to chapter topics.

One last statement on the book's content is warranted. The journey we're on together crosses all national borders and brings together brothers from all races, ethnicities, and faiths. For me, one of the most beautiful aspects of doing this work is the opportunity it gives me to walk—as a white Christian—alongside my friends from other denominations and races with their wide range of perspectives, beliefs, and non–belief. I've written this book with the hope that men from every background can use it by incorporating wisdom found in diverse cultures, philosophies, and religions over many ages. In my view there is much we can learn from each other. Although our beliefs could divide us, we are stronger when we hold together. I encourage you to look for the commonalities among our beliefs and for the truths you can learn from faiths that may be different from your own.

Finally, none of what you learn in this book will be of any real use to you if you don't make it active in your life. Change will come as you move the knowledge in your head downward into your chest, your guts, and your limbs through action. You will have to put it to work. I encourage you to choose to believe that right now is the perfect time to do so. Let's begin.

---

[1] http://www.gallup.com/poll/160517/lgbt-percentage-highest-lowest-north-dakota.aspx.

[2] Moore and Gillette have written a series of five books on these archetypes, titled *King Warrior Magician Lover* (1990), *The King Within* (1992), *The Warrior Within* (1992), *The Magician Within* (1993), and *The Lover Within* (1993). To me their term, "Magician," confuses the intended concept. I have substituted the term "Magian," which is a singular form of the word "Magi."

Chapter 1

The Archetypes: Shadows and Wholeness

For any individual the archetypes may be creative and life–enhancing or destructive and death–dealing…. [I]f we fail to learn how to use these vast energy resources, or misuse them, we will be courting our own destruction, and we may take others with us.

Moore & Gillette, *The King Within*

Let the states of equilibrium and harmony exist in perfection, and a happy order will prevail throughout heaven and earth, and all things will be nourished and flourish.

Confucius, *The Doctrine of the Mean*

hat is a whole man? In truth, that is a question few in our age can answer. I suggest that wholeness means living the fullness of our masculine potential. This implies that all of our essential male traits are online and active, integrated into a functioning, unified Self.

A whole man is disciplined, powerful, and strong to be sure. He's also compassionate, relational, and deeply connected to the feelings of his body and the intuition of his spirit. He can acquire and use knowledge through his intellect and reason. He governs himself and those over whom he has responsibility with order, balance, and benevolence. A whole man is tuned into a Higher Power beyond himself, and he accesses that power to bless his life and the lives of those around him.

Why should you be concerning yourself with heady concepts like wholeness when your immediate problem is unwanted sexual attractions toward other men?

Because the very attractions you want to diminish are, in all likelihood, the result of a lack of wholeness.

Carl Jung

In order to help you more readily understand and identify with the plethora of traits that make up a whole man, I'll use the concept of archetypes. The Swiss psychiatrist, Carl Jung (1875–1961), developed this idea and applied it in contemporary psychology to describe the structure of the human psyche or mind. Jung believed that unconscious forces influence our thoughts, feelings, desires, and behavior. Jung grouped these unconscious forces into sets of innate human traits, which are sometimes described as instincts, energies, drives, or internal forces. Jung called these sets of traits "archetypes." For example, the masculine traits of discipline, power, and strength are grouped together in the archetype called "Warrior," while the masculine traits of empathy, passion, and connection to feeling and intuition are grouped together in the archetype called "Lover."

Authors Robert Moore and Douglas Gillette have expanded on the teachings of Jung in a series of books about four masculine archetypes, which include the Warrior and Lover, as well as the King, and what they call the Magician or Shaman. They, like Jung, believe that these archetypal traits are part of a "collective unconscious" that is universal among all humans—passed from one generation to the next like a collected memory of humankind. Moore and Gillette support this belief by amply demonstrating that the archetypes have appeared across cultures and throughout history. They postulate that these traits are hard–wired into us and even suggest which structures within the brain may give rise to the various archetypes.[1]

The archetypes help us understand the way maleness happens. They represent the universal principles underlying masculinity.

These masculine archetypal energies reveal to us the "*Tao* of maleness." The term Tao comes from the ancient Chinese philosopher Lao Tzu, who lived during the sixth century BC. In his book *Tao Te Ching* (pronounced *dow de jing*), he describes *Tao* as the universal principle underlying all things. *Tao* is typically translated as "the way," meaning the way things happen, the way of the universe, the way of God. So the archetypes help us understand the way maleness happens. They represent the universal principles underlying masculinity.

The traits represented by the archetypes are the birthright of every man. You possess and can further develop every trait. You may already feel these energies within you, or they may be just on the brink of developing. Keep in mind that wholeness is not about accentuating and living from your "gift" archetype—the energy that comes most readily to you. Rather, wholeness comes from understanding and developing each archetypal capacity and trait while also balancing and integrating them.

In this book I refer to the archetypes in a number of ways. Sometimes I'll refer to an archetypal "energy" or speak as though an archetype is within us. Other times I describe archetypes in terms of roles and functions. Often I refer to them almost as though they are actual men, even using pronouns such as "he." Don't be confused by all of this. I'm not suggesting that the archetypes are anything other than groupings of male–typical traits that have been described and named. Therefore, you are free to think of them in any way that suits your imagination and belief system.

I'll invite you to become awake to yourself—to your inherent archetypal energies. You have the capacity to develop them fully. They are part of your body, mind, and soul. With patience and love, call them forth within yourself. But always stand in healthy proximity to the archetypes, neither too close nor too far. They are like the sun—a source of energy and power. If you get too close, you will be burned up by your attempts at perfection. If you stay too far away, you will become frozen and lifeless.

Let me briefly introduce you to the masculine traits that we call "the archetypes."

King

Two over–arching functions comprise the archetype of the King. The first function is that of creating order. Foundational to that function is the sense of being centered in ourselves and connected to a Higher Power. This function also provides balance, moderation, integration, and discernment. It organizes our lives and is our capacity to choose. This aspect of the King ties us to law and creates civilization. The second major function of the King is that of providing, which includes the energy of creating or giving form to things. It includes inspiring, affirming, and blessing others. And it entails providing for our own needs and for the needs of those who depend on us.

Warrior

The Warrior archetype represents the masculine power that comes from discipline and productive aggression. It's our courage and ability to detach from feeling when it's necessary in order to get a job done. Warrior energy is truly awake in life and is always fully authentic. The Warrior archetype is comprised of two primary

The traits represented by the archetypes are the birthright of every man.

3

functions. First, it protects our boundaries internally, interpersonally, and within society. Second, it serves the King by carrying out the will and vision that comes from our center and our Higher Power. In this function, Warrior is the archetype of mission and commitment to a cause.

Magian

The word *Magian* refers to ancient Zoroastrian priests known originally for their connection to God and devotion to truth and science. Magians later gained a reputation as sorcerers, tricksters, and practitioners of what later came to be called magic. The masculine attributes we identify as the Magian include consciousness, cognition, introversion, and absolute commitment to truth. These attributes serve in fulfilling two main functions, the first of which is to possess knowledge. Magian energy is on a quest to understand unchanging principles, patterns, and universal laws. With that knowledge, the Magian can detect and expose illogic, pretense, and contradictions. Knowledge also empowers the Magian's second main function, which is to bring about transformation. An understanding of essential principles, patterns, and laws enables the Magian to manipulate and channel various forces and energies, leading to new creations that transform our lives and our world. The Magian transforms others by initiating them into his special knowledge.

Lover

Lover energy represents the experience of every type of sensation, including feelings of pain, of pleasure, and every nuance in between. It's our experience of external stimuli: sights, sounds, tastes, and smells, as well as tactile and spiritual sensations. And it's the awareness of our internal emotional states. Lover is also the force of "libido," which refers to life energy and instincts—the experience of appetite, passion, and urge. And Lover is the desire for union and connection with all things. It's the energy that unifies all opposites and makes a whole of the many parts. It is the archetype that moves us toward relating and friendship.

ARCHETYPAL WHOLENESS AND SHADOW

Shadow: opposite extremes of archetypal energy

The descriptions you just read express what Moore and Gillette describe as the archetypes in their "fullness." I use the word "whole" because it adds a dimension that I'll describe shortly. But archetypes also have "shadows"—this too is part of the *Tao* of maleness. These shadows are described as being opposite extremes of archetypal energy. For example, the Warrior archetype has the two shadow "poles," or opposites, of Sadist and Masochist.

The structure of the archetypes with their two polar shadows is depicted as two diverging lines with the whole archetype at the top and the two shadows on the bottom. The graphic below illustrates this for the archetype of the Warrior.

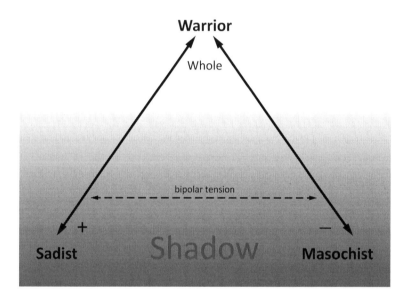

In this drawing, the two vertical arrows represent the two opposite potentials for the Warrior archetype. The extreme of the overly active (+) potential leads to sadism, or too much Warrior, and the extreme of the overly passive (−) potential leads to masochism, or too little Warrior. The further these arrows go down from the Whole Warrior, the more they diverge from one another, the deeper into shadow they progress, the greater the tension becomes between the opposite poles, and the more potentially destructive they become.

This concept harmonizes with Isaac Newton's third law of motion, which states that for every action, there is an equal and opposite reaction. It is also in accordance with what some have called the law of polarity, which is that everything has its opposite. In *Tao Te Ching*, Lao Tzu describes how the opposites give rise to, define, and complement one another. Consider the following from J.H. McDonald's translation:

For every action, there is an equal and opposite reaction.

When people see things as beautiful, ugliness is created.

When people see things as good, evil is created.

Being and non–being produce each other.

Difficult and easy complement each other.

Long and short define each other.

High and low oppose each other.

Fore and aft follow each other.

John Heider described this truth in *The Tao of Leadership* as follows: "All behavior consists of opposites or polarities. If I do anything more and more, over and over, its polarity will appear. For example, striving to be beautiful makes a person ugly, and trying too hard to be kind is a form of selfishness." This is according to natural law. It will always be true.

Unless the archetypal energies split and go down into shadow, these opposing potentials are held in a healthy balance within the nature of the archetype. For example, the active (+) potential of the Warrior is to be aggressive, willing to take risks, healthfully detached from relationships, and unyielding to the distraction of feelings. These are good Warrior qualities, unless they go to their shadowy sadistic extremes of being antisocial, self–destructive, cruel, and emotionally numb. Likewise, the passive (–) potential of the Warrior is to be willing to yield to greater authority, to be self–preserving, to relate well with comrades, and to be emotionally engaged. These are also good Warrior qualities until they progress to their masochistic extremes of being submissive, cowardly, victimized, and emotionally depressed.

All capacities of the opposing energies are good and are intended to be held together in a compound wholeness. We might compare it to the perfect day where the breeze is cool but the sun is warm, or the twenty–four–hour cycle where the day enables action and the night enables rest. When balanced, these energies become something more than their constituent components—the perfect day is not experienced as the bitterness of cold and the oppression of heat because together those opposing qualities balance and complement each other.

Experiencing an archetype in his whole form is much like standing on the top of a mountain. From such a place we see the world with a transcendent perspective that can't be enjoyed in any other way—even if we've been to both sides of the

"If I do anything more and more, over and over, its polarity will appear."
John Heider

All capacities of the opposing energies are good and are intended to be held together in a compound wholeness.

mountain. This is what is depicted in the symbol of yin–yang—a composite of opposing forces held in balance.

The graphic below depicts the four masculine archetypes with their shadows. See if you can imagine it in 3D with the center as a mountain peak from which you can experience all four sides. Since we'll refer to these archetypes and shadows throughout the book, it would be helpful for you to spend a moment familiarizing yourself with all of them. Notice that the King has the active Tyrant shadow and the passive Weakling shadow. The Warrior has the Sadist and the Masochist. The Magician's shadows are the Manipulator and the "Innocent" or Denying One. And the Lover archetype includes the shadows of the Addict and the Impotent One.

Archetypal Shadows

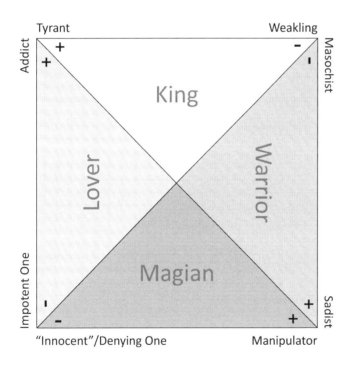

THE MEANINGS OF "SHADOW"

As we discussed previously, authors Moore and Gillette use the term "shadow" to refer to the opposite potentials of the archetypes, or the destructive "shadow poles" of the archetypal energies. But the word "shadow" has another meaning as well. It's also commonly used to refer to the aspects of ourselves of which we're not conscious, or the parts of ourselves that we don't understand. These can include denied impulses

Shadow: aspects of ourselves of which we're not conscious; parts of ourselves that we don't understand

Shadow is every part of us that we have split off and hidden in the cellar of our nonconscious mind.

and repressed feelings and needs. It's the stories we tell ourselves about ourselves and about the world, without knowing we're telling them. It is every part of us that we have split off and hidden in the cellar of our nonconscious mind. I sometimes refer to these as our split–off parts. This is consistent with the meaning given to this term by Carl Jung, who first articulated the concept of the shadow.

These two different meanings of "shadow" overlap. Their main point of intersection is when an archetypal shadow pole—such as the Masochist—is repressed, or made nonconscious. Let me explain how this happens. Painful and shaming life experiences split archetypal energies apart by making it unsafe, bad, or wrong to have or express one or the other energy or trait. As children we stop doing the things that don't get us what we want or that cause us to be rejected or hurt. So we cut off, repress, or deny those traits in ourselves that seem unwanted or unsafe, relegating those parts to our nonconscious shadow. Some refer to this as parts that have been disowned.[2] These parts are experienced as "who I am not." The energies or traits that feel protective or comforting—or at least less dangerous— are engaged in and amplified, becoming aspects of our identity. These parts are experienced as "who I am."

For example, abuse may teach a boy that it's not safe to be open, receptive, or vulnerable. Such abuse might cause him to split off the vulnerable aspects of his personality and create a nonconscious Masochist shadow. This boy might take on the identity of the opposite shadow pole—the Sadist—and become a bully, abusing other victims. Conversely, if abuse taught him that it's not safe to be powerful or angry, he might repress his forceful side, creating a nonconscious Sadist shadow. In such a case, the boy would probably take on the role of the opposite shadow— the Masochist.

The graphic on the next page illustrates the shadows of the boy just described. This boy's Sadist shadow has been repressed and forced out of consciousness where it joins with his other unconscious shadows, represented by the dark circle. His conscious self is identified with the Masochist pole so that he lives out the role of a victim.

In this book I've taken care to be clear about which way I'm using the term "shadow." Frequently the term is used very clearly in the context of archetypal

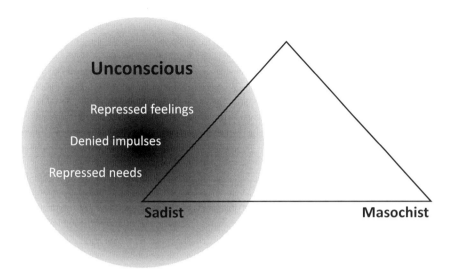

shadows. When it is used in the context of the unconscious, I've used words to make that clear.

SHADOWS SEEK WHOLENESS

Our split–off parts don't go away. Whether they are nonconscious archetypal shadows, denied impulses, or repressed feelings and needs, they remain present with us, though outside of our awareness. Occasionally our split–off aspects are expressed in indirect ways, like strange dreams or "Freudian slips." Sometimes they come out through uncharacteristic behaviors that surprise us—and those around us. At such times it may be said that our repressed parts are "coming out sideways" rather than directly.

Often the opposing energies of our archetypal shadows are experienced through internal conflict. The conflict may manifest itself as splits within our own nature. We may be like Dr. Jekyll and Mr. Hyde. We may be like the Tyrant who, when confronted by a superior power, collapses into nothing, or like the Weakling who is given a little authority and wields his new power like a "little Hitler."

On the other hand, we may project our split–off parts onto other people or groups. Our projections can be both positive and negative. For men with same–sex attraction, positive projections often show up as attractions to other men who possess the positive traits we can't see in ourselves. Our negative projections may show up as resentment or fear of male traits.

Projection: the act of seeing in someone else a feeling, impulse, desire, or personality trait that we hide, repress, or deny in ourselves

Why can't we just jettison these unwanted, shadowy parts of ourselves? We can't because they *are* parts of ourselves, just like our hands, our eyes, and our colon. Our feelings are made to be felt, our impulses need to be recognized and learned from, and our needs must be fulfilled. As for our opposing archetypal energies, they are intended to be held together in a compound wholeness, as mentioned previously. And they must remain balanced. The polar energies of the archetypal shadows create problems for us only when they are split apart. Since they must remain balanced, the further apart they are split, the more conflict they will generate in our lives. A severe Masochistic shadow necessitates a severe Sadistic side to balance him.

Of central importance in all of this are our unmet needs. Where there is repression, denial, and shadow, there will also be unmet needs. And because core needs are non–negotiable, our shadows find ways to meet the needs anyway. Often these ways are destructive, hurtful, and damaging. Our shadows push against our repression and denial just as hard as we clamp down on it—and sometimes much harder. Shadows can sabotage us, wreaking havoc in our lives.

RESTORING WHOLENESS

Wholeness is about balance, moderation, and integration.

Wholeness is the opposite of fragmentation, which is when our energies are split into shadows or when we have pushed away shamed parts of ourselves. But as you may be starting to understand, wholeness is not merely having all the parts assembled. It doesn't mean making a soup of our accumulated weaknesses and strengths or collecting a set of all our shadows and fragments. Wholeness is about balance, moderation, and integration. These three states bring transcendence and a new perspective. This may seem simple enough, but there is much more to them than is at first apparent. Let's look deeper.

Balance and Moderation

Journalists know that a good news story presents contrasting viewpoints in a balanced or equal way. So they will quote an expert who expresses a particular viewpoint, followed by a quote from another expert with a contrasting or contradictory viewpoint. Or they will include the perspective of the politician backing a bill and then counter it with a statement from the politician opposing the measure. When the contrasting viewpoints of both sides have been equally presented, the report is called "balanced."

So balance has two aspects—contrast and equilibrium. Contrast simply means the presence and juxtaposing of diverse or opposing elements or perspectives. In the news story, contrast comes from the two politicians each presenting their opposing views. Equilibrium means that the elements are combined within the whole in such a way that each element is given its appropriate place, prominence, and emphasis—but no more than is appropriate. In a balanced news story, the reporter doesn't spend an inordinate amount of time presenting the opinion of one side while ignoring the opinion of the other side.

Juxtapose: to put two things side by side

Earlier in this chapter I mentioned the symbol of yin–yang, which is a *Taoist* concept from ancient China. The symbol is a juxtaposition of opposing black and white shapes nested together in a single whole circle. The philosophy of yin–yang suggests that the natural world is composed of interconnected opposites that equally balance one another. A balanced life gives attention and expression to all contrasting energies. In practical terms, we can't just ignore a trait because it's uncomfortable or unfamiliar, and our lifestyle can't over–focus on one energy at the expense of others. Remember, if an innate capacity isn't used in positive ways, it will try to get our attention in whatever way it can—often with destructive consequences.

The weakness of this symbol is that it's static, meaning that it doesn't show movement. The philosophy of yin–yang is actually very dynamic, describing cycles of flux and change. The balanced way of living must be dynamic and flexible since each life situation will require a somewhat different force or ability in order to meet it adaptively. In short, the whole man is able to access an entire range of energies as appropriate for the situation. But he must do so in moderation

Now let's turn to the philosophy of moderation. This takes us back to ancient China again to a philosopher named Confucius, who lived from 551 to 479 BC. Central to his teachings is the concept of moderation, which he called 中庸 (*zhōng yōng*) or "doctrine of the mean." (The word "mean" refers to "middle.") Over the next few hundred years, a number of Greek philosophers—including Socrates, Plato, and Aristotle—also taught this concept, which they called "the golden mean." More recently (a mere 800 years ago) a Jewish philosopher named Maimonides again extolled this doctrine.

doctrine of the mean

What is moderation? Simply put, it's the avoidance of extremes. This also implies self–restraint and observing reasonable limits. According to this philosophy, a man should fly the middle course or walk the middle path between the extremes. Every virtue and all of the archetypal energies have their extremes, which are characterized by exaggeration (too much) on one hand and deficiency (too little) on the other. The philosophers teach that the good life is not found in the extremes. The good life is found in the middle path between them. This principle is essential if we are to healthfully access archetypal powers. It's the exaggeration of an archetypal power in our lives that creates the shadowy active pole of that archetype. And it's the deficiency of that same energy that gives rise to passive archetypal shadows.

Integration

I'm going to take you through a bit of semi–heady etymology (which means "word history"). Stick with me here and the point will become clear shortly. In modern English, the word "integration" refers to a process or act of putting together and combining diverse parts into a unified whole. It suggests creating harmony and coordination. It's often used synonymously with the word "synthesis," which comes from a Greek term *syntithenai*, meaning "the act of putting together."

Integer: not touched; unmarred, unimpaired, or in original condition

Integratio: to renew or restore to the original condition

But our modern English is missing something important here about the concept of integration. The Latin root of the word "integration" has quite a different meaning that is very significant to our discussion. To understand this, let's first look at the origins of the word "integrity," which is the base of the word "integration." The Latin root of "integrity" is *integer*, which has two parts: *in* (meaning "not") and *teger* (from the root *tangere*, meaning "to touch.") So "integrity" literally means "not touched"—in other words unmarred, unimpaired, or in original condition. The Latin word *integratio*, which is the root of "integration," adds the concept of renewing or restoring, as in restoring to the original untouched condition.

I suggest we combine both of these meanings of "integration" in our understanding of wholeness. Thus wholeness becomes about restoration—putting diverse elements back together in their *original and untouched condition*. Now let's apply this to the topic of integrating archetypal energies. How is creating a perfect synthesis of our archetypal energies a restoration to our original untouched condition? You may feel like you've never been whole, archetypally speaking. But I believe you have—and so did Carl Jung.

At the beginning of this chapter I talked about Jung's belief in a collective unconscious—a universal inherited psychic system of which the archetypes are a significant part. I suggested there that the archetypal energies are the birthright of every man, which includes you. If these archetypes are an inherited birthright, then they must be part of your original blueprint, which still resides at your core in its original whole condition—untouched, unmarred, and unimpaired.

I see this concept as resonating with the Biblical statement that God created man in his own image (Genesis 1:27). I consider God's image to be one of wholeness. And it's clear to me that the traits described as the four archetypes are apparent in God's nature. Therefore, as the inheritors of that image, wholeness is in our basic design. Maybe that explains why you've chosen to work on overcoming your issues—you want to be restored to who you are at your core.

So now let's get a little more practical—let's talk about where we start the process of integration. We start by accepting where we are today. Many of us who have walked this journey out of homosexuality ahead of you have found that, until we love and accept ourselves just as we are, *right now, unchanged*, we can make little progress.

Each of our weaknesses, each of our shadows and fragments, has something to teach us and some bit of wholeness to return to us. Behind each shadow is a golden gift. Our job is to receive each gift by accepting and loving every part of ourselves *right now*. By calling forth our shadows for a loving look, we activate the change process and begin moving toward wholeness.

Synergy

Let me summarize what I've said so far about wholeness by defining it as the integration of contrasting virtues and energies, held in balance and accessed with moderation. This kind of relationship to our diverse energies and attributes creates a transcendence that I likened earlier to the view from the top of a mountain where we can experience the surrounding terrain in a holistic way that is otherwise impossible—even if we've been to both sides of the mountain. Only from the top of a mountain can we really get the lay of the land. Only there can we see how all the little tributaries connect and flow together to form a stream. Only from that elevation do we have the perspective to see where the winding road we are on is taking us.

> Until we love and accept ourselves just as we are, we can make little progress.

Synergy: the value of the whole is greater than the sum of the parts

Balance, moderation, integration, and a transcendent perspective are the conditions that create what's known as "synergy"—the value of the whole is greater than the sum of the parts. The synergy created by the integration of archetypal energies makes life work much better than when these energies are split into their extremes. The energies will always be present and balanced in our lives—this is according to natural law and is therefore unavoidable. Those powers may be present as faded shadowy traces, dramatic polar conflicts, or as a moderate integration of forces, but they will always be present, and they will tend to be equal. Only when they are integrated in a balanced way and accessed with moderation will these forces work to our good and the good of those around us.

The computer I'm using to write this book is a perfect metaphor of synergy. It's an elegant and sophisticated amalgamation of metal and silicon, integrated in such a way that its whole is immeasurably greater than the sum of its parts. Each element is carefully measured—neither too much nor too little. The demands of its software are balanced by what its hardware provides. Only in this way can I, the user, enjoy an optimal writing experience. The wholeness of the computer makes it work properly.

Now let's look at synergy in human terms using traits of the Warrior archetype which we discussed earlier. The table below lists eight Warrior traits (e.g., *Power*, *Feeling*, *Anger*, etc.). In the row beside each trait are four words that describe the range of potential attributes for each trait, ranging from *Sadistic* (far left) to *Masochistic* (far right). The words in the middle columns describe more moderate but still contrasting attributes. For example, the trait of *Power* is followed by the

Warrior Trait Scales

Traits	Sadist		Moderation		Masochist
1. Power	Overpowering	Disciplined	Relenting		Powerless
2. Feeling	Numb	Detached	Aware		Ruled by Feelings
3. Anger	Rageful	Aggressive	Calm		Depressed
4. Allegiance	Defiant	Independent	Loyal		Dependent
5. Trust	Paranoid	Vigilant	Open		Gullible
6. Self-care	Reckless	Courageous	Self-preserving		Cowardly
7. Relationality	Controlling/Cruel	Detached	Receptive		Victimized
8. Sociability	Antisocial	Assertive	Yielding		Disempowered

words *Overpowering* (which is sadistic), *Disciplined* and *Relenting* (which are more moderate), and *Powerless* (which is masochistic). Take a moment now and review the seven scales to get a feel for the range of each trait.

These trait scales give us the lay of the Warrior landscape. They allow us to see how the divergent Warrior capacities connect and flow into each other like tributaries into a stream. They also provide a perspective so we can see where the road of Warrior is taking us. A trait scale like this is included in each of the chapters on the four archetypes.

Let's see how these traits work in a hypothetical situation. Imagine an average guy named Guy who regularly goes biking with a friend. Let's imagine that we sit Guy down and interview him about how his Warrior traits show up in their adventures. Here is the gist of what he tells us:

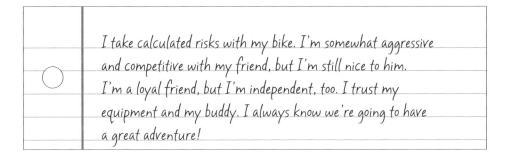

I take calculated risks with my bike. I'm somewhat aggressive and competitive with my friend, but I'm still nice to him. I'm a loyal friend, but I'm independent, too. I trust my equipment and my buddy. I always know we're going to have a great adventure!

Now let's look at how Guy's various Warrior attributes are integrated through moderation and balance to create an optimal, synergistic experience for him. First, let's look at how the principle of *moderation* creates synergy for Guy. He told us that he takes calculated risks with his bike. This is an act of moderation in the trait of self–care. Imagine that instead of practicing moderation, he lives in either extreme—reckless or cowardly. In either position, he will always be subject to pain, whether from physical injury or from a coward's self–reproach. The synergy created by Guy's moderation allows him to experience a sustainable and healthy exhilaration that cannot be had in either extreme.

Now let's look at how the principle of *balance* creates synergy for Guy. He told us that he is "somewhat aggressive and competitive with my friend, but I'm still nice to him." Guy is balancing his aggressive and assertive traits with his receptive trait. Imagine what a different experience it would be for Guy and his friend if Guy was always aggressive, or even overpowering. On the other hand, how would the relationship be different if Guy was constantly oversensitive to his buddy's feelings? Yuck! Or imagine that Guy made polar swings from one extreme to the other—full–on aggression one day and all teddy bear hugs the next. The balance of Warrior traits allows for friendly competition, which is one of the male–to–male love languages. A man's attitude of "I love ya dude…now I'm gonna kick your butt" is part of what can make friendships interesting and exciting. ✍ 1.1

Your Growth Toward Wholeness

> We can't spend our whole lives on the top of a mountain. We actually spend most of our time in the valleys of our lives.

Now let's throw a wrench into the works with an entirely different viewpoint. Consider this—we can't spend our whole lives on the top of a mountain. As much as I've been extolling the importance of a transcendent perspective, we actually spend most of our time in very non–transcendent places, down in the valleys of our lives. This is as it should be because we need our valley experiences to teach us.

Think about it this way—we can't appreciate the height of a mountain unless we've seen it from its base. We can't understand the forest unless we've been down in the middle of it. And we can't fully comprehend the winding of a road unless we have—at some point—wound along its tracks. The importance of our mountaintop experiences is the perspective they give—a perspective that we can carry with us even when we're no longer on the top of the mountain. A truly transcendent perspective integrates and balances the views from both the mountaintop and the valley floor.

In practical and personal terms, this means that any confusion, mistakes, or blindness you may have experienced in your life is not wasted. These experiences from the dark shadows of your valley floor provide a perspective that will help you in ways that you may not be able to comprehend right now. Most readily, they can help you to see your growth. ✍ 1.2

Synergy is the King

The significance of wholeness in the process of resolving concerns about same–sex attraction can't be stressed too much. Wholeness makes life work properly—and it makes transitioning from same–sex attraction more possible. My personal experience with same–sex attraction—and most of what I have seen cause those attractions in other men—can be attributed to a lack of wholeness. You will find as you progress through this book that the principle of wholeness underlies almost everything we discuss. By calling forth your shadows for a loving look—accepting and loving every part of yourself as you are *right now*—you activate the change process and move toward the fullness of your masculine potential. Wholeness is a lifelong process that is never quite finished. But much of the joy and interest in life comes through the journey itself.

The prospect may seem daunting—growing slowly toward wholeness through daily trudging along winding roads in dark valleys with occasional mountaintop epiphanies. Just remember that as you integrate your shadows, new capacities come on line. And as you continue to have mountaintop experiences, you will find a new energy or power within you that seems to come out of nowhere. That's the product of synergy, as we discussed a few pages back. Remember, synergy means that the value of the whole is greater than the sum of the parts.

The synergy we're talking about here could be referred to archetypally as the transcendent power of King energy. The King's powers encompass those of the other three archetypes, but transcend them also—he adds something above and beyond. It's King energy that governs the other three archetypal energies by integrating them, balancing them, and accessing them in moderation. The process works in reverse as well—as we discover, integrate, and balance the other archetypes, we empower the King. Therefore, the King is the archetype of wholeness. The development of this wholeness is essentially the purpose and process of this book.

> King energy governs the other three archetypal energies by integrating them, balancing them, and accessing them in moderation.

We've been referring to King capacities as something that comes from within our own psyches. But I believe there is more to the story than that. The word "synergism" refers to an ancient theological doctrine, which states that divine grace cooperates with human activity in the process of spiritual regeneration. My experience tells me that there are King powers beyond our own psyches that cooperate with our own efforts in creating personal wholeness. I've repeatedly experienced those powers in clear and unmistakable ways and am convinced that they truly exist. I know many others who have also experienced those powers. I call the source of those King powers "God." You may believe whatever you like about those powers, but I assure you that they are real and that you can access them by aligning your inner King with the Universal King. But that is the subject of the next chapter.

> *Synergism:* divine grace cooperates with human activity in the process of spiritual regeneration

---

[1] For more detail on this subject, I refer you to the four books in Moore and Gillette's series on the archetypes: *The King Within*, *The Warrior Within*, *The Lover Within*, and *The Magician Within*. Chapter Two, titled "Decoding the Male Psyche," is identical in each book. In this chapter the authors elaborate at length on the origins, structure, and functions of the archetypes and shadows. Appendix B in each book discusses a possible relationship between the limbic system and the archetypes. Appendix C looks at the feminine archetypal element within men, which is called the Anima.

[2] See *Embracing Our Selves: The Voice Dialogue Manual*, by Hal Stone and Sidra L. Stone.

Chapter 2

THE KING

In myth and legend it is the king who constellates the Center of the world. He is the point in the world where sacred and profane energies meet in a dramatic exchange of Libido.

Moore and Gillette, *The King Within*

 n every major religion there exists a concept of a sacred connection point between heaven and earth. It's at this point of intersection that the divine realm interacts with the profane or human realm to give laws, impart knowledge, and provide blessing. And it's around this center point—sometimes called a hub, pole, or navel—that all things are ordered and revolve. Such points of divine intersection have been called the "axis mundi," which literally means "turning point of the world."

The purpose and nature of these points of connection vary according to the tradition. For example, the Garden of Eden is the center point of creation in the Judeo–Christian and Islamic faiths. The Tree of Knowledge is seen in those same faiths as the source–point of conscience, understanding, or enlightenment. Certain cities have been viewed as sacred or as centers of civilization, such as Jerusalem, Mecca, Rome, and the ancient Chinese city of Chang'an. Places such as Mount Sinai and the Oracle at Delphi are, or have been, seen as points where divine revelation is received. For Christians, the Garden of Gethsemane and the cross on which Jesus was crucified are sacred places of redemption and reconciliation with God. Synagogues, churches, temples, mosques, and shrines continue to be recognized as sacred points where people commune with God.

Mount Sinai

Archetypally speaking, the King holds our axis mundi—our connection to divine or Higher Powers and the core or central hub around which our lives are organized. As a connection to divine power, axis mundi may be described as our gut wisdom or what we know in our hearts. It is sometimes called "the Spirit" and "Source." For men of faith, it's our relationship with God—it's revelation and epiphanies.

Synergism: from the Greek root *synergos*, which means "working together"

As a central hub, the King archetype brings together and governs the powers of the Warrior, Magian, and Lover—balancing, moderating, and integrating their energies. King is the point around which all things revolve, and therefore it's the archetype of wholeness. It could be said that the King is the blueprint of our whole self. King power is synergistic, making things work together and bringing grace from somewhere outside ourselves so that the value of the whole becomes greater than the sum of the parts. It's the transcendent and organizing view from the top of a mountain. And it's the light that dawns on us as we stand in such places. It's the power that makes life work properly.

Creator of Order
- Axis mundi
- Source of balance
- Moderator
- Integrator
- One who discerns
- Sovereign
- Organizer
- Keeper and giver of law
- Builder of civilization

In this chapter we'll explore the two essential functions of the King as described by Moore and Gillette. The first function is *ordering*, or creating order. This function begins with the King's role as keeper of our axis mundi, which entails connecting with our deep, unchanging, essential Self and fostering a connection with our Higher Power. These connections create a strong Center through which we may access our own core wisdom and the wisdom of the universe. This strong Center also forms a reference point, enabling the King to create balance, moderation, and integration in our lives. The King's *ordering* function also includes discernment, which means differentiating and making distinctions among things. It includes assuming the power, right, and responsibility of governing our lives as our internal "sovereign." It entails keeping our lives logistically organized and conforming to natural laws. And it involves the work of civilizing us by promoting our progression, advancement, and development.

The King's second essential function is that of *providing*, which is fulfilled through creating, inspiring and blessing others, and providing material means. Moore and Gillette refer to this aspect of the King as "the generative man."[1] Through acts of creation, the King gives form to intentions, thoughts, desires, patterns, feelings, impulses, and inspirations. What once was only in the mind becomes real and tangible. King energy inspires us to live our lives as authentic examples of wholeness, which in turn may inspire those around us to live their lives in similar ways. It also inspires us to truly behold and affirm the good in all, which may encourage others to be their best selves. The King blesses us, and others, through touch, words, and commitment. And the King provides the means for our material wellbeing and that of those for whom we have responsibility.

Following our discussion of the King in his whole form, we'll consider what this energy becomes when it splits and goes into shadow. The two opposing shadows of the King are the Tyrant Usurper and the Weakling Abdicator. The Tyrant seizes authority that rightfully belongs to others. Those of us who are caught at this pole may become over-inflated, or too full of ourselves. We may be self-centered and constantly feel the need to prove our validity to others. We may be controlling of everything in our lives and narcissistically focused on advancing only ourselves. We might unfairly discriminate, rigidly demand uniformity and compliance, or act with arrogant disrespect for the boundaries of others.

The King's passive shadow pole—the Weakling Abdicator—lacks a connection to our Self, leaving us deflated and uncentered. Those of us who are caught at this pole may be negligent in handling opposition, contradiction, and conflict. We may be sterile and unable to create anything. We might be confused and unable to discern. Our lives may be chaotic and disorganized. All of these manifold weaknesses may cause us to abandon our power and the responsibilities that we alone must fulfill.

This chapter is the longest and most involved in the book. This is so because—as the central or governing archetype—the King is the most far-reaching and complex of all the archetypes. So take your time reading and allow yourself to absorb it. You might even want to return to this chapter for a second reading after you have read the other chapters.

Now as we begin our exploration of the King in earnest, let me leave you with this suggestion: the outcome of the growth process in which you're engaged is not merely to overcome same-sex attraction. That goal is far too narrow to be successful or to bring lasting joy. I suggest that the outcome of your growth is to manifest true kingship. So pay close attention to the teachings that follow.

The Provider
- Creator
- Inspirer
- Giver of blessing
- Provider of means

I suggest that the outcome of your growth is to manifest true kingship.

CREATOR OF ORDER
Axis Mundi

The King within us wants to prevent chaos and allow us to experience ultimate joy by providing clarity and vision and by confirming to us our validity, worth, and purpose. This can come in no other way than through maintaining a psychic connection to our centering Self and a spiritual connection to our Higher Power. These two connections create the internal guidance system we are calling axis mundi.

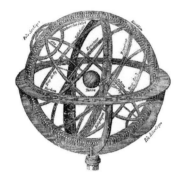

In Chapter One I talked about *zhōng yōng*, or the "doctrine of the mean," which was taught by Confucius. The term *zhōng yōng* has also been translated as "the unwobbling pivot," which means a stable center point around which things move or revolve, like the axis of a globe or the fulcrum of a lever. This Far Eastern philosophy corresponds in certain ways with the concept of axis mundi.

In religious traditions, axis mundi is a physical place or object where, or through which, spiritual energies are channeled. Within us, axis mundi is not a physical place, but a capacity or ability that can only exist if it is carefully fostered. Since understanding these concepts is utterly essential for wholeness, let's consider them carefully.

Connection to Our Self: Many writers have described the concept of the self in a wide and complex variety of ways. Most broadly, it could be defined as the totality of what we are with both unique and common features. For simplicity's sake, we will say the self consists of just two components: the ego and the core Self, which I referred to in the beginning of this chapter as "our deep, unchanging, essential Self." It's this core Self that's involved in axis mundi, and we'll soon turn our attention there. But in order to accurately comprehend what this core Self is, we must first understand what it's *not*. It's not the ego. ✍ 2.1

Ego: all psychological processes concerned with self and identity

The term "ego" is defined in many different ways by many different people. For our purposes, I will define it as all the psychological processes concerned with self and identity. It includes both conscious and nonconscious processes. On the conscious level, the ego includes memory and awareness of our past and present behaviors, traits, and preferences. It's the part of us that thinks, reasons, and plans. It solves problems, feels desires and aspirations, reacts to people and situations, and behaves according to our will. It protects, maintains, and fosters our identity or sense of self. On the nonconscious level, the ego holds a mental record of all our life experiences. These nonconscious memories have a tremendous impact on shaping our ego, even though we don't remember them. Combined with our conscious memories and conscious reasoning, they form our belief system.

In reality, every person has multiple egos, sometimes called "ego states," which represent various aspects of our personalities, social roles, and moods. For example, when I'm at my job I'm usually in a specific ego state that might be described as "professional." When I'm playing with my kids I'm in a very different ego state, which could be described as playful and relaxed. I have many other ego states that handle and express the full range of my personality. Rage, sexuality, humility, aggression, celebration, defensiveness, shame, sadness, and worship are all ego states. Although in reality the ego is complex, for ease in communication I'll speak of it as a single thing.

One of the ego's main functions is to protect our sense of validity, worth, and purpose so we can continue feeling good about ourselves. The ego does this by defending against anything that threatens this good feeling. That's why we sometimes get defensive or angry toward others—they are threatening some aspect of our validity, worth, or purpose. It's also why we banish certain of our feelings, impulses, needs, and archetypal capacities to our nonconscious shadows—they may threaten aspects of our sense of goodness. Such behaviors are sometimes called "ego games." Most of us are completely unaware of how hard our ego functions to keep us feeling good about ourselves. We'll explore this in great depth over the course of this book.

Our ego is shaped through the same kinds of life experiences as those that create our shadows, which I discussed in Chapter One. As adults we have the capacity to be aware of our ego, although we may not use that term for it. We may say, "Oh, I'm in my grumpy mood," or "I'm all business today." Such statements are expressions of ego states. But despite our ability to express or even name our ego states, few of us really understand how our ego functions and affects us. We think it's just who we are. We identify with it, thinking that this accumulation of personality traits, roles, and moods is our self. And most us use our ego as a pseudo axis mundi to guide our lives. But, as I indicated earlier, the ego is not the part of us involved in axis mundi. In fact, our ego is the part of us most likely to thwart access to the wisdom available at our core.

> Every person has multiple egos, sometimes called "ego states," which represent various aspects of our personalities, social roles, and moods.

> Most of us are completely unaware of how hard our ego functions to keep us feeling good about ourselves.

Now let's consider the Self—the unmoving, unchanging center that can safely guide and direct the rest of our psyche. As I've described previously, the Self provides clarity and vision about our course through life and instills a sense of validity, worth, and purpose. It helps us to maintain balance and moderation and to integrate all aspects of ourselves into a unified and functional whole.

Self: the central guiding core

self: the total person or some other aspect of that entirety, typically some aspect of the ego

Jung used the term *Self* (capitalized) to signify this central organizing structure. I've adopted that term here by differentiating in print between the Self (capitalized), which refers to the central guiding core, and the self (not capitalized), which refers to the total person or some other aspect of that entirety, typically some aspect of the ego.

As a psychotherapist, on rare and sacred occasions I've witnessed men as they accessed their Self. Often this occurs in active visualizations where they see who they truly are—free from all their problems and issues, healed from all their wounds, and standing in the light of absolute truth. In these moments, validity, worth, and purpose are second nature; clarity and vision are automatic. But the highest defining experience of these occasions is love and generosity.

An essential aspect of healing and maturation is coming to know the self in its entirety—including our many ego states and our core Self. The goal of most substantial forms of psychotherapy is to help us bring the self from a state of disorganization and mystery to a state of integration and familiarity. Most of all, healing processes need to help us gain access to our Self. By connecting with this essential element, which Moore and Gillette referred to as "the tranquil but dynamic Self at the psyche's Center," we can experience the pull of our egos' contradictory feelings, impulses, and needs and then respond to them from a core awareness of truth and rightness. I believe this way of life is better than simply allowing our egos to react to the people and events around us.

By understanding ourselves, we can *anticipate* our own responses and behaviors, rather than being surprised at what our various ego states think, feel, do, and say. And we can experience ourselves as single identities, meaning that we feel like we have *one* whole (though complex) self, rather than many disjointed versions of self. We come to know our self mostly through paying careful attention to our feelings and then seeking understanding of what those feelings mean. Because our feelings typically arise from below the level of our conscious mind, they are a fairly accurate reflection of what's going on in our inner world, which is why it's often said that our feelings never lie to us. But keep in mind that our feelings are usually reactions to our belief systems. So if our beliefs are accurate, our feelings will be accurate. But if our beliefs are inaccurate, our feelings can lead us astray.

For example, if I believe that a man is about to harm me, I'm likely to feel vulnerable and afraid. My fear is an accurate reflection of my inner reality. It's telling me my truth. But what if I'm fully capable of protecting myself from the other man? Or what if he doesn't actually intend to harm me at all? In either case, my feelings—though truthful—aren't accurate in the present situation. Deeper reflection on those feelings may reveal that my emotional reaction is an echo from my past. The situation may have reminded me of a time earlier in my life when a man *did* harm me. My feelings of vulnerability and fear were accurate then, and the truth these emotions are showing me in the present is that I am still living in that past moment and need to resolve that memory. The self—and most particularly the Self at our self's center—is a source of much wisdom for the man who diligently seeks to understand it.

Connection to Our Higher Power: Axis mundi, as you recall, is an intersection between the divine and the profane realms. In plainer terms, it is an ability to feel connected to a Higher Power—to God or some other external power or principle that helps to provide personal stability and spiritual sustenance. We need to be able to rely on, surrender to, and receive guidance from that transcendent source. Guidance from our Higher Power may come as stunning flashes of revelation, as whisperings of inspiration or intuition, or as simple feelings of peace and calmness.

If we're to live a centered life, we must foster a spiritual connection to something higher, more powerful, and more meaningful than ourselves by creating what could be called "sacred space" within our own bodies and minds. To live a truly abundant life necessitates that we draw on the energy and potential of our Higher Power. We must bring it into our lives through vision and faith. We need that transcendent source of wisdom and guidance in the same way that a compass needs the magnetic pull of the north or a child needs the direction and correction of his parents. Even with a strong core self, without the guidance of a transcendent power we're bound to wander and make less of our lives than we otherwise could. I'll discuss this topic in far greater detail in the next chapter. ✍ 2.2

> Our feelings are usually reactions to our belief systems.

> To live a truly abundant life necessitates that we draw on the energy and potential of our Higher Power.

Clarity and Vision: Fostering axis mundi—by developing our ability to hear, recognize, and distinguish the voice of our Self and the voice of our Higher Power—provides a degree of clarity in our lives that we could not experience in any other way. Together, they make clear to us what we must have in our lives and what we must exclude. They tell us what's good and bad, right and wrong. These voices illuminate what's important to us—what should come first in our lives and what we can let go of. And they provide a sense of what's *enough* and when we've gone too far. Such awareness is the foundation of our needs, values, priorities, and boundaries.

"Where there is no vision, the people perish."

Proverbs 29:18, *KJV*

Knowing the voice of our Selves and our Higher Power can also provide us with *vision*. Definitions of vision might include a perspective on life and our place in the world, a powerful and motivating idea that we feel compelled to create, and a goal or sense of where we're going. These goals, perspectives, and ideas all derive from truths that are revealed to us from some higher source. A verse from *The Proverbs* in *The Old Testament* expresses the significance of vision. It says simply, "Where there is no vision, the people perish." Think about it this way—if you couldn't see, would you drive a car? Do you walk around town with your eyes closed? Even visually impaired persons don't go out unless they have a cane or guide dog, which provide them with vicarious vision.

It is vision that pulls us forward in life. With no vision, we tend to navel gaze at the failings and meager merits of our ego. But with a strong vision we're drawn toward something transcendent, something better than where and what we are in the present or who we were in the past. If you don't have a vision for yourself right now, don't worry about it. Continue reading and implementing the concepts in this book, keeping in mind the idea of finding a vision for yourself, and it's very likely that a vision will eventually find you. ✐ 2.3

Validity, Worth, and Purpose: It's my opinion that each human being has inherent validity, worth, and purpose. Validity means having strength and power and being pertinent. Worth implies having value and being deserving of respect and esteem. Purpose means that there is design and meaning in your existence; that you are here for a reason. It implies that you have a special future.

Because these factors are inherent in each of us, contact with our deep Self and with our Higher Power confirms them to us automatically. Having a vision for our lives intensifies our sense of them. I know this because I've experienced it myself in profound ways and because I've known many other people who experience it, too. Life circumstances may alienate us from our sense of validity, worth, and purpose. We can become caught in ego games, compulsively defending our sense of goodness. But this doesn't change our intrinsic value—it only obscures it.

Intrinisic: essential to the nature of a thing; built in

These are very powerful and essential factors in our lives, and their significance can't be expressed too strongly. Connection with our inherent validity, worth, and purpose can have a tremendous regenerating capacity to renew our energy and keep us moving forward through life's greatest challenges. Such a connection can become a reserve of psychic power that we can use to push the darkness from our lives. And the assurance gained from this connection intensifies the gravity, or centering capacity, of the Self. Without that assurance, we'll likely find ourselves either lacking a Center or obsessively centered on the ego–driven struggle to prove our validity, worth, and purpose. ✍ 2.4

Source of Balance

The "unwobbling pivot" of our Center provides a sort of spiritual and psychological fulcrum by which we can balance all things in our lives. Let me give you a visual example for this. On the illustration of the seesaw (or teeter–totter) below, notice the two ends, labeled points A and B, with the fulcrum in the middle. The fulcrum represents *zhōng yōng*—the center reference point or axis mundi. This is what I described in the previous section. In Chapter One I mentioned that balance has two aspects: contrast and equilibrium. *The two ends, A and B, represent contrast and the board itself helps us understand equilibrium.*

Our Center provides a sort of spiritual and psychological fulcrum by which we can balance all things in our lives.

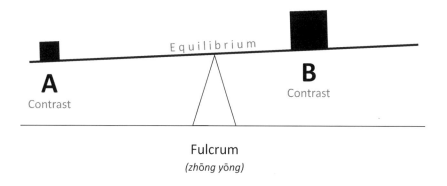

Equilibrium

A
Contrast

B
Contrast

Fulcrum
(zhōng yōng)

Contrast: The old adage, "All work and no play makes Jack a dull boy" is stressing the importance of contrast. Contrast means that diverse and even opposing energies, forces, and traits are present in our lives. Everything in life has its opposite. This is what gives life richness and perspective. Imagine the seesaw with no point *B*.

There would be no balance and point *A* would never get off the ground. Without diversity, life becomes like a one–ended seesaw.

This implies that we accept and embrace the opposing states and energies that naturally occur in life—and we're enriched by this diversity. According to the principle of yin–yang, we understand that our internal and external worlds abound with opposing states and forces, like old and young, beginning and end, hard and soft, holding on and letting go, firmness and yielding, pain and pleasure, humor and solemnity, reverence and rowdiness, spiritual and physical, fulfillment and sacrifice, and masculine and feminine. We honor all of these.

Contrast also implies that we're involved in diverse activities and pursue a range of interests and goals in our lives. It means that we're well rounded. For example, our lives include diverse activities like work and play, intimacy and alone time, giving and receiving, exercise and rest, masculine activities and time with a woman, self–expression and quiet reflection, worship and sensual pleasure, assertion and surrender. 2.5

Equilibrium: In our daily living we need to feel, express, and engage in the contrasting elements described above in healthy proportions—not too much, not too little. A good metaphor for this would be making cookie dough, which includes contrasting elements like sugar and salt. The dough won't be good without both ingredients, but it also won't be good if the sugar and salt aren't included in proper proportions. Very little salt is necessary to balance the sugar.

Likewise, in our lives we must give each element its appropriate place, prominence, and emphasis—but no more than is appropriate. For example, we don't pursue work to the complete exclusion of play. And we don't play to the degree that our work is ignored. We balance humility with accurate self–worth. Our firmness gives way to yielding when needed. All things are held in appropriate relationship to one another—no part overwhelms another.

But our internal and external worlds are constantly in a state of flux. So in order to maintain equilibrium, all of these diverse and opposing elements need to be held in a dynamic and flexible tension with one another. In other words, we have to be able to adjust and adapt.

Let's return to the seesaw. Look at the graphic again and notice that on point *A* there is a small object that's further from the fulcrum while point *B* has a larger object that's closer to the center. If you've ever been on a seesaw, you probably recall that you have to balance the weight of the kid on the other end by moving back and forth on the board, toward or away from the fulcrum. If you're lighter than the other kid, you slide up the board away from the center. If you're heavier than the other kid, you slide down the board toward the center. Similarly, we need to be flexible and adapt ourselves to changing circumstances. ✍ 2.6

The Moderator

The first rule of the seesaw is this: the longer the board, the bigger the swings; the bigger the swings, the harder the crash. The doctrine of the mean suggests that the wise man lives life by walking the middle path. In other words, he rides a seesaw with a short board.

The principle of moderation is well illustrated by the Greek myth of Icarus, who was imprisoned with his father Daedalus on the island of Crete. Daedalus, who was an excellent craftsman, made wings for himself and Icarus so that they could fly to freedom. The wings were made of feathers fastened to a wooden frame with wax.

Icarus and Daedalus

Before they began their flight, Daedalus warned Icarus to fly the middle course between the waves and the sun. By flying too low he would be in danger of crashing into the sea, and by flying too high he would be in danger of the sun melting the wax that held his wings together. (The Greeks were a bit naïve about the actual location of the sun.) But Icarus was an unwise youth and, having never read Confucius or this book, he lacked moderation. He flew too high, the wax melted, and he plummeted into the sea.

The principle of moderation is essential to a well–lived life. Moore and Gillette warn in each of their books about the danger of accessing archetypal energy too directly or intensely. The raw power of the archetypes is too great for any human soul to channel or contain. We men are flawed conduits that burn up quickly when infused with raw archetypal amperage. When we mainline an archetype, we go quickly into shadow, and then we burn out fast. Think of the out–of–control addict or the man who goes "postal." Lacking any moderation, they bring themselves down—and often bring others down with them.

The principle of
moderation is essential
to a well-lived life.

You might worry that moderation will create a bland life of vague pleasantness. My own experience with developing greater moderation is that I've traded drama for peacefulness, flash for substance, and chaos for calmness. In truth, life is immeasurably more rich and full.

Now let's look at moderation in more real terms. Moderation is created and maintained through boundaries, which entail self–restraint and observing reasonable limits. Knowledge of which boundaries are proper for us comes from our Center— the unmoving, unchanging core that guides and directs the rest of our psyche. The gravity of a strong Center pulls our extremes toward it and into moderation. So knowing and setting boundaries is King work. Enforcing our boundaries is the work of the Warrior, and we'll discuss his role in maintaining boundaries in Chapter Five. For now, let's overview two broad categories of boundaries: internal and external.

Internal Boundaries: What we do is a result of what we think and feel. Put differently, our thoughts and feelings precede our behavior. So if we're to live with moderation, we must have boundaries in all of these internal aspects of our lives— in our thoughts, our feelings, and in the behaviors that result from them.

Mental and emotional boundaries may be the most difficult to set and keep because our thoughts and feelings are so strongly influenced by the nonconscious mind and by biology, both of which can be mysterious and difficult to control. But if we carefully observe our thoughts and feelings, we may begin to notice patterns in our thinking and our feelings and in the relationships between the two. Learning about our patterns is a vital first step in assuring a moderate lifestyle.

As we observe ourselves, we may notice that our thoughts and feelings tend to be over–controlled, suggesting boundaries that are too rigid. For example, we might find that we tend to hold onto ideas or beliefs even when evidence suggests we're wrong. We might find that we're inflexible in our opinions and outlook. We could discover that we avoid thinking about things we just don't want to deal with. We might realize we view feelings as something dangerous to be avoided. It could become apparent that our feelings are locked down and very difficult to connect with. And of course others might straight out tell us we're stubborn or emotionally disconnected.

Moderation is created and maintained through boundaries.

We must have boundaries in our thoughts, our feelings, and in the behaviors that result from them.

On the other hand, our observations may reveal a lack of control of our thoughts and feelings, suggesting boundaries that are too weak. For example, we may notice that our thoughts are out of control or obsessive or that we can't stop ruminating. We may find that we can't or won't control our daydreams or fantasies. We might recognize that we can't seem to make up our mind or that we're constantly changing our opinion. We might discover that we tend to react to certain thoughts with strong emotions or that our emotions seem generally out of control. We could even find that we enjoy feeling very intense feelings or that we tend to create a lot of emotional drama in our lives. It may become apparent that we can't control feelings like fear, anxiety, worry, shame, lust, anger, sadness, or depression.

Our behavior tends to follow the patterns of our thoughts and emotions. So, if our mental and emotional boundaries are rigid, we may find that our behavior seems strict, controlled, or stiff—that we rarely or never act spontaneously. We may recognize that we don't allow ourselves the joy of healthy, normal behaviors like rest, pleasure, or socializing with friends. Or we may discover that we routinely avoid doing things that are outside our comfort zone. If our mental and emotional boundaries are weak, we're likely to discover that our behavioral boundaries are weak as well. We may find ourselves unable to control, limit, or stop certain behaviors. And we may discover that we have compulsions or addictions.

You may find that neither the description of rigid or weak internal boundaries resonates with you. This may be a sign that your internal boundaries are already moderate. But if any aspects of the descriptions above seemed to fit you, be sure to read Chapter Four carefully where we'll discuss issues like counter–emotions, difficulty feeling, negative core beliefs, sexual addiction and compulsion, bipolar disorder, anxiety, and obsessive–compulsive disorder—all of which relate to difficulty moderating our internal lives. ✍ 2.7

External Boundaries: If we're to live with moderation, we must also exercise appropriate boundaries in our interpersonal relationships and in our interactions with society in general. Having healthy boundaries with the external world depends on us maintaining strong internal boundaries, like those we discussed above. We have to understand and be able to appropriately limit our own thoughts, feelings, and behaviors in order to live moderately with others. In addition to those internal boundary skills, we must also develop a whole range of interpersonal and social responses, from complete openness, to total detachment and perhaps even

We must also exercise appropriate boundaries in our interpersonal relationships and in our interactions with society in general.

fierce self–defense. Some relationships or social situations will invite us to be open, receptive, and flexible with our boundaries while others may require us to be aware, even wary, and firm with our boundaries. In still other situations we'll need to be vigilant, on guard, and hold very rigid boundaries. On occasion, we may have to disconnect ourselves completely from others.

Moderation in our personal relationships means that we can have intimacy with limits, expectations with flexibility, and commitment with independence. We neither avoid nor become addicted to intimacy. Rather, we enjoy the blessings of friendship and the beauties of other people without fixation, obsession, or enmeshment, and without attempting to own or control them. We allow others to have their own space, to think their own thoughts, and to make their own decisions. There is give–and–take in our relationships. We can hold onto our expectations of others when appropriate, and yield those expectations when it's the right thing to do. We can also hold onto our position in a dispute or disagreement when we know that we're right and yield our position when we see that we're wrong. In our relationship with our Higher Power, we can be open, receptive, and trusting, while also maintaining an appropriate sense of self–reliance. Over all, good boundaries allow our relationships to be peaceful and satisfying.

> Moderation in our personal relationships means that we can have intimacy with limits, expectations with flexibility, and commitment with independence.

In our interactions with society, moderation means that we're aware of and comply with laws, rules, and expectations without becoming obsessed or stifled by them. We respect and comply with customs and traditions intelligently and with intention, understanding their value and purpose rather than just following blindly. We may be actively involved in fostering social progress without falling into radicalism. We engage in our professional marketplace in assertive but respectful ways—actively pursuing what we want without becoming obsessed with competing against others. And we properly protect ourselves from fraud, repression, and abuse—and assist others who are being poorly treated—while remaining generally positive and open. ✍ 2.8

> Moderation with society means that we're aware of and comply with laws, rules, and expectations without becoming obsessed or stifled by them.

The Integrator

To review, balance provides contrast and equilibrium in our lives and moderation provides us with protective internal and external boundaries. As a result, we experience ongoing health and an abiding sense of wellbeing because balance and moderation allow for persistence. In simpler terms, we don't burn ourselves out with too much of one thing or get to the end of our rope from ignoring the things that replenish us. Rather than craving or longing for the fulfillment of unmet needs, we regularly experience a sense of refreshment and enjoyment of life. This makes our lifestyles sustainable.

The principle of integration goes a step further by working to synthesize all the various parts of our lives and personalities into a unified and functional whole. As you remember from the previous chapter, integration has a dual meaning, referring to both an act or process of combining diverse parts into a whole and to restoring something back to its original and untouched condition. This aspect of the King brings order to our lives by helping us hold together our archetypal energies so their opposing forces can operate as a single, unified whole. It also makes the archetypal forces more moderate. For example, the emotion, sensuality, and relationality of the Lover humanize the Magian and soften the Warrior, while the Warrior's discipline and the Magian's wisdom give boundaries and reality to the Lover. The result is three more moderate energies. Integration is important in both our inner and outer worlds

> Integration means working to synthesize all the various parts of our lives and personalities into a unified and functional whole.

Internal Integrity: This implies that we're put together and unified *within ourselves* rather than feeling conflicted and at odds with our own thoughts, feelings, desires, impulses, and behaviors. We experience ourselves as moving all in the same direction rather than being pulled in opposite directions by vastly conflicting urges. For example, consider the following questions:

> Internal integrity implies that we're put together and unified within ourselves.

- Can you simultaneously experience feelings of anger and love toward a close friend without feeling conflicted? Can you accept both of these emotions as part of an intimate relationship?
- Can you experience and appropriately respond to sexual feelings while feeling at peace with your Higher Power?
- Can you feel gratitude and joy for your own strengths and gifts while meekly accepting your deficiencies?
- Can you identify the *satisfying* response and the *right* response in a situation—which might be contradictory—then choose the response that's ultimately the most beneficial?
- Can you satisfy your bodily appetites in ways that are in keeping with your spiritual values?

Having this internal unity can make us feel like things work well inside us. It can make us feel whole and put together "right." We can see ourselves as being what God designed us to be. ✍ 2.9

Integrated Lifestyle: Although our lifestyles may include diverse interests, activities, and relationships, all of the pieces fit together in some sensible way. We don't have parts of our lives that are split off or kept secret from the rest. This allows us to feel calm and peaceful, settled and secure. Consider the following questions that suggest an integrated lifestyle:

- Does your wife, or do your parents, know your friends? Do your friends know each other?
- Do your friends and co–workers know your religious convictions?
- Do your parents understand the problems you're facing in your life?
- Do you keep your job because you like it, not just because you have to? Does it make you feel productive and alive?
- Does your lifestyle match your spiritual values?

Now consider these questions that suggest a non–integrated lifestyle:

- Is your addiction a secret?
- Do you have different and incompatible sets of friends?
- Do you spend all day working at a job you hate while dreaming about being more creative?
- Is there a complete lack of connection between your work life and your home life? ✍ 2.10

Range of Capacities: When our archetypal energies are integrated, we can access a diverse set of abilities in order to respond appropriately in any situation we encounter. For example, we can access passion when we want it and calmness when we need it, aggression when required and submission when appropriate. When we're integrated, these and all other capacities are available to us in the moment they are needed. And it all feels like one whole self. Consider the following as possibilities for your life:

> All of the diverse interests, activities, and relationships in our lives fit together in some sensible way.

> We can access a diverse set of abilities in order to respond appropriately in any situation we encounter.

34

- Your Lover qualities of passion and intimacy can humanize your diligently cerebral and intellectual Magian, allowing you to love your work and connect personally to your colleagues.
- Your Warrior's discipline and your Magian's wisdom can provide boundaries and reality to your Lover's desire for closeness, allowing him to deeply enjoy others without becoming obsessed.
- Your Magian's intelligence can mitigate the zeal of your Warrior so that you know when it's time to surrender an ambition you can't achieve.
- The compassion of your Lover can soften your Warrior's indignation, allowing you to say "No" with kindness.
- Your King can lead your life with a Magian's wisdom, a Warrior's discipline, and a Lover's passion.

Below is a list of some of the capacities that a man might need to access and integrate in order to live a balanced life.

Kindness	Forgiveness	Surrender	Tolerance of pain
Meekness	Reverence	Compassion	Opposite sex attraction
Diligence	Humility	Awareness	Fortitude
Creativity	Imagination	Courage	Commitment
Persistence	Faith	Authenticity	Calmness
Tenacity	Fierceness	Passion	Submissiveness
Empathy	Love	Zeal	Intelligence
Intimacy	Wisdom	Discipline	Indignation
Ambition	Hope	Vision	Ability to feel guilt
Openness	Sensuality		

Your inner King understands the design of your unified self, and he wants to create it according to your birthright as a man. ✍ 2.11

The One Who Discerns

To discern means to detect or discover something with the senses, or to distinguish or know something within the mind. It implies differentiating and discriminating one thing from another and making value distinctions between them. This is foundational to the King's role as the Creator of Order because discernment is what enables us to create a mental structure for everything we know and experience. Without the ability to tell one thing from another, our minds and lives would be

Discern: to detect or discover with the senses, or to distinguish or know something within the mind

complete chaos. Moore and Gillette refer to discernment as "the sword that cuts through confusion."

Discernment is an innate human capacity. Early in childhood we begin to differentiate among things, laying down our basic cognitive map of the world. We discern that a cat is not a dog and a barn is different from a house. We differentiate happy from sad and good from bad. We learn that we like some things and don't like other things. So discernment is foundational for learning. It's also essential in making decisions, establishing priorities, and gaining insight. And it's the foundation of true consciousness and self–awareness, since without the ability to discern we can't notice our thoughts or understand our actions. Our capacity to discern is greatly enhanced by the clarity and vision that come from a strong connection to our Self and our Higher Power.

This King trait is absolutely necessary if we're to understand our emotions, impulses, desires, intentions, and values, and those of the people around us. In order to have true balance in our lives, we need discernment, since balance can only be understood and chosen if there is comprehension of the opposites being balanced. Discernment also enables us to learn what brings true peace and joy, as opposed to what's merely exciting or makes us happy for the moment. Without the wise judgment of practiced discernment, we'll be prone to make decisions based solely on what pleases and displeases us at the time. And perhaps most important for our discussion here, discernment is essential in the process of healing our lives and overcoming unwanted same–sex attraction. 2.12

The Sovereign

A King has sovereignty over his realm, which means that he has ultimate power or right to govern himself. Each man is a sovereign in his own life. This is true because we have been endowed by the Creator with volition, which means the capacity to choose. That power cannot be taken from us. Our freedoms may be curtailed, but not our capacity to choose.

An example may help clarify. Imagine a prisoner in maximum security who is locked in a cell and shackled to the wall. This man has very little freedom, meaning that his range of options is minimal. Even so, his capacity to make choices based on those options is unimpaired. He can choose to think anything he wants to think.

King George V of England

He can choose to whisper, shout, sing, or recite poetry. And he can choose to foster feelings of anger, resentment, and hatred, or remorse, contrition, and forgiveness.

Even chained to the wall, the prisoner still has sovereignty over his mind and heart. Obviously he is subject—as are all of us—to a number of factors that limit his options. But the same is true for an emperor—somewhere there is an end to his influence and a world beyond his authority. The difference between the prisoner and an emperor is the extent of his limitations versus the number of options open to him. The prisoner has major limitations and few options, which restricts his power. The emperor's situation is the reverse—he has few limitations and a vast number of options, giving him extensive power. Even so, both the prisoner and the emperor are sovereign within their sphere.

With sovereignty comes duty and responsibility. We're answerable for our actions and become bound by what we do. We can't control or endlessly avoid the consequences that follow our choices. This is obviously true for the prisoner. But the principle is equally true for the emperor as well. For example, he can't control how his people feel about his laws or whether they will eventually rebel and overthrow him. The only way for any man to control consequences is to change his behavior so that it's in line with the consequences he desires.

> With sovereignty comes duty and responsibility. We're answerable for our actions and become bound by what we do.

Because we have the capacity to choose, we can make our lives whatever we want them to be within the range of our limitations and options. This power is an essential aspect of the King's ordering function. Without it we can't govern or guide our lives. But with it we can gradually overcome our limitations and increase our options, thus expanding our freedom and power. As freedom and power are gained, the King will be vigilant to maintain his hard–won advances by protecting his boundaries from the encroachment of others and from situations that would diminish his power. He will also be vigilant against the erosion of his power through his own neglect.

As a King advances his freedom and power, he will interact with the boundaries of other people and of established systems, such as business entities, government agencies, and social customs. We aren't sovereign in those realms, and so in order to get what we want, we're obliged to make "alliances and treaties." A king will never allow himself to become enslaved or unnecessarily beholden to these "foreign powers." For example, he won't allow himself to become "owned" by the company or to remain dependent on a welfare system for very long. He looks to his own capabilities and relies foremost on his own power. ✐ 2.13

The Organizer

There is no joy in chaos. Chaos doesn't provide for need fulfillment except in purely haphazard ways. Some degree of practical organization is necessary in order to maintain a lifestyle amenable to providing for our needs and the needs of those who depend on us. Our careers, our home lives, and our relationships all require organization if we're to feel truly content and happy. Organization applies to logistical concerns like scheduling, finances, time use, possessions, and living environment. How can we know if our lives are appropriately organized?

We know we're organized when the logistics of our lives feel calm and in control. Things flow smoothly—we have what we need to have, we're where we need to be, and we can do what we need to do. Our careers are moving in meaningful directions. We're on time more often than not. We're in control of our money and our time. Our possessions are well kept, and we can find a screwdriver when we need one. Our homes are restful—they are clean and relatively free of clutter.

But it's not good to be *over*–organized. (The principle of moderation applies here, too!) While chaos doesn't allow for more than haphazard fulfillment of our needs, being too rigid and shunning spontaneity can rob us of the *joy* of that fulfillment. Organization itself can become a Tyrant Usurper if we feel compelled to maintain things in some exact way. Compulsive organization can also be hard on our relationships if others don't share our same standards of organization. If our organization is too rigid, we block ourselves from experiencing peaceful and spontaneous fulfillment and joy. ✐ 2.14

The Builder of Civilization

In the year AD 527, a new ruler took the throne in the Byzantine Empire. Known as Justinian the Great, this emperor labored throughout his thirty–eight–year reign to restore the greatness of the classical Roman Empire. Through military campaigns, he retook many territories that had been part of ancient Rome but had been lost to usurping rulers. He completely revised Roman law and attempted to settle long–term disputes of religious dogma. He caused many cathedrals, churches, and monasteries to be built, ordered the construction of bridges and water supplies,

There is no joy in chaos.

While chaos doesn't allow for more than haphazard fulfillment of our needs, being too rigid can rob us of the joy of that fulfillment.

founded at least one new city, and strengthened the kingdom's borders with military fortresses. He also actively supported the arts and literature.

Though by modern standards this type of aggressive kingdom building would be considered utter tyranny, it was the mark of great rulers for millennia. The intention of these rulers is presumed to have been to overcome chaos by spreading the benefits of civilization throughout the known world. Indeed, these kinds of efforts did spread language, science, technology, and culture from more advanced civilizations to those that were less developed. Under the best circumstances, they also ensured the rule of law and the safety and prosperity of the people. Such rulers were strongly connected to the King archetype's function as a builder of civilization.

Justinian the Great

Within our psyches and in our temporal lives, we need to connect with this role of the King archetype. It's this energy that can help us to overcome chaos and advance order and prosperity in our own lives and in the world around us. This role is the source of all progression, advancement, and development.

The King is the source of all progression, advancement, and development.

In our physical environment, this might include finishing the basement or adding a needed bedroom, planting a garden, or petitioning to get a sidewalk put in. In the professional and legal world, this might mean starting a new company, codifying laws, writing policies and procedures, developing new software, conducting scientific research, or creating a new invention.

Interpersonally, this could mean improving our relationships with our wives and children, establishing better boundaries with a friend, reconciling a lost friendship, or making new acquaintances. Internally, this might include changing a troubling habit or increasing our ability to surrender an addiction. It could mean dialoging with split–off parts within us, or becoming more discerning, conscious, and self–aware. It would include increasing our awareness and compliance with natural law. It might mean becoming more balanced, moderate, and integrated in our attitudes and behavior. And it could include deepening and expanding our relationship with our Higher Power. ✎ 2.15

The Keeper and Giver of Law

The universe works according to natural laws, and a king orders his world according to these laws. As sovereign entities, mortal kings make laws to govern their people.

Nine Natural Laws

• Polarity

• Relativity

• Cause and Effect

• Vacuum

• Manifestation

• Abundance

• Perpetual
  Transmutation

• Gestation

• Rhythm

But kings are themselves governed by these higher natural laws, which they can't control. These universal laws have been set by a Universal King or a universal force. Scientists, philosophers, holy people, and everyday folks have observed these natural laws for millennia. Some of these laws govern our daily lives in very direct ways, such as the law of gravity and the other physical laws of our world. Disobeying these laws tends to more or less quickly result in death. Other laws have effects that aren't as immediately noticeable. It's about some of these more subtle—but still tremendously powerful—laws that this section is dedicated.

James Allen wrote in his classic book, *As A Man Thinketh*:

> Law, not confusion, is the dominating principle of the universe. ...
> This being so, man has but to right himself to find that the universe
> is right. And during the process of putting himself right, he will
> find that as he alters his thoughts towards things and other people,
> things and other people will alter towards him.

Most of the frustration we experience in our lives comes upon us as a consequence of not following the laws or principles that would allow our lives to run better. We may be very sincere and even committed to the idea of changing our lives, but if we don't follow the right principles, our lives won't change.

Take time to carefully consider the nine laws described below.[2] As you do, realize that they are impacting your life every day, whether you know it or not. Consider how you could use these laws to move your life in the direction *you want to go*.

For everything that exists there is an opposite of equal value or degree.

Law of Polarity: For everything that exists there is an opposite of equal value or degree. We discussed this in Chapter One in the context of the archetypes and their bipolar shadows. I quoted there from the *Tao Te Ching*, where Lao Tzu states that opposites create and define each other, as *beauty* creates *ugliness* and *white* helps to define *black*. Opposites also complement and follow each other, as *easy* complements *difficult* and *end* follows *beginning*. We can add to Lao Tzu that some opposites seek fulfillment or completion through each other, in the way that *lack* seeks fulfillment through *plenty* or *weakness* seeks completion through *strength*. This law suggests that for each of our shadows we have the potential for wholeness, for each of our weaknesses we have a potential strength, and for each of our misfortunes there awaits a potential blessing. ✎ 2.16

Law of Relativity: Things gain value only in comparison with other things. Most of what we experience in our lives is not fundamentally good or bad. Without comparison, we simply accept things as they are. But when we compare, we begin to make judgments. It's the judgments that make us feel good or bad about the things in our lives. The stoic philosopher Epictetus (AD 55–135) said, "We are disturbed not by events, but by the views which we take of them." We're neither handsome nor ugly until we compare ourselves with another man. Nor are we rich or poor, smart or stupid, lucky or cursed, fortunate or condemned, until we compare ourselves to someone else.

Because we live in society and have endless situations with which to compare our own, we cannot avoid making judgments. But we can choose to what and whom we'll compare ourselves. And we can choose what we tell ourselves about those comparisons. ✎ 2.17

Law of Cause and Effect: Everything that we do has an impact of some kind. We may not always see those effects, at least not immediately, but an effect is created nonetheless. We discussed this concept in Chapter One along with the principle of polarity. I paraphrased Newton's third law of motion, which states essentially that for every action there is an equal and opposite reaction. Another way of saying this is that we reap what we sow. This is also known in Eastern religions as the principle of karma. That which we do is returned to us in some way. By giving we receive. By serving we lead. By caring for others we are loved. Selfishness leaves us empty, but gratitude brings an endless flow of blessings. ✎ 2.18

Law of the Vacuum: Whenever an empty space is made, something will come in to fill that space. The removal of an undesirable habit leaves an opening, and one of several things can happen: the same habit will return, another undesirable habit will take its place, or we'll consciously replace it with a new desirable habit of our own creation. The same is true of our belongings, our friendships, our beliefs, and even our emotions. In order to obtain the things we want in our lives, we must first remove from our lives the things we don't want. Then we must consciously create the things we do want. ✎ 2.19

Law of Manifestation: Our sustained and consistent thoughts create the world in which we live. Our thoughts do this in two ways: first, by affecting our perception of the real world around us, and second, by actually bringing to us the things we

Things gain value only in comparison with other things.

Everything that we do has an impact of some kind.

Whenever an empty space is made, something will come in to fill that space.

Our thoughts create the world in which we live.

think about. The more intense and focused our thoughts are—whether positive or negative—the more intensely they will impact our reality. This is also referred to as the Law of Attraction.

For example, the way you perceive yourself and other men, and the beliefs you form about these perceptions, will create the reality in which you live your life. Whether you see men as safe or threatening, honorable or suspect, accepting or rejecting, and whether you see yourself as equal to, or somehow defective and less than other men—these beliefs create the world of men as you know it. We sometimes call these beliefs "the stories I tell myself," because they really are just the stories that we create inside our heads to make sense of the world around us. Change your beliefs and you change the world as you know it. Change the stories you tell yourself about yourself and the people around you, and you change your reality. 2.20

Law of Abundance: The universe has an endless supply of the essential elements from which all physical substance is formed. Therefore, there is no scarcity except that which we create by our beliefs. In reality there is only abundance. The universe also has an endless supply of emotions. There is endless joy, love, anger, sadness, and fear. Furthermore, the universe has an endless supply of ideas and creative opportunities. There are endless works of art, technological inventions, and business deals to be created. Whether abundance—physical, emotional, or creative—flows through our lives or evades us is a product of our own thinking and our willingness to observe the other pertinent laws. 2.21

Law of Perpetual Transmutation: Everything that exists is either coming into form or going out of form. Another way to say this is that everything has a "life cycle" of some sort. Physical things start in diffusion and slowly gather, coming into form. They exist in material form for a period of time as they continue to grow, then begin to decay. Eventually they break down into diffusion again. We can see this in a physical body, which gradually grows in a womb as elements are gathered from their diffuse state in the mother's body. The body emerges in material form at birth and continues to grow until a certain age, at which time it begins to break down. After death the elements of the body break down further and are diffused back into the environment.

The universe has an endless supply of the essential elements. There is no scarcity.

Everything that exists is either coming into form or going out of form.

The things we create have a similar life cycle. They begin as diffuse concepts or principles. At some point, concepts begin to coalesce and an idea is formed. The idea may continue to grow for some time until it's brought into physical form through the actions of people. Our creation may remain in physical form for a very short or a very long time, but eventually what we create will decay and return to its diffuse form. This is exemplified by the building of a structure. It begins with an idea. Then plans are made. The elements needed to construct it are gathered, and the structure is erected. The building may stand for a few years or many centuries before it crumbles or is torn down and its elements are scattered. ✍ 2.22

Law of Gestation: Everything that's created has an incubation period, which is a set and finite length of time. Also, everything that's created must be nurtured and nourished in some way, just as a growing fetus must be nourished. Our creations follow the same principles that things in nature follow. If we want to create something, we need to remember that it will take a finite period of time and the right amount of nurture to bring it into material form. Since we often don't know what the set gestation period is, we can become frustrated, and sometimes we may lose hope and stop nurturing the thing we're trying to create.

> Everything that's created has an incubation period.

When we give up on our creations, they begin to go out of form back into diffusion. In other words, our plans and hopes fall apart. Sometimes we use this as evidence that it wasn't going to happen anyway. We may say to ourselves, "See, I can't accomplish that. It's never gonna happen." But giving up on the things we want to create is like a farmer planting a seed, then plowing up the field in frustration the next week because all he sees are tiny sprouts instead of ripened vegetables. We have to give our creations time to come into form. ✍ 2.23

Law of Rhythm: Natural processes happen in cycles that are constantly being repeated. This law is closely related to the Law of Perpetual Transmutation. The Law of Rhythm is easily seen in the cycle of the seasons, the water cycle, and the reproductive cycle. This law applies to events that happen in our lives as well. For every low there is a high. Sadness will give way to joy. Fatigue will return to strength. Loss will be compensated with something new. This is sometimes referred to as the vicissitudes of life—in other words, life's ups and downs. We can impact the rhythms that occur in our lives by our thoughts. It's possible—through our thoughts—to get ourselves stuck in painful cycles. It's also possible to consciously use our thoughts to make each "up" bring us a little higher and cause

> Natural processes happen in cycles that are constantly being repeated.

each "down" to be a little less low. We will always cycle, but we can cause life's rhythms to move us gradually upward.

In music, rhythm is considered to be the energizer and organizer. Think about that concept for a moment. The rhythm or beat of a song is what carries it forward and gives the sounds meaningful organization. The rhythms of life can have the same effect, if we choose to see them in a proper light—as indicators that life is unfolding and moving forward. If we see ups and downs as just a meaningless cycle, or interpret the downs that follow the ups as mere setbacks, we're bound to feel frustrated. But if we choose instead to recognize that these natural rhythms are an indication that life is proceeding on a natural and meaningful course, these rhythms can at least feel tolerable or perhaps even comforting and reassuring.

Let me give a brief example. I find that my connection with God cycles through feelings of intense union and ecstatic closeness, followed by feelings of distance and aloneness, followed by a return to closeness. For many years I interpreted that cycle as an indication of my inadequacy as a disciple. With an understanding of the Law of Rhythm, I now recognize the periods of distance as part of the process of spiritual growth. I need those "alone times" to test my resolve and strengthen my will. ✍ 2.24

The Provider

The Provider

- Energy of libido
- Creator
- Inspirer
- Giver of blessing
- Provider of means

To review what we've discussed so far, the King's *ordering* function includes his role as our Center, or axis mundi. He provides balance, moderation, and integration. And he discerns and differentiates, organizes our lives logistically, maintains our sovereignty, observes natural laws, and extends the bounds of civilization. These are critical roles on all levels, from our internal psychological functioning to the functioning of society as a whole. But in my opinion, the King's crowning and most noble roles are those of his second essential function as the *provider*, or what Moore and Gillette call "the generative man."

The King fulfills this function through several roles. First, he's a creator. He gives form to intentions, thoughts, desires, patterns, feelings, inspirations, and impulses. He also inspires us, and those around us, by living his life as an authentic example of wholeness and by beholding and affirming the good he sees in us. He blesses us, and others, through touch, words, and commitment. And he provides the means for our material wellbeing and that of those for whom we have responsibility. We'll explore each of these roles in some detail. But first I must introduce you to the source from which all of these powers spring—the energy of "libido."

Libido

The roles of creating, inspiring, blessing, and providing are motivated by an instinctual energy that pushes us toward life, creativity, and individuation. Carl Jung used the term "libido" to refer to this energy, which may appear as appetite, passion, desire, motivation, and interest in relating with others. It might be described as "the lust for life" or the inspiration to exert ourselves, to fulfill our needs, and to bring abundance into our lives. Libido is also the urge to procreate, provide for, and inspire the next generation. It's this life energy that causes us to truly engage in our careers, to pursue avocations, recreation, and meaningful leisure, and to give ourselves to important causes. Without this energy we feel weakened, unmotivated, lifeless, and lost. Without libido we have no power to create, inspire, bless, or provide.

Libido: may appear as appetite, passion, desire, motivation, and interest in relating with others

While it's libido that motivates us to fulfill our roles as creators and givers of blessing, it's acts of personal sacrifice that shape the way we fulfill those roles— and that shape us as men *through* those roles. Allow me to explain this. We are finite. So everything we create limits our ability to create something else. Whatever time and resources we sacrifice to create one thing we cannot use to make another thing. To inspire others, we must choose to sacrifice those aspects of ourselves that make us common and uninspiring. To provide for others, we must give away some of what we have. To behold and bless others, we must take our eyes off ourselves. These are all acts of personal sacrifice, and they shape us as men. The higher and more ennobling our choices are, the nobler we'll become. ✍ 2.25

Creator

A primary expectation of a King has always been to produce an heir so that the kingdom can continue. Without an heir, the succession of leadership is broken and the kingdom risks being thrown into chaos. The entire procreative act is desirable to emotionally healthy men. Certainly the sex act and process of insemination draws the bulk of a man's procreative attention. But it's also very instinctual for emotionally mature men to want to have and raise children. We want to pass along our collected life experience to another generation. We want to see them become more and better than ourselves. Through this creative act, we leave the world better and more whole than we found it.

In *The King Within*, Moore and Gillette describe the creative act as "Libido in the process of incarnating itself." The term "incarnate," as Moore and Gillette use it, means to give physical form to something that's non–physical. For example, Christians speak of Jesus Christ as "God incarnate," by which we mean that the divine has taken physical form in Jesus. Sometimes when we speak of a particularly evil person we'll refer to him or her as "the devil incarnate." The act of begetting children is an incarnation of the man's desire for continuation and eternal life, for through the existence of the child the man will live on.

Every time we create something that's new to us, it could be said that we're incarnating an intention, thought, desire, pattern, feeling, impulse, or inspiration. This capacity is instinctual, and it is godly in that we're emulating the Higher Power that created all things. Our acts of creation may be in any number of different areas, from the world of science to the world of arts and entertainment. ✍ 2.26

Inspirer

The act of creation is not limited to incarnating in the physical world. We can also create within the realm of the human psyche. Inspiring others is an act of creation in that it helps to bring our vision of the world, and our vision of other people's potential, into physical form. It does this by evoking from within that person a unique vision of their best self so that it can grow into reality. On the most essential level, we inspire others by the example of our own lives. We also inspire them by deeply seeing them in affirming ways. Moore and Gillette use the term "beholding" to describe this level of seeing.

But the generative man doesn't only provide inspiration to others—he's also inspired by others and by himself. It's a kingly trait to be able to see the goodness in others and be lifted by their examples to higher aspirations. And it's a kingly thing to be able to provide inspiration for ourselves. So the role of inspirer may operate in three ways: we may inspire others, we may be inspired by others, and we may inspire ourselves.

Inspiring others is a kingly act that any man can do. This potential is not limited to leaders and luminaries. While I've often been inspired in the ways described above by men of great stature, I've also commonly been inspired by men I consider to be my peers. And I've very often been inspired by men who actually considered me to be *their* leader or teacher. Also, consider that inspiring others is as much

The creative act is "libido in the process of incarnating itself."

Moore and Gillette,
The King Within

We may inspire others, we may be inspired by others, and we may inspire ourselves.

a blessing to the inspirer as it is to the inspired—if not more. As I take seriously my role of leadership in my community—by attempting to live an exemplary life and by seeing, affirming, and blessing others—I find myself becoming a more capable and a happier man. I encourage you to develop the capacity and practice of inspiring others for the blessings you can give to others and for the strength it will create in you.

Authentic Example: Let me speak personally for a moment. I grew up being told that I was an example to others. I don't really know why that happened. I didn't really make much of it until I was well into my career and it became apparent that many men knew who I was and were watching me. I was becoming more known as a therapist as well as from things I had written and from leading experiential weekends. A small reputation was beginning to follow me. That's when I faced a choice: to be or to act. Having been involved in theater and film earlier in my life, I think my first impulse was to simply act like a leader. I unconsciously followed that approach for a while, attempting to do and say what I thought a leader would do and say. But at some point I realized that I was faking it—and I realized that leadership can't be faked. Those that try to fake it will eventually fail—life will eventually poke holes in their shtick, and their truth will be seen. The news is full of men learning that lesson the hard way.

> I realized that leadership can't be faked.

So I realized I had to either beef up my shtick and hope no one ever saw through it, or I had to surrender the act and instead truly be a leader by developing myself from the inside. Making the choice to let go of pretense and just work on actualizing my potential has brought tremendous benefits, the greatest of which is that I feel immeasurably more peaceful, confident, and calm. Pretense is draining; truth is relaxing. I don't have to worry about who is watching. I just try to authentically live what I teach.

Being an authentic example to others is a strange dichotomy. On one hand it implies that we're living our lives with an awareness that others are watching. In essence, it could be said that we're living our lives *for others*. But on the other hand, if our interest is in living as an *authentic* example, we're doing it for *ourselves* and we reap the benefits, which are tremendous. For me, this is a very energizing and motivating combination and not at all contradictory because it's simply reality. And it's a reality that any man can live. ✒ 2.27

Beholding: Overflowing with the positive and benevolent energy of his own libido, the King naturally showers blessings of recognition and affirmation on his subjects. To "behold" another entails seeing that person with complete acceptance of who he or she truly is in the present while also envisioning and affirming the person's greatest potential. Through acknowledging and openly praising them, the good King inspires and motivates his subjects, affirming for them a vision of their best potential. With their view of life now enriched by the King's graces, the subjects experience their own libido and they flourish, becoming more empowered, motivated, and capable of meeting their own needs.

> When our vision is firmly fixed on our greatest potential, we give ourselves something truly compelling to move toward.

This pattern is a good paradigm for lifting and motivating those around us and for earning their love and loyalty. This same pattern works internally as well. By seeing and completely accepting ourselves as we are right now, while also envisioning our own highest potential, we earn our own love and loyalty. In more practical terms, this means that we see and accept all parts of ourselves—including our weaknesses, flaws, and failures—with complete love and acceptance. Yet our attention doesn't linger on our weaknesses but on our strengths. We take time to notice our assets—our proficiency, growth, talents, and gifts. This is what motivates us to develop ourselves further. When our vision is firmly fixed on our greatest potential, we give ourselves something truly compelling to move toward. 2.28

Giver of Blessing

> Elements of blessing:
> - Meaningful touch
> - A spoken message
> - Expressions of worth and value
> - Picturing a special future
> - An active commitment

In their book, *The Blessing*, John Trent and Gary Smalley detail how we may bless our children, spouses, friends, and others. They studied Biblical accounts of various types of blessing as well as the lives of Orthodox Jewish families, in which blessing is a customary event. Through their research, they discovered five essential elements of blessing. The first element is "meaningful touch," which typically means placing hands on the head of the one receiving the blessing. The second element is "a spoken message." They point out that the message must be said out loud so that it can be heard by the one receiving. The spoken message contains statements that express to the one being blessed his or her intrinsic worth and high value. This is the third element of blessing. The fourth element is "picturing a special future for the one being blessed." This provides the individual with a sense of a positive and meaningful life ahead of them. And the fifth element of blessing is "an active commitment" to assist the individual in fulfilling the blessing.

Blessing may be a formal or ritual event, such as the blessings by patriarchs to their children described in the Bible. Ritual blessing also occurs in our own day in a variety of ways within the Orthodox Jewish community. It also happens regularly within the Mormon community[3] as well as within many other Christian churches. But acts of blessing need not be formal or ritual. All five of the elements of blessing can also be an informal part of daily life. For example, meaningful touch may be given and received daily in many different ways, including handshakes, hugs, pats on the back, and so forth.

Trent and Smalley quote a number of studies citing the significance of physical touch in the development of children as well as in the lives of adults. One study they refer to found that men and women need to receive eight to ten meaningful touches each day in order to maintain emotional and physical health. The need for touch is a significant issue for many men who are moving away from unwanted same–sex attraction, and we'll discuss this topic in greater depth in Chapter Eight.

The other elements of blessing can be provided informally as well. Spoken words of blessing that express to others their intrinsic worth and high value, and that help others to see a special future for themselves, are easily given and always welcome. If you've rarely received or given such words in the past, you may need some practice doing so. Trent and Smalley provide some useful suggestions about developing this ability, and I suggest that you read their book if you have an interest in further developing this kingly skill.[4] The fifth element of blessing, active commitment, is always an informal part of daily life. Daily commitment consists of devoting time, energy, and resources to caring for those we wish to bless.

As the king in your own life, you have a responsibility to provide blessing to yourself. I know of three ways in which this can be done. The first is by doing each of the five elements directly for yourself. We can be actively committed to ourselves. We can speak words of affirmation to ourselves that express our worth, value, and special future. And, though the idea may sound strange, we can even provide meaningful touch to ourselves. For example, try closing your eyes, thinking loving and affirming thoughts about yourself, and giving yourself a hug or gently stroking your own face.

> As the king in your own life, you have a responsibility to provide blessing to yourself.

A second way to provide blessing for yourself is to seek it from other people. Ask someone you trust and who cares about you to speak words of blessing to you. If you know someone who practices a faith that blesses, ask him for a blessing. You might also seek out touch in safe situations. And the third way to provide blessing for yourself is to bless others. The power of blessing is reciprocal. As you actively devote yourself to providing the five elements of blessing to other people, you're likely to find that your own King energy grows much stronger. ✍ 2.29

Provider of Means

The benevolent king also showers material blessings on his people—he's the dispenser of riches and the source of abundance in life. This represents real acts of giving to the self as well as to those in our lives for whom we possess King energy as a father, husband, friend, leader, or co–worker. These "riches" can be temporal, physical, mental, emotional, and spiritual. Let's break this section down into two directions of giving—internal (as self–care) and external (as giving to others).

Self–Care: We are responsible for our recovery and wellbeing. Ultimately, only we can make sure that our needs are met. It's typical of males for our first concern to be about our own wellbeing. Although this may sound selfish, on a certain level it makes sense and is appropriate since we have to preserve our own wellbeing if we're going to be there for those who depend on us. If we let ourselves go and overly sacrifice for others, we ultimately sabotage their wellbeing along with our own. So we need to consciously and proactively devote time, energy, and other resources to providing for the fulfillment of our needs. We have to treat ourselves as a generous king would treat his people—with an unwavering commitment to our own wellbeing. Then as we feel blessed and fulfilled, we naturally want to bless the lives of those around us. ✍ 2.30

> Only we can make sure our needs are met.

Giving to Others: At the same time, it's important that we recognize that we aren't on this planet just to take care of ourselves. There are people in our lives and in the world around us that we're meant to help and bless. This is the role of a mature man. That's why we often leap into action when we feel like someone needs our help. As soon as we give to others, we actually bless our own lives. Because of the Law of Cause and Effect, which we discussed a few pages ago, giving to others is actually another form of self–care. The Bible teaches that whatever a man sows, he will reap the same. The *Tao* teaches that when we give of ourselves, we become more. On the simplest level, I personally know that when I give, I feel good, I feel powerful, and I feel masculine. But on a more transcendent level I know that wise

> There are people in our lives that we're meant to help and bless.

generosity brings abundance, kindness returns kindness, and teaching causes me to learn.   ✐   2.31

SHADOWS OF THE KING

In the previous chapter, I introduced you to the concept of archetypal wholeness and shadow. You will recall that the word "shadow" has two meanings. It refers both to our nonconscious thoughts and traits and to the polarized extremes of the archetypes. Here I'm speaking of the second meaning. The opposing archetypal extremes always consist of an active side and a passive side. It's healthy for archetypal energies to have opposing—even conflicting—characteristics. In Chapter One I gave examples of opposing Warrior traits, including being disciplined versus relenting, being healthfully detached from feeling versus being aware of feeling, and being aggressive versus being calm. Opposites like these are meant to be held in balance and accessed in moderation.

Shadows seek wholeness. Our split–off parts don't go away. They simply seek their opposites according to the Laws of Polarity and Cause and Effect. If painful and shaming life experiences have caused us to split apart our archetypal King energy, we'll forever seek a balance between two opposing weak and tyrannical forces. This is according to natural law. And as water takes the most direct course into the lowest place, so too our psyche seeks the simplest and most direct remedy to its splits, even if that remedy is not healthy or real.

> Shadows seek wholeness. Our split-off parts don't go away. They simply seek their opposites.

The opposing extremes of the King archetype are referred to as the "Tyrant Usurper" and the "Weakling Abdicator." Both shadow poles of the King archetype arise out of a loss of healthy connection to the childhood archetype that Moore and Gillette call "The Divine Child." Normal parents see each of their children as something very special and treat them—at least for a period of time—as if they are the center of their world. Infants, in their innocence, know nothing but their own feelings and wants. They too see themselves as the center of all things. This is the Divine Child. And it's a healthy and appropriate stage of our development.

> The opposing extremes of the King archetype are referred to as the "Tyrant Usurper" and the "Weakling Abdictor."

How a child moves out of this phase determines how he will respond in adulthood to archetypal King energy. If he's eased out of that "divine" position with some dignity, he will likely develop a healthy relationship in adulthood to his inner King. Such a man will have gradually let go of his childhood pretentions of divinity, but will retain a spark of kingly energy at his core in the form of personal worth, legitimacy, and autonomy. His sense of greatness and potential is balanced by a realistic humility.

But too often a young person's Divine Child is squelched too harshly, taken away too early, tolerated for too long, or perhaps not permitted at all. These are the circumstances from which a Tyrant or Weakling arises. The parents may dethrone the Divine Child in their boy through abuse or neglect. The child may respond with resistance or passive submission. Alternatively, the parents may play into a child's grandiosity, leaving him unsure of the boundaries of his will. But in any case, the child is eventually left shamed and insecure about his validity, worth, and purpose. This is the underlying wound. Whether the individual responds to this wound in a predominantly tyrannical way or as an abdicating weakling depends on a variety of personal and situational factors too numerous to account for.

In response to a painful end to his Divine Child, the Tyrant actively clutches his crown and becomes preoccupied with keeping himself at the center of his universe. The passive Weakling, on the other hand, represses his pain by denying the memory of his divine beginnings. The spark of the King is dampened. Both shadows are obsessed with *self*. The Tyrant is beset by a crusade to advance his self in competition and opposition with the rest of the world and with God Himself. At the other pole, the Weakling comforts his wounded self through ignorance and vindicates his inner victim with false noble suffering. Both shadow poles are distanced from a Higher Power. The Tyrant has taken the role over and placed himself on God's throne, while the Weakling is more likely to not understand or simply not care about the existence of any transcendent power.

Projection: the act of seeing in someone else a feeling, desire, or trait that I hide, repress, or deny in myself. More simply, it's imposing my own traits onto someone else.

If we aren't accessing King energy in its fullness as described earlier in this chapter, we'll experience its split shadow forms, often by identifying with one pole and projecting the other pole onto people around us with whom we'll experience conflict. Another way to say this is that we'll live out the role of one of the shadow extremes while experiencing people around us as the other extreme. It's through the conflict between us and them that we maintain a shaky semblance of wholeness. They are the yin to our yang, the day to our night. The Tyrant and the Weakling—like all polar shadows—need and depend on each other. One pole cannot exist without the other also being present in some form. To a man with only a hammer, everything looks like a nail. And a man with only nails is constantly looking for a hammer. So too, for a man possessed by the Tyrant, everyone looks like a Weakling to be exploited. And a Weakling is constantly seeking to complete himself through a Tyrant whom he can fear and resent. But in either case, they are really just looking for their lost other half.

On the other hand, our psyches may attempt to hold onto both of these shadows through conflicts we create *within ourselves*. We don't need to look any further than our own minds to find both shadow poles of any archetype. We may spend most of our time in one shadow, but the other side is hidden within us, waiting for some unforeseen life situation to bring it out. Moore and Gillette eloquently state this principle in *The King Within*: "Scratch a tyrant and you'll find a weakling. Pressure a weakling and you'll find a tyrant."

As I've described already, our King potential splits into opposing shadows in reaction to childhood wounds. Some of us tend to react to those wounds in more "active" ways, leading to a predominantly Tyrant shadow. Others tend to react in more "passive" ways, leading to a predominantly Weakling shadow. But the picture is actually more complex than that. Some of us mix the passive and active poles throughout our lives. We may be tyrants in the workplace and weaklings at home. We may passively allow ourselves to be victimized for months then suddenly fly into a tyrannical rage. The possible combinations are endless. We all have both shadows available within us. Those of us who cannot connect at all with one of our shadows are simply doing a superb job of projecting it elsewhere.

The further apart our pain has split our King energy, the more dramatic and chaotic the conflict will be and the more challenging the process of integration is likely to be. This is true because, as much as these energies are attracted to each other, they also oppose or repel one another. Keep in mind that from the beginning the split was a remedy for pain or shame. We repressed or disowned the traits of one side of the archetype because they were unsafe, wrong, or bad. So the concept of re–integrating these traits raises the fear of re–experiencing the original shame or pain. Everything in us wants to avoid that—except for the part of us that hungers for a restoration to wholeness.

But if we're proactive and conscious, we can, with intention, bring about a balanced and moderate integration of these opposing energies. Any other response simply allows the repellant force of our splits to win out. The end result of that course will always be shadow. In that light, consider the following crucial point—if you

"Scratch a tyrant and you'll find a weakling. Pressure a weakling and you'll find a tyrant."
Moore and Gillette,
The King Within

don't access and manifest appropriate King energy, you leave the power to direct your life open to a usurping force, either from outside or from within yourself. The belief that you can passively flow through life giving little thought to the principles taught in this chapter is a dangerous philosophy. With this warning in mind, let's expand our view of the King archetype's entire constellation by delving into his shadow poles.

The Tyrant Usurper

Throughout human history there have always been tyrants—men willing to wield absolute power over others. Without restraint from law or outside forces, they take what they want for the gratification of their own desires, oppressing the people over whom they have power or responsibility. Tyrants are also usurpers, which means that they take power that rightfully belongs to another.

King Henry IV of England

King Henry IV of England exemplifies the extremes of these traits well. Henry was a man of considerable power—a duke and member of the immensely wealthy House of Lancaster. Henry had been banished from England for insurrection by his cousin Richard II, who was the rightful monarch. But while Richard was fighting battles in Ireland in 1399, Henry returned to England, seized power, threatened all who opposed him, and took the throne. He then imprisoned Richard and later ordered his assassination.

Tyranny can also appear in less blatant forms, such as the leader, boss, or parent who is preoccupied with his authority being recognized or with maintaining control of those he leads or for whom he's responsible. It can appear in the form of a "king killer," which is the community or group member who undermines the rightful authority or dignity of a leader through gossip, passive–aggressive acts, belittling comments, or simply refusing to follow his lead. And it can appear as the pushy friend whose opinion is always right and who has to always one–up your every success.

It's typical that a Tyrant Usurper causes suffering for those around him. Indeed, the entire kingdom must pay for his arrogance. This is on display throughout the world in countries where a powerful would–be king stages a *coup d'état*, usurping power from the current leader. The *coup* itself may produce casualties, but over the long–term it's the citizens of the country who usually suffer the most because the tyrant's central goal is to serve his own needs rather than those of the people.

Most tyranny is not that dramatic, but its effects are still felt. The overbearing, authoritarian, or controlling leader, boss, or parent usurps his underling's opportunity to develop his own King capacities. The King killer creates confusion and insecurity among the group and undermines the leader's own growth into leadership (not to mention his own). And the pushy friend may keep you always off–center, doubting yourself, and battling your own inner Weakling.

When we're in the power of the Tyrant Usurper, we make a mistake similar to King Henry's—we inflate ourselves with pride and entitlement, believing that *we are the King*. This is what Moore and Gillette refer to as becoming identified with archetypal power. But kingship isn't ours to possess. It's an energy that we may only access with balance and moderation and with humble awareness that actual sovereignty belongs only to the Archetypal King.

The Tyrant Usurper manifests seven basic traits: he's over–inflated, self–centered, controlling, narcissistic, discriminatory, rigid, and arrogant. Take a moment to consider each trait as I describe it below. Ask yourself whether these traits might sometimes show up in your personality or behavior. Also consider whether you notice these traits in the people around you. If you find that you're bothered often or intensely by other people who manifest these traits, it may be an indication that you're projecting aspects of the Tyrant shadow onto them. This will require some real humility and rigorous honesty on your part to accomplish. ✍ 2.32

Tyrant Usurper
- Over-inflated
- Self-centered
- Controlling
- Narcissistic
- Discriminatory
- Rigid
- Arrogant

Over–inflated: The Tyrant is too full of himself. Like Icarus, he's flying too high and too close to the sun. His identity and self–worth are wrapped up in the more passionate traits of the archetype: power, authority, and generative urges. His intentions and actions are oriented around a gradually failing attempt to re–enthrone his Divine Child and to repress weakness in himself and others. He may find himself preoccupied with issues related to his power and ability to control his world. He grips power tightly and wants to make sure those around him know he's in charge. These tendencies have been described using terms like "hubris," which may be defined as excessive self–confidence, and "vainglory," which is exaggerated pride in one's achievements. Under the surface there is a deep and overwhelming fear of his own weakness.

Self–centered: The Tyrant and Weakling share an underlying wound of shame and insecurity about their validity, worth, and purpose. This wound can leave us disconnected from or Selves—the unmoving, unchanging core that guides and directs the rest of the psyche. Likewise, this wound can cause our connection to powers greater than ourselves to be plagued by the same unhealthy dynamics that characterized our relationships with our dethroning parents.

For the Tyrant, the doubt this wound creates centers his ego on aggressively proving to himself, and vicariously to others, his validity, worth, and purpose. He's likely to be paranoid that his peers will move in on his territory or challenge his position. He will typically respond to those in authority with resentment and resistance. God may seem threatening. Humility may feel degrading. He supplants the voice of his Self and his Higher Power with the loud voice of his own ego. And so he's aware of only his loudest passions, urges, and wants. He worships himself.

The Tyrant is trying to prove to himself, and to others, his validity, worth, and purpose.

The Tyrant has not given up his battle against the demotion of his Divine Child. But this is a goal he will never achieve without access to his Self and his Higher Power. Lacking that connection, he's very vulnerable to basing his validity, worth, and purpose on false values. Despite his constant self–focus, he can never authentically understand himself.

Controlling: The Tyrant wants what he wants. He refuses conflict, contradiction, and opposition because they threaten to plunge him into the underlying fear that he's not valid or worthy. So he usurps the role of higher powers, including God, because any authority higher than himself calls his own desires into question and challenges his supposed sovereignty.

The Tyrant wants what he wants.

He is controlling of his circumstances and life experience, and therefore he doesn't have any true balance. The diversity he allows in his life will be self–serving and not for the sake of being well rounded or whole. He will go overboard with the things that please him, actively pursuing excess. He will enjoy contrast—life's opposing energies, forces, and traits—only to the degree that it is amusing. This may be particularly true in his relationships with the feminine. Otherwise, he may be impatient with contrast or it may even arouse in him feelings of disgust, suspicion, or hatred.

He's not integrated. His beliefs, feelings, and impulses lack cohesion and unity. Those around him may describe him as being "all over the place." He tends to act in the moment in self–indulgent and self–serving ways. He may develop only those capacities that are easy or pleasing or that advance his aims. He's like the man who goes to the gym often but only works out the muscles that make him look better. The rest of the body is ignored. So it is also with contrasting or opposing perspectives, interests, and ideas—he may ignore them or even actively silence or put them down. The Tyrant shuts out whatever displeases him.

Whatever harmony exists in his life is forced. His life may look perfect, but it will be a false perfection. In fact, his life is probably very out of balance, and if he lets down his control, things are likely to topple. So the Tyrant must be extremely persistent. This is not a sustainable position and will eventually tip sideways. When that happens, or whenever he feels overwhelmed by conflict or opposition, the Tyrant will shift into passive negligence.

Narcissistic: The generativity of the Tyrant is purely narcissistic—it's all about repressing his shame and insecurity by proving his validity, worth, and purpose. His ego is programmed to create only himself. He's fixated on incarnating his own likeness all over the world. In its grandest expressions, this may look like a Trump Tower in every major city, a designer's name on every t–shirt at the mall, or an oversized statue of a living dictator in the public square. The Tyrant's libido is unrestrained. Sex is purely selfish for him. He wants to express himself fully and to excess. He wants to possess the whole world if he can. The deeper his wound, the greedier he may become. This makes him extremely vulnerable to addiction.

...a Trump Tower in every major city, a designer's name on every t–shirt at the mall, or an oversized statue of a living dictator in the public square.

His own shame and insecurity prevent him from inspiring or blessing others. Because he's disconnected from his Center, he won't be able to conceptualize living life as an authentic example. That, combined with his compulsion to constantly prove his validity, worth, and purpose, will keep his attention fixed squarely on maintaining an image. Beholding others may raise a fear of losing himself—more specifically his position as Divine Child. Somehow he erroneously learned that there can only be one Divine Child. So if he affirms the greatness of another person, he fears he's dethroning himself. He may be consumed with jealousy toward those around him who excel in any way. If he works with or through other people, he will use them to elevate himself. He may even be jealous of his own children, subordinates, students, protégés, or followers. He may tend to focus on their weaknesses and failures in an unconscious attempt to elevate himself. He doesn't understand that there is enough magnificence to go around—every child is divine.

He may provide a living for his family, he may provide employment and sustenance to others, or he may even provide wealth for thousands. But somehow everyone knows that it's really all about him. Everything must flow to him to prove his validity, worth, and purpose.

Discriminatory: I use the term "discriminatory" here in its most negative and selfish sense, as it's commonly used today to describe acts of unfair treatment of others. As is generally true of the way in which the Tyrant uses his capacities, his use of the gift of discernment is self–serving. He's hyper–aware of differences in classes and qualities of people, material goods, opportunities, behaviors, and priorities. But his paradigm for valuing these differences is colored by his wound. Things are good if they make him feel more secure and worthy. Things are bad if they raise his shame or make him feel insecure. So he will tend to judge in reactionary ways. He's likely to be racist and sexist. He will have strong favorites, and he will hate things with equal fervor. He will justify behavior that gets him what he wants. And his priorities will reflect his narcissism.

Rigid: Control and rigidity are general traits of the Tyrant. And that's particularly likely to be true in the way he organizes his life. It's all about power. Regarding things for which he alone is responsible, his organization may be compulsive. When other people are involved, he will always want it done *his* way—whether or not that's the best or most practical way. He will be demanding and inconsiderate. Allowing others to organize things their own way may feel undermining or insubordinate. So his approach will be to demand uniform compliance. Spontaneity and flexibility may feel threatening or may raise his insecurity, so they will be frowned on. While his standards may be admirable and his methods exemplary, the people around him will probably still resent him because they will sense the compulsive madness behind his method.

The people around a Tyrant will probably resent him because they will sense the compulsive madness behind his method.

Arrogant: In denial about his own limitations, the Tyrant believes he can choose whatever he wants with impunity. He sets himself above the laws that govern his existence. Indeed, he believes that he is the law. His conscious or nonconscious credo is, "I am THE King." With this mentality, he goes too far in his attempts to civilize his world, encroaching on the kingdoms of others and defying the established systems within his society.

His relationships with other people will always be problematic. Most basically, he doesn't recognize that they too are sovereign, and so it's easy for him to disrespect their boundaries. He tends to view others as merely things to be used in getting what he wants. He may try to expand his realm to the point where he overtakes the rights and responsibilities of others, limiting them and curtailing their options through his control and domination.

Like all the archetypal shadows, a Tyrant tends to project. He may project his own hostile intentions toward others, which leads to feelings of paranoia and beliefs that others are trying to encroach on his domain and freedoms. Insubordination will be a major concern for him. He may be preoccupied with ensuring that his orders are followed or that he's recognized as the final word.

A Tyrant may also project his own weakness onto others. He has never come to terms with the reality of his own limitations and potential for complete failure. As a result, he will fear the weaknesses of those around him. His fear may grow into disgust, hatred, repression, and persecution of those who are weak or failing. This, of course, is the source of the Tyrant's perennial oppression of the Weakling.

The Weakling Abdicator

No better than the Tyrant Usurper's seizure of the power, leadership, and rights of others is the Weakling Abdicator's abandonment of responsibilities that he alone must fulfill. An abdicator is one who gives up, abandons, or relinquishes his responsibilities and power.

King Edward VIII of England (1894–1972) provides a good example. As Prince of Wales he was extremely popular and was the most photographed celebrity of his time. His compulsive womanizing, controversial public statements, and other reckless behavior earned him the distrust of his father, King George V, as well as that of the Prime Minister and other high–ranking government officials. After he had become king, government ministers were reluctant to send confidential documents and state papers to him for fear they would be seen by his mistress and his many houseguests.

Edward VIII of England

Edward abdicated the throne in 1936 after only eleven months as king. He had fallen in love with a twice–divorced American named Wallis Simpson—one of many married women with whom he'd had an affair. But the British Cabinet refused to allow the two to marry on grounds that it violated Church of England doctrine and would not be acceptable to his subjects. In his abdication speech he stated, "I have found it impossible to carry the heavy burden of responsibility and to discharge my duties as king as I would wish to do without the help and support of the woman I love."

During World War II, Edward, now reduced to the rank of Duke, favored appeasement of the Nazi government. Against the wishes of the British government, he went to Germany to visit with Adolf Hitler, who considered Edward friendly to the Nazi cause. Edward was suspected of leaking strategic war documents and other secrets to the German forces. Years later, Edward remarked to a close friend, "I never thought Hitler was such a bad chap."[5]

Weakling Abdicator

- Deflated
- Uncentered
- Negligent
- Sterile
- Confused
- Chaotic
- Abandoning

In today's society, the Weakling may show up in the employee who, when given the smallest amount of responsibility, will still find a way to not come through. It may appear in the man who can't keep his life together—he's always disorganized, out of money, and behind on everything. Or the Weakling may manifest itself in the man who is always getting the raw end of every deal.

The Weakling Abdicator has seven main characteristics. He's deflated, uncentered, negligent, sterile, confused, chaotic, and abandoning. Once again, take a moment to consider each of these traits as I describe them below and assess how they show up in your life. Consider whether you may manifest these traits in your own personality. Also consider whether you notice these traits in others—an indication that you could be projecting them onto those around you. ✍ 2.33

Deflated: He can't try anymore. He may have tried to hold on to his Divine Child or his budding King power, but life circumstances eventually ripped it from his grasp. Now his interactions with the power of Kingship are limited to exchanges between himself and other people, institutions, and life situations that repress and abuse him. Unlike Icarus, he has chosen to fly too low and often finds himself crashing into the rocks. His depression of spirit may result in laziness and fatigue. He finds it very difficult to be productive or to make a life for himself. He may be plagued by feelings of impotence and beset with fruitless urges to break out of his lethargy through fantasies of power and domination. But when threatened or pushed too far by the tyrants he has gathered around him, the Weakling may suddenly unleash the full force of his repressed tyrannical power in a surprising polar shift.

Uncentered: Like the Tyrant, the Weakling has a wound of shame and insecurity about his validity, worth, and purpose, which has left him disconnected from the guidance of his deep Self. And like the Tyrant, his connections to powers greater than himself are plagued by the unhealthy dynamics that characterized the relationship with his parents.

Out of the doubt caused by his wound, the Weakling has abandoned the battle for his Divine Child, so there is nothing to center him. A primary focus of his ego will likely be to avoid the topics of worth, validity, and purpose—those topics are fraught with conflict and pain and threaten to catapult him into the Tyrant pole, for which he simply doesn't have the energy.

Deeper aspects of himself are quite mysterious to the Weakling, and he feels empty inside. He will tend to have difficulty centering his faith in a Higher Power, even if he's religious. Without an internal guiding factor, his life may be an aimless series of wanderings. He's likely to often find himself distracted and controlled by more powerful external circumstances, events, and people. Lacking a sense of purpose and worth, he will tend to be slothful and underachieving.

Negligent: Like the Tyrant, the Weakling's wound has left him uneasy with or frightened by opposition, contradiction, and conflict. He may respond to this in at least two different ways. One response may be to withdraw from life into passive denial, ignorance, and naïveté. Because he's out of touch with his Center, he has no healthy way to understand or resolve opposition. With no personal validity, worth, or purpose, he doesn't see the point in exposing himself to the discomfort inherent in becoming more integrated or in exerting the effort that would be required to create authentic balance and harmony in his life. He has no persistence and lets everything slide. The result may be that he tolerates a passive life full of contradiction.

A second response may be to revel in contradiction and conflict and take pleasure in disunity. He may enjoy seeing things go nowhere and may consciously create disagreement. Just a few steps further in this direction and he begins to enter the zone of the Tyrant.

Neither of these two responses is sustainable. Both neglect the need for true harmony. But balance is inevitable—even for the Weakling Abdicator. Yet when balance happens to him, it will always be created in accidental and uncontrolled

> The Weakling has a wound which has left him disconnected from the guidance of his deep Self.

> He has no persistence and lets everything slide. He tolerates a passive life full of contradiction.

ways, often with him as a victim. If he's pushed too far or comes under too much stress, he may react with a polar shift into control and rigidity, suddenly and forcefully "clamping down" or seizing power.

Sterile: He is impotent. This is not referring to a biological condition of erectile dysfunction or infertility. Rather it's referring to a lack of libido that's far more than just sexual. He's forbidden by an unconscious vow to engage in any generative act. This vow was likely instilled in him by dethroning parents or the influences of a stifling culture. His only substantial creative act will be the Tyrants he creates with his projections. It's to them he looks for the creation and re–creation of his victimized Weakling self.

If he produces things, they will be hackneyed reproductions of others' creativity. And he won't produce them for himself—he won't permit himself to take joy in anything he makes. His productivity will all be for others—his parents, his wife or boss, the company, or the government. He may lack the capacity to create or nurture another generation. His wound has left him too empty to do so. He may have children, but he won't be a father. He can't behold or bless others. Like the Tyrant, he has no Center and thus no ability to be an authentic example to others. And he can't pretend to be great—he simply lacks the energy for pretense.

His ability to provide for himself and others will be diminished. He will likely have difficulty making money, but even if he does have a good occupation and income, he won't be able to make life feel abundant.

Confused: His wounds have convinced him that his judgment is not valid or worthy of consideration. So the Weakling doesn't trust himself to make meaningful sense of the distinctions he perceives. He may become so doubtful of his capacity to discern that he stops noticing things altogether. If he does discern things, he's not likely to act on his awareness. If he deliberates, he will probably do so at great length and without meaningful conclusion. His choices will tend to be random and not well thought out. He will try to avoid making choices whenever he can. He may simply say, "It's all good."

As he continues deeper into this shadow, his ability to discern begins to return but his judgment will be inverted. There, in the darkest corner of this shadow, good and evil are upside down. So extreme will be his confusion that the Weakling will

A Weakling's only substantial creative act will be the Tyrants he creates with his projections.

His wounds have convinced him that his judgment is not valid or worthy of consideration.

unconsciously embrace the dark and destructive forces—what Moore and Gillette refer to as "the collective Shadow."

Chaotic: Lacking a sense of validity, worth, and purpose, the Weakling lacks the impulse or motivation to organize his life. What would be the point? He's passive and apathetic. Everything is out of control. He often finds himself without the things he needs and therefore unable to accomplish what he needs to get done. Rarely is he on time. His finances are probably out of control and his physical domain is likely to be unkempt and cluttered. Yet with all of this chaos he seems passively content. Things aren't coming together for him, and there is no real plan. Life is a series of unforeseen situations.

The people around him may resent him for the inconveniences he creates. When they impose organization on him, he may comply temporarily and to a minimal degree, although he will resent it. But at some point, in a passive–aggressive swipe at the Tyrant, he may subtly and unconsciously sabotage the organization that has been set up for him by failing to keep it up.

Abandoning: He is afraid to choose. The shame and insecurity from his wounds have left him insecure about his validity, worth, and purpose. He abdicates his capacity to choose and with it his own sovereignty. He will tend to be either naïvely ignorant of the laws and principles that govern his life or he will see them as oppressively slanted against him. Far from being civilized, his life feels out of control and ungovernable, and it tends over time to slide further into disarray. As the hackneyed saying goes, "Failing to choose is choosing to fail." His failures increase his limitations and diminish his options. As a result, his power and kingdom shrink.

The Weakling's power is split–off and projected onto the Tyrant whom he fears and resents. The truth behind the projection is that he fears his own power—or more specifically he fears that if he takes up his power, he will be shamed and belittled once again. The problems in his relationships with other people arise from this fear. He withdraws from attempting to fulfill the responsibilities that are incumbent on him and refuses to lead or to take any responsibility or authority with other people. This further hampers his ability to build a life for himself and often results in his betraying and abandoning those who have expectations of him.

> The Weakling lacks the impulse or motivation to organize his life.

> "Failing to choose is choosing to fail."

When he's not feeling threatened, his relationships with peers and superiors may be characterized by apathy or passive resentment. But because he's unable to establish or enforce boundaries, he will often feel provoked or threatened. At those times he will retreat into the same victim role he was placed in as a child. From that place he may passively look for deliverance from an all–powerful supreme being. At the furthest extent of the Weakling shadow, all King energy is extinguished, including that of the Higher Power. For men in this place, God is dead. One step deeper into this shadow actually brings a man around to the active pole of King shadow. There in the arrogance of the Tyrant, he unconsciously assumes that if God is dead, then he has the right to assume God's place.

THE SYNERGISTIC KING

In Chapter One, I talked about how the archetypal energies are meant to be held together in a compound wholeness. Remember, it's healthy for archetypal energies to have opposing—even conflicting—characteristics. Accessing those opposing energies in moderation and integrating them in balanced ways in our lives is what creates the synergistic powers of the archetypes.

Take some time right now to view the King archetype from a mountaintop perspective by reviewing his various traits in their extremes and in moderation. The intent here is for you to gain a clearer sense of the type of synergy that's possible when the opposing active and passive potentials of the King's various archetypal traits can be accessed in moderation rather than in their extreme shadows. On the next page is a table with seven trait scales, similar to the table of Warrior trait scales you saw in Chapter One. This table depicts various shadowy and moderate ways in which individuals might respond to the archetypal powers of the King.

Take a few minutes now to familiarize yourself with the table. A good way to do this is to first look at it vertically by column. Review the *Tyrant* column, then the *Weakling* column. Next review both of the *Moderation* columns together. After you've done that, review the table horizontally one trait scale at a time, considering the full range of the attributes associated with that trait. Use the numbered paragraphs below the table to help you understand the details of each scale.

As you review the scales, I encourage you to consider how each trait may be manifested in your life. Find your tendencies on each scale, remembering that we often have a range and may slide back and forth from one side to another, depending on our circumstances. ✍ 2.34

King Trait Scales

	Tyrant	Moderation		Weakling
1. Archetype Connection	Over-inflated	Noble	Humble	Deflated
2. Centeredness	Self-centered	Self-aware	Submissive	Uncentered
3. Harmony	Controlling	Reconciling	Accepting	Negligent
4. Generativity	Narcissistic	Creative	Self-sacrificing	Sterile
5. Discernment	Discriminatory	Differentiating	Deliberative	Confused
6. Organization	Rigid	Organized	Flexible	Chaotic
7. Sovereignty	Arrogant	Self-magnifying	Yielding	Abandoning

(Traits)

1. Archetype Connection

This scale relates to how intensely connected a man is to the archetypal energy of the King. The Tyrant is *over–inflated*, or too full of himself. He's preoccupied with proving to himself and others just how kingly he is. In moderation, this side of the King archetype is strongly connected to his *nobility* and kingly powers, which he actively uses in service of himself and others. He's aware of a desire to be his best self.

The Weakling is completely *deflated*. He has projected his King energy onto others, whom he experiences as oppressive. He feels impotent and lacks the energy or drive to make a life for himself. In greater moderation this tendency engenders *humility* and leads to recognition of his finite and imperfect nature. It evokes compassion and benevolence toward himself and others. It reminds him of the reality that he's not *the* King.

2. Centeredness

This scale relates to a man's awareness of his deep Self and his connection with a Higher Power. The Tyrant is *self–centered*, stuck in an ego–driven battle to prove his validity, worth, and purpose, and goes through life trying to keep his Divine Child on the throne. He's disconnected from his Self and his Higher Power and listens only to the passions, urges, and wants of his ego. In moderation, these tendencies show up as a strong *awareness of Self*—a King knows who he is and what he wants. He's internally guided and self–directed. He trusts himself and can assert his desires and will. He's motivated to experience his validity, worth, and purpose and to demonstrate these through meaningful achievement.

The Weakling is *uncentered*. He lacks connection to his deep Self and feels empty inside. He avoids thinking about his worth, validity, and purpose. He wanders through his life, controlled by more powerful forces. True *submission* to transcendent powers is a more moderate quality. The King can let go of his ego and empty himself of his passions, urges, and wants. This allows him to hear other voices, especially that of his Higher Power. He accepts that his own validity, worth, and purpose are nothing in comparison with God's greatness.

3. Harmony

This scale relates to a man's ability to balance and integrate opposing energies in his life. The Tyrant *controls* things in his life to avoid undesirable disharmony. He refuses conflict, contradiction, and opposition and shuts out whatever displeases him. He forces harmony through rigidity. In more moderate amounts, this trait is a hunger to *reconcile* things into perfect harmony. It's a patient insistence on unity and equilibrium. It urges balance, cooperation, and the integration of opposites.

The Weakling is *negligent* in his responsibility to create true harmony. Either he tolerates a life of passive contradiction, or he may even revel in the contradictions and conflicts in life, taking pleasure in disunity and enjoying seeing things go nowhere. A more moderate response to this energy brings *acceptance* of opposition and contradiction, patience with imbalance, and acceptance of things that don't yet harmonize. Things don't always have to conform to expectations. There is an appreciation of the process and willingness to let things flow naturally toward wholeness.

4. Generativity

This scale refers to all aspects of a man's role as a creator and giver of blessing. The Tyrant's generativity is *narcissistic*. He's fixated on incarnating his likeness wherever he can. He wants to possess the whole world. He can't inspire others because that feels like a demotion of himself. He is jealous. Everything he provides is an attempt to repress his shame and insecurity. In moderation, this trait of the King provides a deep sense of confidence and personal fulfillment through *creative* assertion. He accepts his personal majesty and expresses it in dignified ways.

Inspiring and blessing others expands his own joy. He's propelled by a continual desire for greater abundance to provide well for himself and those he loves.

The Weakling is *sterile* and lacking in libido. Anything he produces will be for others and will be done begrudgingly, bringing him no joy. He cannot nurture others, and he has no Center from which to inspire or bless. He has a diminished ability to provide an abundant life. In moderation, the King is *self-sacrificing*. He accepts that his ability to create is ultimately limited and that much of what he produces must be for others. He can be satisfied with having only part of what he really wants, so he's willing to let go of one thing in order to obtain something he wants more. And he recognizes and lovingly accepts the limitations in others.

5. Discernment

This scale relates to the judgments a man makes about things, people, and situations. The Tyrant is *discriminatory*, but makes his judgments based on what serves his interests. Things that make him feel secure and worthy are "good;" things that raise his shame or insecurity are "bad." With greater moderation, this side of discernment enables the King to quickly *differentiate* those things that are truly beneficial for his kingdom and himself from those things that are of no value or may even be harmful.

The Weakling is *confused* and doubts his capacity to make good judgments. He may even lose his ability to accurately sense distinctions, causing him to make poor decisions. Further into the shadow, his perceptions of things may become inverted. In moderation, this side of discernment allows the King to question his perceptions and judgment and to make decisions after appropriate *deliberation*. He's receptive and tolerant and able to fully understand, and even feel, all sides of an issue. His decisions are more inclusive and integrated.

6. Organization

This scale relates to the degree of control and flexibility a man exercises in organizing his life. The Tyrant's method of organizing his life is *rigid*. He will likely be compulsive in his own domain and will always want it done his way when other people are involved. With moderation, this trait makes the King's life *organized* and well structured. High standards of order and personal control are adhered to.

The Weakling resists organization, so his life is *chaotic*. He's passively content to have things out of control. His life lacks a plan. When organization is imposed on him, he resents it and may eventually undermine it. In greater moderation, this trait becomes *flexibility*, spontaneity, and an ability to accept imperfect circumstances. He's peaceful and serene in uncontrollable situations.

7. Sovereignty

This scale has to do with a man's use of power in governing his life and his function as the Creator of Civilization. The Tyrant is arrogant and wants to make choices with impunity. He tends to encroach on the rights of others and defy established systems. He ignores the sovereignty of those around him. He's paranoid and fears insubordination. And he hates and persecutes those around him who are weak. A more moderate King magnifies himself by working aggressively to civilize his world. Comfortable with his own strength and power, he willingly steps into authority and leads others. He's assertive and not hobbled by unduly constraining interpersonal boundaries. But he's compassionately aware and protective of the weak around him.

The Weakling abandons his sovereignty and his capacity to choose. He sees laws as oppressive stumbling blocks, and his life is unmanageable. He fears his own power and projects it onto Tyrants, whom he resents. He fails to fulfill his responsibilities and betrays others. He cannot establish boundaries. In greater moderation, this tendency allows a King to yield and humbly submit to overriding laws. He accepts the reality of his weakness and recognizes that ultimately life is unmanageable and requires reliance on a Higher Power. He's thoughtful about his choices and humbly aware of his capacity to fail. He's capable of tolerance when others cross his boundaries.

TRUE LEADERSHIP

True leadership has nothing to do with authority.

King is the archetype of leadership, whether we're leading a worldwide movement, a community, a group, a family, or just our own lives. This chapter has pointed out much of what creates true leadership. But we never talked about authority. That is because the King archetype—like true leadership—has nothing to do with authority, except that every now and then there is a man who has both. Authority is the right to govern, which comes by default, by assignment, by consent, or by dominance. Authority can be maintained and executed without any of the positive qualities I've attempted to teach in this chapter. Tyrants and Weaklings both can have authority.

True leadership is true Kingship. As you've learned from the preceding pages, a king is centered and connected to a Higher Source of wisdom and insight. A king observes balance in his life and is integrated. He practices moderation through appropriate boundaries. He's discerning and organized, accepts the duty and responsibility of choice, conforms his life to natural law, and extends the bounds of civilization within his world. A king is a creator, and he provides for himself and for others. These King capacities are the foundation or prerequisite of leadership. But they aren't enough to make a man into a true leader.

True leadership begins with vision. As I wrote near the beginning of this chapter, vision can mean a goal or sense of where we're going, a perspective on life and our place in the world, a powerful and motivating idea that we feel compelled to create, or truth that's revealed to us from a Higher Source. Men and women are hungry for vision. Whether or not a person has read *The Proverbs*, they seem to instinctually understand the need for vision. Because this need is innate and universal, people with compelling visions tend to naturally become leaders. Having a vision turns a normal man into an axis mundi.

> True leadership begins with vision.

Enlivened by vision, the true leader liberally shares his vision with others. Then he empowers those who resonate with his vision so that they can make that vision their own. He empowers them first by exemplifying his vision through the way he lives his life. Being an example cannot be faked—at least not for long. It must be lived from the core. The leader's example inspires others. And he further inspires and empowers them by *beholding* them. Fully accepting their present self, while simultaneously seeing their highest potential, the true leader *delights* in those around him. His love for them prompts him to bless them through touch and through words that affirm their value and worth, praise their growth, and help them to discover their own special future. But he doesn't bless them through touch and words alone. His actions provide opportunities for them to reach that special future. And all of this is part of his vision.

> Enlivened by vision, the true leader liberally shares his vision with others.

To summarize all that I've said here in a few words, the true leader *lives his vision and actively loves others*. If he must operate within an established hierarchy, he will respect the chain of command, but he will neither be motivated nor stifled by it. And he won't be worried about issues of authority and respect. He understands that leadership cannot be expected or demanded. In its purest forms, it comes only as a natural flow when great qualities are recognized and sought out by men who need an example to follow.

The virtues of true leadership are intended to be developed by every willing person.

The world needs much more of this type of leadership. Lao Tzu taught it twenty–five hundred years ago in his book *Tao Te Ching*.[6] Jesus Christ exemplified it beautifully through his life and teachings. If you look at the beginnings of almost every positive religion or movement, you will find such a man or woman. But the virtues of true leadership can be developed by anyone. In fact, they are intended to be developed by *every willing person*. The Universal King wants to expand civilization throughout all of creation. He does this by synergistically cooperating with our own efforts to civilize ourselves and our world. In other words, He *wants* you to rise to your full King capacities. But He is waiting for you to cooperate with Him in that process. So seek the King Archetype and let him shape you into a king and a true leader. ✍ 2.35

---

[1] The authors borrow this term from Erik Erikson, who described the concept in his book, *Identity: Youth and Crisis.*

[2] These laws are described in many places. The best collection of them is found in *Hidden Treasures* by Leslie Householder. I've used her labels for the most part. Some of these principles are also found in *The Science of Getting Rich* by Wallace Wattles, *As A Man Thinketh* by James Allen, and *The Tao of Leadership* by John Heider.

[3] Members of The Church of Jesus Christ of Latter–day Saints (Mormons) receive a "patriarchal blessing" in young adulthood, which contains the same elements Trent and Smalley describe. Priesthood holders within that church also regularly give other members blessings of comfort and healing, which typically contain most of the elements.

[4] *The Blessing* is written from a Christian perspective, but its message is universal. It is simple and direct.

[5] Patrick Balfour, Lord Kinross, *Love conquers all* in *Books and Bookmen*, vol. 20, p. 50.

[6] *The Tao of Leadership*, by John Heider, is a modern adaptation of the *Tao Te Ching*. Although the book suffers from an unfortunate plethora of typos, it is of great worth to anyone who wishes to lead in any capacity and I strongly recommend it.

CHAPTER 3

NEED FULFILLMENT

Instead of asking what you think you ought to do to become a better
man... I want to ask, *What makes you come alive?* What stirs your
heart? The journey we face now is into a land foreign to most of us.
We must head into country that has no clear trail.

John Eldredge, *Wild at Heart*

 ing is the energy of axis mundi—our Self and our connection
with our Higher Power. As our Center, the King is *zhōng yōng*,
an unwobbling pivot in the middle of us from which we gain
clarity and vision, and which provides us with validity, worth, and
purpose. This stable point enables us to balance our lives. Through
that balance, we are aware of contrasting energies and can thus choose to engage
in diverse activities and interests in healthy proportions, allowing ourselves to
maintain equilibrium.

In our lifestyle, as well as within our own mind and heart, we are integrated. Our
lives feel put together, and we're unified within. We are able to manifest a full
range of diverse capacities according to what's appropriate in each situation we
encounter. We practice moderation, flying the middle course through behavioral,
emotional, and relational boundaries, and yielding when appropriate. We discern
and distinguish what's good from what's harmful, and we make wise choices
within the range of our sovereignty.

Our lives are logistically organized without being overly rigid. We understand and
follow natural laws, using them, as a wise king would, to govern our lives. And
we build greater civilization in our lives by continuously promoting progression,
advancement, and development. These are the roles and capacities of the King's
function as creator of order.

But the King is far more than merely a source of structure and organization. His other essential function is that of a *provider*, which is an unimpressive term for creator of all things, inspirer of all that is good, giver of blessings to mankind, and source of sustenance. These two functions of the King—creating order and providing—are the foundation of need fulfillment. While the functions of other archetypes are also required if our needs are to be met, it's the capacities of King that make it happen.

In his function of creating order, he connects us to our Self and to our Higher Power. Through these connections he's able to discern our true needs. As a sovereign, he makes the hard choices that enable us to balance ourselves in the pursuit of our often–divergent needs. As an integrator, he unifies us and coordinates our capacities as we seek fulfillment. As a moderator, he keeps us from going to extremes. He also organizes our efforts—in a disorderly life, needs are likely to be met poorly and haphazardly. As the keeper and giver of law, he sees that we abide by the natural laws governing the fulfillment of each need. And his civilizing impulse pushes us forward in pursuit of ever–greater fulfillment.

In his function as provider, the King incarnates libido in acts of creativity that are essential to need fulfillment. He inspires us with visions of what our lives can be when we actively commit ourselves to meeting our needs. And he provides the required means that enable us to pursue the things we require in order to experience joy through need fulfillment.

The more we develop the traits of the King, the more whole we become and the more capable we are of knowing our true needs and fulfilling them.

The more we develop the traits of the King, the more whole we become and the more capable we are of knowing our true needs and fulfilling them. If we could fully embody the King archetype, our needs would be completely met and abundance would flow to us spontaneously. But this is not our reality, since—by the very nature of our human imperfection—we're all caught in the tension between a Weakling Abdicator and a Tyrant Usurper. So for the conscious man, life becomes a continual process of integrating our shadowy tendencies as we struggle toward greater wholeness and greater fulfillment of our needs.

Need fulfillment is inextricably tied to joy and wellbeing. In fact, the word "need" could be defined as that which is required in order to maintain joy. I consider joy to be central to the purpose of human existence. In order to better understand our true needs and their relationship to joy, we first have to shed three false perspectives about needs.

The first falsehood is that happiness comes from fulfilling our every craving. When I speak of needs, I'm not talking about the things we *crave*. Fulfilling our cravings through self–indulgence doesn't bring joy because cravings can only lead to suffering. Here we're borrowing from the wisdom of Buddha, who taught that cravings arise from being overly attached to things we can't truly possess or control.[1] For example, we might cling to people, possessions, status, reputation, expectations, or appearance. The inevitable loss of these things is what causes our suffering. According to Buddha, happiness results from surrendering our cravings and thus eliminating our suffering.

The second untruth is the shadowy polar opposite of the first—that there is some virtue in denying our true needs. Buddha balanced this teaching about cravings with an acknowledgement that we must fulfill our true needs. Extreme self–denial is no more a virtue than self–indulgence. So true need fulfillment comes from walking the middle path between too much and too little.

The third wrong belief that we must shed has to do with modern consumerism, which teaches that our needs are conditions that can be satisfied by goods and services. For example, consumerism teaches that the need to eat is satisfied by food (goods) and the need for physical health is satisfied by the care of a physician (services). But while buying groceries and visiting the doctor may be necessary to maintain health, they alone aren't enough to fulfill our need for physical self–care. In this chapter, we'll view needs from a perspective that's very different from these three false ideas.

The meeting of our needs in balanced ways provides internal stamina and emotional resources for facing life challenges. When our needs are fulfilled, we become more robust and resilient. Our inner kingdom becomes stronger, which allows our emotional resources to be used for healing and for growth. When we stray from the middle path—whether through indulging our cravings or denying our needs—we experience pain, which piles on top of old wounds. This forces us to direct our emotional resources toward handling or defending against the pain and sadness, leaving us even less capable of meeting our needs.

Three False Perspectives About Needs

- Happiness comes from fulfilling our cravings.
- There is virtue in denying our true needs.
- Needs can be satisfied by goods and services.

But when we do the work required to appropriately meet our needs, we feel a sense of wellbeing that naturally motivates us to continue doing what's necessary to meet our needs. In that joyful state, the King within us naturally wants to bless the lives of those around us, which further increases our own joy because giving is naturally satisfying. And when we feel and express gratitude to the source of our fulfillment, we invite more of those blessings into our lives.

NEED FULFILLMENT IN PRACTICAL TERMS

Let's get more specific and practical about the role of the King archetype in meeting our needs. Let's consider six needs that can't be satisfied by goods or services—they can only be satisfied by individual action and by walking the middle path. While these needs are important for anyone wishing to live a joyful life, they are absolutely essential for men who want to live according to the *Tao* of maleness. Women might come up with a different list. But we're not women.

Six Essential Needs

- A mission
- An adventure
- Comrades
- Spiritual connection
- Physical care
- Genderedness and complementarity

Three of the needs we'll discuss have been borrowed from John Eldredge's book, *Wild at Heart*, which I consider a must read for any man who wants to grow beyond his impasses around masculinity.[2] Eldredge states that, "in the heart of every man is a desperate desire for a *battle to fight*, an *adventure to live*, and a *beauty to rescue*" [italics added]. Notice that each of these needs involves taking personal action. Eldredge doesn't say that men need a battle to *watch*, an adventure to *fantasize about*, and a beauty to *look at*!

For the purpose of our discussion, I'll use some terms and concepts that are slightly different from Eldredge's. I'll use his term "adventure." But, rather than the term "battle," I'll use the more specific term "mission." And rather than speaking of "a beauty to rescue," I'll discuss the broader need of experiencing "genderedness," which refers to the differences between the sexes, and "complementarity," which refers to the way the two sexes complete and balance each other. The other three needs I'll introduce are the need for comrades, the need for spiritual connection, and the need for physical care.

Certainly there are other more basic needs we have as humans, such as the needs for safety and sustenance. I'm assuming those needs are already met for you. The six needs we'll discuss are of a slightly higher order. These are the needs that tend to be most significant for men who are growing beyond unwanted same–sex attraction and toward masculine wholeness.

It's possible that you may not be in touch with some of these needs at this point in your journey. Or perhaps you may even feel a strong block or resistance about pursuing one or more of these needs. For example, a lot of men with unwanted same–sex attraction feel resistance toward spirituality or toward genderedness and complementarity. If you notice resistance or resentment coming up as you read any of the sections below, see if you can understand what that's about. Don't pressure yourself about it. Just make note of it as something to be worked on at some point.

Mission

Men need to work. Most of us have to work so that we can make money. But even if we happen to be independently wealthy, I believe we all need to be engaged in a productive activity that allows us to feel effective and useful. My own observations suggest that we feel a greater sense of joy, satisfaction, and purpose when the work we do resonates with our personality, suits our capacities and aptitudes, stimulates our minds and bodies, and makes us feel like we're doing something good in the world. Some of us are fortunate enough to fulfill all of that through our jobs. But many of us take on avocations or hobbies to add a level of satisfaction that our jobs don't provide.

Martin Luther King, Jr.

Finding fulfillment through our careers and avocations seems like a tall enough order already. But when Eldredge says that men need a "battle to fight," he's talking about something beyond just our occupations and hobbies. He says, "A man must have a battle to fight, a great mission to his life that involves and yet transcends even home and family. He must have a cause to which he is devoted even unto death, for this is written into the fabric of his being." When I read this, I get the feeling that he isn't describing a nine–to–five job with a round of golf on the weekend.

> "A man must have a... great mission to his life that...transcends even home and family."
>
> John Eldredge, *Wild at Heart*

I believe John Eldredge. Particularly, I believe that this battle—this mission—must be in the service of something higher and bigger than my own ego. In my judgment, it isn't a mission if it begins and ends with me alone. Don't get me wrong, I believe men do *get by* without having a mission—in fact that's the way most men live. That's why western male culture is so preoccupied with recreation, fantasy, sports leagues, and sexual conquest. These are our pseudo–missions. And they are killing the masculine spirit. While a pseudo–mission may be a tremendously fun past–time, I doubt whether it can create any lasting sense of validity, worth, or purpose. These come only through disciplined service to something bigger than myself.

So, what are some of the types of causes that might provide a man with a more true sense of mission? Eldredge mentions "home and family," and certainly these things are bigger than self, whether family means our own wives and children, or our siblings, nieces and nephews, and other extended relatives. Family can be a significant mission, especially when it involves pouring into the next generation. But again, Eldredge is talking about something that transcends home and family. For such a mission a man might look to things like community involvement, social movements, religious service, politics, philanthropy, environmentalism, and any other cause or movement that benefits something beyond ourselves.

Balancing and integrating a job, hobbies, and a mission can be a tricky thing for all the obvious reasons. If you've figured out how to earn your living by serving a cause about which you feel passionate, you may already be living your true mission. But if you haven't yet created that opportunity for yourself, you may choose to continue working for someone else's mission in order to earn a living while pursuing your soul's passion on the side.

A mission is a transcendent personal vision that is put into action.

So how can you find or create a mission for yourself? By putting a personal transcendent vision into action. Vision is the seed of a mission. In Chapter Two, I said that vision might be defined as a goal or sense of where we're going, a perspective on life and our place in the world, a powerful and motivating idea that we feel compelled to create, or truth that is revealed to us from a Higher Source.

But a vision does little good if we never take action. So we must access the King function that I described in Chapter Two as "the provider" or "the generative man." That King function is the catalyst of our need for a mission. It's fueled by the urge and passion of libido, which wants to be incarnated through creative ventures. It's the source of inspiration to us, and others, to emulate higher ways and to fulfill our highest potential. It's the impulse to bless others and to remain committed to assisting in the fulfillment of the blessing. And it provides the means required for living an abundant life. These aspects of the King archetype instinctually urge us to bring our vision into reality through action. They are also a good gage for measuring the fullness or richness of a mission. The more of these aspects that are present in a mission, the more fulfilling that mission is likely to be.

In Chapter Five we'll discuss the topic of mission again as part of our exploration of the Warrior archetype. Here we have considered mission from the perspective of the King. But a mission is actually a project on which King and Warrior energies cooperate.   ✍ 3.1

Adventure

"Life is not a problem to be solved," John Eldredge writes. "It is an adventure to be lived." This sounds inspiring and exciting, but why is adventure a masculine need? Because it's an intense source of energy, and without that kind of energy, men become lifeless, dull, depressed, false, and useless to themselves, their loved ones, and society. If you're unsure of that statement, just take a close look at the men you know—those who are alive and energetic will undoubtedly have some type of adventure in their lives. (Whether it's a healthy or a perverse adventure is another question.)

"Life is not a problem to be solved. It is an adventure to be lived."

John Eldredge, *Wild at Heart*

So how does adventure generate the energy that I'm talking about? It does it by stimulating feelings of *creativity* and *power*—both of which are innate sources of male energy. Now don't misunderstand me—creativity and power are also sources of *female* energy. I've been with the same woman now for over twenty–five years and believe me, she is creative and powerful. So is our daughter. But the energy they feel from their creativity and power is different from the energy my sons and I feel from ours. The difference in these energies is a manifestation of the amazing distinction between the *Tao* of maleness and the *Tao* of femaleness.

Creativity is the ability to bring something into existence or to "make out of nothing and for the first time." Adventure stimulates creativity by exposing us to new challenges and unfamiliar circumstances, which require us to bring into existence new responses and to make new solutions. The risks inherent in adventure invite innovation. The reverse is also true: innovation invites the taking of risks. So not only does adventure generate creativity, but creativity itself is an adventure.

The kind of power that adventure stimulates is not the kind of power associated with the Tyrant. True power comes from our Center—it is balanced, integrated, and moderate as we discussed in Chapter Two. It creates an energy of confidence, courage, discipline, generosity, aliveness, self–expression, and good will toward others. In a nutshell, it creates the positive energies of all the archetypes.

One energy that true power doesn't create is the energy of control. Control is an illusion—there are no real guarantees in life. Eldredge talks about this in *Wild at Heart*. Quoting David Whyte, he distinguishes between a false wish "to have power over experience," and the "wish to have power through experience no matter what that may be." The desire to have power over our experience is the intention "to control all events and consequences." This is the opposite of adventure. Adventure implies uncertainty and facing the unknown. It calls upon our creativity as we must devise solutions to unforeseen situations.

"Originality and creativity are essential to personhood and to masculine strength," Eldredge writes. But this inevitably means that we must accept risk. And accepting risk means that we must face fear. For many men with unwanted same–sex attraction, risk and fear are the deal killers of progress. But I can tell you that after more than twenty years of personally pursuing the way of maleness, I'm convinced that growth will only occur—and masculinity will only be felt—when a man learns to accept and enjoy risk and to face the fears that come with it.

I learned this truth early in my own journey out of same–sex attraction. Dan Gray was my therapist at the time, and he had organized a sports group that played basketball in the winter, softball in the spring, and football in the summer. Basketball was the biggest adventure for me. I'm six–feet–four–inches tall, and while growing up, my height seemed to entitle everyone to ask, "Do you play basketball?" Of course I *didn't*, and the amount of shame I felt about that was as big as I was tall. So when I finally learned how to play at a tolerable level, my shame went away and I felt a surge of masculinity.

For awhile I thought this increase in manliness was because I had learned to play basketball. To use David Whyte's terms, I thought it was because I had gained power over the experience of basketball. That was a control–centered belief. But I later realized that I wasn't feeling more manly because I could control an orange ball. I felt more manly because I was learning how to live the way men live—through embracing risks and facing fear! There are endless opportunities for us to face our fears, if we're willing and aware. There are physical ways, like riding a motorcycle or skydiving. There are emotional ways, like feeling our grief or exploring our bottled–up anger. There are interpersonal ways, like opening up to a friend or speaking out in awkward situations. And of course, there are ways to face fears through our careers, like pushing through our blocks to advancement or starting a new business.

The words of Jeff Konrad from his groundbreaking book, *You Don't Have to Be Gay*, are essential to this topic. He said, "Run toward the things that frighten you

---

We must accept risk. And accepting risk means that we must face fear.

"Run toward the things that frighten you the most."

Jeff Konrad, *You Don't Have to Be Gay*

the most." When I first read those words, I was horrified. But the truth of the principle resonated very deeply inside me and brought me to life. Learning this has changed my life—and I'm still learning it. David Whyte summarizes this principle most elegantly: "The price of our vitality is the sum of all our fears."

My own adventure was one of letting go of control, taking risks, and facing fears, which opened to me a whole new world of masculine creativity and power. It wasn't until many years later that I understood the other principle of adventure— faith. The principle of faith means to have hope or confidence in something that hasn't been manifested yet. It means having trust in true things that are unseen or unproven. Faith itself is an energy source. I can have faith in the reality of my own power and creativity to get me through a challenge. And for me, as I'm sure has been true for many other men, acquiring that level of self–confidence was a substantial accomplishment. But there is a far greater level of faith that I found, and I access that energy through the axis mundi of my inner King.

> Faith means to have hope or confidence in something that hasn't been manifested yet.

The higher level of faith I'm talking about requires us to rely on powers beyond our own capacities. It invites us to trust in a Higher Power. Through this type of faith, God replaces control. This faith asks us to remember that, although we are kings, we are not *the* King. At first, the idea of faith in a Higher Power can be disturbing or even maddening—particularly for those of us who want control. But it isn't any crazier than trusting our life to an airplane. Think about it—when we get on a plane we trust forces that we can't see and can't control. The only reason air travel doesn't seem insane is because we know that people do it all the time and it works—we have mastered the principles of flight. Faith works, too, although our lack of mastery of its principles makes it seem unpredictable. But that is the very essence of adventure. ✎ 3.2

Comrades

I'm extremely fond of a statement I've often heard a friend of mine make: "Masculinity is a team sport." Simply and truly, men need men. We need to be seen, understood, and accepted by each other. We need the mentoring, support, and challenges we give each other. As the writer of *Proverbs* chapter twenty–seven advises, "Iron sharpeneth iron; so a man sharpeneth the countenance of his friend" (*KJV*). In pursuing our mission and our adventure, we must have comrades.

Six elements make for strong friendships and strong male communities. They are commonality, trust, authenticity, reciprocity, boundaries, and unconditional love and compassion. Let's discuss each one briefly.

Commonality pulls the friendship together—it's the primary bonding agent without which a friendship would not exist. Commonality might be created by sharing a mission or adventure, by living in the same neighborhood, or by working or worshipping together. And it's increased when we have similar recreational interests, values, temperaments, maturity levels, personality strengths, and senses of humor. Strong friendships can be developed from even a reasonably close match in just a few areas. And the more similarities we share with another man, the closer we tend to become. At the same time, some degree of diversity in our interests and personalities can add depth and enjoyment to the friendship.

Trust is the first choice of any friendship. Without trust, two men won't engage each other, even if commonality exists. Minimal trust—typically referred to as "safety"—is the assurance that the other man won't hurt us. A higher level of trust would be based in the confidence that the new friend will accept us and treat us with equality. Higher still would be trust that's based on reliance that our friend loves and honors us. The word "trust" is both a verb and a noun. As a noun it describes a sense or feeling of safety or confidence. As a verb it describes an act or a choice.

Trust is a very simple human ability, but its applications in a person's life can be complex. For example, I may trust a friend with the key to my house, but I may not trust him to arrive on time. I may trust someone more after he reveals that he has lied to me. And I may trust others less on days when my self–esteem is low than on days when it is high.

Authenticity implies both an internal awareness of our feelings, wants, and desires, as well as an openness about these with the people around us. Authenticity in friendships includes sharing thoughts, experiences, feelings, desires, and goals. These disclosures may be extensive and deeply personal, covering many intimate facets of our personal lives. Or the communication may not be so deep—perhaps even limited to just a few shared interests. Sometimes authenticity requires friends to challenge or confront each other. The vulnerability that's inherent in

---

Trust is the first choice of any friendship.

Authenticity implies both an internal awareness of our feelings, wants, and desires, as well as an openness about these with the people around us.

authentic relationships depends on trust as each man chooses to open himself freely to the other.

Authenticity often requires a certain level of assertion, especially if we're going to make our wants known. Rich Wyler tells of a young same–sex attracted man he knew who had been eyeing a group of boys who sat closely together at church activities, whispering and joking with each other. The young man silently watched them from afar, passively wishing he could be included and wondering why they didn't reach out to him and invite him to join them. Then one day a new boy showed up at church. The new boy walked right over to the group of young men and said, "Make room." The group of boys made space, and the new guy plopped himself down among them. That was it—he was in. Sometimes we make authentic assertion a much bigger deal than it needs to be.

Reciprocity refers to mutuality or give–and–take in a relationship. It implies that, as friends, we share a similar interest in each other and in our friendship. We want to spend time together and each of us initiates doing things with the other. Both of us take responsibility for making our friendship work by investing time, effort, and other resources. We each do what we reasonably can to be available and helpful to the other; we're true to our mutual commitments. There is equality and balance in such things as talking and listening. Power is equally shared with each of us having a say in decision–making. But most importantly, we both feel like we're equally giving and receiving.

Healthy boundaries are an essential part of genuine friendships. Boundaries are limits on such things as time, energy, interaction, disclosure, intimacy, physical space, and electronic communication. Respect for each other's time might mean being punctual and not staying too long. Boundaries on intimacy may include sharing and asking about only what's appropriate given the degree of openness in the relationship. Physical space boundaries could include standing at an appropriate distance, touching only in ways that are comfortable for both, and respecting the privacy of each other's home or work environments. Boundaries in a relationship enable individuals to maintain privacy, retreat when necessary, and say "No" when it's appropriate.

Unconditional love and compassion begin with a full acceptance of all that our friends—in trust and authenticity—reveal about themselves. We may occasionally

> Reciprocity refers to mutuality or give-and-take in a relationship.

disagree with their opinions, we may not like all of their choices, and we may have difficulty with some of their weaknesses. But we let our feelings and actions toward them be guided and inspired by our love of their "true Self" qualities. Their good traits eclipse their personal flaws in our view of them. And it's primarily through these good traits that we relate to them. This instills a mutual sense of freedom to share and the comfort of being understood.

Love and compassion soften the edges of authenticity and boundaries. When authenticity creates fear and vulnerability, love responds with safety and attunement, strengthening trust. When boundaries require confrontation, compassion protects, heals, and holds the friendship together. Love and compassion—balanced by the other five elements—raise friendships to their highest and most healing levels. Loving bonds with comrades put men more deeply in touch with the *Tao* of maleness as we resonate with one another's masculinity. 3.3

Spiritual Connection

Of the six needs, this one may be the most difficult to describe and explain to a group of readers as diverse as that for which I'm writing. For instance, if you're already well grounded in this need, you could find my viewpoint off–target. If you don't appreciate spirituality, you might find my words meddlesome. I encourage you to use this as an opportunity to consider your own spiritual life rather than to get caught in disagreements with my premises, even if that means ignoring everything written here and just pondering the topic on your own.

Let's start by defining the subject. Spirituality could be described as the reality beyond our five senses—a transcendent universe that connects all things together. It's also our personal connection to that reality. And it's the meaning, beliefs, and practices that come from our experiences with that transcendent reality.

Different people understand this transcendent reality in different ways. To some it's understood as a universe created and governed by God. Some people also believe in the presence of unseen entities besides God, such as spirits and angels. There are those who understand the forces of this transcendent realm to be a non–personal governing power in the universe. And still others consider spiritual phenomena to be creations of our minds. Regardless of how we explain the phenomena that we classify as "spiritual," they do occur and are very real and very helpful and comforting for many of us.

Why do I assert that we have spiritual needs? To begin with, I assert this because the King archetype has always been associated with spiritual powers. He is the axis mundi—the connection to the divine realm. When a belief such as this shows up in so many cultures and religions across time, I consider it very unwise to ignore it. More significantly, I assert that spirituality is a need because of the many benefits and blessings that a spiritual awareness can bring. So what are those benefits and blessings?

To begin with, spirituality brings a sense of connection to something bigger than ourselves. This can provide a sense of comfort that we're not alone in the universe. A spiritual grounding can give meaning and a sense of purpose by assuring us that life and creation are going somewhere—there is an eternal continuation. A belief that there is more to our existence than what we see in the temporal here–and–now offers ways to understand the suffering we see in this life. It gives a hopeful context for what otherwise might seem meaningless and vain.

When our spirituality has been well developed, it can be a source of guidance in the form of inspiration, intuition, or a sense of inner knowing. This might be experienced as conscience, inner clarity, epiphany, or as divine communication. Sacred texts speak of revelations and visions where God imparts wisdom to man and makes known his plan for our happiness. In this fashion, spirituality can be a profound compass. It can also be the foundation of a man's mission when he feels called by God to champion a certain cause. Some experience spirituality in ways even more real than these—as a source of real power beyond our own. The Bible tells many stories of mortals being blessed by God with special powers and gifts.

> Spirituality can be a source of guidance in the form of inspiration, intuition, or a sense of inner knowing.

Faith is one of the greatest benefits of a spiritual life. We talked about faith in the section on adventure. There I said that faith means to have hope or confidence in something that hasn't been manifested yet—to trust in true things that are unseen or unproven. I suggested that faith in a God, or a Higher Power, can replace our need to control everything in our lives. With faith we can overcome the fear of accepting that we actually have very little control in this world. We can accept this because we believe that our Higher Power has control over *all* things and that he wants us to grow and develop—even through hardship. So we can put ourselves in His hands and trust him.

My life experiences have convinced me beyond doubt that there is a benevolent power in the universe. Through repeated interactions with this unseen force, I'm equally certain that I'm known and loved in a very intimate and personal way. I understand this loving power to be God. I've tried life with and without a spiritual connection, and with almost predictable precision my life goes far better when I'm spiritually grounded and connected with God. Not only do I have a stronger sense of joy, hope, and purpose, I actually experience guidance, intervention, and spiritual powers beyond my own from the unseen force. Sometimes the interventions from the spiritual realm are astonishing. But more commonly they are very subtle. To notice such interventions, one must be very still and listen for the "still small voice" spoken of in the Bible (see 1 Kings 19:12).

I can also attest to the impact that faith in a Higher Power has on the healing process. The second step of Alcoholics Anonymous reads, "We came to believe that a Power greater than ourselves could restore us to sanity." I've seen that happen in dramatic ways for men with various addictions. I've also seen the healing influence of that Higher Power in the process of growth out of unwanted same–sex attraction. Though most men aren't simply lifted out of homosexuality by prayer alone, those who apply faith to their journey experience real help.

Wherever you are spiritually, I encourage you to risk, even if only slightly, and venture toward a deeper connection with the spiritual realm. Even if all you can do is to want to believe, give room for that desire in your heart. Nourish that desire the way you would nourish a seed you had planted. Seek connection to your Higher Power and see if the seed grows. You will know it's growing because it will feel good and your belief will deepen. Keep in mind that spirituality is dynamic and our needs can change throughout our lives. Different ages and stages of life bring different levels of awareness and desire. Be aware of the place you are in right now. ✍ 3.4

Physical Care

> It's through our bodies that we fulfill all of our core needs.

Our bodies are the instruments through which we interact with the world—the foundation of everything we experience in this life. It's through our bodies that we fulfill all of our core needs. Think about it—each of the needs we've discussed involves our bodies in some way. Fulfilling a *mission* and living an *adventure* both require physical action and mental alertness (remember that your brain is part of your physical self). The foundation of the need for *genderedness*, which we'll discuss next, is the physical differences between men and women. Plus it's through our bodies that we engage in sexual intercourse—the ultimate act of genderedness. Men tend to relate to their *comrades* through action, which naturally involves the body. Even the transcendent experiences of *spirituality* are played out in our hearts and minds—in other words, in our bodies.

But our physical needs—perhaps more than any of our other needs—tend to be shrouded in shadows, such as the belief that the body is shameful, genitals are dirty, pleasure is evil, touch is bad, or that it's vain to care about how we look. We'll never be able to fulfill our physical needs until we move past our shadows and develop an attitude of kindness and care toward our bodies. We need to relate to our bodies as a benevolent king would relate to the people of his kingdom—with a sense of love and stewardship toward a precious gift that has been entrusted to our care. But what does that mean in everyday life?

It means that we must have a positive emotional connection to our bodies. Think about the emotional relationship you have with your body. Is it based on feelings like joy, confidence, gratitude, and love? Or do you more often feel shame, guilt, and disgust about your body? You might even dissociate from your body, which means that you lack a sense of connection to it, as if your body didn't really exist. The nature of your emotional relationship with your body is important because it determines how well you will take care of it. Our bodies need constant care, and if we're going to be loving stewards of our bodies we have to accept that reality.

On the other hand, if we treat our bodies the way a Weakling Abdicator treats his kingdom, we'll have to contend with the consequences of poor physical, psychological, and emotional health that result from such self–betrayal. We can't choose the genetic givens of our bodies or the demands those givens place on us. But we *do* choose what we do with the genetic cards we were dealt. Think about it this way: Would you rather drive a well–tuned car or a clunker? You don't get to decide whether the car is a Lamborghini or a Kia. You only get to determine how well you take care of it. Since most of what we do in life just requires our bodies to get us from point A to point B, the make of the car is less important than how well it's maintained.

> Would you rather drive a well-tuned car or a clunker? The make of the car is less important than how well it's maintained.

So now let's get specific about what proper care of the body looks like. Let's start with staying physically fit. The three pillars of fitness are exercise, nutrition, and rest. The benefits of exercise can hardly be overstated. First of all, it combats chronic diseases by lowering blood pressure, increasing the good type of cholesterol (high–density lipoprotein), and preventing build up of plaques in our arteries. And it helps manage weight, which in turn tends to prevent a host of other diseases. What's more, exercise tends to increase energy levels, leaving us feeling more alert and alive. It improves mood and decreases the likelihood of depression. And it has been shown to improve sleep, making it easier to fall asleep and causing deeper sleep. Exercise has also been shown to improve sexual desire and prevent erectile dysfunction.[3]

Proper nutrition is important for sustaining energy throughout the day and plays a key role in maintaining optimal body weight. Diet also has a very direct impact on our health by making us either more susceptible or more resilient to a variety of diseases. When thinking about nutrition, we need to consider the type of food (for example, fats, proteins, carbohydrates, and sweets), the quality of the food (for example, fast and prepared foods versus fresh and organic), and when we eat it (for example, morning versus late at night). All of these factors directly impact our health and wellbeing.

Rest and relaxation are also essential to long–term wellbeing. This includes waking downtime as well as sleep. Following exercise, it's important to allow sufficient time for recuperation before working out again. Without adequate rest our bodies never have time to replenish their energy. We become worn down and vulnerable to illness, injury, and disease. I encourage you to find the right amount of time that your body needs for both sleep and waking downtime and observe those needs. Much more could be said about exercise, nutrition, and rest. Scores of books have been written on these topics. But for our discussion it's enough for you to consider how mindful you are of fulfilling these aspects of your physical care.

For men with unwanted same–sex attraction, the benefits of having a healthy emotional connection to their bodies and being physically fit can go well beyond what we've already talked about. In my own experience, when I feel deeply connected to my own body and I'm actively engaged in keeping my body healthy and strong, I feel far less interest in the bodies of other men. I've heard others say similar things. I don't have to make my body perfect. The fact that I have a sense of mastery over it seems to be enough. I believe the reason this works is because the sense of self–mastery helps me own my masculinity rather than

The three pillars of fitness are exercise, nutrition, and rest.

I don't have to make my body perfect. The fact that I have a sense of mastery over it seems to be enough.

projecting it onto other men. Also, when I feel good about myself physically, I interact more confidently with other people, which improves my relationships and further increases my sense of masculinity.

There is one more physical need we have to address—touch. We talked a little about this in Chapter Two. Human beings are wired to need touch. Touch deprivation in childhood can lead to very serious physical, emotional, and psychological problems. While touch is especially important during our earliest years, I believe the need for touch continues throughout our lives. People who did not receive adequate touch in childhood may be especially prone to cravings for touch and physical closeness in adulthood.

Human beings are wired to need touch.

Many men in the process of overcoming unwanted same–sex attraction find that experiencing appropriate non–sexualized touch from other men diminishes their desire for sex with men. That's confirmed by my observations of men I've worked with and by my own personal experiences with male–male touch. The key to making this work lies in creating situations that are completely non–sexual. This starts in the minds of those engaging in the touch. ✍ 3.5

Genderedness and Complementarity

John Eldredge's concept of "a beauty to rescue" could be a bit off–putting to some men. I can't tell you how many times I've heard men say essentially, "Oh great, I've gotta have a pathetic woman in my life who I'm gonna have to bail out again and again. Shoot me now—and I'll gladly pay for the bullet!" Likewise, some women may roll their eyes at the prospect of waiting helplessly to be rescued by Dudley Do–Right. But that's not what it's really like when the man and the woman are living out of the wholeness of their masculinity and femininity. The *Tao* of maleness and femaleness are such that each brings about the fullness of the other. Complete Kingship emerges from a balance of all four masculine archetypes, but it also requires some type of relationship with a feminine archetype. This is how we as men become our very best and most whole selves.

To explain this further, let me introduce the terms "genderedness" and "complementarity." Genderedness is the natural state of having two sexes that are distinct and different from one another. Complementarity refers to a favorable relationship between the two sexes where the natural traits of each sex fulfill, balance, and perfect the other. It implies that we see the opposite sex as desirable

Genderedness: the natural state of having two sexes

Complementarity: a favorable relationship between the two sexes and as having something valuable to contribute to us. Together the two sexes make a complete unit. It takes these two energies together to be truly whole. In *Wild at Heart*, John Eldredge writes beautifully and sensually about this interplay of the genders.

> The beauty of a woman arouses a man to play the man; the strength of a man, offered tenderly to his woman, allows her to be beautiful; it brings life to her and to many. This is far, far more than sex and orgasm. It is a reality that extends to every aspect of our lives.

> There is no wholeness in masculinity alone. The woman is our opposite. And she is the other half of a greater whole.

There is no wholeness in masculinity alone. The woman is our opposite. And she is the other half of a greater whole. The *Book of Genesis* in the Bible and the Torah says in chapter two, verse eighteen that it is not good for man to be alone. Jewish and Christian translations of the next sentence read (italics added):

"I will make a *compatible* helper for him."

"I will make him a helper *corresponding* to him."

"I will make an help *meet* for him."

What this verse is telling us is that woman's relationship to man is not merely to be the recipients of our semen and bearers of our offspring. They are our helpers and they are made in such a way as to be well suited and worthy of us. So how is she our well–suited helper? Precisely because she is our opposite. Her experience of life is different from our own. Her physical and emotional makeup give her perspectives that are exotic and mysterious to us. Only by bringing together the gifts of the two genders can we experience wholeness in life. For example, the feminine trait of openness and receptiveness must be matched by the masculine trait of assertion and penetration in order to bring pleasure to both and to create life.

Let's go back to the symbol of yin–yang. As we discussed in Chapter One, the symbol represents union and interrelation of opposites. Chief among those opposites is gender. In Taoism, the dark yin is associated with femininity while the light yang is associated with masculine traits. The symbol is telling us two essential truths: the genders are different and they belong together. Notice that the presence of the black helps to define the shape of the white parts of the symbol. Correspondingly, the presence of the white creates the outline and dimensions of the black. In this same way, the distinction of the feminine helps to define the masculine just as the distinction of the masculine helps to define the feminine.

It has been noted that the white masculine yang penetrates the black feminine yin as the man penetrates the body of the woman. At the same time, the feminine yin penetrates the masculine yang as the woman penetrates the man's heart. What all of this doctrine is teaching us as men is that we can experience the utmost fullness of our masculinity only through its interrelationship with the feminine yin in our lives. This calls on us to explore, embrace, and enjoy the differences between the genders.

Now let's look at the problems you may have with the idea of rescuing a "beauty." The issues that same–sex attracted men may have with women are diverse. Every man's story is unique. You may have wounds from girls or women that lessen or cripple your ability to see them as desirable companions. You may have experienced life too much through the female mind, leaving you without a sense of arousal by the feminine mystery. You may feel emasculated or overwhelmed by them. Or perhaps you believe that you started this journey too late in life to ever find a woman to be with.

> The issues that same-sex attracted men have with women are diverse. Every man's story is unique.

Each of these situations requires a different process for working through and resolving. For now, let it be okay if your life has not yet prepared you to fully be a man with a woman. Continue your discovery of the Tao of maleness through living your mission, experiencing adventure, gaining strength from comrades, deepening your spiritual connection, and caring for your physical self. Love and accept yourself just as you are and spend your energy grounding yourself in your own masculine yang and moving toward an appreciation of your opposite. What happens after that is a mystery, just like the feminine.

Finally, consider that—depending on their life circumstance—some men will fulfill the need for genderedness through their wife or girlfriend. Others may fulfill it through healthy women in their family or community. You don't necessarily have to be married to enjoy and benefit from the feminine. ✍ 3.6

We have reviewed a long list of King traits and capacities in this and the previous chapter. This review has been an invitation to consider how well you're doing at meeting your needs. You may have noticed areas of strength and areas where you want to improve. This kind of awareness could feel overwhelming. I encourage you to apply the principles of balance and moderation as you think about the changes you want to make in your life. Also, remember the Law of Gestation and allow yourself plenty of time to "incubate" your King archetype. And finally, bless yourself with praise and recognition for the growth you've already accomplished and for your sincere intention to move forward.

NEED FULFILLMENT AND JOY

To finish this chapter, let's return to the essential connection between the fulfillment of our needs and joy. Joy may be defined as the experience of satisfaction, wellbeing, and completion; the sense that life is good, that it has purpose and meaning. I'm speaking of joy in its mature, bigger–than–self form—not mere satisfaction of cravings through excitement, stimulation, or even bliss, although each of these may be part of joy.

Joy results, in part, from the fulfillment of our needs. It's not necessary that *all* of our needs are met in order to experience joy. And fulfilling our needs doesn't guarantee that we'll feel joy. But when we do feel joy, it's because some need has been fulfilled and its fulfillment has been experienced. Need fulfillment and joy tend to create some very powerful cycles in our lives. These cycles start with our active commitment to fulfill our needs. Consider the three cycles described below.

Fulfillment Cycle

Through fulfilling our needs, we experience a sense of wellbeing, which may include feelings of calmness, contentment, satisfaction, and energy to continue. We're less likely to experience cravings and more likely to feel love for ourselves. Because these feelings are so positive, we naturally want to experience them again, which provides strong motivation to continue fulfilling our own needs. At the same time, our belief in our capacity to fulfill our needs also increases. This entire cycle increases our joy.

Blessing Cycle

When we feel truly joyful, we tend to want to bless others. It's a natural trait among emotionally mature people that when we're truly happy and fulfilled, we want those around us to enjoy the same blessings we enjoy. So we reach out and give to others. The act of giving increases our feelings of joy and fulfillment because giving is inherently satisfying. That satisfaction increases our desire to give to others.

ˆvcle

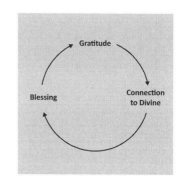

ˉait among emotionally mature people to feel gratitude toward ˉings and fulfillment. Feeling and expressing gratitude to ˉn we depend for everything we have puts us in direct ˉ of the universe. And gratitude invites more of that ˉs blessings—into our lives, which, once again,

---

ˍachings of Buddha are contained in *The Four Noble Truths*. A second text, *The ˍ Eightfold Path*, teaches how to live life in such a way as to achieve an end to personal ˍfering.

[2] Eldredge is a Christian writer and his book contains many Biblical references. Non–Christian readers have told me that they also found the book very valuable, even though they didn't entirely resonate with its Christian elements.

[3] This information is from the Mayo Clinic. See www.mayoclinic.com.

Chapter 4

Just as I Am

In order to change, I found that I needed to let others walk with me through my deepest shame. With trusted friends, I brought my shame out of darkness, into the light, and exposed it. Then I surrendered it.

Doing so was very painful. But on the other side, I found that *I am valuable and good, just as I am*. And I found that I have brothers who see my shadows and accept me, *just as I am*. Only as I accept myself *just as I am*, can I allow you to see and accept me in the same way.

Journey Into Manhood

ou are the king and you have a job to do. The job to which this chapter calls your inner king is to become aware of any dangers your kingdom may be facing from internal shadows that may be bent on usurping the power in your life. In other words, this chapter is intended to help you find any psychological problems you may be dealing with. Psychological problems—such as shame, depression, anxiety, and obsessive–compulsiveness—can usurp power by diverting your attention from kingdom building to inner turmoil. A powerful king would never allow that.

In order to complete this chapter, you will need to access some of the kingly traits you just learned about in Chapter Two. You will need the King's capacity to *discern* because you will be asked to look closely at many aspects of yourself. You may need the capacity of *moderation* in order to pace yourself as you go through the chapter so that you don't go too fast and become overwhelmed or go too slow and avoid learning the truth. Later on, you may need to be the *provider of means* that are necessary in order to get the help you may need to deal with any problems that are revealed.

> Psychological problems can usurp power by diverting your attention from kingdom building to inner turmoil.

But most importantly, you need to access the King's roles as the *inspirer* and *giver of blessing*. You must hold the vision that there is purpose in everything you face in your life. You need to *behold* yourself from a place of love and acceptance, affirming your own highest potential even as you frankly view your own weaknesses. And you need to *bless* yourself with an active commitment to moving through your issues and into your own special future. To begin with, I suggest that you access your axis mundi—ground yourself in the knowledge of your validity, worth, and purpose—so that what you do arises from a stillness, a knowing, inside you. It flings

This chapter will be different from the others since it contains a number of short questionnaires to help reveal problems of which you may not be fully aware. We'll consider a variety of issues, including shame, negative core beliefs, addiction, depression, various anxiety disorders, obsessive–compulsiveness, post–traumatic disturbance, and harmful relationships.

It's beyond the scope of this chapter to provide specific help for each of the issues to be considered. But a lot of information is now available on the internet, and you should be able to find resources to help you.

> If you find the realizations that come from this chapter overwhelming, frightening, or disturbing, stop working on it and reach out to someone you trust.

None of what we'll discuss in this chapter is unique to men with unwanted same–sex attraction—heterosexual men and women also suffer from these problems. But, in my clinical experience, these issues do occur with far greater frequency among men with unwanted same–sex attraction than among the general population. These problems can make working through unwanted same–sex attraction difficult, if not impossible, if they are not addressed. So give careful attention to the topics raised in this chapter. Be introspective and honest with yourself. Go all the way through this chapter, even if you think you aren't dealing with anything other than unwanted same–sex attraction. You may discover something new and important.

Be aware that some men may find the realizations that come from this chapter overwhelming, frightening, or disturbing. If that happens to you, stop working on it and reach out to someone you trust. If you have a therapist, talk to him or her about your feelings. If you don't currently have a support network of any kind and you're prone to anxiety, depression, or suicidal thoughts, I urge you **not** to complete this chapter until you're able to create support for yourself. Just skip to Chapter Five. As you go through this chapter you may discover that you need the help of a professional to progress through certain issues you're having.

There are many different types of mental health professionals, but they can all be divided into roughly three groups. First are psychiatrists, who are medical doctors with special training in psychology. Typically, psychiatrists are consulted when medication is required for certain mental disorders like depression, anxiety, OCD, and bipolar disorder—they typically don't provide psychotherapy. These are usually the most highly trained mental health practitioners, but their training tends to be more medical than psychological.

The second group, which can be lumped under the term "psychotherapists," includes clinical psychologists, marriage and family therapists, social workers, and counselors. Among these there is a broad range of university training, but all of them are licensed by a government agency, and they are trained to assess, diagnose, and treat emotional, mental, and relational difficulties. The third group includes life coaches and other non–professional practitioners. These individuals aren't licensed by the government and usually don't have university training in mental health. But they often have specific training or experience in some type of helping modality.

The level of an individual's training and licensure should definitely be considered when determining which professional is right for you. Certain issues really do require the help of a highly–trained person while other issues can be worked through quite effectively with a less trained caregiver. And keep in mind that traits like insight, intuition, wisdom, and life experience are essential in helping professionals, and those may be possessed by—or lacking in—professionals of all levels. As we go through the various sections in this chapter, I'll note the level or type of care that I recommend for those specific issues.

One final thought before we begin: remember moderation. It's not intended that you overcome all these issues right now. Overcoming them will require meaningful and sustained attention over a span of months or even years. This chapter is just intended to start a process of recovery and growth.

Now, let's start our discussion of the various issues you might be facing by considering the nature and role of feelings. This is a good place to start because our feelings, which include emotions, counter–emotions, and defenses, often play a very substantial role in all of the other issues we'll discuss afterward.

Mental Health Professionals

- Psychiatrists are doctors that dispense medication for mental disorders.
- Psychotherapists are university trained and licensed to assess, diagnose, and treat mental disorders.
- Life coaches are non-licensed professionals with varying degrees of training.

FEELINGS

In the process of change, feelings can be one of our best allies or greatest stumbling blocks. We're capable of a broad range of feelings. Some of our feelings are healthy and even essential for healing and growth. Other feelings can keep us stuck, lead us astray, or even cause us great pain. So understanding our feelings is a matter of great importance. In this section we'll first review what is healthy and helpful, then consider some of the major problems we can experience with our feelings.

Core Emotions

The term "emotion" may be the most loosely defined term in modern psychology. The word itself derives from Latin and Middle French roots that mean, "to start out, incite, stir up," or "move out." The term "core emotion" may be used to designate those feelings that are informative, healing, or that bring us to a state of wellbeing. The core emotions include fear, anger, sadness, joy, shame, and disgust.[1] These emotions, when they are fully felt, always lead to some type of transformation. Sometimes that will be a transformation into a deeper feeling. But eventually it will be a transformation into a state of peacefulness or resolution. In reality, there are more emotional states than just the core emotions, including such feelings as love, peacefulness, sexual desire, and surprise. In men's work, we tend to focus just on the core emotions for simplicity and because they are most applicable to the process of healing.

We usually experience emotion in three ways: as thoughts in our minds, sensations in our bodies, and impulses in our minds and bodies. Let's discuss these in a bit more detail. First, we're usually aware mentally when we're experiencing emotion—we typically know when we're feeling happy or sad. But on a less conscious level, our thoughts actually lead to our emotions. The mental stories we tell ourselves—about ourselves, our situation, our relationships and so forth—create the emotional reality in which we live our lives. This is just another way of saying that our thoughts strongly affect our feelings. Thinking that life is good and that we're blessed will usually create feelings of joy. Thinking that we have been mistreated or abused will frequently lead to feelings of anger. Thoughts about loss will lead to sadness, and a story about being in danger will lead to fear.

But our emotions also reciprocally affect our thinking. Anger tends to cause our thoughts to be less rational. When we're angry, we also tend to be more willing

Core emotions: those feelings that are informative, healing, or bring us to a state of wellbeing

to engage thoughts we wouldn't otherwise entertain. True fear often causes our thoughts to be very clear and quick (anxiety on the other hand often makes our minds go blank). Sadness has a tendency to slow our thoughts down as we focus our mental attention on the loss. And joy often creates mental clarity and peacefulness.

Second, all emotions can create physical sensations in our bodies—the heat and electricity of anger, the emptiness or pangs of sadness, the jolt of fear, or the expansive sensations of joy. Emotions can also bring about physiological changes in our bodies. For example, anger might cause our muscles to tighten, sadness often causes tears to form in our eyes, and fear usually increases our heart and respiratory rates.

Third, our emotional impulses tend to come from both our minds and our bodies. They show up in our minds as thoughts of how we want to express the feeling we're having. They show up in our bodies as compelling physical urges to follow through on those thoughts. With anger the thoughts may be about hurting or punishing those with whom we are angry. Physically, angry impulses may show up as a clenched fist or a desire to yell. With fear, impulses may show up as thoughts about escape from the situation. The bodily impulse of fear may be a compelling urge to run!

With sadness, the mental impulses may be focused on wanting to see, touch, or hold a lost loved one or animal, or thoughts of wanting to go back and undo a tragic situation. (Part of what makes sadness so painful is the impossibility of fulfilling these desires.) The physical impulses of sadness may be the urge to touch or hold, or perhaps the urge to collapse and express the feeling through tears and sound. Joyful impulses may focus, in both thought and physical urge, on giving voice to the feeling as a song, a shout, or a quiet expression of gratitude. Or they may focus on giving action to the feeling through jumping, expanding your body, or lying still as tears of joy stream down your face.

Emotions can tell us deeper truths about ourselves than we can learn from our thoughts alone. Because our thoughts are conscious, we're able to repress and deny those we don't like. Our feelings are not conscious and therefore often escape the scrutiny of our minds. It's often said that the body doesn't lie, and there is much truth in this. However, our feelings often require interpretation in order to be properly understood.

> Emotions can tell us deeper truths about ourselves than we can learn from our thoughts alone.

For example, if I get angry at someone who got in my way, I may think that I hate him and need to hurt him. With proper interpretation I may realize that I'm actually angry about something entirely unrelated to that person. The value of the angry sensations, thoughts, and impulses in that case was that they brought the anger to my awareness. But then I needed my mind to understand what the feeling was really about. And I need emotional control to keep me from punching the guy.

Emotions can protect and inform us. Fear alerts us to dangers. Anger and sadness bring our awareness to our wounds. Joy is our signpost of progress and wellbeing. Emotions move us toward greater maturity and wholeness. For example, sadness moves us through the experience of loss by expanding our emotional capacity to feel and encompass the loss. We become more emotionally capable than we were before the loss. And emotion is often curative in itself—feeling is healing. The kind of learning that causes deep and lasting change involves both our intellect and our feelings. ✍ 4.1

Counter–Emotions and Defenses

Not all of our feelings are so helpful. Some of our feelings don't inform us accurately, don't heal us, and don't transform us into states of wellbeing. Those feelings could be called "counter–emotions." Counter–emotions are typically reactions to situations that we never learned how to handle in more positive, authentic, or empowered ways. Often they are used to cover up or replace core emotions that our unconscious mind deems too painful or scary to feel. We learn how to contain or repress the real emotion through feeling a counter–emotion replacement.

Counter-emotions: feelings that don't inform us accurately, don't heal us, and don't transform us into states of wellbeing.

So when our fear is too scary, when our anger makes us feel guilty or afraid, or when our sadness is too overwhelming, we learn to hide it or stuff it deep down inside us, and instead we feel something else. We may experience these feelings as sensations in our bodies, just like authentic emotions. But instead of moving us toward greater wholeness, they keep us stuck. I use the term *counter*–emotion because these feelings don't transform or expand us, they shrink us. They don't increase our understanding of our self. They cloud it. They don't tell us about our deeper truths. They tell us lies.

Anxiety is an example of a counter–emotion. Anxiety is different from fear, which impels us to either fight or flee. Anxiety causes us to freeze. Shame is another counter–emotion—and a particularly destructive one. Shame is the painful awareness of the exposure of our flaws—a condemnation of our very being. Depression is also a counter–emotion. Depression is different from sadness, which is healing. When we're depressed, we become static and shut down. In that state, no healing can happen. Lust is a counter–emotion, too. Lust is self–centered. It's about what we want to take from the object of our lust. It's about *using* instead of giving, sharing, or brotherhood. Lust blocks out other feelings so we can't feel our discomfort or pain.

Sometimes the situation can be a bit muddier. Core emotions can function as counter–emotions. For example, we might use anger to defend against a deeper sadness or an overwhelming fear. Or we might go into a false sadness to avoid feeling the intensity of our rage. This happens because our unconscious is trying to find the least painful way through an emotionally overwhelming situation. So if we unconsciously believe that anger is less threatening than our sadness or fear, anger is what our body will produce. This is just another of our mind's natural attempts to keep life from being too intolerable.

But our counter–emotions can become intolerable as well. So we may build an even stronger wall against feeling our emotions through the use of defensive behaviors like using drugs or alcohol, overworking, fantasizing, denial, intellectualizing, compulsive sex, or numbing out in front of the television. Like counter–emotions, defenses are used unconsciously to handle emotional situations we are unprepared to handle in more effective ways. When our wounds create painful or frightening emotions, we often build defensive walls to protect ourselves from the pain.

Eventually we may build a formidable wall of counter–emotions and defenses around our authentic core emotions to protect ourselves against feeling our fear, anger, sadness, and disgust. If we were to draw this system of counter–emotions and defenses, it might look something like the diagram on the next page.

As the diagram illustrates, our counter–emotions and defenses keep us well insulated. But are we happy? Usually not, because when we cut off our core emotions we also cut off our joy. We may tell ourselves that, given enough time, the past hurts of our lives will all go away. We may believe that the fear, anger, and sadness will weaken and die eventually, if we just keep them buried long enough, allowing us to feel joy again. But they don't die. Past hurts become stronger, not weaker. They fester

Depression is a counter-emotion. It's different from sadness, which is healing.

Defenses are used unconsciously to handle emotional situations we are unprepared to handle in more effective ways.

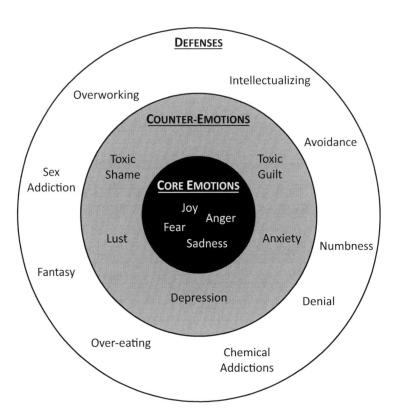

and rot and find sneaky ways to express themselves and sabotage our lives. They demand to be heard, honored, and released from the prison we've built for them.

We have to trust our own capacity to handle our authentic feelings. And we may need to put trust in others who can help us to find them. We have to trust that we can survive letting down our walls—one layer at a time—and feeling the pain underneath. We have to trust that all emotions are finite: any feeling fully felt will always shift into a deeper feeling. By continuing a process of dropping down through our emotional layers, we eventually come to a core state of peace, empowerment, and joy. By embracing *all* of our core emotions, we experience our most authentic selves—our true selves. 🖋 4.2

> We have to trust that all emotions are finite: any feeling fully felt will always shift into a deeper feeling.

Difficulty Feeling

Some of us have difficulty experiencing our emotions. We may know mentally when we are having an emotion, we may even be aware of certain impulses, but we don't feel any sensations in our bodies. Or we may feel sensations in our bodies, but not be able to name what the feeling is or know what it's about. There are those of us who feel lots of impulses, but can't relate them to our feelings. And then there are those of us who can neither feel our emotions in our bodies nor experience them mentally. Those who experience this may go through life almost entirely without feeling.

Of course, there are varying degrees of each situation I've described. And some of us have a combination of these difficulties depending on the emotion or the situation. For example, a man may be able to feel his fear but not know what it is. He may know when he's sad but can't feel it in his body. And he may be completely unaware that he has any anger, or maybe he can feel anger in some situations but not in others.

For some of us, these are very comfortable ways to live because we don't have to deal with feelings that can seem very tricky and unruly. But this condition makes healing very difficult, if not impossible. It's not wholeness. It's caused by splitting–off feelings and impulses, which is what creates shadows of unconsciousness, as we discussed in Chapter One. ✎ 4.3

SHAME

Of all the counter–emotions, shame is the most destructive and the most difficult to break through. In his groundbreaking book, *Healing The Shame That Binds You*, John Bradshaw describes two types of shame: healthy shame and toxic shame. It's normal for people to experience the core emotion of healthy shame. Healthy shame is the type of shyness and embarrassment that causes us to maintain appropriate boundaries. It stops us from walking down the street naked or acting in other "shameless" ways. Healthy shame is important for community—it keeps us from behaving in ways that are repulsive, offensive, or hurtful to others.

Healthy shame is also our recognition that we have weaknesses, that our capabilities are limited, and that we don't know everything. This awareness creates a type of humility that is essential for growth and creativity in that it causes us to seek more understanding and to improve our abilities. It's also necessary for spirituality in that it urges us to seek for things higher and more powerful than ourselves. It causes us to reach toward God or some other power greater than our own.

The counter–emotion of toxic shame is very different. In their book, *Facing Shame*, authors Merle Fossum and Marilyn Mason describe this type of shame as "an inner sense of being completely diminished or insufficient as a person. It is the self judging the self." Toxic shame is commonly distinguished from healthy shame

> Healthy shame is the type of shyness and embarrassment that causes us to maintain appropriate boundaries.

> "[Toxic] Shame is the ongoing premise that one is fundamentally bad, inadequate, defective, unworthy, or not fully valid as a human being."
>
> Fossum and Mason, *Facing Shame*

in this way: healthy shame is the knowledge that we have *done* bad; toxic shame is the belief that we *are* bad. To quote Fossum and Mason again, "Shame is the ongoing premise that one is fundamentally bad, inadequate, defective, unworthy, or not fully valid as a human being."

The authors also distinguish between short moments of shame and shame that is lasting and pervasive. Shame moments are brief experiences where our flaws are exposed in humiliating and dignity–destroying ways. This can happen when we're embarrassed in public or when we get in trouble at a very unexpected moment for something we didn't understand to be wrong. Pervasive or lasting shame on the other hand is an ongoing sense of fundamental badness, inadequacy, defectiveness, or unworthiness. Pervasive shame is often created by a series of shame moments which become woven into our sense of who we are. Over time, shame can become a core facet of our identity.

When this is the case, shame has moved from an occasional feeling to a core aspect of our character and personality. Thereafter it will color our beliefs and expectations of ourselves and the way we experience our relationships with others. These and other aspects of our lives will be filtered through our shame. We may then have very little or no frame of reference outside our shame.

As you may now understand, toxic shame can change our personalities, crippling our innate capacities for intimacy, self–esteem, and assertion, and blocking our ability to experience authentic emotions or to feel peace and contentment. For some of us, the effects of shame run across our entire personalities. For others, shame impacts only specific aspects of our characters. ✍ 4.4

The Roots of Shame

> Those of us who grew up in shame-bound families may experience an intense need to hide or cover up things about ourselves.

The type of toxic shame that is lasting and pervasive originates within a shame–bound family system. Fossum and Mason describe these families as systems that perpetuate and transmit shame from one generation to the next. This is done through an unspoken—and often unconscious—system of rules and expectations. The central requirement of these rules and expectations is complete personal control and perfection. Anything less than this is considered dangerous or "bad" and must be denied or blamed on others. Those of us who grew up in such families may experience this internally as an intense need to hide or cover up things about ourselves: who we are, what we do, and what we feel.

When we talk about families that are governed by rules of complete personal control and perfection, it gives an impression of high achievement and personal development. But what "control" and "perfection" are really about in these families is avoiding disapproval, rejection, and physical and emotional harm. For example, perfection may mean getting flawless grades so that a child receives the strokes he needs to avoid feeling totally worthless. Control might mean staying completely silent so that his father doesn't beat him.

I described these shame–bound families in Chapter One in the section "The Meanings of Shadow." There I explained how, as children, we may cut off, repress, or deny the traits in ourselves that seem unwanted or unsafe within our families, relegating those parts to our unconscious shadow. This is one of the ways in which archetypal energies get split apart. Children who experience this type of splitting often live with a sense of being a fraud or having a secret life, which in turn creates feelings of anxiety and tension in addition to shame and guilt.

Children who experience splitting often live with a sense of being a fraud or having a secret life, which in turn creates feelings of anxiety and tension in addition to shame and guilt.

We begin to acquire shame very early in life through a process detailed in John Bradshaw's book. Bradshaw explains that we begin to take it on, perhaps from the moment of our birth, through interactions with shame–based caregivers—our parents and others. This is how it becomes woven into our very identities; we grow up with it as a given, as a basic premise of our existence.

Some of us may have difficulty understanding why we personally are experiencing shame—our families were not abusive, our parents loved us, and we didn't experience any big traumas. If you're thinking this, it's important for you to understand that although abuse and trauma are often a part of the lives of shame–bound families, shame can be—and often is—transmitted from one generation to the next without abuse or trauma. It's the system of rules and expectations that transmit shame, and those rules and expectations can be very intense even in apparently loving families.

Another point of confusion arises when the system of rules and expectations is not obvious. In some families the shame–based dynamic is very blatant to both the family members and to outsiders. But the shame–based rules of other families can be so subtle and unconscious that it's invisible to outsiders and even to the family members themselves. This is somewhat like the fish that doesn't realize he's living in water—he's blind to his own obvious reality. ✍ 4.5

Self–Alienation

The splitting off, hiding, and covering up that result from a shame–based upbringing typically cause children to experience what Bradshaw describes as "self–alienation." He writes that, "When one suffers from alienation, it means that one experiences parts of one's self as alien to one's self."

As we discussed earlier, the rules of shame–bound families require complete personal control and perfection. But as children we have lots of feelings, impulses, and needs that are difficult to control. So those of us who grow up in shame–based families resort to suppression or denial of any aspects of ourselves that violate the family rules and expectations. We cut off and hide everything that would bother, disappoint, or anger the people around us. This may include our emotions, desires, aspirations, fears, needs, impulses, and any other aspects of ourselves that we believe are vulnerable to attack. The more severe the family rules are, the more intense our suppression and denial will be.

Those of us who grow up in the most intensely shame–bound families get the message that there is something wrong with our very nature, with what or who we are. We're taught to hate, hide, repress, and deny essential aspects of our humanity, including our bodies and personalities. All of this hiding cuts us off from our core Selves. We don't just hide from others—we repudiate or reject ourselves. This further alienation from self may be accompanied by chronic depression and by what Bradshaw calls "a sense of unreality," or the feeling that we aren't really in our own lives. It also blocks the fulfillment of core needs. ✍ 4.6

Shame and Healing

Shame is like a virus that can infect anything. It can contaminate our beliefs and attitudes about our bodies, personalities, families, and jobs. It can corrupt our perspective on our past and present behaviors and life experiences. It commonly seizes upon our weaknesses, but can even attack our strengths and talents. Once the intense feelings of shame have taken hold of something in our lives, we lose the ability to think rationally about that part of ourselves. We see everything through those feelings and obey the shame at all costs. Yes, we *obey* our shame. We believe it's the absolute truth, and we do whatever it tells us—we hide, lie, avoid, quit, cover up, keep secrets, and turn down opportunities. This curtails our freedom

---

Those of us who grow up in shame–based families resort to suppression or denial of any aspects of ourselves that violate the family rules and expectations.

Shame is like a virus that can infect anything. It can contaminate our beliefs and attitudes about our bodies, personalities, families, and jobs.

and makes growth difficult. So breaking the grip of shame is essential to any psychological healing process.

For some men, shame is a main motivating factor behind their desire to heal unwanted same–sex attraction. But shame will never produce positive change because shame only begets more shame, and because shame actually fuels homosexual feelings and compulsive behaviors. So, shame must be overcome.

But here is the good news—shame collapses and dissolves once we stop obeying it. As soon as we accept that *shame is a lie*, we start to get our freedom back. This tiny quantum leap in our thinking can give us enough courage to take the next big step, which is to expose our shame in trusting relationships with other men. Through this exposure we gain more courage and we release more of our shame. This becomes a positive cycle, like the joy cycles you read about in the previous chapter. Gradually the chains of shame dissolve, and we emerge as free men.

Exposing your shame to other men can be very scary, especially since feeling accepted and affirmed by other men is such a core need for many of us. These two needs—to reveal your shame and to feel accepted by other men—may seem mutually exclusive. On the one hand, you may fear that if you reveal your shame to other men, you won't be accepted and affirmed—you'll be rejected and disliked, making your shame deeper than ever. But then if you hide your shame, you may never be able to accept the affirmation you get because in the back of your mind you'll always be thinking, "If they only knew." It may seem like there is no way out—if you don't know what to trust.

Remember, shame is a counter–emotion, and therefore it is lie. If you trust that lie more than you trust in the goodness of other men, you will remain stuck in shame. But if you choose instead to trust other men enough to let them walk with you through your deepest shame, you can create a way out of the shame. And you may also discover that these two seemingly mutually exclusive needs are actually synergistic in the process of healing.

Now, a little advice: you can't trust everyone. But there are many trustworthy men in this world if you look for them. And when you open your secrets to them you're likely to find that they are also carrying shameful secrets that they are anxious and

> Shame collapses and dissolves once we stop obeying it. As soon as we accept that shame is a lie, we start to get our freedom back.

ready to reveal. They *can* understand you, and even love you. And you can love yourself more—just as you are.

Getting Help

If the material in this section raised your awareness that shame is a significant issue for you, I recommend Bradshaw's *Healing the Shame That Binds You*, and *Facing Shame: Families in Recovery* by Fossum and Mason. You might also search for "shame" at online bookstores. Many good resources are available. One of the most powerful ways of diminishing shame is to work on it directly in therapy with either a psychotherapist or an appropriately experienced life coach. Men's groups and experiential weekends, such as *Journey Into Manhood*, can also be very helpful in growing beyond are.

NEGATIVE CORE BELIEFS

Painful and shaming life experiences can cause us to form negatively distorted beliefs about ourselves.

The kinds of painful and shaming life experiences we've been discussing can cause us to form negatively distorted beliefs about ourselves that become firm and unchanging. These are called negative core beliefs. These mistaken beliefs develop because, as children, we tend to see every event in life as somehow related to ourselves, which makes us very susceptible to blaming ourselves for things that go wrong. To make matters worse, when we're young, our minds are unable to cope with the sense of vulnerability that comes from living in an unsafe world. So when bad things happen to us, rather than accepting that the world can be a dangerous place, we assume that we are the problem. This allows us to maintain an illusion that the world is safe and that, if we can just be better or do better, everything will be okay.

For example, when a child has been abused by his parent, rather than accepting that he's living in an unpredictable and risky situation, the child may create the belief that he did something wrong. Or when a child has been molested—rather than accepting that he cannot control his surroundings and what happens to him, he may create the belief that he's responsible or that he deserved it. Although these self-shaming beliefs are painful, they are less disturbing to a small child than the truth.

Once these negatively distorted beliefs have been created in childhood, we tend to reinforce them through selective awareness of the events that happen in our lives. In other words, we tend to notice everything that confirms our negative beliefs. We tend to distort neutral events to make them conform to our negative beliefs. And we typically disregard or perhaps don't even notice those events that contradict our negative beliefs.

As these negative beliefs are continually reinforced year after year, they become internalized and harden into negative core beliefs, which we now assume to be absolutely true about us. We construct layers of defenses to insulate ourselves from the awareness and pain of these core beliefs and to prevent others from seeing them.

Negative core beliefs can be based on a variety of things. Most commonly they are based on a sense of defectiveness, vulnerability, or helplessness and hopelessness. Men with same–sex attraction also tend to have negative core beliefs about our own maleness, about relating with other men, and about women.

John Eldredge uses the term "agreements" to describe essentially the same thing I'm talking about here. As a Christian writer, he believes that these are agreements we unconsciously make with Satan that stifle our relationship with God. He offers a very simple process of breaking these agreements with Satan. The process essentially involves asking for God's help in becoming aware of the agreement, breaking and renouncing the agreement, inviting God's power to heal and remove all of the history behind the agreement, and then replacing the old agreement with a new, positive agreement.[2] This is a distinctly Christian process. But for the non–Christian or the non–religious person I would offer that the same result can be achieved using your own conceptualization of God or a Higher Power. ✎ 4.7

SEXUAL ADDICTION AND COMPULSION

Addictive and compulsive sexual behaviors can become a man's most serious barrier to growth and are very common among those with same–sex attraction. Let's start with a brief discussion of the whole spectrum of human sexual desire and behavior to help you understand how addiction differs from compulsive sexuality and from normal sexual behavior.

The graphic on the next page depicts this spectrum as a scale going from sexual anorexia on the far left to sexual addiction on the far right. Near the middle of the scale you find normal sexual behavior. But you will notice by looking at the scale

---

Negative Core Beliefs

Defectiveness
I am a bad person
I am not loveable
I only deserve bad things
I am a disappointment
I am worthless

Vulnerability (Unsafe)
I am in danger
I can't protect myself
It's not safe to show my emotions
I am misunderstood

Helplessness and Hopelessness
I can't do anything about it
I can't change
I'll never accomplish much
I won't ever have good things
I will always be alone

My Maleness
I am weak
I am not masculine enough
I am a sissy
I don't look like a man
I can't assert myself
I have no power in my life

Relating to Men
I can't trust men
Men will reject me
I don't understand men
I can only relate with other same-sex attracted men
Men are dangerous

Relating with Women
I can't trust women
Women are disgusting
Women will drain and use me
Women are overwhelming
It's bad to want sex with a woman

that "normal" covers a wide span of the spectrum. Even within the normal range, humans differ greatly in our level of sexual desire and the extent of our sexual behavior. Now let's turn our attention to the extremes.

Human Sexual Behavior Scale

| Sexual Anorexia | Normal Sexual Behavior | Compulsive Sexuality | Sexual Addiction |

Sexual anorexia is a diminishing or loss of interest in sex and intimacy.

Sexual addiction is the loss of control of sexual behavior.

Sexual anorexia is a diminishing or loss of interest in sex and intimacy. It can be as substantial a problem for those who experience it as sexual compulsion or addiction, and it's also treatable by professionals who have the right training. Sexual addiction on the other end of the spectrum is the loss of control of sexual behavior, which then becomes worse over time. Those of us with extreme sexual addiction literally cannot stop the continual intensification of our sexual acting out, even when our behavior has cost us our job, relationships, financial security, and even our freedom. We'll discuss this further in a moment.

Compulsive sexual behavior is not unmanageable in the way that sexual addiction is. Although those of us with sexual compulsivity usually cannot stop our sexual behavior without help, the behavior doesn't worsen over time, and its consequences tend not to be as extreme as for the addict. Compulsive sexual behavior may remain essentially the same for many years. Even so, it can still be a serious obstacle to growth.

Before discussing sexual addiction and compulsion further, let's look at the process that sets people up for those troubling conditions.

The Control–Release Cycle

Control–release is a normal human dynamic. We first experience the control–release dynamic during toilet training, which requires control and release of bladder and bowels. Another example of this dynamic is sports and performance arts where control of the body is balanced with release or expression of power or emotional expression. Language provides a third example in that it requires us to control letters, words, and punctuation in order for us to express (or release) ourselves. The control and release dynamic is often experienced as exhilarating or empowering.

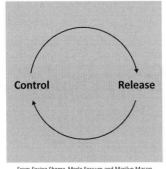

From *Facing Shame*, Merle Fossum and Marilyn Mason

Shame sets off a different type of control–release cycle—one that may provide occasional exhilaration, but is never empowering. When we feel shame, we naturally try to compensate or cover up our shame with certain types of control behaviors. Control behaviors can include overly strict avoidance of "bad" behaviors, repression of "wrong" thoughts, compulsive performance of "good" acts, making demands of other people, and avoiding situations that might expose our shame.

The more intense the shame, the more intensely we'll try to control ourselves and our situations. But the control behaviors are inauthentic, out of balance, and can't be maintained indefinitely. This leads eventually to a tipping point where we can no longer keep them up. At that point we go into the release phase of the cycle. The release provides relief from our intense attempts to control ourselves. It also provides pleasure and a temporary sense of wellbeing and power, which momentarily alleviates our shame. The more intense our control has been, the more intensely we'll feel compelled to release. And the more intense the release is, the more intensely we'll control things when we return to the control phase.

Once these shame–based cycles have been established, they can take on a life of their own as addictions and compulsions. All types of addictive behaviors are the result of a shame–based control–release cycle. The addictive behaviors in turn maintain and increase the shame from which they originated, creating a type of continuous feedback loop.

These control–release cycles create and maintain equilibrium for individuals and families. Although very painful, this equilibrium can remain stable for generations. As long as this dynamic remains in place, we'll be unable to overcome our negative behavior patterns, and our growth and healing will be curtailed.

The phases of control and release correlate with the shadow poles of the four primary masculine archetypes. The control phase correlates with the passive shadow poles, since behaviors typical of this phase are masochistic, impotent, "innocent–denying," and "weak." The release phase correlates with the active shadow poles, since behaviors typical of this pole are sadistic, addictive, manipulative, and tyrannical. ✍ 4.8

Once these shame–based cycles have been established, they can take on a life of their own as addictions and compulsions.

Identifying Addictive and Compulsive Sexual Behavior

Addictive and compulsive sexual behaviors can include masturbation, pornography, internet chat, cruising, sexual activity with other people, engaging in intense romantic relationships, and other behaviors.

Review the list of symptoms that follows, and put a check in the box next to each symptom that applies to you.

☐ Unable to stop engaging in relationships or sexual behaviors that you feel are wrong

☐ Loss of control over the frequency of your sexual behavior

☐ Your sexual behavior becomes more extreme over time because the old behaviors no longer provide the same high

☐ Shifting back and forth between feeling that your sexual problem is out of control and believing you have it under control

☐ Using sexual behavior or relationships on a regular basis to deaden painful feelings or forget your own problems

☐ Keeping your sexual behavior or relationships secret and perhaps even lying to cover them up

☐ Spending large amounts of time or money pursuing sexual behavior or relationships

☐ Making promises to yourself or others that are later broken because of your sexual behavior

☐ Life becomes unmanageable because of your sexual behavior—work and family responsibilities are neglected

☐ Serious consequences result from your sexual behavior, like the loss of a job, financial distress, the breakup of a marriage, or being arrested

If you check even a couple of these symptoms, you may be dealing with addictive or compulsive sexual behavior. The more you checked, the more likely it is that you need help to regain control of your sexual behavior. ✍ 4.9

In the years I've been helping men overcome sexual addictions and compulsions, I've noticed a few factors that increase the likelihood of success in getting free. Those are listed below.

- Attend twelve–step meetings frequently. I typically recommend attending 90 meetings in the first 90 days of recovery.

- Read from recovery literature *every day*.

- Get a sponsor with long sobriety who is willing to confront and push you and who can be available to you at all times.

- Work the twelve steps and pass them off with your sponsor.

- Work with a therapist who is familiar with addiction and processing trauma.

- Find books, resources and other information by searching online for "sexual addiction." The LifeStar Network is one such resource. You can get more information at www.lifestarnetwork.org. Another valuable resource is Sexaholics Anonymous. You can find them at www.sa.org.

  ✎ 4.10

OTHER PSYCHOLOGICAL ISSUES

Shame, negative core beliefs, and sexual addictions and compulsions can create serious difficulties for men trying to overcome unwanted same–sex attraction. Unfortunately, there are quite a number of other psychological issues that can also become real roadblocks to change. Below are lists of symptoms for the most common of these issues. When men are experiencing these conditions, their ability to overcome same–sex attraction can be greatly diminished. These problems can deplete energy, diminish enjoyment of relationships, create negative and sometimes chaotic life circumstances, and focus attention away from more basic needs, thereby blocking fulfillment of those needs. I encourage you to carefully review these sections, even if you think you don't have a problem in an area—you may discover some things of which you're unaware.

The psychological issues discussed in the sections that follow generally require the help of more highly trained psychotherapists. When the issues are particularly severe, using medication temporarily or permanently may be a good idea, which would require visiting with a psychiatrist.

The questionnaires on the following pages are intended to help you get a sense of whether you might need to seek help with any of the issues described. The questions are based on information contained in the *American Psychiatric Association: Diagnostic and Statistical Manual of Mental Disorders, Fifth Edition*. However, these are not scientific assessments and are not intended to diagnose any psychological disorders. After completing these questionnaires, if you believe that you might be dealing with one of these issues, you should see a licensed mental health professional for an actual assessment and diagnosis.

Depression

Depression may result from unresolved childhood issues, current life circumstances, or chemical imbalances in the brain. Depression can take a few different forms depending on the number of symptoms and how long they last. Circle the number corresponding to the severity of each symptom that you've experienced within the past few months (see the scale at the top of the list). Then on the line underneath each symptom describe the frequency and length, for example: "rarely for an hour or so" or "daily for several years."

⓪ – None ① – Mild ② – Distracting ③ – Distressing ④ – Debilitating

⓪ ① ② ③ ④   Feeling depressed, sad, or empty often or all the time, or frequently tearful

Frequency and length: _____

⓪ ① ② ③ ④   Lack of interest in pleasurable activities

Frequency and length: _____

⓪ ① ② ③ ④   Decrease or increase in appetite or significant weight loss (not due to dieting) or weight gain

Frequency and length: _____

⓪ ① ② ③ ④   Difficulties with sleeping: either unable to sleep or sleeping too much

Frequency and length: _____

Moving very slowly, like you are in slow motion; or being agitated and moving around restlessly   ⓪ ① ② ③ ④

Frequency and length: _____

Feeling fatigued or without energy   ⓪ ① ② ③ ④

Frequency and length: _____

Feeling worthless or guilty   ⓪ ① ② ③ ④

Frequency and length: _____

Having difficulty thinking or making decisions   ⓪ ① ② ③ ④

Frequency and length: _____

Thinking about death or suicide   ⓪ ① ② ③ ④

Frequency and length: _____

The more of these symptoms you checked and the more severe or longer lasting these symptoms are, the more important it is for you to seek professional help. Even checking two of these symptoms could indicate a need for help if the symptoms are distressing, debilitating, or long lasting.

Bipolar Disorder

Like depression, bipolar disorder can take a number of forms. Some people experience the symptoms below for a period of time then switch to experiencing symptoms of depression like those listed above. Others experience only the types of symptoms described below. Put a check in the box next to each symptom that you've ever experienced for *four days or longer*.

☐ Feeling unusually good about yourself; feeling more important than usual; feeling invincible

☐ Needing less sleep than usual

☐ Being more talkative than is typical for you or feeling like you can't stop talking

☐ Having ideas racing through your mind, feeling unable to slow down your thinking

☐   Being easily distracted by things happening around you

☐   Setting big goals, starting big projects, or feeling very restless or agitated

☐   Compulsively pursuing pleasurable or risky activities such as spending sprees, intense sexual behavior, or risky business transactions

If you've experienced three or more of these symptoms within the past few years—particularly if you've also experienced depression during that time—I strongly encourage you to seek a well–trained psychotherapist.

General Anxiety

Anxiety can take many forms and affect us in many different ways. Circle the number corresponding to the severity of each symptom that you've experienced within the past few months. Then on the line underneath each symptom describe the frequency and length, for example: "rarely for an hour or so" or "daily for several years."

⓪ – None   ① – Mild   ② – Distracting   ③ – Distressing   ④ – Debilitating

⓪ ① ② ③ ④   Feeling anxious or worried and having difficulty controlling the worry. This might be about one specific thing or about a number of different concerns.

Frequency and length: _____

⓪ ① ② ③ ④   Feeling restless, keyed up, or on edge

Frequency and length: _____

⓪ ① ② ③ ④   Getting tired or fatigued easily

Frequency and length: _____

⓪ ① ② ③ ④   Having a difficult time concentrating or finding that your mind goes blank

Frequency and length: _____

⓪ ① ② ③ ④   Being easily irritated

Frequency and length: _____

⓪ ① ② ③ ④   Holding tension in your body

Frequency and length: _____

Having difficulty falling or staying asleep or waking in the morning not feeling rested　⓪ ① ② ③ ④

Frequency and length: _____

If you've experienced three or more of these symptoms within the past few months, you should consider seeking help from a psychotherapist, particularly if the symptom has been distressing or debilitating.

Social Anxiety

Fear of social situations can make it very difficult for men to fulfill their needs for closeness with others. Review the list of symptoms below, and check the box if the symptom applies to you.

- ☐ You fear being embarrassed or humiliated in a social situation (particularly with unfamiliar people) or a situation in which you believe your performance is being observed or scrutinized

- ☐ You experience anxiety or panic when you are in such situations

- ☐ You try to avoid these types of social or performance situations out of fear of becoming anxious

- ☐ These problems interfere with your daily routine, your social life, or your schooling or occupation

If you checked most or all of these symptoms, you should consider contacting a psychotherapist for help.

Obsessive–Compulsive Disorder (OCD)

Obsessive–compulsive disorder (OCD) is somewhat common among men with same–sex attraction and can create severe obstacles to change. OCD has two parts: obsessions and compulsions. The symptoms for these are listed separately.

Obsessions are thoughts, impulses, or images that seem to come to your mind regularly and are difficult or impossible to get rid of. Check the box next to each of the following types of obsession that apply to you.

- ☐ Preoccupation with being contaminated by body fluids, dirt, germs, insects, animals, sticky substances, a disease, etc.

☐ Fear of getting an illness

☐ Needing to save or collect things, feeling worried about throwing things away

☐ Needing to have things in order, symmetrical, exact, or lined up

☐ Having to write perfectly, needing to start over if you make a mistake

☐ Feeling excessively afraid about being wrong or bad, having bad thoughts, saying bad things, being punished; dwelling excessively on thoughts about God or religion

☐ Fear that you will harm yourself or someone else or worry that you have been or will be responsible for someone being harmed because of your actions

☐ Fear that you will do something that you can't control

☐ Having unwanted sexual thoughts that are not enjoyable and that you cannot control

☐ Needing to count objects, steps, stairs, or behaviors

☐ Worry about saying things wrong or leaving out important details

☐ Worry about losing things or making mistakes

☐ Being easily bothered by certain sounds or by the texture of things on your skin

☐ Excessive superstitious fears or beliefs

☐ Other: _____

_____

☐ Other: _____

_____

Compulsions are things that you feel unable to stop yourself from doing or things that you have to do in a very specific way. You may feel driven to do it in response to an obsession, like those listed above—in other words the obsession *drives* you to do the compulsive behavior. You may have to do it so that you can stop feeling anxious about it. Or you might just do it automatically without even thinking about it. Compulsions can either be outward physical behaviors (like washing your hands or checking locks) or internal mental rituals (like counting or thinking through past events over and over again).

Sometimes people don't recognize that their compulsions are excessive until they take into consideration what *most* people do or until others tell them that it's excessive. If you wonder whether some of your behaviors are compulsive, ask someone you trust to give you an honest answer. Check the box next to each of the following types of compulsive behaviors that apply to you.

☐ Excessive personal cleanliness and grooming practices, either done frequently or done in a very specific way (hand washing, showering, brushing teeth, shaving, etc.)

☐ Excessive cleaning or care of the house, yard, car, or objects; having to clean certain items yourself rather than allowing others to do it, or cleaning or caring for things in a very specific way or using very specific tools or products

☐ Avoidance of contamination or germs by avoiding certain objects, staying away from certain places, wearing gloves or special clothing, using excessive protective barriers (like on toilet seats), etc.

☐ Checking to be sure you haven't been harmed or haven't harmed someone else

☐ Checking locks, doors, windows, blinds, light switches, stoves, and other appliances or equipment, etc.

☐ Checking yourself for illness or disease

☐ Saving useless items, buying or collecting items that you don't use, or having difficulty getting rid of items that are no longer useful

☐ Reading or writing things over and over, having to rewrite something because you made a small mistake, keeping excessive lists or journals

☐ Repeating activities or behaviors over and over for no reason other than a feeling of compulsion, repeating something you've said several times because you don't feel heard

☐ Counting objects, items, or behaviors

☐ Arranging items in specific orders or patterns, compulsively arranging things symmetrically

☐ Excessive repetitive thoughts, like prayers or reassuring statements

☐ Frequent confessing of bad deeds or wrong behavior, even when those actions are not considered wrong to others

☐ Other: _____

_____

☐ Other: _____

_____

How much time each day do you think you spend engaged in your obsessions and compulsions?

_____

Obsessive–compulsive disorder can be a serious roadblock, but it's also very treatable. If you checked even a single item in the two lists above, this could be an indication of obsessive–compulsive *tendencies*. If you checked a few items on each list, it's a strong sign that you may be dealing with OCD. I encourage you to talk to a group facilitator, therapist, or another trusted person to get another opinion on whether the thought or behavior is obsessive or compulsive. If you're dealing with obsessive–compulsiveness, you need to be working with a psychotherapist who has specific training in this area.

Obsessive–Compulsive Personality Disorder (OCPD)

OCPD is different from OCD, which I described above, mostly in the attitude that the person has toward his behaviors. OCD would make you feel very anxious, and you would do the compulsive behavior in order to make yourself feel less anxious. You would probably recognize that your behavior is not normal, and you would likely want to change it. But if you're dealing with OCPD, an obsessive–compulsive personality, you might not feel anxious about your behavior (unless someone tries to make you change it). You probably believe that what you're doing is perfectly acceptable and the best way to do things. In fact, you might even wonder what's wrong with people who don't behave in the same way.

My own clinical experience with men that have same–sex attraction has shown that as many as two–thirds are dealing with one or the other—or both—types of obsessive–compulsiveness. Among most of the men I've worked with who are obsessive–compulsive, the main symptoms are perfectionism, rigid and stubborn thinking, and rumination, which means, "obsessive or abnormal reflection upon an idea or deliberation over a choice." Check the box next to each of the following symptoms that apply to you.

☐ Being preoccupied with things like details, following rules, keeping a schedule, having things in a particular order, or being organized

☐ Being perfectionistic, especially if it gets to the point that you have a difficult time completing projects or tasks

☐ Being so devoted to work and productivity that you ignore leisure, family, and friendships

☐ Being overly conscientious, overly principled, and inflexible about morality and doing what's right

☐ Saving objects that have no worth or sentimental value (also called hoarding)

☐ Being reluctant to delegate things to other people or to work with others unless you know they will do things exactly your way

☐ Hoarding money or being overly cautious in your spending

☐ Being generally rigid or stubborn in your beliefs and attitudes, including unrelenting negative thoughts or attitudes about yourself, pervasive doubts, or pessimism

Even one of these symptoms could indicate a tendency toward obsessive–compulsiveness in your personality, although that doesn't mean you need to seek psychological help for it. Some of these traits are actually very beneficial if you know how to control the tendencies and balance yourself. If you have several of these traits, or perhaps just one trait that's very intense, it could indicate that you need help from a well–educated licensed professional. When the tendencies are strong, OCPD can make growing out of same–sex attraction very difficult or impossible until the OCPD is diminished. This is particularly true if you find that it's difficult for you to change your thinking about yourself, your situation, or things that have happened to you.

Anxiety About Your Body

Some people experience a strong preoccupation with their bodies or with specific bodily features or flaws. Therapists refer to this condition as "body dysmorphic disorder." Check all of the following symptoms that apply to you.

☐ Excessive concern and shame about a defect or flaw on your face or body that others have either never noticed or have repeatedly told you is just fine or normal

☐ Preoccupation with being too fat or too thin, even though others would consider you to be within a normal weight range

☐ Excessive worry that your muscles are not big enough, even if others would see you as being muscular, fit, or having a nice physique

☐ Going to excessive lengths to hide perceived physical flaws

☐ Being preoccupied with trying to get an accurate view of your body and feeling like you can never see it accurately

Body dysmorphic disorder is closely related to OCD and can be a particularly difficult problem for men trying to overcome unwanted same–sex attraction. Our feelings about our bodies are often tied to our feelings about our masculinity. So shame, worry, or preoccupation about our bodies can have a devastating impact on how we feel about ourselves as men. If you checked any symptoms in the list above, contact a trained psychotherapist for help.

Posttraumatic Disturbance

People who have experienced abuse or other types of traumatic events earlier in their lives sometimes suffer from a variety of difficult symptoms as a result of those experiences. Circle the number corresponding to the *frequency* of each symptom that you've ever experienced for a period of time *longer than one month*.

⓪ – None   ① – Mild   ② – Distracting   ③ – Distressing   ④ – Debilitating

⓪ ① ② ③ ④   Recalling traumatic events through flashbacks (which might include images, sounds, or even smells), disturbing dreams, or frightening thoughts related to the events.

Reliving painful past events as if they were happening in the present. Sometimes this can even include seeing images from the trauma and experiencing the same feelings.   ⓪ ① ② ③ ④

Becoming very upset or disturbed by things that remind you of the trauma. This can include places, people, objects, sounds, and smells. It can include being touched in certain ways or being in certain physical or emotional situations.   ⓪ ① ② ③ ④

Avoiding talking or thinking about the trauma or having only vague memories of it.   ⓪ ① ② ③ ④

Avoiding places, situations, activities, or people that remind you of the trauma.   ⓪ ① ② ③ ④

Feeling a loss of interest in certain activities that you previously enjoyed. These activities may or may not have anything to do with the traumatic events.   ⓪ ① ② ③ ④

Being unable to feel certain emotions, such as anger, love, or joy, or having sudden outbursts of irritation or anger.   ⓪ ① ② ③ ④

Feeling disconnected or alienated from other people.   ⓪ ① ② ③ ④

Not seeing yourself as having a future or being unable to imagine future events, such as a career, being married, seeing your children grow up, or growing old. Expecting yourself to die young.   ⓪ ① ② ③ ④

Having difficulty falling asleep or staying asleep because of disturbing thoughts.   ⓪ ① ② ③ ④

Having difficulty concentrating because of disturbing thoughts.   ⓪ ① ② ③ ④

Being jumpy or easily startled.   ⓪ ① ② ③ ④

Being intensely aware of—or sensitive to—your circumstances; being on the constant lookout for danger. This can create anxiety and exhaustion.   ⓪ ① ② ③ ④

When a person frequently experiences a number of the symptoms described above, the condition is known as posttraumatic stress disorder (PTSD). But even occasionally experiencing just a few of these symptoms can make life difficult and detract from your ability to overcome unwanted same–sex attraction. If you marked a one or higher on any of the above items, it would be a good idea for you to consult a therapist. If you marked a few items—especially if you marked higher numbers—I strongly encourage you to seek help from a professional trained in trauma recovery work.

Traumatic memories can be repressed for long periods of time and then come back into awareness. Some people—and sadly even some therapists—believe there is no such thing as repressed memories. But I can assure you from extensive experience that our minds can forget terrifying or painful events. Sometimes a person will have only a vague awareness of the trauma or perhaps he will remember just a foggy image from the event. It's very common for these repressed memories to surface in a safe relationship with a trusted therapist. Therapy can be tremendously helpful in alleviating the symptoms that result from trauma. Eye Movement Desensitization and Reprocessing (EMDR) is a particularly beneficial type of therapy for posttraumatic disturbance. A newer modality called Brainspotting is also showing very encouraging results.

Dissociation

Dissociation can be described as a disruption in consciousness, or a separation of one part of self from other parts. There are many different types of dissociation. The simplest and most common would be "zoning out" and the most complex would be having multiple personalities. Many therapists believe that dissociation is a natural mental mechanism that protects the mind from being overwhelmed by stressful or traumatic circumstances. Dissociation is commonly seen among individuals with post–traumatic disturbance. Check the box next to each of the symptoms that you've experienced in the past few months.[4]

- ☐ Losing track of things that have happened, such as arriving somewhere and not remembering what happened on the trip there or not knowing how you got there, not hearing things that were said to you, or not remembering putting on the clothes you are wearing

- ☐ Having objects you don't remember buying, finding, or being given

- ☐ Feeling like you're outside your body watching yourself, feeling like your body doesn't belong to you, or feeling like you're a robot

- ☐ Feeling like the world around you is not real, having the world appear as foggy or far away, or being in a place you know but having it seem somehow strange or unfamiliar

☐ Being accused of lying or of not telling the entire story when you believe you're telling the whole truth

☐ Lacking memories of significant life events or of long periods of time

☐ Not recognizing yourself in the mirror

☐ Remembering past events with intense clarity and vividness as if it was happening right now

☐ Being unsure whether things you remember are real, imagined, or occurred in a dream

☐ Zoning out and losing awareness of time or finding that time has passed and you don't know what you did during that time

☐ Acting so different in various situations that you almost feel like you're two different people

☐ Being unsure whether you actually did or said something or just thought about doing or saying it

☐ Finding out that you did something you don't remember doing

☐ Hearing voices inside your head talking about what you're doing or about what you should or shouldn't do

Each of the symptoms described above is a strong indicator of dissociation. If you marked any of the boxes, I strongly urge you to seek help from a psychotherapist familiar with these issues and to do so very soon. ✍ 4.11

HARMFUL RELATIONSHIPS

Relationships are essential for our growth in two significant ways. First, we need the support and nurture that strong, positive relationships can give us in order to face life challenges and grow through our problems. Supportive relationships can occur with many different types of people and in many different situations. And second, we often need male friendships in order to meet needs for closeness with other men. But relationships can also be extremely *harmful* to our growth and wellbeing if they are unhealthy.

Consider the following unhealthy or unhelpful relationship features to see if you recognize these within any of your own relationships. The problems listed here tend to be common among men with same–sex attraction. As you review this list, keep in mind that a single relationship might have more than one of these features. Also remember that our relationships are often a mix of positive and unhealthy features. For example, a parent can be both loving and controlling.   4.12

Conflictual: You feel angry, resentful, afraid, or untrusting. You experience the other person or people as antagonistic, angry, attacking, or even dangerous. This may occur within your family of origin, with a wife and children, or even with friends. Often conflictual relationships are experienced in work settings where a boss or co–workers seem to always be creating difficulty for you. Arguments, complaining, and hostile silence are typical of these types of relationships.

Unsupportive: You feel let down, uncared for; you ask for support and don't receive it, or you believe support won't be given and so you don't ask. You experience other people as unhelpful, disengaged, or uncaring. This too can occur in families, friendships, and work settings. It can be particularly distressing in relationships on which you're relying for help with personal issues. Among men with same–sex attraction who are married, this can be a particularly difficult problem. You may experience your wife as unsupportive of your needs, especially your need for time and connection with other men. But the problem is not one–sided—your wife is probably feeling unsupported, unimportant, or even unwanted by you, which can make it very difficult for her to feel good about giving you the support you need.

Discourages Growth: You feel pulled by the person toward accepting a gay lifestyle; or you feel emasculated, drained, weakened, or feminized. You may experience the other person or people as very comfortable or comforting in an unhealthy way. You may feel like their influence weakens your commitment or feeds into your issues. This is sometimes experienced with gay friends or with females who like you just the way you are and don't understand why you would want to change. Occasionally heterosexual male friends who have been indoctrinated by pro–gay rhetoric express opposition to the concept of changing your sexual orientation. And sometimes mothers unconsciously continue relationship patterns that discourage change and development.

Controlling: You feel dominated or manipulated; you feel like you don't have a choice. You experience the other person as overpowering, overwhelming, or impossible to communicate with. This pattern is common during the childhood of boys who grow up to experience same–sex attraction. But childhood patterns can continue into adulthood. Fathers, mothers, and older sisters can retain a controlling influence over men with same–sex attraction. Sometimes adult friends may also exert unhealthy control over us. Constant corrections of your speech or behavior, overly restricting your involvement with friends, telling you what you do or don't feel, and trying to mandate your interests and activities are typical of controlling relationships.

Shaming: You feel intimidated, humiliated, embarrassed, small, or inferior. You may experience people as superior, better, or manlier than you. Or you may experience them as looking down on you or criticizing you. Shame–bound families, as described earlier in this chapter, are often the root of shame and may be a continuing source of shame throughout adulthood. Peers, in both childhood and adulthood, can also be painful sources of shame. Perhaps even your friends may create feelings of shame for you without even intending to. You may be particularly vulnerable to this if your childhood deeply sensitized you to interpret what's said about you as being critical or attacking.

Obsessive/Tempting: You feel strongly drawn to a man in a sexual or obsessive way. You may experience him as seductive or as being so intensely desirable that you can't stop thinking about him. This kind of obsession can occur whether or not the other man is gay. Sometimes the worst obsessions can focus on men who are straight, especially when the man is very friendly or intimate.

Knowing what to do with an unhealthy relationship can be a difficult thing. Sometimes it's necessary to separate yourself completely from a person or to allow a relationship to gradually fade away. Other times it may just require a simple shift in perspective or a clarification of boundaries. A relationship might be improved by working through the issues you have with that person or these types of people in therapy. Or you may need to develop the ability to forgive. Occasionally, working on the relationship in therapy will be required, with or without the participation of the other person.

YOUR FEELINGS NOW

How did your King hold out? Take a moment right now and tune into him. Let him ground you again in the knowledge of your worth and validity. Let him remind you of the vision that there is purpose in the things you're facing in your life. Let him behold you with love and acceptance. And let him reaffirm his commitment to helping you achieve your highest potential.

This chapter has taken you through quite a number of areas where you might be having some difficulties. The purpose has been to bring to light significant issues that you may not have been very clear on in the past. Sometimes getting such a clear view of ourselves can be a little hard to take. On the other hand, it can be quite relieving to finally have an explanation and understanding of things we've always sensed, but couldn't really explain.

> Even in the middle of whatever challenges or weakness you believe you're facing, you still have innate goodness and value.

If this chapter made you aware of new or deeper challenges, I hope you will view this as an opportunity for growth and change. And I hope that you will remember the affirmation included in the quote at the beginning of this chapter: *"I am valuable and good just as I am."* Even in the middle of whatever challenges or weakness you believe you're facing, you still have innate goodness and value. If you begin to doubt that, connect yourself back with your King, to your Center. Connect to your deep Self and your Higher Power to find your worth and validity and to understand what purpose these difficulties have in your life.

Yes, these difficulties do have a purpose in your life. If you choose to see that purpose and to fulfill it, you will find that facing these struggles makes you a far better man. On the other hand, if you choose to believe that it's all meaningless or that you're just being abused or punished by some cruel god, you will grow doubtful and bitter. Either way, you will still have the same issues to face. The perspective you take on the issues is of utmost importance. Choose to see them as your path to your own special future. ✍ 4.13

---

[1] See *The Transforming Power of Affect: A Model for Accelerated Change* by Diana Fosha.

[2] Most of this process is described in his book *Walking with God* (pages 57–60). He also teaches about this process on his *Wild at Heart Advanced Bootcamp*. Go to www.randsomedheart.com for more information.

[3] Professionals in the field of sexual health differ in how they categorize and name the phenomena described in this section. I've used the categories that make the most sense to me. Also, the term "hypersexuality" is becoming more widely used now, rather than "sexual addiction." I've used "sexual addiction" because it's more easily understood.

[4] This assessment was modified from the *Dissociative Experiences Scale (DES)* by Eve B. Carlson, Ph.D. and Frank W. Putnam, M.D.

Chapter 5

The Warrior

Evidently the Warrior has been with us for a long time. He is here to stay. We cannot wish him away.... We cannot neutralize him through social engineering, and if we tranquilize him we suffer a variety of attendant consequences.... The questions are, how can we harness his aggressive potential for creative action? How can we avoid the brutal excesses of the *Shadow Warrior*? How can we wed might with right and power with goodness?

Moore and Gillette, *The Warrior Within*

Even the most casual observation of men reveals that we want to have our Warrior energy stimulated on a regular basis. Some of us are more outward and physical in this pursuit while others channel our Warrior energy inward through more mental activities. Some men do extreme sports or join the police force or the military, while other men play violent video games and watch action movies.

Today many of us experience the Warrior mostly through our recreation. I suggest that this may be because our true Warrior is underdeveloped and underutilized. Many of us can make it through an entire workweek without needing to access any Warrior energy. Even worse, some of us work in situations where Warrior energy is consciously discouraged. But like all of the archetypal energies, Warrior is intrinsic to our masculine souls—men need Warrior. We *will* engage it somewhere in our lives. It is wise, in my judgment, to find positive and proactive ways to use this energy in our everyday pursuits. Otherwise, we run the risk of allowing this vital energy to be expressed only through its shadow poles.

Of the four archetypes, it's the Warrior's traits that are most commonly viewed in society as being "masculine." And Warrior is the archetype that is furthest from the traits we stereotypically associate with femininity. When men describe the things that make us feel masculine, it's usually Warrior traits we'll list—traits like power, courage, discipline, awareness, aggression, and freedom from emotion.

The Whole Warrior

- Source of power
- Protector of boundaries
- Servant of the King

The Whole Warrior has three main functions. First, his strengths and discipline are our source of power. Second, he uses his power to set and enforce boundaries for the protection of vulnerable things in the world. He's the watchman of internal boundaries around our thoughts, feelings, and behavior; the enforcer of limits in our interpersonal relationships; and a guardian of the weak, the good, and the beautiful in society. And third, the Warrior commits his power to the King in service of something greater than himself—a Higher Power or higher cause. This is what gives rise to the Warrior's mission.

The Warrior can be a powerful force for protection and progression. But his shadows can be equally powerful forces for destruction and regression. The passive pole of the Warrior's shadow—called the Masochist—has no power, is overcome by negative feelings, and lives life as a coward and a victim. The active shadow pole of the Warrior—the Sadist—uses his power in excessive ways that are cruel and controlling of others, disruptive to society, and dangerous to himself. He acts out his anger in displays of rage, but is numb to most other feelings. He trusts no one, punishes the weak, and defies authority.

At the heart of the Warrior archetype is a central dynamic, which is the interplay between power and vulnerability.

At the heart of the assortment of traits just described—both whole and in shadow—is a central dynamic, which is the interplay between *power* and *vulnerability*. The various functions, roles, and capacities of the Warrior all seem to be called forth and aroused by that dynamic. This interplay is vital in shaping the Warrior, but it's also interwoven with the process of creating masculinity, which may be why masculinity and Warrior seem to be so closely tied together. Imbalances in the interplay between power and vulnerability cause the Warrior's two shadows to emerge. Understanding this dynamic and its development is essential to comprehending our own Warrior with its shadowy potentials, as well as our sense of masculinity. We will turn our attention to this dynamic and to some other key processes in the development of Warrior before moving on to the archetype's various functions, roles, and capacities.

ORIGINS OF THE WARRIOR

As with all the archetypes, the traits and capacities of the Warrior are innate to us as men. Foundational to those traits is the instinctual masculine tendency toward aggression. Although it's naturally present in both males and females, aggression is typically stronger in males because of our higher levels of testosterone. Generally speaking, males are also anatomically and temperamentally built for strength, action, and physical activity—all of which are essential to Warrior. This combination of traits is necessary for the survival of our species in a hostile world.

Power and Vulnerability

Though males come into life genetically and hormonally pre–loaded with these Warrior potentials, we are nevertheless born helpless and completely dependent on others. So here, from the moment of our birth, is the setup for the dynamic between power and vulnerability: we are built for power but born vulnerable. From this state of total helplessness, we gradually develop a modicum of power through mastering the tasks of childhood. At first these tasks are very basic, like controlling body movements, sitting up, and crawling. Later, as we start to acquire more physical strength and coordination, we graduate into more advanced skills, like walking, speaking, and controlling our bowels. This development fosters autonomy and confidence and creates outlets for our aggressive impulses, producing a sense of personal power. Of course, our failures, accidents, and physical limitations will occasionally remind us that, in reality, we are actually still very vulnerable.

> Here is the setup for the dynamic between power and vulnerability: we are built for power but born vulnerable.

Our interactions with adults are critical in this process. When adults allow children a certain amount of independence to try out their new skills—providing at least permission, if not also opportunity and affirmation—a sense of power will develop quite naturally. But *all* adults are going to intervene at some point to stop children from fully exploring their powers in the world. Whether out of laziness, fear, or simple good judgment, mom or dad will at some point stop "Little Tommy" from carrying out the risky boyish plots his mind hatches. Their interference protects "Tommy's" vulnerability, but it also curtails his power.

In addition to protecting vulnerable boys from their own power, the concerned involvement of parents and other adults in the boy's life models aspects of the power–vulnerability dynamic. It models the setting of boundaries around power— the boy can't do everything his testosterone desires. It models the wielding of power within a social system and how to be strong while also submitting to something greater than yourself. And it models how powerful people care for the weak—how compassion is extended toward those who are vulnerable. Adults will never model these things perfectly. Sometimes they will model them well. But far too often they will model the shadowy inverse of these Warrior abilities. ✍ 5.1

Leaving Mother to Join Father

Developing Whole Warrior and complete masculinity requires boys to leave their mother's female world and join their father's male world. To properly convey the nature and impact of this journey requires a foundation of understanding. To begin with, let's create a simple way to talk about mothers and fathers. Attempting to discuss actual human moms and dads in all their variety would lead us into an endless morass of contradiction, exceptions, and overlap. To avoid that complexity, we'll speak in archetypal terms, grouping all that is quintessentially motherly and fatherly into a Mother archetype and a Father archetype. To be sure there is no confusion, I'll capitalize "Mother" and "Father" when I mean the archetypes. This will allow us to draw clear and universal patterns to which you can then apply the peculiarities of your own background and life situation.

As defined in Chapter One, archetypes are sets of innate human capacities and traits, which may be described as instincts, energies, drives, or internal forces. Seeing things in archetypal terms highlights contrasting forces and tendencies that might otherwise go unnoticed. The Mother and Father archetypes allow us to notice the contrast created by gender that is inherent and essential in these two forms of parenting.

So now let's define these two archetypes. The Mother archetype represents feminine traits of acceptance, inclusion, nurture, and satiation of desires. She fosters or allows dependency, passivity, and freedom from care. These traits may be found in biological, adoptive, or foster mothers, grandmothers and aunts, and teachers, nannies, and babysitters. The Father archetype represents masculine traits of expectation, decisiveness, self–reliance, and self–denial. He fosters or requires independence, action, and responsibility. These traits may be found in biological, adoptive, or foster fathers. In the absence of such men, male relatives, neighbors, religious leaders, celebrities, or fictional male characters might fill the role. In our age, mothers are increasingly called on to provide these traits.

Developing Whole Warrior and complete masculinity requires boys to leave their mother's female world and join their father's male world.

The Mother archetype represents feminine traits of acceptance, inclusion, nurture, and satiation of desires.

It's not crucial that the traits and capacities of these two archetypes are exhibited perfectly and distinctly in a boy's life in order to be effective. Dad doesn't need to be exclusive and quintessential *Father* and mom doesn't need to be pure and perfect *Mother*. The presence of an adequate amount of these traits from people who exhibit at least a moderate degree of gender contrast may suffice for most boys to get the idea and receive the needed effect.

With that foundation now laid, let's return to the journey boys must take from Mother to Father. Boys begin life in the Mother's world. It's comfortable, safe, and familiar. It's their source of nurture and security. It is home. The Father's world is an exotic, foreign place, and its existence presents the boy with a crisis. Instinctually he knows—whether consciously or unconsciously—that the Father's world is his intended destination. He also senses that, in order to go there, he must sacrifice and deny himself of the Mother's world.

> The Father's world is an exotic, foreign place, and its existence presents the boy with a crisis.

Boys respond to this crisis in a wide variety of ways. Some boys naturally segue into the Father's world without conscious awareness of the crisis or the sacrifice. Some experience the crisis and sense the sacrifice more consciously and in varying degrees of intensity. These boys face conflicting feelings and must eventually choose a course. Most boys will choose to move forward into Father and some will choose to remain with Mother. A few boys, seemingly immune to the crisis and oblivious to the Father's world, stay contentedly entrenched in the Mother's world.

The significance of this journey and its outcome can't be overstated. It impacts boys in several important ways. Three of these relate to Warrior only tangentially, but they are important enough to our overall purpose in this book that they bear mentioning here. First, it creates awareness of contrast between the sexes. Father is different from Mother. When boys move into Father's world, it becomes home, and Mother's world—the world of women—becomes foreign and exotic. This is the source of genderedness and complementarity, which we explored in Chapter Three and will pursue further in Chapter Six.

Second, the outcome of the boy's crisis—specifically the degree to which he chooses Father's world over Mother's—impacts the development of his masculine identity. We'll discuss this much further in Chapters Six and Seven. And third, the choice to leave Mother's world and the ensuing unconscious longing to reconnect with that blissful state is one catalyst in the development of the Lover archetype. We'll delve into this when we discuss the birth of Lover in Chapter Ten.

As for the development of Warrior specifically, the boy's sacrifice of the comforts and security associated with Mother in order to join Father is a primal act of Warrior discipline, courage, detachment from feeling, and boundary setting. The boy must walk away from a sweet deal in the lap of the Mother and accept a relatively austere lifestyle at the side of the Father. The choices to do so, though they are largely outside any conscious understanding, catalyze and activate Warrior energy in the boy.

The choice to sacrifice Mother and join Father also leads to identification with the male group and abstinence from the female group. This primes the Warrior's sense of belonging to a team and being different from an "other." The "us versus them" perspective that arises from this situation may be problematic socially—and is absolutely counter to both King and Lover energy—but it is a necessary perspective for the Warrior. 5.2

The choice to sacrifice Mother and join Father leads to identification with the male group.

Father and the Development of Warrior

It should be abundantly clear by now that a connection with men who convey archetypal Father energy is a critical part of the process of male development generally, and Warrior development specifically. So far we've been looking at the significance of the Father's world as a destination for boys leaving Mother's world. The characteristics and traits of men in the Father role also have great significance in these developmental processes.

Mature older men can model traits of all the archetypes and thus shape the boy's paradigm of masculinity as a whole.

Mature older men who are actively involved in a boy's life can model traits of all the archetypes and thus shape the boy's paradigm of masculinity as a whole. Young boys seem especially drawn to traits of the Warrior: power, strength, courage, discipline, confidence, aggression, and emotional control. It may be that boys are instinctually wired to look for and bond with the power figures in their life. But they also need to see examples of more refined Warrior traits, like honor, self-sacrifice, and devotion to duty. When these traits are modeled in bonded male relationships, boys can internalize them almost automatically as they grow up.

Men with Father energy can also model ways of handling the power–vulnerability dynamic. Boys need to see men wield power confidently yet with moderation and restraint. They need to see those same men recognize and accept their vulnerabilities, weaknesses, and failures with humility and openness, compensating for them in wholesome ways. Healthy modeling of this interplay between power and vulnerability gives boys permission to be their best selves while also owning their foibles. This is a great asset for a developing Warrior.

Finally, boys are introduced in the Father's world to what has been called "the reality principle." This principle is very simple: life expects certain things of males. Men must conform to reality—at least to some degree. Adults of both sexes can introduce this principle to young men. But adult male involvement in this process is especially important because only from a man can a boy learn how to live up to the expectations of the male world—a world that the boy will eventually need to navigate. The reality principle requires boys to develop Warrior traits. ✎ 5.3

The reality principle: life expects certain things of males.

Anger, Individuation, and Masculinity

At play during this same time period is yet another dynamic of great importance to the development of both masculinity and Warrior. That dynamic is the boy's anger and how it is handled in the home.

Our bodies are equipped with the emotion of anger in order to help us summon up the capacities we need in moments when our power or wellbeing are threatened or oppressed. Anger is defined as "a strong feeling of displeasure and usually of antagonism." In other words, it's a strong reaction against things that displease us. Physiologically, anger causes adrenaline to flow, increases our heart and respiratory rates, raises our blood pressure, and causes muscle tension—all preparing us for intense action and full engagement. We think and act more quickly, though not always more rationally. The energy and focus provided by these physiological changes gives us the will to do frightening things that we might otherwise avoid, whether that's standing up to an abusive boss, fighting off an attacker, or killing an enemy.

Anger is the emotion of protection and boundary setting. As we mature, we need to protect and set boundaries around our own independence. Anger is central to that process. At about age two, we discover a magical word—an incantation that miraculously and mysteriously turns us into independent beings, separate from mommy. That magical word is, "No!" This is part of what psychologists call the process of *individuation*, or becoming a separate individual. For boys, this is also the beginning of masculinity. This kind of anger is pure Hero[1] energy, and as boys we must use this energy again and again to break away from our mothers throughout early and middle childhood. We don't need to be angry throughout our entire boyhood to make this separation—a few good "No's" can go a long way. But the more our wills and freedom are encroached on, the more we will feel the need to resort to anger to assert our masculine independence.

As we discussed earlier, separation from mother is necessary for the development of male identity and masculinity. As boys we must assert two things in our journey away from Mother: "I am not you," and "I am not *like* you." The first assertion ("I am not you") is brought on by our increasing awareness that we are physically, mentally, emotionally, and behaviorally separate from our mothers. We realize that we still exist when she leaves the room. We can get up and walk away from her. We can think things she doesn't know. We can do things she doesn't like. And we can be things she can't become. Most of all, we can exert our own will and ability to choose.

The second assertion ("I am not like you") is the beginning of our awareness of gender, as has already been mentioned. In other words, it's our awareness that humans come in two different flavors—boys and girls. Mommy is a girl and I'm a boy. This usually occurs by around three years of age, but boys will keep proving this difference to ourselves over and over for many years thereafter. And it will typically involve more than just mother—sisters and other girls also become players in this process. Anger is not the only tool boys use to get this job done, but it's a handy one.

This separation process is facilitated by the willingness that anger provides boys to cut off, or to "kill," the warm and nurturing relationship with our mothers. As I suggested earlier, we have to set boundaries with our mothers. Without some degree of anger, we may lack motivation to make the effort. This process needs the active support of older people of both sexes. Mothers especially can help this process by graciously letting go, maybe even pushing away gently. But this is not always an easy thing for mothers, who are disposed by their very natures to hold on and to protect. After all, it's a mother's job to tell her son not to take risks. But it's a son's job to take them anyway.

As boys we must assert two things in our journey away from Mother: I am not you, and I am not *like* you.

It's a mother's job to tell her son not to take risks. But it's a son's job to take them anyway.

In his book, *The Wonder of Boys*, Michael Gurian provides an eloquent example of a boy individuating through anger. He relates the story of a mother who had noticed her teenage son's behavior toward her becoming increasingly angry. One day the mother mentioned this to the son. She wisely observed, "You need me, but you hate me because you need me." The boy acknowledged that this was true. His anger toward his mother was a reaction against his continued vulnerability and need for mother's help, an attempt to infuse power into his budding independence, and an emotional boundary between him and the Mother's world. ✍ 5.4

Maturing Anger into Warrior Power

The basic human capacity that underlies anger is an innate and innocent energy that is vital to our safety and wellbeing as individuals and as a society. It's a capacity that, like so many other human capacities, can be used in ways that bless and benefit or that hurt and destroy. You could argue that in a perfect world anger would not be needed because there would never be encroachments or threats, and thus there would be no need to protect or impose boundaries. But in the world as we know it today we rely on the feeling of anger to protect us physically and emotionally. It's only when anger has been hijacked by the Sadist that it creates trouble in the world. The rage of the Sadist is a continuation of the unfinished business of childhood.

In order to benefit us, anger must be matured. As we grow up, if those around us appropriately respond to our anger—respectfully hearing it while also placing loving boundaries around it—our childish anger matures naturally. We develop the ability to experience our anger without acting it out on other people, and then to move through our anger and return to feelings of calmness and kindness toward others. Our anger gradually transforms into capacities that augment our personal power. These capacities include the intense focus of energy, the adrenaline–based physiological arousal, and the effortless assertion of our wills that anger produces.

In order to benefit us, anger must be matured.

Experiencing these capacities helps us navigate the complex interplay between power and vulnerability. As boys, we face vulnerability whether we stay close and controlled by our mothers or leave her side to venture into the Father's world. Anger can encourage us to push through that vulnerability, separate from our mothers, and face life's risks. And our anger can teach us that we aren't entirely vulnerable in the world. We have a sword in our hands—or maybe, we have a nuclear bomb in our mouth. Knowing that weapon is there—that we can back up our will with action—produces a certain empowering confidence, even if we seldom or never actually use our anger. Internalizing that sense of power diminishes our need to rely on anger as a source of strength, though we may occasionally resort to it when threatened. This mature power is a key source of our positive aggression and assertion, which are essential traits of the Warrior.

Jack and the Beanstalk is a story of male initiation.

Let's return again to Michael Gurian's *The Wonder of Boys* for an illustration of these concepts. Gurian retells and interprets the ancient folktale *Jack and the Beanstalk* as a story of male initiation. Jack's mother, you may recall, gives Jack the responsibility to take their cow to the market to sell it. Instead, Jack trades the cow for magic seeds. This displeases his mother, who throws the seeds out the window and sends him to bed without supper. The discarded seeds grow overnight into a huge beanstalk, which Jack finds looming outside his window in the morning. Jack puts on his clothes and begins climbing the beanstalk into the clouds, where his adventures with the Giant ensue.

Jack does what he has to do—his time has come and he quietly leaves.

What does this show us about growing beyond anger and into power? Let's look closer. Jack obeys his mother when she sends him to bed without supper. He doesn't lash out at her when she punishes him. There is no fit or tantrum—he respectfully does as he's told without pointless disobedience or angry disrespect. Then the next morning, when he discovers the beanstalk outside his window, he simply walks out of the house and starts climbing. Again, there is no display of rage, no angry announcement of plans to run away or flipping off mother on his way up the beanstalk. Jack does what he has to do—his time has come and he quietly leaves. Jack knows his mother doesn't want him to take risks. But he knows he has to take them anyway—and he no longer needs anger to push him to do it.

Jack has outgrown the use of anger as a tool of individuation. But he has also transcended the power–vulnerability dynamic. Again, let's look closely at the story. Jack is neither immobilized by the awareness of his vulnerability to a disapproving mother and an unknown future in the clouds nor must he resort to rage in order to escape his mother's control. He's able to act calmly and without hesitation in the interest of solidifying his masculine independence. Certainly he knows that by climbing the beanstalk he will displease his mother yet again. Even so, he takes action. In so doing, he communicates unequivocally to his mother, "I am my own man"—in other words, "I am not you, and I am not *like* you." This is appropriate Hero action: protecting and advancing the powerful sovereign male self.

Less–than–optimal childhood circumstances can aggravate our anger, leaving it over–inflated and in the shadow of the Sadist. If this is the case, we may need to develop skills to cool our anger and bring it into the exclusive service of our Higher Power. I see this situation so rarely among men with same–sex attraction that I won't discuss it further here. Much is written on the management of inflated anger elsewhere.

More common among men I know who are overcoming unwanted same–sex attraction is the situation where life circumstances disabled our anger—and therefore our power. This leaves us primarily in the passive shadow of the Masochist, although we may shift on occasion to the active Sadist pole. Those of us who have experienced this disabling of our anger—whether our anger was punished, ignored, or rejected—need to reconnect to our anger and mature it into feelings of personal power. Often this may require that we find opportunities to discover and express our anger in safe places, such as men's groups and individual counseling or psychotherapy. In addition to creating feelings of power, this work can also help us complete the vital process of individuation and deepen our sense of masculinity.

Experiencing anger that has been repressed since childhood can feel very frightening. It tends to bring back the disturbing feelings and beliefs that caused us to repress it in the first place. During this process, men commonly experience intensified shame and guilt or will get stuck on the negative beliefs they were taught about anger. If this is your experience, courage and persistence can lead you through the discomfort and into a place of greater peace and mature masculine power. If you don't work through your repressed anger, you may retain an essentially hostile attitude toward others. Or you may project your hostility onto others and fear them.

> Experiencing anger that has been repressed since childhood can feel very frightening, but can lead us into a place of greater peace and mature masculine power.

Let me simplify and exemplify this whole relationship between anger, power, and vulnerability with a hypothetical situation. Anytime we are triggered with feelings of displeasure toward another person, we can be sure that our Warrior has been awakened. If we react to that trigger with anger, we're moving toward the Sadist shadow. If we pander to our vulnerability by playing nice, shutting down, or dissociating, we have gone into Masochist. If we feel the displeasure and can respond with power and true calmness, we are in pure Warrior.

All of this talk about maturing our anger may sound like a lot of work. But if we're to become whole as men, it's work that we must do. To have safe and effective Warrior energy, we must befriend our anger and harness its power for use in the service of feelings and values higher than our own ego, such as reason, truth, love, duty, justice, or compassion. For the true Warrior, anger is not his weapon or his rightful attitude—it's his source of power, his call to arms, and then, his most essential sacrifice. ✍ 5.5

What About Your Life?

If you are like most men in the world, chances are high that at least some of the processes we've been exploring didn't succeed in ways that favored the development of a strong Warrior. It could be that physiologically or temperamentally you feel you're just not "that kind of guy." It could be that the adults in your environment reinforced your vulnerabilities rather than your power. Perhaps you got discouraged, diverted, or abandoned somewhere along the journey from Mother to Father. Maybe there were no men around to show you the way. Maybe the male world was made to seem dangerous, disgusting, or impossible to endure. Or maybe you were told, in so many words, not to go there. Your anger may have been ignored, punished, or shamed. And perhaps you were never allowed, or never allowed yourself, to separate and individuate from mother.

A billion things could have gone wrong with these processes in your life. Nevertheless, you are still taking breath so there is still time for growth. Your next step may be to review the section "Origins of the Warrior" again, considering which of the processes described there worked well in your life and which didn't work so well. The value in being clear about what went wrong is that it can provide meaningful clues about how to compensate going forward. Please believe that even though things got derailed in childhood, you can still find ways to reach the desired outcome, which is to continually become more whole.

Keep exploring this chapter with the intention of finding *your* Warrior. Warrior is far more an attitude and belief than anything else. It doesn't take muscles, fighting skills, or an awesome father. And it definitely doesn't take a perfect upbringing. Consider something I said in Chapter One:

> Each of our weaknesses, each of our shadows and fragments, has something to teach us, and some bit of wholeness to return to us.

To have safe and effective Warrior energy, we must befriend our anger and harness its power.

Being clear about what went wrong can provide meaningful clues about how to compensate going forward.

Behind each shadow is a golden gift. Our job is to receive each gift by accepting and loving every part of ourselves right now. By calling forth our shadows for a loving look, we activate the change process and begin moving toward wholeness. ✍ 5.6

WARRIOR AS A SOURCE OF POWER

Having now delved into the Warrior's origins—most particularly the power–vulnerability dynamic at his core—we are ready to explore his key traits. They are sources of pure power for the man who develops them. What are these traits? The Warrior is awake: conscious, vigilant, and appreciative of life. He's a disciplined master of his body and mind. He's aggressive in positive and productive ways. He's able to detach from feeling and tolerate pain. He's courageous and pushes through his fears. And he's authentic with others and adventurous in his approach to life. A key element in many of these traits is anger that has matured into masculine power.

Let's look at how these traits might be manifested in our lives as modern men. Keep in mind as you read that the traits and energies we'll be talking about are—like core needs—non–negotiable. They are essential to the masculine psyche. They may be repressed, but they will still show up in their shadow forms, as I described in Chapter One. It's far better to accept these capacities and try to integrate them so that they can be accessed in balanced and moderate ways.

Awake

The Warrior is conscious, vigilant, and aware of his own finite nature, which traits cause him to be awake in life. He's conscious of the things happening in and around him—he's observant, perceptive, and discerning. He's conscious of what pleases and displeases him, what's suitable and unsuitable, and what's desirable and undesirable. That consciousness requires a healthy and mature relationship with his anger so he can—with minimal casualties—refuse what displeases him, reject what's unsuitable, and decline what's undesirable. If a man's anger is in an active shadow, that consciousness may lead to over–inflated rage, perpetual dissatisfaction, and hurtful aggression. Conversely, if a man's anger is in a passive shadow, he may entirely lack that consciousness, and may experience instead a dull and passive sense of disappointment.

The Warrior is vigilant to the possibility of danger and is always on the lookout for it. If we're aware of the reality of our own anger and hostile potential, we

---

Source of Power
- Awake
- Disciplined
- Aggressive
- Detached from feeling
- Courageous
- Authentic
- Adventurous

The Warrior is conscious, vigilant, and aware of his own finite nature.

will also be aware that others have the same potential and might be capable of doing us harm. In other words, by knowing our own dark possibilities, we can anticipate the motives and actions of our enemy. If we have owned and come to terms with those possibilities within ourselves by moderating, balancing, and integrating them, we won't be blind to those possibilities in others, nor will we be hyper–vigilant, looking for danger and offense lurking behind every comment and sideways glance.

The Warrior is aware that time is finite and that it's running out. He apprehends the immediate possibility of his own death. This awareness allows us to more fully value life, energizes us, and gives our every action intense clarity, focus, and purpose. This awareness of the finite quality of life also prioritizes all our possibilities, and our values become organized accordingly. We become serious, determined, and tenacious.

The Warrior traits of consciousness, vigilance, and awareness of our finite nature truly make us very awake in our lives. There is an "edge" to us when our Warrior is active. We are able and willing to respond with precision and directness when needed. There's no "messing around" when we're in this mode—we're always carrying our swords. But our "edge" is balanced by restraint, kindness, and compassion so that we're never unnecessarily cutting or offensive. ✍ 5.7

Disciplined

It is Warrior energy that causes us to commit to the rigors necessary for developing mastery over our bodies, minds, and emotions. Through intense focus, we can train our bodies to perform the functions that our life situations demand of it, whether those functions require skill, power, accuracy, control, or endurance. We can train our minds to be awake as described previously: observant, perceptive, discerning, vigilant, and aware. Emotionally, we can train ourselves to recognize our anger and then to practice restraint, kindness, and compassion. Through this discipline we know when and how to act and when to hold back. This allows us to risk wisely and to avoid unnecessary error. Also, we know whom we serve, and we serve no other.

The dynamic between power and vulnerability is important to acknowledge as we discipline ourselves and others. Discipline implies the use of power to overcome weakness. So here again there must be balance. The Whole Warrior would never punish himself for being weak. If he's disciplining another person, he wouldn't punish them for their weakness either. And he never over–disciplines himself or anyone else. Over–discipline comes from ignoring the bounds of human limitations, and it leads to resentment, rebellion, and regression. We must be able to relent and let go at a certain point so that we don't burn ourselves out or drive others away from us.

Discipline doesn't lock the Warrior into a rigid approach. He's able to quickly adjust his tactics and even his strategy as needed. He's aware that there may be an infinite number of ways to achieve the goal of his higher purpose. Thus, he's never dissuaded by the failure of one approach. Rather, he fixes his eye more keenly on the end goal and, with unrelenting cleverness, formulates a new plan. ✍ 5.8

Aggressive

The Warrior's approach to life is one of positive aggression and continual forward movement. The energy behind his anger has been channeled toward advancement and taking on life challenges. Metaphorically speaking, he advances the bounds of civilization, subjecting the "barbarian horde" to the rule of the King. In modern, everyday terms, this refers to aggressive *self–civilization*—in other words, our Warrior wants to expand our personal capacities as a man, whether those capacities are physical, intellectual, financial, emotional, relational, or spiritual. Our inner Warrior wants to eradicate our unruly and uncivilized traits. He urges us toward aggressive development of the talents and abilities we use in our career, pastimes, relationships, and spiritual life.

Barbarian horde: an uncivilized and brutal tribe or clan

The Warrior's aggressive stance also pushes us toward assertion in the outside world. This may mean speaking up for an interest or cause, putting ourselves forward for career advancement, or stepping up to a new level of responsibility. It's the energy that compels us to seek and acquire the things we need in order to survive and thrive. Proper Warrior assertion is not necessarily competitive. In a world with endless opportunity, the success of one man doesn't require the failure of another. Yet, as our Warrior asserts what's best in us, we will naturally rise above others who are less developed or who are corrupt. These others may eventually fail, not because they *must*, but because their own Warrior is in shadow. Through the pursuit of excellence and advancement, the Warrior destroys the corruption in the world around him. This concept is summarized well in *The Warrior Within*, where Moore and Gillette write: "The Warrior, when properly integrated into the whole, is on a self–affirmative, world–building mission."

As our Warrior asserts what's best in us, we will naturally rise above others who are less developed or who are corrupt.

As with all traits, our positive aggression is balanced by the ability to surrender our drivenness—to let down and relax. The Whole Warrior is capable of calmness, too, and doesn't let his eagerness for success carry him too far, too fast. ✍ 5.9

Detached from Feeling

Tolerance of pain and detachment from emotion and relationships are essential characteristics of the Warrior. This concept can be difficult to understand, so allow me to explain further. Responsiveness to pain, the ability to feel our emotions, and the capacity to engage in relationships are all valuable and necessary in a man's life. These traits belong mostly to the Lover archetype—they are not part of the Warrior. To function optimally in the world, it's necessary for us, at times, to set aside the influence of all feelings in order to have an objective view. The man who can't do this risks acting with Warrior aggression in the service of his own pain, fear, grief, or anger—a potentially disastrous mistake.

> Rather than permitting our feelings to possess us, we must learn to set them aside when necessary.

This ability to *consciously* detach and step back from ourselves is, in my experience, one of the most beneficial assets a man can develop if he wishes to overcome unwanted same–sex attraction. And the lack of this ability is one of the greatest blocks to progress. Rather than permitting our feelings to possess us, we must learn to set them aside when necessary. In *King Warrior Magician Lover*, Moore and Gillette explain how samurai warriors were taught to separate from their feelings. Rather than saying, "'I am afraid,' or 'I am despairing'" they were taught to say, "'There is someone who is afraid,' or 'There is someone who is despairing.'" Following this method allows us to view our own life with greater objectivity, enabling far clearer judgment and an improved ability to choose what will ultimately promote our growth.

This may seem surprising or counter–intuitive to you, especially since in so many therapeutic circles we place great emphasis on the exact opposite skill of accessing and feeling our emotions. But as you are learning, wholeness is never found in one capacity alone—both abilities are essential at different times.

Some degree of emotional detachment from our own bodies is also both healthy and necessary. This implies seeing the body as our instruments for living and attacking life. The primary beauty of the Warrior's body lies not in its aesthetics, but in its usefulness. Acceptance of this principle can allow us to focus our energies on developing our internal wholeness. ✍ 5.10

Courageous

A strong connection to Warrior energy can enable us to persevere in the face of fear and pain. Nelson Mandela said, "I learned that courage was not the absence of fear, but the triumph over it. The brave man is not he who does not feel afraid, but he who conquers that fear." Courage requires the ability to detach from feeling as we discussed previously. It also requires confidence and a determination to achieve our purpose though the costs may be high. It's not ignorance of the difficulty or danger, but willingness to face difficulty and danger when the risks are perfectly clear to us.

"I learned that courage was not the absence of fear, but the triumph over it."

Nelson Mandela

A strong motivating factor, such as a mission or cause, can increase our courage. How many people are able to do amazingly courageous acts when push comes to shove and they need to protect their own life or interests, or the life or safety of a loved one? How many behave courageously when they are acting in the service of a cause they feel passionate about? The power that comes from matured anger can bring great courage. We might call this type of anger "indignation," which implies that the anger is just or righteous.

It might be useful to distinguish courage from other kinds of fearlessness. I suggest that acts of courage serve a necessity or a higher purpose. For example, walking down a dark alley when it's the only way home, rescuing someone from danger, and protesting against a totalitarian regime are acts of courage. This is different from another type of fearlessness that we could call "daring," which is more about personal entertainment. Skydiving, rock climbing, and extreme sports are more often acts of daring. These kinds of intentional and self–inflicted bravery can prepare us to be more courageous by teaching us to subdue our emotions and overcome our natural resistance to danger.

A third type of fearlessness, which we could call "rashness," is done with disregard for the consequences and is often a response to ego. For example, picking a fight with a bigger man, purposely cutting someone off on the freeway, and cliff diving without knowing the water depth are rash behaviors. There is no virtue or benefit in rashly disregarding your wellbeing, particularly not when it might endanger others as well. ✍ 5.11

Authentic

The Warrior is without pretense, guile, or hidden agendas—he is exactly who he presents himself to be.

Although authenticity is primarily a trait of the Whole Magian, it also shows up in the Warrior. He is without pretense, guile, or hidden agendas—he is exactly who he presents himself to be without the distorting effect of exaggerated ego states. Adjusting a phrase from Moore and Gillette in *King Warrior Magician Lover*— he wears his sword for all to see. In his commitment to reveal and advance the cause of his true and highest Self, the Warrior bursts free of all the false selves we create to hide him, speaking the truth without fear. We will touch on the trait of authenticity again in Chapter Eight and then devote ourselves entirely to it as a principle of growth in Chapter Nine. ✍ 5.12

Adventurous

Adventure is a primary passion of the Warrior. We discussed adventure at length in Chapter Three, where I suggested that adventure generates masculine energy by stimulating feelings of power in the form of confidence, courage, discipline, aliveness, and self–expression. Adventure implies uncertainty and facing the unknown, which reminds us that we aren't in control and calls upon our creativity in order to devise solutions to unforeseen situations. Inevitably, this means that we must accept risk, which requires us to face our fears. Letting go of control, taking risks, and facing fears are key Warrior behaviors. ✍ 5.13

PROTECTOR OF BOUNDARIES

Protector of Boundaries
- Mental boundaries
- Emotional boundaries
- Behavioral boundaries
- Interpersonal boundaries
- Societal boundaries

As a protector, the Warrior sets and enforces boundaries. Here again we see the dynamic between power and vulnerability. When we're in Whole Warrior energy, we fully own our power and use it to protect the weaknesses and vulnerabilities within ourselves and in those around us. Metaphorically speaking, the Warrior does this through fighting and killing. Modern, real–life warriors still use those means when necessary to enforce boundaries. But in everyday life, you and I use the weapons of intention, will, and words. Our everyday battleground doesn't pit us against a barbarian horde, but against other people—who are more or less civilized—and against our own selves. Yet the same traits that enable a warrior to kill an enemy are also required of us on our more polite battlegrounds if we are to survive and thrive. Surviving and thriving in a modern, everyday context may mean protecting things like self–esteem, emotional integrity, career stability, and financial freedom.

We set the groundwork for understanding the concept of protecting boundaries when we discussed moderation in Chapter Two. There I said that the King's role as the moderator is to set boundaries, which entails self–restraint and observing reasonable limits. So the principle of boundaries is a crossover between King and Warrior energies. In addition to moderation, the King functions involved in boundaries are those of bringing order within ourselves and having a stable center. It's these capacities that create our awareness of the need for boundaries and inform us as to what the boundaries should be.

But those boundaries can only be imposed and maintained through the aggressive energy of the Warrior. Without the Warrior to enforce the limits determined by the King, we would fall prey to the chaotic inclinations of our barbarian natural self. And without a Warrior at his right hand, a King is nothing more than a Weakling Abdicator.

The Warrior's mission then is to support the vision of the King by submitting to his will in service of the weak and defenseless. The Warrior fulfills this mission by protecting our kingdom against dangers from two directions: internally and externally. Internally, the Warrior must enforce mental, emotional, and behavioral boundaries. Externally, he's responsible to maintain interpersonal and societal boundaries. Let's discuss these in greater detail. Then we will consider the Warrior's special role of setting boundaries as part of the healing process.

> The Warrior's mission is to support the vision of the King by submitting to his will in service of the weak and defenseless.

Mental Boundaries

Powerful and clean Warrior energy is the antidote to all internal invasions of shadow energy. This must begin by holding boundaries around our own thoughts. Our minds can be wild and unruly places, and to some degree this just comes with the territory of being human. Consider that our brains hold a complete record of everything we've ever experienced, that our minds are highly creative, and that our thoughts don't have to conform to the rules of reality. This enables our brains to put together and produce a wide range of thoughts. Some are rational, logical, and desirable. Others may be irrational, illogical, or disturbing. And some of our thoughts may even be disgusting or terrifying.

We will never be able to control every thought that pops into our heads. Thoughts can be compared to earthquakes: we can never predict them. But unlike earthquakes, we can learn to control our thoughts once they "strike," we can choose how much damage they do, and we can even change the nature of our thoughts over time through the right therapeutic approaches. This is what mental boundaries are all about.

Some specific types of thoughts we might want to develop boundaries around include thoughts that violate our values, negative and self–defeating thoughts, and obsessive or ruminative thoughts. Thoughts that violate our values might include sexual fantasies that leave us with feelings of guilt or dirtiness, selfish thoughts, unkind thoughts about others, and violent thoughts.

Negative and self–defeating thoughts might include the kinds of thoughts we considered in the section on "Negative Core Beliefs" in Chapter Four. They could also include "thinking errors," which can be described as ways of thinking that are incorrect and damaging to our hope and self–esteem. This might include pessimism, black–and–white thinking, and perfectionistic expectations.[2]

We discussed obsessive or ruminative thinking in Chapter Four. To review briefly, obsessions are thoughts, impulses, or images that seem to come to your mind regularly and are difficult or impossible to get rid of. These thoughts sometimes seem illogical and absurd, but they can also seem logical and completely realistic. Obsessions can also manifest as very rigid or stubborn ways of thinking.

All types of unwanted or out–of–control thinking are a sort of mental bondage and are offensive to the Warrior within us, who is dedicated to maintaining the integrity and freedom of our internal kingdom. For some of us, the Warrior can easily maintain mental boundaries by simply choosing to shift our thinking from unwanted thoughts to thoughts that are more values–congruent or more positive and productive. But some of us may have certain thoughts that are more difficult to control or eliminate. This is often the case with sexual triggers and fantasies and with obsessive thoughts that lead to compulsive behaviors (OCD or OCPD). Men facing these situations may need help from a psychiatrist, therapist, coach, or twelve–step group to eliminate or learn to control these thoughts. ⚔ 5.14

Emotional Boundaries

In order to live free of shadow energy, we must also hold boundaries around our feelings. Strong emotional boundaries allow us to experience a full range of feeling without excess by moderating what we feel. We can experience love without

---

Thoughts are like earthquakes: we can never predict them. But, unlike earthquakes, we can learn to control them once they strike. And we can choose how much damage they do.

All types of unwanted or out–of–control thinking are a sort of mental bondage and are offensive to the Warrior within us.

obsession, sadness without depression, anger without blind rage, fear without paralysis, desire without compulsion, and energy without mania. We maintain values–congruent boundaries around our sexual feelings. And most importantly, we're able to shift ourselves from one feeling state to another by following a natural emotional process. It's entirely possible for most of us to learn how to regulate our emotions, although at first it may be difficult. This doesn't mean we can always choose which emotions pop up throughout the day, but it does mean that we can—through discipline—learn how to surrender or shift ourselves out of emotions that aren't in our best interest.

Some of us tend toward a more "active" emotionality, often finding ourselves feeling intensely runaway emotions that we can't shift out of—we have to just wait until the feelings pass. In the face of any such unhealthy emotional states, the Warrior's duty is to courageously detach from feeling, impose discipline, and restore balance and moderation. We may need to learn how to surrender these emotions. Surrendering an emotion is different from repressing it. When we repress emotions, we stuff them down and refuse to acknowledge their existence, which can be damaging, dangerous, and painful. Surrendering an emotion requires a full awareness of its existence and a conscious choice to let it go.

> The Warrior's duty is to courageously detach from feeling, impose discipline, and restore balance and moderation.

On the other hand, some of us tend toward a more "passive" emotionality, often finding ourselves repressing or blocking our feelings. We may feel shut down emotionally and unable to access our feelings. Those of us in this situation may need to learn to courageously trust our feelings—to allow them to surface and then discipline ourselves to just observe them without judgment. We may need to learn how to shift down through the layers of our emotions until we arrive at a core feeling of peace and calmness.

I should note here that some of us are biologically unable to balance emotion in a healthful way due to chemical imbalances in the brain and may need external help. For example, those with major depression, bipolar disorder, and intense anxiety can often be helped through proper medication and other therapeutic approaches. ✍ 5.15

Behavioral Boundaries

The Warrior assists the King in maintaining a moderate lifestyle by holding limits around the things we do to meet our needs, satisfy our desires, and fulfill our duties. Because cravings can only lead to suffering, the Warrior's job is to see that we pursue the things we need and desire within appropriate limits. And since excessive self–denial is no better for us than self–indulgence, the Warrior must also keep an eye on his own pursuit of discipline and effort in fulfilling his duties.

The most fundamental, and perhaps most difficult, behavioral boundaries for many to maintain are boundaries around the ways in which we satisfy basic bodily needs and give ourselves sensual stimulation. These boundaries include eating amounts and types of foods that maintain health and optimal body weight and keeping our sexual expression within reasonable limits that are congruent with our values. They include avoiding overuse of alcohol and misuse of chemicals, whether obtained illegally or by prescription. And they include moderation in pursuing the natural highs that come from exercise and thrill seeking. We're also responsible for keeping boundaries around the things we do to satisfy our egos, such as pursuing status, power, wealth, and appearance. These boundaries are about remaining truthful and authentic and committing ourselves to fair and ethical behavior.

> The most fundamental behavioral boundaries are around the ways in which we satisfy basic bodily needs and give ourselves sensual stimulation.

The Warrior must also impose boundaries that maintain balance between work, discipline, and sacrifice on the one hand and rest, diversion, and self–preservation on the other. We must work, but we must also rest; we must sacrifice, but we must also survive. So in order to be effective and productive, we have to maintain boundaries around our diversions and escapes, including entertainment, play, relaxation, adventure, and "toys." Consciousness of the resources required to provide these diversions is central to holding good boundaries here. Money, time, and attention must be used prudently within the bounds of their availability. It helps to remember that, ultimately, a Warrior's purpose is to serve something greater than himself.

> The Warrior must also impose boundaries that maintain balance between work, discipline, and sacrifice on the one hand and rest, diversion, and self–preservation on the other.

But long–term effectiveness also requires us to keep good boundaries around our drive to fulfill our duties and obligations through work, discipline, and sacrifice. Consciousness of personal limits regarding commitment, pursuit of perfection, and expenditure of energy and effort are important here. We need to be aware of our physical, mental, and emotional capacities so that we don't overdo what's tolerable. Needless self–sacrifice is not healthy Warrior behavior. This is because, if death is not required of him, the Warrior wants to live to fight another day. ✍ 5.16

Interpersonal Boundaries

In our relationships with others, we need the vigilance and courage of our inner Warrior to protect our boundaries. Most of us only rarely encounter people who have bad intentions, who physically threaten us, or who threaten our loved ones, our property, or our financial security. But when we do encounter such situations, it's normal for the full aggression of the Warrior to awaken. It's his duty to fight the invader in order to protect and secure ourselves and those we love.

More commonly, we may face people in our daily lives who mean well but who, without consciousness, try to manipulate, dominate, or control us—or people who want more interaction, more of our time, or greater closeness with us than is good for us. We may get involved with people who ask more than we're capable of giving, who want more from us than we contracted for, or who want to become enmeshed or co–dependent with us. Even more innocently, our friends and loved ones may unintentionally ignore our limits and cross boundaries related to our possessions, our time, and our feelings. These situations also bring the Warrior on–line to set interpersonal boundaries, which a true Warrior will always try to do peacefully and without resorting to anger.

The ability to set limits with other people is necessary if we are to protect ourselves from invasion, manipulation, and abuse in our relationships. But we also need to be aware of how our own thoughts, feelings, and behaviors toward others might impact their boundaries. Without strong internal boundaries, we run the risk of invading, manipulating, or abusing others. Good internal and interpersonal boundaries are necessary if we're to enjoy intimacy, trust, and closeness in our relationships. That may seem strange, so allow me to explain. When we know we have the ability to hold firm limits with ourselves and others, we don't have to worry about invading or being invaded, injuring or being injured by others. This enables us to feel safe in our relationships, which is a basic human need. That safety creates trust, and trust opens the way for attachment and intimacy.

> Good internal and interpersonal boundaries are necessary if we're to enjoy intimacy, trust, and closeness in our relationships.

The bottom–line teaching here is that a strong and capable Warrior creates the setting in which the Lover archetype is free to fulfill his purpose of relating intimately with others. Without a healthy Warrior, there can be no healthy Lover. 5.17

Societal Boundaries

The Warrior is a steward of society. In that role, he brings to bear all of his other boundary skills—his internal boundaries around his own thoughts, emotions, and behavior and his ability to maintain interpersonal limits. But he goes a step further. He watches the boundaries of others, vigilantly guarding against abuses among individuals and groups within society. In all of this, he balances the trait of aggression with the ability to yield. He can lead with great power and force. But he can also follow, submitting himself to powers and forces that are greater than himself. Notice the integration of all these capacities in what I describe below.

> The Warrior is a steward of society. He watches the boundaries of others, vigilantly guarding against abuses among individuals and groups within society.

As a steward of society, he protects and upholds honored societal boundaries. He yields to appropriate social norms and customs, is respectful of honorable institutions, and obeys the law. He's protective of all that is beneficial, beautiful, wise, and sacred in community, religion, and culture. He's particularly protective of the traditional family structure, which is the foundation of every strong civilization. At the same time, he's assertive within society. He protects us from the tyranny of corrupt social customs and abusive institutions. He fights against unjust laws. And he protects his community, religion, and culture from elements that would be disruptive or degrading to them. He's progressive without being destructive of time-honored constructs.

> The Warrior sees all people as being of one kind, regardless of the situation they may occupy in society.

In his community, the Warrior sees all people as being of one kind, regardless of the situation they may occupy in society. He respects human diversity and is tolerant of every non-destructive viewpoint. This makes him mindful of the equality and rights of all people. He's particularly vigilant and aware of protecting the rights of groups who are in minority, particularly if that group is vulnerable to abuse or mistreatment. He fights against discrimination wherever he encounters it.

A bit more must be said about the Warrior's role in guarding against abusive institutions that are so common in today's culture. Our inner Warriors must be vigilant of institutions that try to take advantage of us financially or in other ways, that try to manipulate our thinking, or that attempt to addict us to their products. This can include everything from the brazenness of online scammers and porn sites to the subtle manipulation of mainstream entertainment, advertisement, and news sources. In such situations, the Warrior's response may be as simple as hanging up the phone, deleting the email, or turning off the TV or computer.

The Warrior enforces the King's view on the Law of Abundance. You may recall this law from Chapter Two. It suggests that the universe has an endless supply of the essential elements from which all physical substance is formed. Therefore, there is no scarcity; there is only abundance. If your inner King is in shadow regarding the Law of Abundance and instead believes that supplies are scarce, then your Warrior will likely place rigid boundaries around the supplies you have acquired. Your Warrior may also pursue the acquisition of more substance in ways that tend to press against the boundaries of others. Within society, this leads to unnecessary competition.

But if your King has learned to live the Law of Abundance, truly accepting that there is plenty, then your Warrior will likely have more open boundaries related to material substance. He will probably be assertive in gathering the material things that flow to him. And he will also be a wise steward in managing and dispensing the things he has to others. Such permeable boundaries would allow you to generously receive and to give freely within your society. ✍ 5.18

Boundaries and Healing

Within our minds, we carry around a whole society, comprised of all the people with whom we've ever interacted. Their voices and actions resound in our memories—some louder and more forceful than others. Some of these people have crossed our boundaries and wounded us, leaving us with destructive beliefs and feelings about ourselves. Boundaries are an integral part of healing the effects of those wounds.

> Boundaries are an integral part of healing the effects of our wounds.

The destructive beliefs and feelings created by our wounds include toxic shame and guilt. Toxic shame comes from internalizing negative messages about our worth. An example would be the belief that you're bad because you're fat or that you're defective because you were abused. In Chapter Four, I quoted authors Fossum and Mason, who described toxic shame as "the self judging the self."

> *Toxic shame:* "the self judging the self"
> Fossum and Mason

Toxic guilt is somewhat different—it's a feeling of having done wrong in a situation where we are innocent. Examples of this would include believing that you somehow caused your parents' divorce, feeling responsible for your mother's unhappiness, or thinking that the abuse was your own fault.

> *Toxic guilt:* the feeling of having done wrong in a situation where you are innocent

Toxic shame and guilt cause children to hate and blame themselves for things that aren't true or are not their fault. The guilt and shame really belong to others—to the people who wounded them through criticism, abuse, neglect, or abandonment.

The process of healing toxic shame and guilt requires safe therapeutic situations where anger and culpability can be directed toward their true targets: those who wounded us. This can unleash deeply buried resentment or even rage toward parents and others. As men, we often protect ourselves from the discomfort of facing those feelings by reasoning that "it doesn't do any good to blame others." This reasoning is both right and wrong.

> The process of healing toxic shame and guilt requires safe therapeutic situations where anger and culpability can be directed toward their true targets: those who wounded us.

To be sure, blame is never a desired outcome of a healing process—the desired end goal is freedom from our shame and guilt as well as from our anger. But achieving that end may require us to first access the Warrior's ability to identify threats to our wellbeing, many of which are the toxic stories that have invaded our minds. Then we must channel our anger into boundaries that protect us from those threats. Most of the time, those boundaries will result in internal scuffles as we say "No more!" to the toxic stories. Thus our capacity to feel anger can become a temporary tool in the Warrior's quest for healing and growth.

In addition to healing toxic guilt and shame, boundaries are also important in resolving many of the other problems discussed in Chapter Four. For example, harmful relationships require the application of interpersonal boundaries. And the process of healing sexual addictions and compulsions relies on the principle of surrender, of which boundaries are an essential component. You will learn much more about surrender in Chapter Eleven, so I won't address it further here. ✍ 5.19

SERVANT OF THE KING

> A true Warrior never serves himself. He is a servant to the King.

A true Warrior never serves himself. The very nature of the archetype is that of a servant to the King, who himself is bound to a power greater than himself—to his God or Higher Power. Moore and Gillette have used the terms "Transpersonal Commitment" and "Transpersonal Other" to denote the things the Warrior serves. "Transpersonal" is a rather clunky and unglamorous term, but it's so precise that I felt obliged to use it. The term refers to things that transcend or go beyond what's personal or individual. So a Transpersonal Commitment is a purpose that's larger than ourselves. A Transpersonal Other is a being higher than ourselves. The

Warrior's service to this higher purpose and higher being follow the vision of his inner King in the form of a mission, similar to what we discussed in Chapter Three. Let's spend a bit of time now unfolding these concepts further.

Transpersonal Other

The concept of a Transpersonal Other or Transpersonal Commitment, as described in *The Warrior Within*, seems to indicate loyalty and fidelity to a higher being, or a higher way of being, both within and outside of ourselves. Put more simply, the Warrior doesn't serve his own ego. He's bound by his duty to serve the King. In *King Warrior Magician Lover*, we read:

> He lives not to gratify his personal needs and wishes or his physical appetites but to hone himself into an efficient spiritual machine, trained to bear the unbearable in the service of the transpersonal goal.

Within our own psyche this transpersonal goal is to bring our lives into alignment with our Center, to become wiser, stronger, more conscious, capable—better in every way. It's the advancement of our own King functions. Outside ourselves, the Transpersonal Other to which we give our complete loyalty is ultimately God or some other Higher Power or greater good. So, the Transpersonal Other may be seen as both our own internal King functions and our Higher Power.

> The goal is to bring our lives into alignment with our Center, to become wiser, stronger, more conscious, capable—better in every way.

A Warrior's commitment to this Transpersonal Other is crucial. Without the combination of passion and subordination that characterize this commitment, Warrior energy soon slips into shadow. Passionate devotion keeps the Warrior from going to sleep and sliding into the Masochist shadow. And loyal subordination keeps the Warrior from possessing us entirely, which would give rise to the Sadist shadow.

King David in *The Old Testament* exemplifies this submission to a Higher Power. In Psalms 40:8 David says: "I delight to do thy will, O my God: yea, thy law is within my heart" (KJV). In *The New Testament*, Jesus Christ demonstrates this same quality. In John 5:30 Jesus says: "I seek not mine own will, but the will of the Father which hath sent me" (*KJV*).

A story in *King Warrior Magician Lover* provides a further illustration of this principle. The story tells of a samurai who tracked his lord's assassin for a length

of time and through many difficult circumstances, illustrating the samurai's loyalty to his lord. But in the very moment when his mission could be accomplished—when the samurai had the assassin at the tip of his sword—the assassin angered the samurai by spitting in his face. In that moment, the samurai's devotion to the principles his lord represented required that he walk away rather than slay the assassin in anger.

To kill the assassin at that moment would have brought justice to the assassin and completed the samurai's immediate mission. But it would have caused the samurai to fail his higher mission, which was to serve only the lord to whom he was bound. The samurai's anger had raised his personal passion and diverted his focus away from exclusive service to his Transpersonal Other. His actions in that moment would have been impure and so he abstained.

How can you know when you have found your true Transpersonal Other? You will know it when you love that Other enough that service to it feels innately rewarding. Love and a desire to serve always go together. The love you feel will propel you into action. As a side note, the affirmation you will feel for your service to your Transpersonal Other will come from your relationship with the Transpersonal Other—your inner King and your Higher Power. This will be your source of validity, worth, and purpose. The gratitude of those you serve—if they do express gratitude—will be secondary. 🖊 5.20

Vision And Mission

In Chapter Three we talked about mission as one of six core masculine needs. Moore and Gillette consider mission to be an essential component of masculinity. In *The Warrior Within*, they state: "Mature masculine functioning … requires that a man have a mission that is beyond the merely private and self–preserving agenda—one that serves the most worthy authority and ideals that he recognizes.… Anything less is in fact a bastardization of an instinctual potential that contains the code for much of the nobility of our species."

A mission is created by putting into action a personal transcendent vision. It's the King archetype that provides the vision that guides us to our missions. The King's libido and generative functions—creating, inspiring, blessing, and providing—instinctually urge us to incarnate that vision. But it's the disciplined and active Warrior archetype that enables us to carry our visions into action. Together the vision of the King and the action of the Warrior create a mission. The work of carrying out our missions is the Warrior's essential and ultimate purpose within our psyches.

Let's delve more deeply into the role that the King's vision plays in creating our mission. Consistent with his commitment to serve a Transpersonal Other, a true Warrior serves only the King—he never serves himself. The King is the axis mundi—the Center and source of clarity and vision and connection to our Higher Power. Therefore, a Warrior's true mission will serve the King's vision. He will serve those truths that his King believes in most deeply, the goals that matter most to him, the things that the King feels compelled to create or to change in the world. It's this kind of transcendent vision that a Warrior is willing to give his life to—or give his life *for*.

Let's consider for a moment the way our wounds can impact our vision and shape our missions. The painful things that happen to us will certainly impact the way we see the world. If we choose to see those wounds as reminders of our vulnerability to the darkness that surrounds us, our vision—and likewise our missions—will be dark and shadowy. Worse still, if our vision is colored by anger, our mission will serve not the King, but the Sadist. A true mission can never proceed from a vision based in pain or anger.

But if we choose to see our wounds as having something beneficial to teach us, then our vision and missions can be full of light, love, and hope. This usually requires profound conscious effort and the faith to allow our Transpersonal Other—whether that's our inner King or a Higher Power—to use our wounds for our growth. If we can see life this way, then the pain that comes from our wounds can be a great teacher and clarifier. This is one of the meanings of the phrase, "there is a fountain of gold behind our wounds." Among the greatest gold we gain from our wounds may be an awareness of our deepest and most transcendent values, which awareness often comes only through struggle and hardship. But even greater gold may be the loving bond we create with our Transpersonal Other as we patiently allow him to shape our vision by teaching us through, and then healing, our wounds. ✍ 5.21

Action And Mission

As I mentioned previously, a mission is created by putting into action a personal transcendent vision. This is what the sidebar to the right depicts. So what is the

Vision
(the world I want to create)

+

Action
(what I do to create it)

=

Mission

If we choose to see our wounds as having something beneficial to teach us, then our vision and missions can be full of light, love, and hope.

Warrior's role in putting the King's vision into action? He's the source of power that propels our missions forward. All of the Warrior's capacities may be called on if we're to fulfill our missions. We will need the power that comes in part by maturing our anger into focused energy and assertion. We must be awake, disciplined, and aggressive in positive and beneficial ways. Sometimes we may have to detach ourselves from our feelings, and perhaps even from relationships, in order to progress. We will need to be courageous, authentic, and adventurous. We will need to be mindful of boundaries in some way. And we will need to be sure that our missions serve something higher than ourselves.

But the Warrior archetype is not alone in bringing the King's vision to life. Though our missions will be pushed forward by the power of the Warrior, they may be full of Magian and Lover qualities. It makes sense that a truly balanced mission would involve aspects of all the archetypes.

> The actions that will provide for the most compelling mission will be actions that you're passionate about doing.

The actions that will provide for the most compelling mission will be actions that you're passionate about doing. As Frederick Buechner observed in his book, *Wishful Thinking*, "The place God calls you to is where your deep gladness and the world's deep hunger meet." These will be things that are tremendously satisfying or meaningful to you; actions that you find rewarding in and of themselves, rather than things that you do only because of what they bring you. These actions may not line up with your professional duties—a mission is different from a job description. They could be very basic human behaviors like loving others, being authentic, judging others fairly, creating things, pushing your limits, adventuring, teaching others, mentoring, or giving.

Sometimes a man's mission must begin with himself. The first battles we must fight to make the world a better place are often those we fight within our own minds and hearts. ✎ 5.22-23

SHADOWS OF THE WARRIOR

> The dynamic between power and vulnerability is an inherent contradiction.

The dynamic between power and vulnerability that creates the Whole Warrior is also the dynamic from which both of the Warrior's shadows emerge. This dynamic is inherently a contradiction—to feel powerful and strong while also being acquainted with your vulnerability and weakness. All of us have to face this conflict as boys. Some pass through it easily and gracefully, emerging into manhood with an ability to balance their sense of power with the reality of their vulnerability. These boys may have good parenting or a strong personality or temperament to thank for their success. Or perhaps their smooth sailing is due to a blissful unconsciousness of the whole dynamic—life simply never forced them to think about it.

But for most of us, this process doesn't go so well. We face the conflict head on—often harshly and usually too early in life. Experience teaches us that we can be wounded and that whatever boyish strengths we possess are puny in comparison with the overwhelming powers around us. This psychologically disfiguring lesson can come from many sources. Emotionally immature parents are at the top of the list, although it must be noted that parents are usually quite unaware of the effect their actions will have on their children. Nevertheless, when parents are abusive, harsh, authoritarian, or manipulative, they may instill in their boys a rage–based sense of power. When parents punish, threaten, or reject their sons for being angry, independent, or trying to set boundaries, they may inculcate a hopeless sense of vulnerability.

Furthermore, mothers who are weak or needy of male help, companionship, or affirmation may unconsciously manipulate their sons out of their power and independence by teaching them to feel guilty for trying to create a separate life for themselves. Overly–anxious mothers may try to protect their vulnerable "little boys" by controlling them too severely, reinforcing and prolonging their childhood dependency. But parents aren't alone in their ability to inflict these wounds. Overly rigid and disciplined educational systems can have a similar effect. And bullies are routinely the teachers of this cruel lesson.

Whatever the cause, many of us did not develop the ability to accept, balance, and deal with both sides of the power–vulnerability dynamic. We became too familiar with our weakness or too immersed in our rage. A crisis emerged that forced us to make choices for which we were not prepared. We were too young and nonconscious to respond in mature and balanced ways. So most of us respond to this situation with some of the simplest of psychological tools: splitting and projection. The splits we created reflect our inner life experience where power is pitted against vulnerability. That splitting happens internally and tends to reverberate through our interactions with other people and with society as a whole. The world becomes a rather polarized place inhabited by the weak and the strong, the victims and the abusers.

> Experience teaches us that we can be wounded and that whatever boyish strengths we possess are puny in comparison with the overwhelming powers around us.

> Most of us respond with some of the simplest of psychological tools: splitting and projection.

The tool of projection is used to safely distance ourselves from the pole we most hate and fear. Some of us fear the pole of power and strength. We may feel entirely overwhelmed by the dominance or ruthlessness of those around us, hating and shunning our abusers. Maybe we don't know how to fight or we're physically too small or weak to prevail. We may be burdened by extreme anxiety or obsessive self–doubt. We may have been overpowered again and again. Expressing anger and hostility seems severely risky and dangerous. Even the idea of standing up for ourselves is terrifying and out of the question. So we may settle into a seemingly safe masochistic vulnerability and project our potential for power onto those who already blatantly possess it.

Others of us fear the pole of vulnerability, hating the weakness within ourselves and projecting it onto other boys whom we also hate. We may push our way through life. We may possess physical strength, tough wits, or a knack for bluster. Maybe we've learned the skills of our own abusers and have made an unconscious pact with them to pass along their hatred and fear of those who are weak. What we don't know is how to accept the reality of our own vulnerability. We sadistically hang that burden around the necks of our victims.

The Sadist represses his
vulnerability and lives in
his power. The Masochist
represses his power and
lives in his vulnerability.

So the Sadist represses his vulnerability and lives in his power. The Masochist represses his power and lives in his vulnerability. But these two shadows are united by the unresolved pain, grief, and reactive rage they carry from their own mistreatment. It's these unresolved feelings that keep the Warrior's shadows alive. The two shadows are also united by their dishonesty, which Moore and Gillette describe in their book *The Warrior Within*. The Masochist, they say, "is dishonest about his passion, aggression, and rage." At the same time, "the Sadist cannot acknowledge his fear, tenderness, or vulnerability." Both deny the truth of the full dynamic, which is that humans are both powerful *and* vulnerable.

These two poles—like the shadow poles of all the archetypes—are inextricably tied together. When one shadow is observable in our personality, the other shadow will be found in the things we project onto those around us. Or the repressed shadow may be dormant within us, waiting for events to trigger a polar shift of shadows and thrust it onto center stage.

The Masochist

Leopold Ritter von Sacher–Masoch (1836–1895) was an Austrian writer whose publications included stories about being dominated by women. He also reportedly had a mistress during one period of his life with whom he made a contract to be her slave. They traveled together with him disguised as her servant. In 1886, a psychiatrist used Sacher–Masoch's name as the root of a new psychiatric term— "masochism"—which he applied to the phenomenon of experiencing sexual pleasure through receiving pain. It was through the writings of Sacher–Masoch that this condition came to be known among psychiatrists.

Today, the term "masochist" is still used as a label for people who gain sexual pleasure from suffering. The term is also commonly used when referring to anyone who causes himself or herself pain or distress or who invites others to do so. As an archetypal shadow, eight key traits of the Masochist stand out. He is powerless, ruled by feelings, depressed, dependent, gullible, cowardly, victimized, and disempowered. As you read the descriptions below for each trait, take just a moment to consider how strongly you experience each trait within yourself. Think about how these traits might show up in you. Also consider whether you're triggered by any of these traits in other people. That may give you an indication of whether you're projecting aspects of the Masochist onto those around you. ✑ 5.24

Powerless: Moore and Gillette refer to the Masochist as a "Dishonest Warrior." He may be dishonest about many things, but central to them all is his dishonesty about his power and his lust for strength. Power is a universal need, but the Masochist falsely denies this need. But his dishonesty is not conscious. Rather it's the result of having been stripped of his power in childhood through mistreatment or abuse. With no other apparent choice available, he succumbed to the humiliation and his identity formed around that powerlessness.

Central to his identity is an agreement that he's not allowed to be powerful.[3] This agreement provides a false sense of safety and stability—he's gotten out of the business of being powerful and feels more secure the further he stays from it. But this security comes at a price. He has to deny and repress the rage he feels toward his abusers. And he must repress his natural male passion and aggression. He has to avoid competition because it thrusts him right back into the "power business."

Leopold Ritter von Sacher– Masoch

The Masochist

- Powerless
- Ruled by feelings
- Depressed
- Dependent
- Gullible
- Cowardly
- Victimized
- Disempowered

To lose would mean suffering another agonizing blow to his power, not to mention his sense of worth and validity. To win would mean breaking his agreement to avoid being powerful and thus violating his identity. On occasion, he may feel confident enough about succeeding in a competitive situation that he will make a go of it. On such occasions, he may be surprised by a sudden onrush of angry impulses as the Sadist pokes a hole through his dishonest passivity.

But most of the time, the Masochist is falsely nice, weak, and overly cooperative, particularly toward those he sees as having power. Whether or not the other people are truly powerful is, of course, irrelevant. The Masochist reacts to those who *look* powerful. They may simply be outgoing, confident, or well dressed. Or maybe they happen to resemble a bully from junior high. The Masochist will tend to respond to these "powerful" people with subservience and excessive compliance as he attempts to please or placate them. He may be trying to avoid becoming the target of their anger or abuse. Or maybe he's attempting to boost his self–worth by winning their approval. Whatever the underlying reason may be, the hidden reality is that he views these people with fear, resentment, or even hatred. Yet at the same time, he may spitefully wish he was as powerful as they. Whereas the Sadist hates the weak and envies the strong, the Masochist hates the strong and envies them, too.

> Wheras the Sadist hates the weak and envies the strong, the Masochist hates the strong and envies them, too.

I've often observed this hatred and envy of powerful males among men with same–sex attraction. It often shows up as simmering anger and cynicism toward men who are confident or in positions of authority. Men with same–sex attraction often sexualize these seemingly more powerful males using fantasies of seduction, eroticized friendship, or discipline and punishment. This sexualization is yet another manifestation of dishonesty because the true desire is not for sex but for the very power and strength the Masochist has denied himself.

Ruled by Feelings: The Masochist tends to live life immersed in passive negative feelings like fear, depression, anxiety, shame, and pain—both emotional and physical. But this may be the extent of his emotional repertoire. Positive emotions—like joy, excitement, love, or true compassion—seem beyond his capacity. And the active emotion of anger is almost always out of reach.

> The Masochist tends to live life immersed in passive negative feelings like fear, depression, anxiety, shame, and pain.

The classic definition of masochism is "one who takes pleasure in pain." On some level, the Masochist has some type of positive association with his negative feelings. If you were to ask the Masochist if he *likes* his painful life he would quickly tell you he doesn't. But if you were to investigate things a bit deeper, you would probably find that he experiences the pain as familiar, safe, or even comforting. In more extreme cases you might discover that feeling bad actually feels good to him and that when he feels good it makes him feel bad.

The Masochist's relationship with his negative feelings may sound almost like an addiction. As you read the following points, notice how strongly these compare with what might be said about addictive behavior.

- He's tried to stop the negative feelings, but he can't.

- Every time he gets close to escaping the negative cycle, he binges on negative feelings again.

- He can't envision a life for himself without the negative feelings.

- He seems to rely on the negative feelings in order to maintain a sense of stability and to repress deeper, more frightening feelings—especially anger.

- The feelings are creating ever–greater destructive consequences in his life.

Depressed: Among the negative feelings just discussed, depression deserves special attention because it's a hallmark of the Masochist. It's also an additional manifestation of his dishonesty. The Masochist's depression is really just another way of hiding his volcanic rage from himself. Moore and Gillette suggest that the Masochist's depression is part of a "repression barrier," which is a defensive wall that keeps him from breaking through to the out–of–control forces of the opposite shadow pole—the Sadist. "The extent of this rage," they say, "can be calculated from the depth of the depression that covers it." To put it more simply, the deeper the depression, the greater the anger beneath it. But this layer of depression blocks more than just the Masochist's rage. It also blocks his libido and all other positive archetypal energies—including power and courage—from being accessed and expressed. What remains is a vague, listless shell.

> The Masochist's depression is a way of hiding his volcanic rage from himself. The deeper the depression, the greater the anger beneath it.

Cynicism emerges in a man under the influence of the Masochist as his repression barrier of depression begins to wear thin. Moore and Gillette refer to cynicism as "the final defense against rage." The nice guy persona disappears and in its place is a negative bitterness. The cynic finds fault with everyone and everything, revealing his own pain through his attacks on any type of goodness, sincerity, kindness, and the possibility of a positive outcome. But cynicism is just an ever so slightly more socially acceptable version of rage, and it wounds others just as certainly as its straightforward counterpart.

Addiction is often a last–ditch effort by the Masochist to avoid a terrifying polar shift from depression to sadistic rage. Here in the transition from the passive to active poles of the Warrior we have a crossover with the Lover's active shadow pole—the Addict. Addiction has many uses, one of which is to cover the deadness of depression with a semblance of life energy while also numbing the underlying rage that's trying to make its way to the surface. Just as with depression, the depth of the rage will determine the extent of the addictive acting out that's needed to anesthetize the pain–based rage. In this circumstance we should define addiction very broadly to include a whole range of unhealthy behaviors that divert the depressed person's attention through fantasy, escape, or sedation. These can include the compulsive use of chemicals, sex, gambling, working, shopping, eating, and even extreme religious behavior.

Dependent: Because of the childhood injuries to his masculine power, the Masochist—like the Sadist—will have difficulty with allegiance to powers greater than his own. But whereas the Sadist defies the power of those in authority, the Masochist may dependently cling to more powerful people. As I mentioned previously, he has an agreement limiting his own ability to be powerful. His main goal is to avoid danger and discomfort at all costs. Since power inherently carries a risk, it must be shunned. Therefore, he must rely on the power of others in order to get what he needs.

> Since power inherently carries a risk, it must be shunned. Therefore, he must rely on the power of others in order to get what he needs.

The Masochist has a Weakling King at his core who lacks vision and offers little in the way of validity, worth, or purpose. So he can't affirm himself. His validity is dependent on regular reassurance from those around him. His worth is determined moment by moment by the positive and negative responses he perceives from others. And his purpose will always be borrowed from the missions of more powerful visionaries. He will submit himself like a slave to other people's expectations and preferences. He's a pleaser—a nice guy. John Eldredge laments about such men in *Wild at Heart*. He says that Christianity offers men only the opportunity to become "Really Nice Guys." Christianity is not the only culture that's guilty of such reduced and hollow expectations of masculinity. Like the

Sadist, the Masochist's mission is self–serving: to confirm the helplessness of the Weakling by denying his own power and clinging to those with greater authority.

Gullible: As I've amply pointed out, the Masochist shadow entails the repression of anger and hostility. Sometimes the Masochist is also out of touch with his fear. This combination will leave him naïve and foolishly open to other people. And the more deeply repressed his anger and hostility are, the more gullible he will be. His naïveté will diminish his ability to set and hold boundaries. He will be easily deceived and manipulated. His inner King's capacity for discernment is totally disabled.

It's possible that on some level, being gullible may reflect an agreement based on low self–worth. The destruction of his masculine power during childhood may have caused the Masochist to accept an agreement that he's worthy of being taken advantage of. He may believe it's his role to be injured; therefore he passively allows it. And, despite the fact that he has been hurt time and time again, he agrees to never see it coming.

Cowardly: To review, I've said that the Masochist is dishonest about his need for power and lives according to an agreement of powerlessness. He's ruled by passive negative emotions, particularly depression, which block his access to positive archetypal energies, including power and courage. This accumulation of weaknesses disposes the Masochist to dependently cling to more powerful people. Add the trait of fearfulness to this description and you have the definition of a coward.

The Masochist is excessively concerned with his own safety and comfort. Remember, his main goal is to avoid danger and discomfort, probably because he lacks confidence in his ability to handle pain. His fear of getting hurt leads him to erect extremely restrictive internal boundaries around his emotions and behaviors. He won't allow himself to do or feel anything that might bring distress. This may lead him to avoid assertion and to isolate himself in an attempt to go unnoticed by the sadists of the world. He will have lived most of his life through a false self, and so he may have great difficulty perceiving and understanding his needs and wants or genuinely providing for his own wellbeing. In running from the possibility of death, it's actually life he misses.

Victimized: In his individual relationships with other people, the Masochist is unable to maintain his boundaries. He is passive and permits—or even invites—

The more deeply repressed the Masochist's anger and hostility are, the more gullible he will be.

The Masochist's main goal is to avoid danger and discomfort, probably because he lacks confidence in his ability to handle pain.

others to victimize him. The bullies of the world are carrying his opposite shadow and so, in a completely unconscious way, he draws them to himself. Because he lacks proper self–esteem, he may not even recognize the extent or wrongness of the mistreatment he receives. This self–degrading tolerance likely arises from his belief that he's unworthy of boundaries or even that he deserves mistreatment as punishment for his faulty and bad true self.[4]

Experience has taught the Masochist that others can't be trusted, his true self is bad, and other people are cruel. It has also taught him that rejection, abandonment, and victimization will always be his lot. Nevertheless, he tries to minimize the abuse by controlling, hiding, and repressing his faulty true self. This means living without authenticity, which is really just a self–inflicted type of victimization, much like the excessive control the Sadist perpetrates on others. But that's the price the Masochist must pay. He trades authenticity for being liked, accepted, or at least tolerated. He trades his true self for a secure dependency.

As a result, the Masochist won't be able to assert his wants or stand up for himself. He will be afraid to confront others. He may say that he doesn't want to hurt their feelings, but in reality, it's more likely that he fears the other person will turn into a Sadist and tear out his guts. On the other hand, his passivity may be yet another defense against his own repressed rage. Confronting another person might invite an explosion from his own tightly capped cauldron. He fears that an outburst from that volcano would certainly result in him being left alone, in pain, or even dead.

The Masochist's situation is inherently unstable—he can't live that way for long. Eventually the cauldron will begin to release some steam in the form of passive–aggressive behavior. Passive–aggressiveness is a wolf in sheep's clothing—the angry edge of the Sadist shadow beginning to creep through the repression barrier. The Masochist begins to act out his hidden aggressive impulses while still appearing innocent and harmless—or even victimized—on the outside. Most typically, he's not conscious of his harmful intentions as he wounds those around him. He may use a variety of ploys to express his hidden rage, such as subtly shaming or undermining others through embarrassing or humiliating comments or questions. He may speak or act in ways that create chaos or leave others feeling insecure. Or he may express his resentment by neglecting his responsibilities or inconveniencing others by his lateness or forgetfulness. But he will claim—and may genuinely believe—that he means no harm.

The bullies of the world are carrying his opposite shadow and so, in a completely unconscious way, he draws them to himself.

The Masochist begins to act out his hidden aggressive impulses while still appearing innocent and harmless—or even victimized—on the outside.

Moore and Gillette describe a particular passive–aggressive relationship dynamic that I believe has particular relevance to married men with same–sex attraction. The authors describe a relationship in which a man has become a Weakling–Masochist and has passively turned over control of his marital relationship to his wife. She responds, as frightened women tend to do, with outbursts of anger and hurt. On the surface, he plays the role of a passive victim. But deep inside, an aggressive Sadist is plotting. In the words of Moore and Gillette, he's thinking, "Hurt me, darling, then I'll have an excuse to leave you, since I never trusted you in the first place."

Disempowered: In his interactions with society, the Masochist is disempowered. His agreement of powerlessness, his energy–blocking depression, his gullibility, his tendency to depend on others, and his inability to assert personal boundaries may leave him feeling marginalized and ineffectual in professional, institutional, and social settings. This part of the Masochist shadow may be characterized by three traits: compliance, disfranchisement, and fear.

While it's important that members of a society comply with appropriate social customs, norms, and boundaries, the Masochist tends to comply in an overly submissive and self–destructive way, usually out of fear of being wrong or being rejected. For example, he may not speak up when an error has been made that disfavors him. He may submit when someone is taking advantage of him. He may automatically assume that abuses are inevitable and unchangeable. When asked for his opinion, he won't give it, and he may not even know what it is.

> The Masochist tends to comply in an overly submissive and self-destructive way, usually out of fear of being wrong or being rejected.

He sees the world in terms of "Them" versus "Us," or more likely as "Everybody" versus "Me." And he will usually see himself as part of the disfranchised group. Disfranchisement means that your privileges or rights have been withdrawn. It means you don't have a voice, you're not deserving, your opinion doesn't count. The disenfranchised man is a victim of forces bigger than himself, and he may have many conspiracy theories as to why that is. But rarely will he be able to summon up enough anger to actually do something about it.

The Masochist has the mentality of scarcity, which means he believes that all goods and services are limited and must be competed for. He's sure there is not enough to go around and assumes this means he has to go without. To actively try to take something for himself brings up his fear of competition, which, as I mentioned earlier, the Masochist feels compelled to avoid. He will do without rather than risk the humiliation of defeat, failure, or rejection by engaging again in the "power business." For the man in the masochist shadow, competition is an order to give up and lie down.

The Sadist

Donatien Alphonse François—
Marquis de Sade

The Sadist

- Overpowering
- Numb
- Rageful
- Defiant
- Paranoid
- Reckless
- Cruelly controlling
- Antisocial

Like the term "masochism," the word "sadism" was also derived from the name of a well–known writer. In this case, the writer was Donatien Alphonse François— better known as the Marquis de Sade. Born in the year 1740, Sade was a French aristocrat who became famous during his age for his erotic novels and for his bizarre sexual behavior, which included drugging and occasionally torturing prostitutes. He spent much of his life either in prison or in insane asylums, yet he continued his perverse behavior up until his death.

As used today, the term "sadist" refers to an individual who inflicts pain on another person as a source of sexual gratification. The term is also used in a more general way to refer to anyone who takes pleasure in causing any type of pain to others or simply anyone who commits excessive cruelty. Eight traits of the Sadist archetype are important for our discussion. He is overpowering, numb, rageful, defiant, paranoid, reckless, cruelly controlling, and antisocial.　5.25

Now consider the traits of the Sadist described below. As you do, think about ways in which you manifest these traits in your own personality. Also think about whether you experience these traits in other people, which may be an indication that you are projecting Sadist traits onto them.

Overpowering: The main function of the Sadist is to engage and balance vulnerability through excessive power. Where there is weakness, he brings strength. But he forcefully imposes that strength on himself and others in hurtful and destructive ways. He may be running from the fear and disdain he has toward his own weakness, softness, and vulnerability. His overpowering behavior is an attempt to stay a step ahead of his weaknesses and self–doubt. He must maintain a position of superiority, control, and invulnerability.

The Sadist's tendency to overpower others may show up as bullying, relentless criticism, faultfinding, and sarcasm. It may show up as extreme competitiveness and being a sore loser. The Sadist may rig the game or deny having lost. More extreme acts of overpowering include acts of genocide, killing sprees, and protracted torture of victims. Or we may turn our Sadistic impulses on ourselves in a sadist–masochist joint venture of overpowering ourselves through compulsive self–denial, perfectionism, ignoring personal needs, and overworking.

The Sadist's sense of his own power tends to be unrealistic. His repression of his own tenderness and weakness allows him to imagine himself as invulnerable and to live as if he had no fear, which he also represses. But his vulnerable passive shadow doesn't just disappear into his unconscious—it is projected onto the weak people around him, whom he hates and persecutes.

While he hates the weak, he also envies the strong. He fears and resents their strength, but he also wants to take it from them. So his underlying desire becomes to disempower—or take the power—of those people he sees as stronger than himself. The phenomenon of the "king killer" arises from this same desire. A "king killer" is a man who targets and attacks the leader of whatever group he is a member. He may be quick to point out the leader's errors or flaws. He will disagree with him over trivial points or maybe even engage in a direct assault with the leader in front of the group through an argument or a challenge of his authority. In his own mind, the king killer believes he's doing nothing wrong. His emotional numbness prevents him from feeling the anger beneath his attacks or perceiving the resentment of those he injures.

> While he hates the weak, he also envies the strong. He fears and resents their strength, but he also wants to take it from them.

For men with same–sex attraction, the Sadist's envy often shows up as sexualization of powerful men. This may be a way to avoid or soften the sadistic impulses they feel toward those men, perhaps out of a fear of what might happen if they directly expressed their resentment. Or it may be a way of hurting the other man or taking his power by sexually conquering him in fantasy or reality.

Numb: The abuse and abandonment that the Sadist has experienced have left him numb to any tender or exuberant emotions. He is not capable of feeling love, affection, compassion, or kindness toward others. He unconsciously blocks out emotional pain, grief, and sadness as well. And he's likely to be numb to joy and excitement, too. When situations arise that evoke tender feelings in him, he's likely to split those feelings off, which in psychological terminology is called "dissociation." You could say that the Sadist has the Lover in bondage—probably to an addiction.

> The abuse and abandonment that the Sadist has experienced have left him numb to any tender or exuberant emotions.

So, he lacks access to positive emotion. He probably also can't connect with the emotion of fear or with physical pain either since either feeling would tune him into his own vulnerability. The only feeling he can access is his deep and unquenchable anger. This combination of traits—lack of tenderness, disconnection from fear and pain, and unmitigated anger—can make the Sadist a truly dangerous man with no limit to his potential for violent and abusive behavior.

Rageful: Underlying the Sadist's tendency to overpower others is a deep unresolved anger over the loss of his masculine power. His rageful displays may be a way of acting out this anger toward the abusers who stripped him of his power, as if he's on some misguided mission to rescue his own hurt little boy. But rather than setting the little boy free, the Sadist keeps him carefully hidden—even from himself. The inner child's tenderness and vulnerability seem—to the Sadist—like a sure way to get hurt again. So he uses the bluster of his anger to provide an effective defensive shield. His angry personality ensures that no one—including himself—will ever touch that tender boy again. Rage is what motivates and propels the Masochist's actions. It provides the drive and energy that gets him through life.

> The Sadist's rageful displays may be a way of acting out his anger toward the abusers who stripped him of his power, as if he's on some misguided mission to rescue his own hurt little boy.

Typically we think of rage as an angry fury, such as when a person "goes into a rage." Such displays are exaggerated rather than authentic expressions of feeling. But Moore and Gillette explain that rage is not always passionate and fiery. It can also be calm, cold, and calculated, such as when someone hurts others without showing emotion or raising his voice. Whether hot or cold, the Sadist's rage is insane. I mean this in the most literal sense—the Sadist is not in his right (or human) mind. This means that he lacks normal human values and restraints. The further into the shadow he goes, the more capable he becomes of launching increasingly cruel and destructive acts.

Defiant: Rather than having a Transpersonal Other to whom he commits himself, the Sadist defies authority and can't be led. It's very difficult for him to submit or surrender to any power greater than his own because the act of submission strikes at the heart of his own hunger for power. As I explained previously, both the Masochist and the Sadist had their masculine power stripped from them in childhood. Now in adulthood, the Sadist is on a quest to recover that power and prove to his own ego—and to everyone else—that he has it. Overpowering those weaker than him is the source of his self–affirmation.

So his only allegiance is to his own Tyrant King. He has no goal higher than feeling powerful. He has no faith in anything beyond his will and his own sword. And his mission is entirely self–focused: to uphold the power of the Tyrant by defying greater authority and abusing the weak. It's this shadow mission that falsely affirms his sense of validity, worth, and purpose.

Paranoid: Although the Sadist may not feel fear, he does tend to be paranoid. Paranoia is different from fear in that it's not an emotion. Rather, paranoia is a delusional belief system based on a sense of persecution and jealousy and characterized by suspicions of the hostile intentions of others. But the Sadist's paranoia is actually a blatant projection of his own hostility. This projection occurs on a nearly conscious level—the sadist has some degree of awareness of his own ill will and assumes everyone else is just like him. How can he trust others when his own mind is filled with such hostile intentions? As a result of this paranoia, the Sadist tends to be very closed.

Reckless: To review, I've said that the Sadist's sense of his own power tends to be unrealistic, allowing him to ignore his vulnerability, that he tends to be numb to emotional and physical pain, that he tends to act out of anger, is filled with hostile intentions, and is defiant of authority. Clearly, this is a dangerous man. But he's not only dangerous to others—this combination of traits makes him dangerous to himself as well. He lacks internal boundaries around his own emotions and behaviors, so he's prone to reckless and destructive behavior. Relentlessly driven by his one goal—to feel powerful—he will obey every impulse that serves that end.

Without the ability to perceive his own pain, he doesn't experience exhaustion. This allows him to persevere almost endlessly, continuing his compulsive campaigns of cruelty. It's as though he's running toward his own death, willing to risk everything to get what he wants. In the Sadist's habit of poor self–care we see a connection to his opposing shadow, the Masochist, who also can't perceive or respond to his own needs. The Sadist eventually finds himself alienated, alone, and depleted.

Controlling and Cruel: In his individual relationships with other people, the Sadist is disrespectful of personal boundaries. As a result, he's both controlling and cruel. Out of his inability to trust, he may impose excessive control on others in an attempt to maintain ultimate power. In *The Warrior Within*, Moore and Gillette suggest

His only allegiance is to his own Tyrant King, with no goal higher than feeling powerful.

The Sadist lacks internal boundaries around his own emotions and behaviors and so he's prone to reckless and destructive behavior.

that on a deeper level, the impulse to control is really a repression of freedom, independence, and all healthy feeling states—all of which are aspects of healthy power and would undo the shadowy power of the Sadist. We see this at work in countries ruled by totalitarian regimes. The ruling party typically represses not only democracy itself, but also the people's access to many freedoms. If the people are allowed to enjoy much liberty, the logic goes, they will only demand more.

The Sadist's cruelty is enabled by his numbness to feelings of tenderness and vulnerability. This allows him to avoid feeling compassion for his victims or empathizing with their pain. His mission to feel powerful no matter the consequence blocks him from recognizing and respecting the rights and boundaries of others. He views people only through the lens of his shadowy mission and is disconnected from them in every other way. This detachment puts him beyond all the softening influences of the King and Lover archetypes and allows him to persistently victimize whoever is in his way.

Though he may often use deceit to get what he wants, he also has the ability to express himself with a cruel form of *faux* authenticity. This type of authenticity means holding nothing back and expressing exactly what he thinks and feels no matter how raw or rude. Such expressions usually amount to disapproval, disgust, contempt, and rage. I've often seen this type of Sadism pass for the virtue of "speaking my truth" in men's groups, sometimes leaving the recipients of the man's "truth" wounded.

Antisocial: In his interactions with society, the Sadist tends to fit the psychological profile known as "antisocial," which is defined as "disruptive and harmful… to the functioning of a group or society."[5] All of the traits that make him reckless in caring for himself also allow him to be reckless as a member of society: his unrealistic view of his own power, his disconnection from emotion, his tendency to act out his anger and hostility, and his defiance of authority. This part of the Sadist shadow may be characterized by three traits: disrespect, entitlement, and competitiveness.

His disrespect may be aimed at any and all social institutions, whether business, governmental, or religious. He may flaunt or ignore social customs, norms, and boundaries in such ways as cutting in line, disrupting public gatherings, driving aggressively, or disrespecting public figures and authorities. He may disregard professional ethical standards or even disobey the law. His worldview likely

The Sadist views people only through the lens of his shadowy mission and is disconnected from them in every other way.

This part of the Sadist shadow may be characterized by three traits: disrespect, entitlement, and competitiveness.

includes a strong "Us" versus "Them" mentality, or perhaps even a "Me" against "Them" assumption. The way he divides who is "Us" and who is "Them" may be based on any criteria, including race, ethnicity, sex, sexual orientation, age, religion, socioeconomic status, and so forth. His entitlement derives from his status as a member of the "Us" group—or as the all-important "Me." He sees himself as deserving of whatever his Shadow King, Magian, or Lover want. Particularly, he sees himself as entitled to be the powerful one in control.

Another aspect of his worldview that is significant here is his mentality of scarcity. Like the Masochist, he believes there is not enough to go around. This, of course, is what gives rise to his unrelenting and aggressive competitiveness in personal, social, and professional settings. A certain type and amount of competition creates benefits for individuals and society. It encourages us to pursue excellence, and it can make us stronger and more aware. But for the Sadist—lacking boundaries and respect for others and fueled by a sense of entitlement—competition is a hostile and destructive grab for whatever might satisfy his cravings.

> For the Sadist, competition is a hostile and destructive grab for whatever might satisfy his cravings.

Shadow Mission

Earlier in this chapter we discussed the Warrior's function of pursuing a mission in service to the King. Like the Whole Warrior, the Shadow Warrior also has a mission, which consists of putting into action the vision of his Shadow King. In his book, *Overcoming Your Shadow Mission*, John Ortberg describes a shadow mission as "patterns of thought and action based on temptations and our own selfishness that lead us to betray our deepest values."

A shadow mission is what takes over automatically when we aren't actively pursuing an authentic mission. We aren't ever completely stagnant—we are always moving in one direction or another. So without the positive intention of an authentic mission—even if we're barely conscious of that intention—we will soon enough devolve into pursuing shadowy purposes. Again, from *Overcoming Your Shadow Mission*:

> A shadow mission is what takes over automatically when we aren't actively pursuing an authentic mission.

> We cannot live in the absence of purpose. Without an authentic
> mission, we will be tempted to drift on autopilot, to let our lives
> center around something that is unworthy, something selfish,
> something dark—a shadow mission.

Our shadow missions will involve the coordinated efforts of our unhealthy and fragmented parts in their best attempt to defeat us. So in considering what our shadow missions might be, we must assume that they may involve shadow qualities of all the archetypes. Always at the heart of it will be the vision of the Shadow King.

The Shadow King's Vision

The Whole King's vision is his perspective on life and his place in the world, the powerful and motivating ideas that he feels compelled to create, and his goal or sense of where he's going—all of which derive from truths that have come to him from a higher source. For the Shadow King—whether Tyrant or Weakling—the "truth" that has come to him from the higher sources of parents and other adults or children is that he's worthless. This message came along with the wounds that brought a sad end to his Divine Child. So his perspectives, ideas, and goals will all revolve around, and be colored by, that damaged core sense of self.

At the active pole of the Shadow King, the Tyrant aggressively attempts to deny his sense of worthlessness by advancing and aggrandizing himself at the expense of those around him. His vision will therefore consist of perspectives that are narcissistic, ideas that are rigid and over–inflated, and goals that are arrogant and controlling. At the passive pole, the Weakling accepts and collapses into his worthlessness, abdicating his responsibilities and relinquishing his power. So his vision consists of perspectives that are confused and chaotic, ideas that are sterile and lifeless, and goals that are vague and ultimately abandoned.

The visions of both the Tyrant and Weakling are self–centered because neither can see past themselves. Both are held fast in the gravitational pull of insecurity about their lack of validity, worth, and purpose. Both are obsessed with assuring and protecting the status and wellbeing of their wounded selves. So they have nothing left over to contribute to others—they can't create, inspire, bless, or provide for anyone else. ✍ 5.26

Action and Shadow Mission

The unhealthiness of the Shadow King's vision will be propagated and compounded by actions that grow out of the Shadow Warrior's cruelty or self–hatred, the Shadow Magian's manipulations or naiveté, and the Shadow Lover's addictions or impotence. And just as the actions of a healthy mission will be those we're

> For the Shadow King, the "truth" that has come to him from the higher sources of parents and others is that he's worthless.

passionate about doing, so the actions of a shadow mission will be those that please or soothe our wounded shadow parts. Adapting Frederick Buechner's statement quoted earlier, we might say that the place our shadow calls us is where our deep pain and the world's ability to fill our cravings meet.

The actions of our shadow missions will tend to either cover up our wounds or to act out our wounds. Either way, they won't bring healing and growth. They will violate the values and purposes of our Whole King. They will be propelled by negative feelings like doubt, fear, shame, anger, lust, or envy. And they won't truly satisfy the genuine need for mission, but will ultimately leave us empty.

How can we avoid being pulled into our shadow mission? By staying actively engaged in our authentic mission. Positive action is the best antidote against slipping into shadow. But it's also tremendously helpful to be on the lookout for our shadow mission's encroachment on our lives. It is easy to begin sliding into the shadows even while we think we're still pursuing wholesome purposes and intentions. We can begin to "drift on autopilot," as Ortberg suggested, without being aware of it. Knowledge of our shadow mission can provide an early warning system to wake us up before we've drifted too far.

How can we come to know our shadow mission? By knowing our Shadow King's vision and how our Shadow Warrior puts that vision into action. First, consider that a shadow mission is often the exact inverse of the Whole Warrior's mission. Simply turning our mission on its head may give us some ideas. There is also much we can learn by watching for the things that take us out of our authentic mission and by noticing where our thoughts and actions drift on those occasions. By observing the ways we fill our cravings or cover up, soothe, or act out our wounds, we can also gain insights into our shadow mission. 5.27

THE SYNERGISTIC WARRIOR

Now that we've looked in depth at the traits of the Whole Warrior as well as at both of his shadow poles, let's review the Warrior archetype in its entirety from a high–level perspective to see the full spectrum of his traits. The intention here is to help you consider the synergy that's available through accessing and integrating the Warrior's opposing active and passive potentials. As you read this section, keep in mind that the Warrior's two shadows are an interdependent pair. Moore and

---

The place our shadow calls us is where our deep pain and the world's ability to fill our cravings meet.

Shadow Vision
(the darkness I create)

+

Action
(what I do to create it)

=

Shadow Mission

Gillette write in *The Warrior Within* that the Masochist "has a wound exactly the size and shape of the Sadist's sword."

As I've explained previously, when an archetype becomes split, we tend to identify more fully with one pole and to repress the energy of the other pole, which we then project onto people in the world around us. This suggests that if we find ourselves in the Masochist pole experiencing persecution by sadists in our lives, those sadists are only there to represent—or hold the place of—our own repressed active Warrior energy. Integrate that energy, and we will no longer need external sadists to bring our passive Warrior shadow into balance. When we own our shadows, the sadists will disappear.

Below is the same Warrior Trait Scales table you saw in Chapter One. Take a few minutes now to re–familiarize yourself with it. A good way to do this is to first look at it vertically by column. Review the Sadist column, then the Masochist column. Next review both of the Moderation columns together. After you've done that, review the table horizontally one trait scale at a time, considering the full range of the attributes associated with that trait. Use the numbered paragraphs after the table to help you understand the details of each scale.

As you review the scales, I encourage you to consider how each trait may be manifested in your life. Find your tendencies on each scale, remembering that we often have a range and may slide back and forth from one side to another, depending on our circumstances. 5.28

Warrior Trait Scales

Traits	Sadist	Moderation		Masochist
1. Power	Overpowering	Disciplined	Relenting	Powerless
2. Feeling	Numb	Detached	Aware	Ruled by Feelings
3. Anger	Rageful	Aggressive	Calm	Depressed
4. Allegiance	Defiant	Independent	Loyal	Dependent
5. Trust	Paranoid	Vigilant	Open	Gullible
6. Self-care	Reckless	Courageous	Self-preserving	Cowardly
7. Relationality	Controlling/Cruel	Detached	Receptive	Victimized
8. Sociability	Antisocial	Assertive	Yielding	Disempowered

1. Power

This scale relates to how we use power and respond to our own vulnerability. The Sadist *overpowers* others who are weaker than himself. He is in a relentless war against weakness and views himself as invulnerable, living as if he had no fear. He envies and resents those who are stronger than he. In moderation, the active side of the Warrior takes a *disciplined* approach to overcoming vulnerability. He keeps the battle against weakness inside himself where it belongs. He comes to terms with his vulnerability and believes in his innate strength. He seeks to increase his personal power in a focused, aggressive, and balanced way. He doesn't fear stronger men, but sees all men as his equal.

The Masochist lives according to an agreement of *powerlessness*, dishonestly denying his need for power. He avoids competition and is falsely nice, weak, and cooperative. He fears and resents those who are strong. The more moderate passive side of the Warrior is *relenting*, which means that he can surrender, when necessary, to an overwhelming force. He's honest about his desire for power. He's also honest about his vulnerabilities and weaknesses and may even find ways that he and others can benefit from them. He's cooperative, flexible, and pleasant to work with. He respects the strengths he sees in other men.

2. Feeling

This scale relates to our internal experience of feelings, both physical and emotional. The Sadist is *numb* to his feelings. He shuts out tender emotions toward other people as well as feelings of joy and excitement. He also blocks out uncomfortable feelings like pain, grief, sadness, and fear. With moderation, the active side of the Warrior is healthfully *detached* from his feelings when life circumstances require it. But this disconnection is conscious and under his control. He's able to tolerate pain and discomfort, which is necessary for his disciplined approach to life.

The Masochist is *ruled by feelings*—mainly his negative ones. He experiences them as familiar, safe, or even comforting. In moderation, this aspect of the passive Warrior is emotionally *aware* and able to feel. He's informed by his negative emotions and may even be energized by pain and struggle when it feels meaningful or serves a valuable purpose. But he can also tune in to a broader range of emotions, including those that are pleasant and joyful.

3. Anger

This scale describes the range of ways in which we might respond to our anger. The Sadist is *rageful* from a deep unresolved anger over the loss of his masculine power. Some sadistic anger is passionate and fiery. But rage can also be expressed in cold and calculated ways. In moderation, the energy behind the active Warrior's anger is channeled into positive and useful *aggression*. His anger has been matured into personal power, and he uses that power to benefit himself and those around him. He touches the feeling of anger only sparingly, always remembering that it must be sacrificed in order to stay out of shadow.

The Masochist is *depressed*, which is actually an implosion of his own volcanic rage. In moderation, the passive side of the Warrior is *calm*. He possesses a healthy awareness and dislike of anger's destructive potential and consciously surrenders it. He has come to terms with his childhood loss of masculine power and is, therefore, unruffled in situations that require him to be quiet and still.

4. Allegiance

This scale considers the nature of our relationship with our Transpersonal Other. The Sadist is *defiant* of authority and can't be led. His sense of validity and worth depend on proving his own power by defying greater authority. In moderation, this active Warrior trait is a capacity for *independent* action in the service of a shared or personal mission. It's the ability to take initiative and think for himself. He's a leader, actively creating his own mission. He may even be the founder of a higher purpose that other men serve. And he derives a certain amount of affirmation from the fulfillment of his mission.

The Masochist is *dependent* on the help and reassurance of people, organizations, or beings that are more powerful than he. Any mission or sense of purpose he has is borrowed from others. He can't affirm himself or derive validity or worth from his Self. In moderation, this passive Warrior trait becomes a *loyal* allegiance to a strong Transpersonal Other, which may be the source and center of his mission. He possesses strong faith and commitment toward worthy authorities and is responsive to direction from them. His sense of validity and worth are enhanced by—but not dependent on—service to a cause greater than himself.

5. Trust

This scale depicts the degree to which we trust our surroundings and other people with our safety. The Sadist is *paranoid*—suspicious that others have hostile intentions toward him. But his paranoia reflects a projection of his own hostility. A more moderate active Warrior response is to be *vigilant* in situations where harm is possible. Effective vigilance requires him to be alert, conscious, and discerning. He understands and is informed by his own hostile tendencies. And because he has integrated those tendencies, he doesn't project them onto those around him.

The Masochist is *gullible*—naïve and foolishly open to other people. His ability to set and hold boundaries is diminished, and he's easily deceived and manipulated. In moderation, this trait becomes an *open* attitude toward others. It's an ability to see and draw out the genuine goodness, kindness, and generosity in others and a willingness to be open in relationships. This perspective is possible because he's aware of his own good intentions toward those around him.

6. Self–Care

This scale considers the kinds of internal boundaries we might maintain to protect our own wellbeing. The Sadist is *reckless* regarding his own wellbeing. He has poor internal boundaries around his emotions and behaviors and doesn't know when to stop. He's oblivious to his own mortality. As a more moderate active Warrior trait, this is a *courageous* attitude toward danger and risk and an ability to persevere in the face of fatigue. His internal boundaries don't hold him back from risking either injury or death in the fulfillment of his mission. So he doesn't withhold himself in battle.

The Masochist is *cowardly*—excessively concerned with his own safety and comfort. His fear of pain and death cause him to put up very restrictive internal boundaries. In more moderate doses, this passive Warrior trait is *self–preserving*. Internal boundaries are enforced to preserve life and wellbeing. Because he knows that death is always an immediate possibility, he's intensely focused and careful with his life.

7. Relationality

This scale relates to the types of interpersonal boundaries we might manifest. The Sadist is *controlling* and *cruel* in his individual relationships. His disrespect of personal boundaries and inability to trust lead him to exert excessive control over others in order to maintain power. His lack of compassion disables him from recognizing and respecting other's rights. When he's "authentic," it is actually just a rude expression of raw emotion. In moderation, this active trait allows the Warrior to be emotionally *detached* from others when necessary. He observes appropriate boundaries, but they don't inhibit him when he has to confront someone. He's emotionally independent enough that he doesn't become entrapped in unhealthy relationships. And, lacking any underlying sadistic rage, his authenticity is never destructive.

The Masochist permits himself to be *victimized* by the sadists around him, whom he unconsciously draws to himself. He tries to minimize the abuse he receives by hiding and repressing his true self, which he sees as faulty and flawed. Thus, he lives an inauthentic life, which prevents him from standing up for himself. His underlying anger may be expressed through passive–aggressive behavior. In moderation, this is a *receptive* and tolerant personality. The ability to moderate this trait comes from working through underlying anger and developing proper self–esteem. With that work completed, he's able to relate well with others by stepping outside himself and tuning into their feelings. He doesn't lack authenticity, but he can withhold its expression when appropriate. He is not compelled to always be heard. And he's able to express his displeasure in humane yet truthful ways.

8. Sociability

This scale overviews how we relate to society. The Sadist is *antisocial*. He tends to be disrespectful of social customs, norms, and boundaries, disregarding of professional ethics, and disobedient of the law. He may see himself as entitled to have whatever he wants, particularly power and control. And he's often aggressively competitive. A more moderate version of this trait is an *assertive* stance toward society and community. He's respectful of social customs, norms, and boundaries without being constrained by them. He might actively work to change oppressive elements within his society. He views the world as full of abundance and assertively gathers the material things that flow to him.

The Masochist is *disempowered*. He tends to comply with social customs, norms, and boundaries in an overly submissive and self–destructive way. He may see himself as disfranchised—without privileges, rights, a voice, or an opinion. He fears competing in the world and assumes he must go without what he needs and wants. A moderate version of this trait is *yielding* to, and actively defending, appropriate and honored social customs, norms, and boundaries. He doesn't place himself above any other person in society, seeing all as equal and deserving of fair treatment. He patiently accepts those elements of his community that he can't change. And he's willing to wait for the flow of abundance.

YOUR MISSION NOW

The purpose of life for a Whole Warrior is to use our masculine power in pursuit of a mission greater than ourselves. The Warrior understands that service to something higher is the very reason for which our power is intended. In fact, the most conscious and committed Warrior would actually fear even the possibility of misusing or wasting his power.

> The Warrior understands that service to something higher is the very reason for which our power is intended.

That's not to say that Whole Warriors have to always and only use their strength to serve their higher purpose. We can and should enjoy practicing and stretching our Warrior skills through games and sports. Activities that discipline us, increase our courage, and channel our aggression into productive energy build strong Warrior power, and we should definitely be involved in such things. And it's good, on occasion, to watch other men flex their Warrior capacities through sporting events and movies. This can inspire and stir up the Warrior within us.

We do need to be discerning, however, because much of the Warrior behavior that is culturally enjoyed these days is quite shadowy. Most of what we see of the Warrior today is just various shades of sadism. The best way to keep the Warrior pure and whole, especially when accessing him for entertainment, is to keep the King in charge. The King's vision needs to stay at the core of our lives. He needs to remain the source of our validity, worth, and purpose. We need to allow our inner King to keep us balanced, moderated, and integrated. And we must subordinate ourselves to his law.

> The best way to keep the Warrior pure and whole is to keep the King in charge.

Finally, we need to be cautious about how strongly we correlate Warrior and masculinity. As I mentioned at the beginning of this chapter, Warrior traits make us feel masculine in a way that none of the other archetypes do. But the Warrior is only one quadrant of whole masculinity. His energy needs to be strongly present in a man, but it must also be balanced and rounded out with the traits of the other three.

[1] The Hero is an archetype of boyhood and the forerunner to the Warrior. See Moore and Gillette, *King Warrior Magician Lover*.

[2] I describe this type of thinking in greater detail in Chapter Eleven. If you want to know more about it now, peek ahead to the section in that chapter entitled "Weapons of Feeling."

[3] Other forms of this agreement may be that power is dangerous, that it is evil, or that he will be punished or even killed if he shows his power.

[4] We will discuss the concept of *true self* in Chapter Nine. Refer to it if you want context for that concept now.

[5] See *The Penguin Dictionary of Psychology*, p. 43.

Chapter 6

Masculinity

The great passion in a man's life may not be for women or men or
wealth or toys or fame, or even for his children, but for his masculinity,
and at any point in his life he may be tempted to throw over the things
for which he regularly lays down his life for the sake of that masculinity.

Frank Pittman, *Man Enough*

e will follow the previous chapter's discussion of the Warrior
archetype with a discussion of the principle of masculinity. I
connect these two because, according to all my observations,
Warrior is the archetype that most directly creates a felt sense
of masculinity. This is not because Warrior is the masculine
archetype—all of the archetypes are aspects of whole masculinity. Rather, this is
true because the Warrior archetype is the energy that feels most distinct from the
feminine. And as the renowned psychiatrist Robert Stoller humorously observed
in his book, *Presentations of Gender*, "The first order of business in being a man
is: don't be a woman."

But being a man is not just about *not* being female. There is a *Tao* of maleness—a way
in which maleness happens and is expressed. Masculinity is the expression of that
way. Masculinity is a very diverse *way*—so diverse that it defies description except
in the broadest terms. I defined it in the introduction of this book as "that which is
spontaneously manifested by men when they are connected to their manhood."

In this chapter we're going to review some core principles of masculinity—or the
Tao of maleness. We'll use the model I've come to call *gender wholeness* to lay
out the foundation of what seems—from my twenty years of carefully considering
this—to allow men to experience themselves as masculine within a gendered
world—a world of two sexes. Reduced to its most basic concepts, gender wholeness

is about experiencing sufficient masculinity while also comprehending the feminine. Put differently, gender wholeness implies feeling complete with regard to our own gender and experiencing a healthy sense of completion through the opposite sex.

GENDER WHOLENESS

As I mentioned in Chapter One, wholeness underlies most of what we'll discuss in this book. In this chapter we've arrived at one of the most important aspects of wholeness—that is, wholeness related to our sense of gender. But what does that mean? What does it mean to feel sufficient masculinity; to feel complete with regard to your own gender? What does it mean to comprehend the feminine; to experience completion through the opposite sex? Let's open these concepts and consider them carefully.

First, let's consider what it means to feel complete with our own gender. Much of the power behind same–sex attraction, for most of us who have experienced it, seems to be related to two unmet core needs. The first need is to feel deeply connected with our own masculinity. The second core need is to feel connected to other men. When these needs for connection are met, men experience what I call *masculine sufficiency*.

The word "sufficiency" has two meanings: one, to be qualified or competent, and two, to have enough. Likewise, masculine sufficiency also has two meanings. First, it means that we see ourselves as qualified and competent as men. I refer to this internal state of masculinity as *gender congruity*. And second, masculine sufficiency means that we feel like we have enough connection with other men. I refer to this interpersonal state of masculinity as *same–sex affiliation*, or put more simply, having *community* with other men.

If we boil this all down, masculine sufficiency involves experiencing masculinity both internally and interpersonally. It's about feeling like a man and living among men. For most of us with unwanted same–sex attraction, this combination tends to decrease our sexual feelings toward other men and to increase feelings of personal masculinity and brotherhood with other men. This is why understanding and developing masculine sufficiency is so essential to the process of shifting our sexual attractions.

Two core needs:

- To feel deeply connected with our own masculinity

- To feel connected to other men

Now let's consider the second component of gender wholeness, which is having a healthy sense of connection with the opposite sex. Same–sex attraction is not the only gender–related issue most men who deal with it are experiencing. Many of us are also dealing with problems in our ability to relate with the opposite sex—with females and femininity. Men need a healthy comprehension of the feminine. So now, you guessed it, I'm going to define "comprehension." It also has two definitions. First, it can be defined as seeing the nature, significance, or meaning of something—in other words understanding or grasping a principle or concept. And the second definition of comprehension is to include something—as in to be comprehensive or to involve or embrace something in a way that makes things complete.

> Men need a healthy comprehension of the feminine.

Comprehension of the feminine means that we, as men, see the nature and significance of the feminine and grasp its meaning to us. And it means that we include, involve, and embrace the feminine in ways that make us complete. Like masculine sufficiency, comprehension of the feminine may be experienced in both internal and interpersonal ways. Interpersonally, we may experience the significance and meaning of the opposite sex in our lives and enjoy the completeness of the two genders together. This is what I described in Chapter Three as *complementarity* of the feminine with the masculine. I'll add some perspective to this concept later. Internally, we may experience elements of the feminine within ourselves. This feminine within the masculine is referred to as *Anima* and I'll introduce that later as well. The diagram below shows the relationships among the topics we'll be discussing.

> Comprehension of the feminine means that we see the nature and significance of the feminine and grasp its meaning to us.

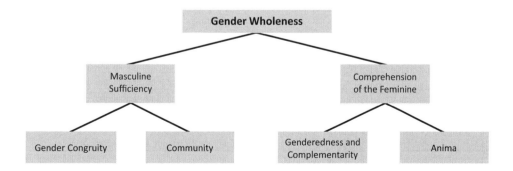

Now, let's begin closest to home with a man's inner sense of masculinity.

Gender Congruity

The word "congruity" means being in a state of harmony or conformity with something else—to match or be comparable. Gender congruity is an inner sense that our gender traits substantially and adequately match the traits that are common among others of our own given sex. This might also be described as a conviction that who and what we are as men corresponds with what we believe men should be.

A man with gender congruity looks at the other men around him and thinks, "I am like them, and they are like me." This doesn't mean he thinks they are exactly alike, but in all the ways that really matter to him, they are close enough. The opposite of gender congruity is *gender incongruity*. A man experiencing gender incongruity thinks, "I am not like other men and they are not like me—I am different." We'll discuss gender incongruity in detail in the next chapter.

> A man with gender congruity looks at the other men around him and thinks, "I am like them, and they are like me."

Gender congruity can be looked at from two perspectives: personal traits and societal roles. We'll discuss the societal roles in a moment, but first let's consider the personal traits that seem to impact a man's sense of congruity.

> We tend to compare our view of ourselves in these areas with our concept of how men are "supposed" to be.

Personal Traits: I've identified six personal traits that seem to show up as areas of concern for men with same–sex attraction. We tend to compare our view of ourselves in these areas with our concept of how men are "supposed" to be. The more closely we see ourselves as matching our perception of the norm, the more congruent we tend to feel. And conversely, the more different we see ourselves as being from our concept of what men should be, the more incongruent we tend to feel. As you read about these traits, think about how congruent or incongruent you feel regarding each one. 6.1

- **Body,** specifically whether our bodies match what we believe a man's body is supposed to be like. This typically includes physical attractiveness in terms of stature, physique, and appearance. But it may also include age, coordination, strength, stamina, and athletic abilities.

- **Power,** which includes traits like confidence, assertion, effectiveness, courage, and independence. It seems to be generally true that when men feel powerful we also feel masculine or gender congruent.

- **Feelings**. This varies greatly from man to man, but each of us has a personal code of conduct regarding how we, as men, are supposed to experience, handle, and express our feelings. Breaking that code can leave us feeling incongruent and shameful.

- **Relationality**. How comfortable and conversant we are in relationships with other men and the ways in which we interact with women are the key factors here. This may include whether we see ourselves as capable of handling relationships with other men in a masculine way and whether we see ourselves as able to engage in relationships with women as we believe a "normal" man should.

- **Capacities and intelligence**. The stories we tell about what we do, what we like, and what we're good at can greatly impact our sense of congruity. Although this varies as well, most men see certain careers, interests, and aptitudes as masculine and others as feminine. We'll talk about this more when we discuss societal roles.

- **Sexuality**. This can include the nature and target of our sexual and romantic attractions, our perspective regarding the frequency and nature of our sexual experiences, the role we assume in sexual situations, and our beliefs about how good we are at sex.

I don't subscribe to the idea that men must or should be a certain way regarding any of the traits outlined above. But our families and society do provide us with some pretty strong expectations, which we tend to adopt. If we're to experience gender congruity, we must deal with those expectations one way or another— either we must conform to them or we must adjust our own expectations. Likely, most of us will do some of both.

Gender Roles: Society also provides us with gender roles, which are essentially expectations of what men and women are supposed to be and do. Each society has its own versions of these roles. Anthropologists who have studied human cultures and societies around the world give us a more long–term perspective on male roles. Four basic roles seem to emerge: presiding, providing, protecting, and mastering the environment. As with the personal traits described previously, we men tend to compare ourselves with each other in terms of these gender roles, with the same outcome of either feeling congruent or incongruent with our gender. ✍ 6.2

> Gender roles are societal expectations of what men and women are supposed to be and do.

- **Presiding** is another way of describing the King's role of bringing order, which you will recall includes the capacities of centering, balancing, moderation, integration, organizing, and giving law. In practical terms today, this can imply leadership and having authority, control, or influence in some sphere—whether within the home, on the job, within an organized religion, in the government, or elsewhere.

- **Providing** represents another aspect of the King archetype—that of "blessing the people." We also talked about this in Chapter Two. Providing also involves the Warrior's transpersonal commitment, which we discussed in Chapter Five, in that we're contributing to something greater than ourselves. In practical terms today, providing includes at very least supplying food, shelter, and other necessities of life for ourselves. It involves taking responsibility for our personal growth and fulfillment. And it may entail insuring the continuation of the species through procreation and caring for the next generation.

- **Protecting** is a significant aspect of the Warrior's function of setting and enforcing boundaries. We also discussed this in Chapter Five. In practical terms today, this might mean establishing and maintaining limits in our thoughts, feelings, and behavior, and in our external life to protect ourselves and those we have responsibility for. Sometimes it may require taking action to protect ourselves and others from physical or emotional harm.

- **Mastering the environment** is a function of the Magian archetype, whose special knowledge of physical and spiritual matters gives him great powers that he can channel in productive ways. This will be discussed in greater detail in Chapter Eight. Mastering the environment also requires the Warrior's self–discipline, discernment, and sometimes his tolerance of pain in order to apply the Magian's knowledge to the needs of daily living. In practical terms today, mastering the environment may mean carving out a place for ourselves in the world, succeeding in our careers, being able to get around in unfamiliar circumstances, and being handy.

Within each of these roles there is great diversity. Some ways of fulfilling these roles may be seen in society as more masculine than others. But the roles themselves are, at least in our world today, rather fixed. It's not essential that we conform to socially–defined ways of fulfilling male roles. But it's important for us to come to terms with those role definitions and, more importantly, we must come to terms with our own ways of fulfilling them.

It's important for us to come to terms with role definitions and our own ways of fulfilling them.

The Need for Male Community

It's natural and normal for people to want to associate with others of our own gender. For men, this is a function of what we call the Lover archetype, which we'll discuss in much greater depth in Chapter Ten. Boys "hang out" together through much of childhood and adolescence. Grown men often seek each other's company for recreation and support. These relationships play an essential role in fulfilling the basic human need for affiliation and companionship. They are also essential in the development of masculinity. In *Man Enough*, Frank Pittman writes, "When men bond, they absorb one another's strengths."

I use the term "same–sex affiliation needs" to describe these normal desires to be in community with others of our own gender. The word "affiliation" means relationship, connection, or association. It implies close contact, including cooperation and companionship, bonding, and love. Affiliation is about being united with or adopted into a relationship or community.

I believe there are four essential same–sex affiliation needs. They are attachment, resonance, approval, and support. I have noticed that adequately meeting these needs tends to diminish homosexual attractions for many men. Remember that core needs are non–negotiable as I pointed out in Chapter Three. So when our needs for community aren't met, our unconscious selves—our shadows—will find ways to approximate meeting the need. Many men I've talked with believe that sexualizing other men is one of those approximations. So let's discuss these important needs one at a time. ✍ 6.3

Same–sex affiliation needs:

- Attachment
- Resonance
- Approval
- Support

Attachment is an emotional tie between two people where there is some degree of healthy inter–dependency with each other for emotional satisfaction. It's a binding affection that includes feelings of tenderness and warmth. Attachments can exist between a father and son, between brothers, and among male friends. Attachments are characterized by enjoyment of each other, wanting to be together, and sadness at being separated.

The story of David and Jonathan in the Bible is an excellent example of attachment. The tie that developed almost immediately between these two men lasted throughout their lives. So strong was their mutual affection that, on learning of Jonathan's death, David lamented, "I am distressed for thee, my brother Jonathan: very pleasant hast thou been unto me: thy love to me was wonderful, passing the love of women" (2 Samuel 1:26 *KJV*).

Resonance is a word that has been borrowed from the world of sound and vibrations to describe a state when the *energy, feelings, and attitudes* within a group of people are set off, maintained, intensified, and enriched by interactions among the group. When a group of boys is playing together, they resonate with each other's energy. It's probable that this is a central aspect of gender identity development. The resonance among them may well be how boys take in the "energy" of being male. It's not enough to just be present with the other boys— it's necessary to "resonate" with them. In this way, a boy sees aspects of himself reflected in the boys around him, creating or deepening both gender congruity and same–sex affiliation.

> Resonance may well be how boys take in the "energy" of being male.

Approval is the favorable attitude or opinion of other people. This implies positive acceptance within a group that wants our presence among them. In a sense, their acceptance is a ratification of our value to them. They are affirming our existence and worth. Validation in male–male relationships comes from feeling affirmed as being like them, being "one of the guys." This approval further contributes to gender congruity.

> Validation in male–male relationships comes from feeling affirmed as being like them, being "one of the guys."

Although men typically don't express their approval for one another through direct statements, their acceptance and enjoyment of each other is often apparent in the way they smile and speak energetically to each other. Sometimes men express their approval of other men through teasing and even through humorous insults. This can be confusing unless we realize that the insult is a way of expressing familiarity. It's as if they are saying, "We're so tight that I can say *anything* to you."

Support implies, at its most basic level, holding up, bolstering, and providing needed help whether that help is temporal, physical, emotional, mental, or spiritual. At times, friendship calls us to comfort and strengthen each other, to provide encouragement or admonition. Support can also mean promoting the wellbeing of a friend, contributing to his success or advancement.

My friendship with a man named Tom typifies the concept of support. Soon after I met him, I wanted to install a microwave oven in my kitchen. Tom is a handyman and he enthusiastically offered to do it for me. That was the first of several projects he helped me with. Some of the projects, like my complete office makeover, were a substantial sacrifice for him. He supported me also through hearing the story of my same–sex attraction at a time when I was really struggling with it. He was a stabilizing factor through my mid–life crisis. He never judged me, but rather expressed words of encouragement and acceptance. Later, when Tom's wife had an affair and subsequently divorced him, it was my opportunity to return the support through listening, encouragement, advice, and direct statements of love.

Elements of Community

Some male communities provide abundantly for the fulfillment of the affiliation needs we've just been discussing, while other communities fulfill these needs in only meager ways. In the section on comrades in Chapter Three, I described six elements that make for strong friendships and strong male communities. The presence of those six elements in our relationships with other men increases the likelihood that we'll be able to fulfill the affiliation needs we talked about previously. I've synopsized those six elements of community below for you to consider in this context.

Elements of Community
- Commonality
- Trust
- Authenticity
- Reciprocity
- Healthy boundaries
- Unconditional love and compassion

Commonality can come from sharing a mission or adventure, living near each other, working or worshiping together, or sharing interests and other personality traits.

Trust is necessary if two men are going to even begin interacting with each other. Trust starts on very basic levels involving physical and emotional safety and then can develop to very high levels that allow for deep sharing and reliance on each other.

Authenticity entails awareness of our own feelings, wants, and desires, and openness about these with the men around us. How authentic two friends become is largely dependent on how much trust they have developed. Authenticity and trust have a reciprocal relationship—each can affect the other in both positive and negative ways.

Reciprocity implies that both men in a friendship share a similar interest in each other and in the friendship. Both men work to make the friendship successful by being available for each other and keeping their commitments.

Healthy Boundaries protect the friendship from being destroyed from within through violations of trust or by the relationship becoming draining, manipulative, or too close.

Unconditional Love and Compassion mean that our feelings and actions toward our friends are guided and inspired by our love of our friend's "true self" qualities. Despite what he reveals about himself and even when we disagree with him, we allow his good traits to eclipse his personal flaws. It's love and compassion that raise friendships to their highest level and make them most healing.

> It's love and compassion that raise friendships to their highest level and make them most healing.

Communities can exist with nominal amounts of these six elements. Even bowling leagues can have a trace of each element. The more fully these elements exist within a community, the more power that community will have to support and heal men and to transform their lives, which includes, for many men with unwanted same–sex attraction, helping them to shift the focus of their sexual feelings. Your challenge is to develop these six elements in relationships that already exist in your life, or to create new relationships that are rich in these qualities.

Community and Mission

There are two forces that we must harness in order to break through the obstacles that stand in the way of living our mission. One force is internal and the other is external. The internal force is the energy of the Warrior that each of us carries. The external force is the energy of a community of men.

> A wise Warrior goes into battle with comrades by his side; he doesn't attempt to do it alone.

A wise Warrior goes into battle with comrades by his side; he doesn't attempt to do it alone. With brothers by his side he can face his foe directly, knowing that someone has his back. And, when necessary, he can attend to his wounds without fears about his own defense. As you continue the process of clarifying and living your mission—your "battle to fight"—don't forget the power you can access through a community of men. ✎ 6.4

Genderedness and Complementarity

It's time for us now to move beyond mere masculine sufficiency and begin exploring the two aspects involved in comprehension of the feminine, beginning with complementarity. We discussed complementarity at length in Chapter Three in the section on "Genderedness and Complementarity," which is one of the six core needs. Here we'll briefly review what we've already learned, adding a few elaborations.

Genderedness, you may remember, is the natural state of having two sexes that are distinct and different from one another. Genderedness is a given of which we're all aware on some level. But to fully experience genderedness we have to get it on all levels—consciously and unconsciously—mentally, emotionally, and physically.

Genderedness begins with a clear sense of belonging to the sex dictated by your body. You must also be aware of the factors that distinguish your own sex from the other.

Genderedness begins with a clear sense of belonging to the sex dictated by your body—if your body is male, you need to feel like you *are* male. You must also be aware of the factors that distinguish your own sex from the other, including the obvious physical differences as well as the differences in personality traits like interests, motivations, emotionality, and relational tendencies. And then you need to believe that your gender traits match, to some degree, those of your own given sex and are sufficiently different from the gender traits of the opposite sex.

This conscious knowledge provides a certain awareness of genderedness—we understand that we are male and that women are very different creatures. But this is just the beginning of experiencing genderedness. There is a far deeper awareness of gender that comes, not from our minds, but from nonconscious places within us. To really comprehend genderedness, our bodies have to *feel* it more than our minds need to *understand* it. Let's look at this from an archetypal perspective.

More than any other archetype, genderedness in men seems to derive from a strong connection to Warrior energy. As I said at the beginning of this chapter, I believe this is true because Warrior is the archetype that feels most distinct from the feminine. Consider the following comparisons between feminine energy and the Warrior masculine:

- The feminine is relational and emotionally aware. Warrior tends to be the opposite—aloof, unrelated, and emotionally distant. He's the source of boundaries and imposing limits.

- The feminine is soft and receptive. Warrior is aggressive—the source of power, focused direction, and forward action.

- The feminine nurtures new life. The Warrior embraces the finality of death. He's the destroyer of old and corrupt ways of life.

- The feminine is unconditionally accepting. The Warrior imposes demands and requires discipline and the development of skills.

When men experience within themselves the Warrior traits described previously, we tend to feel more masculine. We experience greater gender congruity. When we experience ourselves with these traits in the presence of a woman, we feel more gendered. To explain this further, let's switch tracks and look at it from the perspective of resonance, which we discussed a few pages back as one of the same-sex affiliation needs.

I don't understand all of the conscious and nonconscious processes that create resonance between two males, but those same processes are also at work when men interact with the opposite sex. But in the presence of a woman, men typically feel a very different type of resonance—let's call it a "harmonic resonance." When a man is attracted to a woman he definitely is resonating with her, but they aren't on the same note. They are swirling around each other in harmonious counterpoint. If they were on the same note, the attraction would go flat. And this is why many men with same-sex attraction aren't attracted to women—they are too much on the same note with them, and they don't resonate with other men. ✎ 6.5

It's this harmonic resonance that occurs between men and women that creates *complementarity*. The term complementarity refers to a favorable relationship between the two sexes where each completes, fulfills, balances, and perfects the other. It implies that we see the opposite sex as desirable and as having something valuable to contribute to us. For men, it means seeing women as something that can complete and fulfill us—as our other half. And it means seeing ourselves as having something valuable to contribute to women as well and as being strong enough to make our contribution to them without being drained by their needs. We aren't meant to be without our opposite. We're built to complement—or finish—each other just as the black and white of yin-yang make a complete whole.

Now let's take these concepts one step further and look at how they apply in relationships. It's a man's role to complete his woman's femininity by being firmly grounded in his own masculinity. This allows the woman to remain in her feminine energy and complete her man's masculinity. Author and speaker David Deida talks about this concept in his book, *The Way of the Superior Man*. He uses the term

Complementarity implies that we see the opposite sex as desirable and as having something valuable to contribute to us. And it means seeing ourselves as having something valuable to contribute to women as well.

"polarity" to describe the opposing male and female energies. He describes what I, and others, have observed—that when men disconnect from their own masculine power, women naturally summon up masculine energy from within themselves to stabilize the relationship and get things done. So if I slip into my passive shadows, like the Weakling or the Masochist, my wife will strap on her own Warrior sword and march in service to her Queen Self to protect and provide for the kingdom. Believe me, women have these capacities and they can use them—just like men— for good and for ill.

But Deida makes another point in his book that's of essential interest to our discussion. He says that "polarity" is the source of sexual attraction. Polarity, you can probably guess, refers to the opposing energies of the two sexes. He's echoing my own belief that heterosexuality depends on an appreciation of gender and complementarity between the sexes. Through my work I've known many men who have desexualized their attractions toward the same sex. From what I've observed, they seem to do this by creating masculine sufficiency in their lives. But many of these men have *not* developed heterosexuality, and I've wondered over the years why not. It was just in the last few years that I finally understood the central role of the concepts we've been discussing related to genderedness and complementarity in developing opposite–sex attraction.

Now I realize that these men don't develop attractions toward women because they aren't experiencing genderedness and complementarity. I don't mean to blame them for this—in most cases they haven't consciously chosen to avoid them. I think the problem lies in the fact that those of us who have worked with these men have just begun to understand the secrets that might unlock their ability to experience women as a desirable opposite. ✍ 6.6

Anima

There is one final aspect of comprehension of the feminine that we should explore. Like complementarity, this aspect involves the interplay of masculine and feminine. But here the interplay doesn't occur in a male's relationship with a woman. It occurs in a man's relationship with his own inner feminine.

Carl Jung, whom you may recall originated the concept of masculine archetypes, saw all human qualities as being either masculine or feminine. His perspective is not too unusual—many societies and philosophies have held this same view,

> When men disconnect from their own masculine power, women naturally summon up masculine energy from within themselves to stabilize the relationship and to get things done.

including *Taoism*, which we've already discussed several times. Jung believed that although members of each sex express mostly the traits associated with their own gender, they also exhibit some of the traits of the opposite gender. In other words, it's normal for men to have some feminine traits and for women to have some masculine traits. He used the term "Anima" for the feminine qualities within men.[1]

This is another of the important concepts we learn from the folktale, *Jack and the Beanstalk*. In myths and fairy tales, a young man is often called on to rescue a maiden trapped in a castle or a cave that's guarded by a giant or monster. The young man's mission is to confront the giant or monster and free the maiden. In the story of *Jack and the Beanstalk*, Jack finds his maiden trapped in the castle of the Giant. Jack rescues her, they evade the Giant, and climb down the beanstalk together. In this story, the maiden character has a double meaning, representing both the woman Jack will eventually marry as well as his Anima with which he must connect.

The same theme shows up in another folktale—the story of *Parsifal*, as recounted and interpreted in the book *He* by Robert Johnson. Parsifal begins life as a poor fool, but becomes a great knight of the Round Table under King Arthur's rule. During one episode of his life, Parsifal comes to a kingdom that's ruled by a virgin queen named Blanche Fleur. The young knight is smitten by her beauty and purity and swears his allegiance to her defense.

Blanche Fleur likewise falls in love with Parsifal, and as fate would have it, she is in need of such a defender. Blanche Fleur's kingdom has been under siege by an army of savage warriors for many years. She implores the young knight to rescue her kingdom. Of course, he does exactly that and then, having saved Blanche Fleur's kingdom, the young knight returns to receive her honor and gratitude. As an expression of thanks—and of their love—the young knight and Blanche Fleur spend one night together.

They sleep together in the most intimate embrace—head to head, shoulder to shoulder, hip to hip, and knee to knee. Nevertheless, the embrace is chaste and worthy of a vow the young knight had taken years earlier that he would never seduce nor be seduced by a fair maiden. The next day the young knight bids a tearful farewell to his beloved Blanche Fleur and resumes his journey.

It's normal for men to have some feminine traits. "Anima" is the feminine qualities within men.

Blanche Fleur's kingdom has been under siege by an army of savage warriors for many years.

In myths and fairy tales, just as in dreams, every character can be understood as a representation of the man's own inner world—his own psyche. In these two tales, the Maiden and Blanche Fleur represent the energy of the feminine that resides inside every man. This feminine part of a man's mind and emotions helps mitigate the intensity of his masculine energies, creating balance and bringing wholeness. Without it, a man risks being overwhelmed by the severity of his own Warrior.

In various religious traditions we see the softening power of the feminine in representations of a male Creator–God, a nurturing Heavenly Father, and a compassionate, grace–filled Savior. Each of these depictions of God is perfectly masculine yet tempered by feminine qualities. We see this concept graphically depicted in the yin–yang symbol of Eastern cultures in which the white represents the masculine yang—hard, focused, and aggressive—and the black represents the feminine yin—soft, yielding, and passive. White and black rest side by side. But within the white is a spot of black, which we might imagine represents the man's feminine Anima within his greater masculine. Likewise, the woman also holds a spark of the masculine within her greater feminine. This masculine within a woman is called "Animus," and we might imagine that being represented by the white dot within the yin.

The functions and traits of Anima are rather difficult to discern from what has been written about it. I find this quite fitting for such an ethereal, intangible archetype. What I've observed of her suggests that she is unpredictable and can't be controlled or quantified. She can't be forced and she can't be planned on, although if we make our hearts a welcoming place for her, she will visit more often. She makes her appearances and influences our lives through what we might call "spiritual impressions," meaning intangible and often vague and unexplainable thoughts, ideas, and moods. She shows up as inspiration, intuition, and vision. She animates us and brings things to life. Just as a woman can give birth to a child, so Anima gives birth to understanding, insights, and positive intentions. She is the source from which all abundance flows.[2]

As a man matures in the masculine—in his Warrior, Lover, Magian, and King—he also needs to befriend his Anima. Likewise, as a woman grows in the feminine, she will need to welcome her Animus by developing her more masculine potentials. So in myths and fairy tales, when the young hero rescues a maiden, he is, in fact,

Mitigate: to make something less severe, hostile or intense, more gentle or soft

White represents the masculine yang and black the feminine yin.

When the hero rescues a maiden, he is, in fact, rescuing a part of himself.

rescuing a part of himself. He is setting his Anima free from his own giants and monsters—his fears of his own feminine traits.

But what if the man feels monstrous fear of his feminine side—or giant shame about its existence?

On the other hand, what if the giant that the man fears is not the feminine, but his own terrifying masculine?

But what if the man feels such monstrous fear of his feminine side—or such giant shame about its existence—that instead of fighting that monster, he turns on the Maiden and fights *her* instead? Such a man would attack or bury the very gifts of the feminine that could allow him to feel, relate, and love more deeply than his masculine Warrior ever could on its own.

On the other hand, what if the giant that the man fears is not the feminine, but his own terrifying masculine? Instead of rescuing the Maiden, he might *join* her in the cave and become imprisoned with her. Such a man would become consumed or engulfed by his own femininity. The Maiden then becomes the monster, possessing the body of the man in the form of effeminacy.

This is why Parsifal vowed never to seduce or be seduced by a fair maiden and why he remained chaste in his relationship with Blanche Fleur. The folktale is teaching us that a man must be close to his Anima, but must never be seduced or overcome by it. Though he may love it, he must maintain a boundary with it.

For men who are trying to resolve their homosexuality, freeing our inner–Maiden and integrating her energy can be a tricky dynamic. Many of us have been possessed by our Anima for many years. We may be so tied to our femininity that it's hard to imagine a different masculine–feminine balance. On the other hand, we may have locked our Anima in a dungeon in an attempt to eradicate all the feminine within us. Something in us may revolt at the idea of welcoming those traits. Either extreme is out of balance and stops us short of being whole. However we accomplish it, it's essential that we come to terms with our Anima if we are to experience gender wholeness most fully. ✍ 6.7

TAO IS WHOLENESS

In summary, let's return to the belief that there is a *Tao* of maleness—a way in which maleness happens and is expressed. Masculinity is the expression of that way. And it's a diverse way. No two men will do it the same—this is according to God's design. The point isn't sameness. The point is wholeness within our*selves* and wholeness with our opposite. Consider that masculinity may be defined most simply as "unique mature maleness."

---

[1] For a deeper discussion on this topic, see Appendix C in any of the series of four books written by Moore and Gillette on the archetypes: *The King Within*, *The Warrior Within*, *The Lover Within*, and *The Magician Within*.

[2] Some of what I'm describing here as Anima might alternately be described by Christians as the Holy Spirit. In fact, it could be argued that Anima is merely a secular and psychological explanation of the Spirit. For the purposes of this book, I have no reason to argue this point one way or the other. It's the recognition of this phenomenon that's important.

CHAPTER 7

GENDER DISRUPTION

Unadorned suffering is the bedmate of masculine growth. Only by
staying intimate with your personal suffering can you feel through it
to its source. ... Feel your suffering so deeply and thoroughly that you
penetrate it, and realize its fearful foundation.

David Deida, *The Way of the Superior Man*

 commented in the introduction of this book that we already have
enough books on the problems people face related to homosexuality.
So eleven–twelfths of this book is not about those problems. It's
about growing into wholeness as a man. But I feel compelled to
include one chapter focused just on those problems. I do so in the
hope of offering new conceptualizations and greater insights.

In this chapter, I'll describe patterns of thought, feeling, and behavior that seem to
be rather common in the histories of men with same–sex attraction. I recognized
these patterns gradually over the years through my close interactions with hundreds
of men, each with a unique personality and life story. As these patterns became
clear, some resonated with my own life story while others were altogether new to
me. Also, some of the patterns confirmed theories and conceptualizations I'd been
taught about the life histories of homosexual men. But other patterns conflicted
with or even disconfirmed parts of those theories and conceptualizations.

As I considered how these patterns seemed to emerge and develop through
childhood and into young adulthood, I saw evidence of causation. Thoughts,
feelings, and behaviors at younger ages seemed to cause—or at least heavily
influence—thoughts, feelings, and behaviors at older ages, leading sooner or later
to the emergence of homosexuality. The concept that things at younger ages have

an influence on things at older ages is in keeping with the prevailing developmental theories of our day. However, gay affirming theorists and researchers believe sexual orientation is an exception to the developmental model, adopting instead various biological theories for the existence of homosexuality. But the biological theories don't match the way men have portrayed their life experiences to me, which is why I continue to assert the model outlined here.

I am not pretending to present the final word on what makes people homosexual. I don't believe anyone in the psychological or scientific communities has nearly enough data to pronounce a final word on these topics. Much more—and better—research is needed. Rather, I'm contributing my observations and conceptualizations, which, though not obtained through the scientific method, may nevertheless prove valuable. In this chapter I've chosen only to present the pieces of my overall model that seem essential to the greater purposes of this book.

The patterns of life experiences I observed in the men with whom I worked seemed to point to a common phenomenon shared by the vast majority of them. The common phenomenon was a disruption in their experience of gender. The word "disruption" refers to breaking something apart, throwing it into disorder or turmoil, destroying unity or wholeness, and stopping or preventing something from continuing. This perfectly describes the situation I observed in my own life and the lives of nearly every man with whom I worked. Our sense of our own maleness, our relationships with other males, and our relationships with the opposite sex have all been disrupted in quite a variety of ways.

Put more directly, rather than enjoying masculine sufficiency, we struggle with masculine *in*sufficiency. Rather than experiencing gender congruity, we live with gender *in*congruity. Rather than being sustained by community with other men, we endure disaffiliation from others of our own sex. And rather than perceiving genderedness and complementarity with women, we encounter distortions in our experience of genderedness.

In this chapter we will discuss the details of these various causes of disruption, beginning with the two conditions that tend to create masculine insufficiency. The first of those conditions is termed "gender incongruity," and is a sense of being incompatible with or not conforming to your internalized definition of masculinity. It's caused by gender shame, gender double binds, and gender imperatives. We'll

---

For a more complete outline of the model, go to http://genderwholeness.com and click on the "Understanding" tab.

The patterns of life experiences I observed in the men with whom I worked seemed to point to a common phenomenon—a disruption in their experience of gender.

review each of these in turn. The second condition we'll discuss is "same–sex disaffiliation," which is a disruption in our experience of community with other males. After that we'll turn our attention to the problems that some men with same–sex attraction tend to experience with women, which include unhealthy relational responses to females and gender distortion. The diagram below may help you visually grasp the relationships among all of these topics.

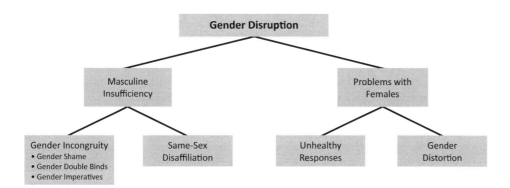

Same–sex attraction is likely to continue as long as men experience masculine insufficiency, but it tends to diminish when our needs for inner and interpersonal masculine connection are sufficiently met. Similarly, diminished or blocked attraction to the opposite sex is also likely to continue as long as our comprehension of the feminine is distorted. Resolving those issues provides the best likelihood of developing opposite–sex attraction. So pay careful attention during these next pages, and see if you can identify core issues that might underlie your own same–sex attraction.

MASCULINE INSUFFICIENCY

It is very likely that few, if any, males spend their entire lives in a perfect state of masculine sufficiency. It is hard to imagine a guy who *always* feels manly enough or who *never* wishes he had more or better connections with other guys. Since we live in an imperfect world, masculine insufficiency is just part of being a man— whether homosexual or heterosexual.

Masculine Insufficiency
- Gender shame
- Gender double binds
- Gender imperatives
- Gender incongruity
- Same–sex disaffiliation

But for men with same–sex attraction, masculine insufficiency is often a very conscious part of our daily lives. Although not all men with same–sex attraction experience disruption in our sense of maleness or connections with other males, the majority of those I've known do. The first four sections below will describe how gender shame, gender double binds, and gender imperatives contribute to gender incongruity. I follow that with a section detailing the specifics of same–sex disaffiliation. I also include two sections with suggestions for dealing with these issues.

Gender Shame

In Chapter Four we discussed shame at some length. We talked about how shame is an ongoing sense of being fundamentally bad, inadequate, defective, or unworthy. Shame can become woven into our sense of who we are. Over time, shame can become a core facet of our identity. We also talked in Chapter Four about how shame can cause us to split off parts of ourselves, leading to what John Bradshaw calls "self–alienation." Shame can become attached specifically to masculinity when a boy internalizes any or all of the following messages: males are bad, it is bad to be male, it is bad for *me* to be male, or I am bad at being male. Each of these messages creates a somewhat different form of gender shame. Let's consider each of these individually.

Males are Bad

Gender shame can develop from a boy's firsthand experience of men behaving badly or stupidly.

Internalizing this message creates a very detached form of gender shame. The man experiencing this feels shame about the gender category of people to which he belongs (males), but he doesn't necessarily include himself in that group. He is detached or disidentified from his own sex so that he isn't one of the "bad males." The message that males are bad can come from hearing others—usually females—berate or insult men as being dumb, brutish, abusive, or inferior in other ways. It may come from hearing women lament about how men have hurt them. And it can develop from a boy's firsthand experience of men behaving badly or stupidly. Experiences like these can turn a boy against his own maleness and negatively color his view of other males. Men may become undesirable figures, blocking the boy's natural desire to emulate them and gradually deepening his disconnection from the world of men. Often the boy will instead look toward females as his role models.

It is Bad to Be Male

With this form of gender shame, the man includes himself in the group of males and feels shame about being in that group and about his own male traits. He thinks, essentially, "I am male and we are bad." This message about maleness is acquired in much the same way as the message that "males are bad," which we discussed previously. Generally, that's by seeing men denigrated by women and seeing them denigrate themselves through their behavior. Because the man experiencing this type of gender shame is not disidentified from his sex, he may feel stronger feelings of conflict and pain. He's essentially living in an intolerable situation— being something that it's bad to be. Here the disconnection from maleness is more internal, sometimes developing into an alienation from his own masculinity.

Denigrate: to bring down the character or reputation of something

It is Bad for *Me* to Be Male

Here the badness about being male is very specific to the boy or man in question. It may be okay for other boys to be male, but for some reason it's not okay for *him* to be male. He may sense that he's not supposed to be male for some reason or that it's not good, acceptable, or safe for him to be masculine. This can occur when a mother communicates to her son in blatant or subtle ways that she wishes he were a girl, that she sees him as a girl, or that she doesn't want him to be or act like a boy. It can develop when sisters or other girls—or sometimes even other boys—tease or humiliate him for acting like a boy. The man who grew up in this situation also lives with the intolerable reality of being what it's bad for him to be. He may try very hard not to be that.

It may be okay for other boys to be male, but for some reason it's not okay for *me* to be male.

Internalizing the three messages I've just described tends to separate men from the maleness within themselves and from the maleness around them. They determine that it's not okay to be it, have it, feel it, or want it. These men often repudiate maleness and masculine traits and hide or repress whatever seems too masculine for approval, trying to fly under the gender radar. The fourth gender shame message, below, is somewhat different.

I Am Bad at Being Male

To understand this message let's refer back to authors Fossum and Mason from Chapter Three. There I quoted them as saying that shame "is an inner sense of being completely diminished or insufficient as a person. It is the self judging the self." Modifying that only slightly we can define this form of gender shame as an inner sense of being completely diminished or insufficient as a male. It's the ego judging our own masculinity. It's the ongoing premise that we're fundamentally bad, inadequate, defective, unworthy, or not fully valid specifically as a male.

Gender shame is an inner sense of being completely diminished or insufficient as a male.

This type of gender shame can come from any source that diminishes a boy's sense of his own masculinity. It can come from females who disparage his maleness. It can come from other boys who taunt, tease, or insult him about his male traits, such as his body, athletic skills, voice, mannerisms, and so forth. And most significantly, this type of gender shame can come from a boy's harsh judgments about his own male attributes.

Internalizing the message, "I am bad at being male," leaves a man with three options: give up, try harder, or try different. The first two options are rather self–evident and probably don't need explanation. The last option, try different, refers to compensating for the perceived lack of masculinity by pursuing non–masculine interests. The nonconscious reasoning goes something like this: "I suck at regular guy stuff, but I'm really good at _____. So that is what I'll do and be."

Gender shame in all the forms described previously disrupts the natural connection that a boy should have with his own masculinity and thereby contributes to gender incongruity. A boy who experiences gender shame can become alienated from his own gender—his own masculinity. From this position, a man might seek things outside himself to make him feel acceptable or whole. This externalization of his masculine wholeness can become sexualized. ✎ 7.1

Gender Double Binds

A double bind is a situation where there is no good way out—where there is pain or trouble no matter what you do. You're damned if you do and damned if you don't. To quote the 1980s punk group, *The Clash*, "If I go there will be trouble / If I stay it will be double." In its most pure form, a double bind occurs when a person is given two messages or commands that contradict or conflict with each other in such a way that responding appropriately to one prevents an appropriate response to the other.

An example of a double bind would be the statement, "You have to do it, but do it because you want to." Let's break this statement down to reveal the conflict. The first message is "You have to do it," which implies that you're being forced, that this is an obligation. An appropriate response to being forced is to feel resistance. But then the second message comes—"do it because you want to." This message suggests freedom and personal choice, and an appropriate response is to feel a sense of internal motivation. The contradiction comes from the reality that personal motivation can't be forced.

> Internalizing the message, "I am bad at being male," leaves a man with three options: give up, try harder, or try different.

> A double bind is a situation where there is no good way out—where there is pain or trouble no matter what you do.

But there is an additional condition to a true double bind, which is that there is no way to address or resolve the contradiction, either because it can't be understood or because it can't be discussed. Often double binds are presented in ways far more subtle than the example given above, so that, although the person in the double bind may sense the conflict, he can't articulate the contradiction. Furthermore, double binds often happen in families where open communication is shamed or punished, or where the family rules demand silent compliance. So even if the boy can articulate the problem, he won't try. This leaves the boy feeling stuck, confused, helpless, and angry.

Let's look at another example of a double bind. Imagine a mother who says "I love you" with a look of disgust on her face. Once again there are two contradictory messages. If you believe the message of her words, the appropriate response is to love her back. If you believe the message on her face, the appropriate response is to feel shamed, hurt, or angry. These responses are in direct conflict—it's very difficult to love her while also feeling wounded by her. And if the family rules are that mother can't be confronted, then there's no resolution—this is a true double bind.

When a boy or a man experiences contradictory messages about males and being male, he's in a gender double bind.

A third example of a double bind would be a mother who cares for your every physical need (the message here is "You are king") but who is critical and emotionally rejecting (the message here is "You are worthless"). This double bind is cinched up if the mother gets angry and pouts when you complain about her rejection and criticism. Here again there is no way to respond properly and there is no way to address the problem.

As you can imagine, double binds leave children feeling helpless and very confused. What adds to their quandary is the reality that double–binding messages are often vague and difficult to identify. As I mentioned previously, they are subtle. You may have noticed in the examples I've given that the messages may not even be spoken. In addition to words, double–bind messages can come from body language (mother's look of disgust), the situation (mother taking care of your needs), and internal wisdom (knowing that personal motivation can't be forced).

Now, back to *gender* double binds. When a boy or a man experiences contradictory messages about males and being male—and he has no way to resolve the contradiction—he's in a gender double bind. The pattern that I've noticed with the contradictory messages that create gender double binds is that one of the messages is "anti–masculine" while the other is "pro–masculine." Let me explain.

Gender shaming messages, like those we talked about in the previous section, are anti–masculine. Remember, the four gender shame messages are: males are bad, it is bad to be male, it is bad for *me* to be male, and I am bad at being male. These "anti–masculine messages" can leave a boy very apprehensive about maleness. A boy who receives such messages fears that something is going to go very wrong if he connects to other males or displays his own masculinity. Maybe he's already experienced rejection or disapproval and he fears getting that response again. Maybe he fears being punished, ridiculed, or humiliated. Or maybe he even fears being abandoned emotionally. Whatever the specific circumstance may be, he doesn't feel a positive connection to some aspect of maleness.

> A boy who receives anti–masculine messages fears that something is going to go very wrong if he connects to other males or displays his own masculinity.

The conflicting pro–masculine message in a gender double bind can be any statement or situation that insists that the boy *is* male, that he has to be male, that he should act like a male, or that he needs males in his life. These pro–masculine messages can be delivered verbally through statements such as "Act like a boy." They can be delivered by situations where maleness is required, such as being in the boy's locker room, participating in a male–dominated sport, or performing "boy chores" around the house. And most significantly, the pro–masculine message may be delivered by the boy's own body and by his internal wisdom that tell him he *is* a boy or that he needs connection with other boys and men.

We could summarize gender double binds by saying that a boy who experiences them is not okay *with* masculinity, but he's not okay *without* it either. And of course, he has no way to address that contradiction. Most likely the conflict can't be addressed because the boy isn't even conscious of it except through feelings of discomfort, shame, or anger. If he's aware of the double bind, he may not have a sufficiently open or trusting relationship with his parents to discuss it. Now, let me give specific examples of gender double binds.

> A boy who experiences gender double binds is not okay *with* masculinity, but he's not okay *without* it either.

Son of a Redneck

Imagine a boy who sees his father and other males around him behaving like rednecks. He judges these men to be "low–class" and feels disgusted by them, seeing himself as more refined. The anti–masculine message the boy takes from this is "Males are bad," and his response is to avoid them. But a barely conscious internal pro–masculine message tells him that he's losing out on something by not being with these men. He needs male closeness, acceptance, inclusion, and masculine mentoring. And his body tells him that he actually does belong among this gender group of which he's ashamed. But there is no resolution because he's pretty sure neither of his parents would understand if he tried to talk about it. So he shuns the males around him with their redneck ways and develops more feminine traits.

"Men are Jerks"

Imagine a boy who hears his mother complain about how cruel his father is. Or maybe he hears his sister complain about how cocky her boyfriends are. Something about the way they voice these complaints sends the anti–masculine message that "It is bad to be male." The boy senses that the appropriate response to this message would be to side with the females against the males, from whom he's already disidentified and probably also estranged. But the boy is at least vaguely aware of some pro–masculine factors that contradict this response. First of all, he himself *is* male. But also, he may be aware of some restrained aggressions he harbors toward his manipulative mother or whining sister and of his own repressed confidence. In other words, deep down he knows that he's one of those "cruel" and "cocky" males. Siding with the females denies his biological and emotional truths. But he believes disagreeing with them would upset them, causing them to reject and abandon him. And again, he can't talk to either parent about his predicament.

> Imagine a boy who hears his mother complain about how cruel his father is.

"You're Special"

Imagine a mother who tells her son *not* to be like his dad, gives him special favors for being different from the other boys in the family, and praises him for being "more like a girl." The boy notices her bitterness and coldness toward his father and brothers, and he gets the anti–masculine message "It is bad for *me* to be male," or more to the point, "It would be bad for me to *act like* a male." The contradictory pro–masculine message arises out of the truth of his own body: he *is* male. The double bind means that he has to choose between what may be his only attachment (to his mother) and his connection to his own body. And once again, he has no one to go to for help. His only tolerable choice is to give in to his most primal need, which in this case is for his mother's care and nurture.

> Imagine a mother who tells her son *not* to be like his dad.

"My Baby"

Imagine a mother who regularly tells her son things like "You're my sweet one" or "You're my little baby." Sweet babies aren't masculine—they are weak, small, and dependent. So the anti–masculine message the son hears is "I am bad at being male." But the father is always telling the son to "grow up," which requires the son to *not* be a baby and insists that he can and must be masculine. So the pro–masculine message is "You're a boy—act like one." Here the boy is forced to choose between his parents as well as his gender: the mother wants the boy helpless and attached, the father wants him masculine and independent. To go with one means to lose the other. And to discuss it with them would bring humiliating attention and conflict.

"Little Faggot"

Imagine schoolyard bullies who tell a boy "Be a man, you little faggot!" The pro–masculine message ("Be a man") is an obvious demand to be masculine. But the contradictory anti–masculine message ("you little faggot") tells the boy that he's impossibly bad at being male. The situation can't be resolved because the bullies have already pegged him as a "little faggot." Therefore, any attempts at being manlier will be mocked. On the other hand, if he doesn't try to change—if he keeps being a "faggot"—they will mock him all the more. He can't address the conflict by imploring his abusers to be fair–minded. And the situation may feel far too humiliating to bring to the attention of adults, or perhaps he tries and their help is ineffective or makes things worse.

The impact of gender double binds on a boy can be devastating to both his sense of masculinity and his ability to connect with other males. He's probably deeply ambivalent—stuck in a limbo between craving his gender and rejecting it. He may feel compelled to learn how to act like a man but hopeless about his prospects of ever doing so. He may yearn to connect with and own the maleness of his own body but be held back by a fear of uncertain consequences if he does. He may feel an intense—if perhaps vague—longing to live like the powerful, secure, and confident men to whom he finds himself drawn. But he may also feel very insecure—or even terrified—about expressing *any* masculine traits or attitudes. This situation leaves him intensely conflicted and, too often, the only resolution he can find is to split off masculine aspects of himself. The duality of craving for and rejection of his own gender may develop into a mix of lust and loathing for men.

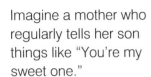

Imagine a mother who regularly tells her son things like "You're my sweet one."

"Be a man, you little faggot!"

The impact of gender double binds on a boy can be devastating to both his sense of masculinity and his ability to connect with other males.

208

The set up for a gender double bind comes from a combination of external and internal sources. The main contributors are rejection, disrespect, and disregard of a boy's gendered self by parents and others in the environment—whether by blunt force or by exquisite unconscious targeting. Societal norms and expectations also play a key role. And the boy's own awareness, perceptions, and interpretations of these outside messages and of his own male traits are an essential factor. Ultimately the double bind is created in the mind and emotions of the boy himself as his internal logic makes meaning of his experience and thereby constructs his own reality. ✍ 7.2

Gender Imperatives

Many men with same–sex attraction tend to become fixated or obsessed with certain male traits. Often we consider these attributes to be necessary in order to be truly masculine or to be considered attractive, desirable, good, valuable, loveable, or complete as a man. When we see someone with the trait—or when we think about the trait—we are prone to experience powerful feelings of pain, longing, curiosity, envy, or lust. Reports from men I've known suggest that this fixation can begin in childhood, although it may not emerge until adolescence or even later. And I've noticed that these obsessions tend to become inflexible and unrealistic and can remain unchanged over many years. I have adopted the term "gender imperatives" to denote these obsessions.

Gender imperatives seem to form in response to masculine traits we see in the males around us but consider ourselves to be lacking in. The dissimilarity and incongruity we sense in relation to these masculine traits becomes a critical factor differentiating us from the males around us. Typically, we tell ourselves the story that these differences make us inferior or wrong, which creates pain and longing. We may tell ourselves that, in order to be truly worthy or whole as a boy or man, we must possess those qualities. But we also see ourselves as incapable of sufficiently obtaining or developing the required traits.

> Gender imperatives seem to form in response to masculine traits we see in the males around us but consider ourselves to be lacking in.

Gender imperatives can develop around specific body traits, such as muscularity, body hair, facial features, or a large penis. They can form around personality traits, such as aggression, athleticism, or confidence. They can even be based on socioeconomic factors, such as education and wealth. And they are often focused on a mysterious and vague quality that has often been described to me using terms like "the male mystique." To wax archetypal for a moment, consider the idea that gender imperatives are archetype fragments—facets of archetypal light and power glimpsed in mortal men. As such, they tend to reinforce a less–than–whole perception of masculinity.

Gender imperatives can function on a very conscious level, such as the conscious belief that men must be good at sports. But they can exist on far less conscious levels, showing up only in our spontaneous responses to the men around us—most typically in our attractions. You might discover your own gender imperatives by noticing your reactions to the men you interact with. For example, if you find yourself drawn again and again to a certain type of man or to specific masculine traits, that may be evidence of a gender imperative you carry. If you look more carefully, you might find that these types or traits are aspects of masculinity that you felt devoid of in boyhood, even if you have obtained those traits for yourself in adulthood. ✍ 7.3

> You might discover your own gender imperatives by noticing your reactions to the men you interact with.

Gender Incongruity

Gender incongruity is a sense of being incompatible with or not conforming to your internalized definition of masculinity. Gender shame, gender double binds, and gender imperatives can cause us to see ourselves as being at odds or out–of–sync with what we believe a man is supposed to be. Men with gender incongruity look at other men and think, "I am not like them and they are not like me. I am different and that difference makes me less." It's likely that nearly all men on occasion feel like they don't fully measure up to their masculine ideal. But gender incongruity is much deeper than just not fully measuring up. It's a pervasive sense that we're lacking in vital qualities or capacities that are essential for masculinity. And it includes a belief that there is no way to sufficiently obtain or grow into these qualities or capacities.

> "I am not like them and they are not like me. I am different and that difference makes me less."

Gender incongruity is a subjective experience, which means that it occurs within our own minds and is based entirely on our own perspective, regardless of what others may perceive about our gender traits. Some men may feel very incongruent with their gender even though their friends would consider them to be totally masculine. Other men may seem quite unmasculine to those around them but don't acknowledge any sense of incongruity. Usually men who are dealing with gender incongruity are conscious of it. But some may not be aware of the incongruity they may harbor.

Gender incongruity creates a psychically unstable situation because feeling congruent with our own gender seems to be a basic and essential human need. If we don't fulfill that need, the psyche will compensate in some other way. Remember, core needs are non–negotiable. In conversations with men with same–sex attraction about their sexual interests in other males, many have described to me a desire to *be* the men for whom they were lusting. Through sexual fantasies, encounters, or relationships, they were trying to absorb the masculinity of those men. Sometimes it actually helped for a while. But it didn't really resolve their gender incongruity, and often they felt like they had become dependent on getting a regular fix of masculinity from some other guy. 7.4

It's possible to heal or grow beyond gender incongruity by developing your sense of masculinity. Developing and integrating attributes of the four archetypes can be a key component in that process, especially the traits associated with Warrior. Some additional processes that I've found helpful for myself and for men I've worked with are described below. These may fit you well or they may spark ideas that will work even better for you.

- **Keep the locus of masculinity within your own body.** "Locus" is a Latin word that means "place or location." So a *locus of masculinity* is a place of masculinity, or a place where masculinity exists or happens.

  Think about the last time you were sexually attracted to another man. In that moment, where was the masculinity happening? Were you feeling deeply connected to your own masculinity? Or was the other guy the place where masculinity was happening in that moment? Keeping the locus of masculinity in your own body means maintaining the perspective that, in your life, the place where masculinity exists is inside you. If you notice yourself fixating on another man, pull the masculinity back inside yourself and own it.

- **Do what seems authentically masculine to you.** This one is very simple. Find those activities and behaviors that seem masculine to you, or that increase or intensify your sense of being a man, and do them. Often men find that activities involving some degree of challenge and risk, or that otherwise create feelings of personal power, are very masculinizing.

Feeling congruent with our own gender seems to be a basic and essential human need. If we don't fulfill that need, the psyche will compensate in some other way.

- **Label yourself, your actions, and your sensations as masculine.** The story you tell about yourself determines who you will believe you are and what you will believe you are capable of. So consciously practice the art of creating masculine labels for everything you *are* and *do*. You may find that some of your traits, feelings, or behaviors are very difficult or impossible to label in this way. You will need to consider these carefully, perhaps with the help of a trusted friend, support group, or therapist. It may be that you just have an irrational block toward some things that are legitimately masculine. On the other hand, it may be that these things are categorically unmasculine *for you* and that you need to avoid them.

- **Feel the masculine sensations of your body.** Allow yourself to explore all of the emotions, energies, urges, pains, and desires of a man. This can be done through athletics, exercise, or just stretching your muscles. It might be accomplished by interacting with nature, whether the activity is aggressive or calm. It can be experienced through sexual expression that feels appropriate to you. Perhaps any values–congruent experience that creates a bodily sense of wellbeing, calmness, exhilaration, relaxation, or intensified focus will accomplish this, as long as your mind is simultaneously focused on the fact that you're a man having a masculine experience.

- **Surrender gender imperatives.** Recognize that your gender imperatives are obsessions or fixations on masculine traits that have taken on far greater meaning than they deserve. Put your imperatives back into balance by choosing to take a more whole perspective on manliness. Choose to see *all* the males around you and to recognize each one as reflecting an aspect of the full masculine potential. Make room in yourself to enjoy the wide variety of men that inhabit the world. Work at extending a feeling of love toward all of them as your brothers and equals and thereby broaden your view of what masculinity means. If you still find yourself obsessed with a specific trait, you may need to uncover its hidden personal meaning through individual therapy. Often, men find that they need to grieve an insufficiency or a loss represented by that trait.

- **Do things with men you respect.** Interacting with men whom you respect and admire can be very masculinizing. This is especially true when the six elements of community are in place and when you feel some degree of mutual attachment, resonance, approval, and support from them. Many men have reported that this helped diminish their gender incongruity. I suspect that being accepted by men we admire creates identification with those men and feelings of worth. ✐ 7.5

Same–Sex Disaffiliation

The last several sections—gender shame, gender double binds, gender imperatives, and gender incongruity—all have to do with our internal sense of ourselves as men. Now we're moving on to disruptions that can occur in our sense of community with other men—in other words, in our male affiliations. The word "affiliation" means "connection or association." It implies a close contact, including cooperation and companionship, bonding, and love. Affiliation is about being united with or adopted into a relationship or group. This describes the type of connections boys need to experience with other males as they grow into manhood.

Painful, frightening, or alienating experiences with other males can lead boys to pull away from their father, brother, peers, and other males, breaking or preventing the normal affiliations and creating a state of "disaffiliation." Elizabeth Moberly and Joseph Nicolosi describe a situation called "defensive detachment" in which the boy not only pulls away, but also puts up an unconscious block against the possibility of ever reconnecting. We need connection with others of our own gender; it's another core and non–negotiable need. So if we're detached, the natural needs for attachment, resonance, approval, and support will go unmet. And if our defensiveness prevents us from reconnecting, we'll remain isolated, without support, and our needs may turn into longings and cravings.

> Painful, frightening, or alienating experiences with other males can lead boys to pull away from their father, brother, peers, and other males, breaking or preventing the normal affiliations and creating a state of "disaffiliation."

Negative stereotypes of boys and men can contribute to same–sex disaffiliation. Not all men with same–sex attraction have negative views of other men, but many do. These stereotypes may have been formed directly from bad personal experiences with other boys or men early in childhood. Or they might have been caused by anti–male complaints and criticisms from females around the young boy. The distance from other men that's created by defensive detachment perpetuates negative stereotypes because it prevents us from getting to know what men are really like. We only know their ugly side. Holding onto negative stereotypes alienates us from our peers, which prevents us from fulfilling core needs.

Gender incongruity, which we discussed in the previous section, can also contribute to same–sex disaffiliation by causing us to avoid other males out of a sense of being different or strange. We may fear that if they get to know us, they'll see our strangeness and reject us. Likewise, same–sex disaffiliation can reinforce gender incongruity since the less time we spend with other males, the less like them we will feel and become. Gender incongruity and same–sex disaffiliation can become a mutually reinforcing negative cycle. 🖎 7.6

Just like gender incongruity, it's possible for you to resolve same–sex disaffiliation through conscious effort. I suggest that your focus in this area should be on doing things that will enable you to meet your needs for attachment, resonance, approval, and support. Some ideas that I and others have used are described below. These may fit your own situation well, or they may provoke thoughts that will lead you to better ideas.

- **Work through past painful relationships**. Conscious and nonconscious memories of painful experiences with other males can deter you from making new relationships or cripple you in the relationships you have. I encourage you to give serious thought to this and take action soon, if you haven't already. You might do this work through personal grieving, group experiences, and individual therapy.

- **Learn about how men interact with each other.** Watching the way men interact can be very eye opening. Pay attention to how they speak to each other and what they talk about, how they engage physically, and when they do and don't touch. Watch for indications of what's going on internally, such as signs of insecurity, compassion, or friendship. It may be even more helpful to you if you journal about this.

- **Establish friendships with other men walking similar paths**. Men who are consciously working to heal past wounds and live in congruity with their values are more likely to be able to understand your situation and provide helpful insights and feedback. But keep in mind that men with relationship wounds can be a two–edged sword. On one hand they may be hungry for connection and willing to befriend you. On the other hand, their own wounds can complicate or even compromise the relationship.

- **Participate in a men's group.** A lot of men's organizations sponsor groups for men. Religious organizations often offer men's groups as well. If nothing like this is available, you might consider starting your own group in your local area. ✎ 7.7

PROBLEMS WITH FEMALES

In addition to the issues with other males that we've been discussing, which the vast majority of men with same–sex attraction seem to experience, many of us also have issues with females that diminish or disrupt our potential for opposite–sex attraction. These issues may be grouped into two categories. First are the unhealthy interpersonal responses to females that grow out of disturbing or painful experiences with females during childhood. And second are the distorted perspectives of gender, which typically result from faulty perceptions of females and faulty beliefs about ourselves in relation to females. These issues are not universal among men with same–sex attraction. So as you read this section, keep in mind that you may identify with much, some, or none of what is discussed here.

> Problems with Females
> - Unhealthy responses to females
> - Gender distortion
> - Diminished or blocked opposite–sex attraction

Unhealthy Responses to Females

To understand the issues with women that so many of us have, we must begin by looking at the relationship experiences that create those issues. We've already set the stage for this in our discussions of gender shame and gender double binds. Both of these situations are often created by females, and they can leave boys feeling resentful, distrustful, and angry toward girls and women. In addition to these injuries, females—including mothers, sisters, extended family members, teachers, babysitters, and others—can wound a boy in a frightening variety of ways. They may overwhelm him with their attention, smothering him with too much love or concern. They may control, dominate, and overprotect him, leaving him feeling emasculated and incapable. They may over–connect with the boy and use him as a confidant, perhaps pulling him into their problems with other males, including conflicts with his own father, grandfather, or brother.

Females may over–connect with a boy and use him as a confidant.

Females may also criticize a boy for any number of weaknesses, causing lasting feelings of shame, insecurity, and self–doubt. Conversely, they may over–praise him with compliments that are overdone, unrealistic, or insincere. They may feminize him by using him in their make–believe play as another girl—sometimes dressing him up as a girl or even telling him he is a girl. And females, especially mothers, sometimes rely on a boy emotionally or even physically, requiring him to take care of them, creating in him a sense of being engulfed and used and fostering feelings of guilt if he tries to be independent.

By failing to observe boundaries and standards of modesty, females may sexualize the relationship with a boy. They may do this by leaving bedroom or bathroom doors open while they are changing, bathing, or using the toilet, or by walking around the house in their underwear or even naked. They may sexualize him by commenting on his body or by talking to him about their sex lives. And occasionally, females also directly abuse boys by engaging them in sexual behavior. ✍ 7.8

Experiences like those I've been describing can cause a boy to grow up responding to women in a wide variety of unhealthy ways. These responses may be grouped into four broad categories: oppositional, avoidant, enmeshed, and comfortable. Some of us respond to women with feelings, impulses, and behaviors from more than one of these categories, depending on the situation. As you read the descriptions below, consider if any of it fits for you.

Unhealthy responses to females:

- Oppositional
- Avoidant
- Enmeshed
- Comfortable

Those of us who become oppositional tend to reject women and push them away. We may do so out of feelings of resentment, dislike, disgust, or even hatred. Or we may do so in reaction to feeling threatened and endangered by women. Some of us are completely conscious and blatant about our antipathy toward females. For others, negative feelings toward women may show up only in subtle behaviors and thoughts of which we are barely aware. And some of us may be completely unconscious of our opposition.

Those of us who are avoidant of women tend to experience feelings of fear and anxiety, which may cause us to keep our distance. Or we may simply feel apathetic and indifferent toward women, perhaps treating them as if they don't exist.

Those who are enmeshed with women tend to feel needy or dependent on their support and approval. We may subordinate ourselves to women, allowing ourselves to be controlled by them. The dependency may go the other direction as well, as in the case where an elderly mother is dependent on her son for assistance in ways that disrupt his ability to live his own life. And the man may be bound to maintain this situation by tremendous feelings of guilt. If he tries to free himself from the entanglement, his guilt overwhelms him and he gives in.

Those of us who are comfortable with women tend to seek out females and female settings as sources of security and consolation. In this case, "comfortable" means something more than simply being at ease with women. It implies an over–familiarity and over–resonance with them, sharing interests and perspectives, or feeling included as "one of the girls." And it often includes using women and female settings as places of resort and safety. ✎ 7.9

Gender Distortion

In addition to causing unhealthy responses to women, disturbing or painful childhood experiences with females can also create distorted perspectives or beliefs about women. Many of us develop beliefs about women that are not accurate for women as a whole, even if they may be true about the women within our own families. For example, we may view all women as dangerous or downright evil—as cruel, vindictive abusers. We may see them as needy and engulfing, manipulative and cajoling. Or we may see women generally as being stupid and weak or as just more trouble than they're worth—moody, complaining, and whining. On the other hand, we may idealize women, viewing them as good, pure, or even sacred. Or we may look to them as our protectors or providers. ✎ 7.10

> Many of us develop beliefs about women that are not accurate for women as a whole, even if they may be true about the women within our own families.

Disturbing or painful childhood experiences with females may also create incorrect or immature perceptions of ourselves in relation to women. The kinds of experiences I described may have left us seeing ourselves as needy and weak in our relationships with women or as undesirable, vulnerable, and inferior to women. We may feel small and incapable of handling the demands of an intimate opposite–sex relationship. On the other extreme, we may see ourselves as being superior to females—as far better or somehow *right*.

Most critical of all the effects of our childhood relationships with females is the way those relationships impact our sense of gender. For many of us, females were the predominant influence in our lives growing up. They provided us with role modeling and friendship while the men in our lives may have had little impact on us. This may have left us without a clear sense of genderedness—the roles and differences between men and women may seem ambiguous.

> Most critical of all effects of our childhood relationships with females is the way those relationships impact our sense of gender.

In addition, gender shame and gender double binds may have disrupted our connection with our own masculine identity or turned us off to the idea of being male. We may have identified ourselves with females or even come to believe that it would be preferable to be female. Some of us may have developed such strong repugnance toward masculinity and such a strong desire to be female that we truly came to see ourselves as a woman stuck in a man's body. More commonly, we probably have a clear recognition of our maleness but feel a much stronger sense of connection and resonance with the opposite sex.

Archetypally speaking, this cross–gender identity could be termed *Anima possession*, a concept we discussed in Chapter Six. The naturally occurring inner feminine has been allowed to expand unnaturally, overwhelming and subduing the masculine. This creates a noticeable effeminacy in the personalities of some men. Other men may show no external sign whatsoever of their inner dilemma. 7.11

Diminished or Blocked Opposite–Sex Attraction

As I mentioned at the beginning of this section, not all men with same–sex attraction experience the issues with females and femininity that I've been describing. But the result for many of us who do experience these issues tends to be a diminishing or complete blocking of opposite–sex attraction. This blocking may occur because all of the problems with females I described previously tend to disrupt genderedness and complementarity, on which heterosexuality seems to be based.

> Problems with females tend to disrupt genderedness and complementarity, on which heterosexuality seems to be based.

> *Genderedness:* the natural state of having two sexes that are distinct and different from one another

> *Complementarity:* a favorable relationship between the two sexes where each completes, fulfills, balances, and perfects the other

We talked about genderedness and complementarity in Chapters Three and Six. I explained that genderedness is the natural state of having two sexes that are distinct and different from one another. Complementarity refers to a favorable relationship between the two sexes where each completes, fulfills, balances, and perfects the other. If you consider any of the issues with females described in the previous sections, you will notice that it either distorts a man's sense of genderedness or it diminishes the possibility of having a favorable and complementary relationship with a woman.

Issues with the opposite sex like those we've been exploring can be resolved. But in most cases, this will require counseling or psychotherapy because the mental programming these issues create tend to become very deeply ingrained, difficult to perceive, and challenging to change. Therapy that provides conscious insight into your beliefs and patterns can be useful, particularly if you're in an opposite–sex relationship that you're trying to improve. But in order to fully transcend these issues, you will likely need the help of a therapist who is trained to work with the unconscious. ✍ 7.12

HOMOSEXUAL THOUGHTS AND BEHAVIOR

Personal and professional experience has convinced me that, in many cases if not all, homosexuality emerges from underlying issues. Often it seems to be an outcome of gender incongruity and same–sex disaffiliation. Sexual abuse, childhood exposure to male pornography, and extensive sex–play with other boys can also play a role, as can discomfort, distress, or negative feelings in childhood opposite–sex relationships.

When we engage in homosexual thoughts and behavior, new issues emerge that tend to strengthen our attractions. I will describe three of these outcomes. First, when we engage in homosexuality mentally (through looking and fantasy) or behaviorally (through masturbation paired with pornography or fantasy, or through sex with other men), the brain becomes increasingly conditioned—or used to—this type of stimulation. Neurons that fire together wire together.[1] In other words, when the brain processes two pieces of information simultaneously, it will remember them in conjunction with each other. For example, you've probably noticed that certain songs will bring back vivid memories of a time and place from earlier in your life. This is because your brain linked that song with things you experienced during the time in your life when you first heard that song. For men with same–sex attraction, this means that the more we experience men in a sexual context, the more our brains remember them in that context.

> When we engage in homosexuality, our brains become increasingly conditioned. Neurons that fire together wire together.

A second outcome of homosexual thoughts and behavior can be the development of sexual compulsions or addictions. Any kind of sexual pleasure is strongly self–reinforcing, which results in the brain and the body wanting more of it. If we add shame to this picture, as we discussed in Chapter Four, our sexuality can be pulled into a control–release cycle in which sex is used to provide pleasure and a temporary sense of wellbeing and power, momentarily alleviating our shame. Over time, more frequent or intense homosexual thoughts or behavior may be required in order to provide the same level of pleasure and relief from shame.

> Any kind of sexual pleasure is strongly self–reinforcing, which results in the brain and the body wanting more of it.

A third consequence of engaging in homosexual thoughts and behavior can be the further diminishing of our masculine sufficiency. If we feel ashamed of our homosexual desires and behaviors, we may see ourselves as different from our male peers, thus increasing our sense of gender incongruity. If we consider our homosexual acts to be a big secret that has to stay hidden from others, we may keep our distance from the men around us, intensifying our same–sex disaffiliation. And if we mentally divide the community of men into just two groups—the "attractive," which we sexualize, and the "unattractive," which we ignore—we may find it very difficult to bond and meet our needs for connection.

If you want to stop being homosexual, you have to stop being homosexual.

For some unexplainable reason, it seems that a lot of men who are trying to grow beyond same–sex attraction don't understand a very simple reality: *if you want to stop being homosexual, you have to stop being homosexual.* In other words, you have to discontinue your homosexual thoughts and behaviors if you want to resolve same–sex attraction. Every time you engage in homosexual thoughts and behaviors, you intensify the issues we've just discussed. ✍ 7.13

Below are a few very practical things you can do to surrender unwanted sexual arousal. You would be wise to practice these a number of times when you're not aroused so that when you're in a situation where you need them you will know how to use them effectively. It's possible that some of these may work for you and others may not; they are not universally effective. Modify these or combine them with each other and with other techniques of your own to create strategies that work for you.

- **Breath and relaxation.** Breathe deeply and slowly while focusing on relaxing your entire body, particularly where you feel the arousal. Continue this until the arousal diminishes, then use the "Distraction" technique described below.

- **Move the energy.** Focus on the sensation of the arousal in your body. Think of it as simple energy—nothing more. It's the story you tell about it that makes it homosexual. Now, imagine moving that energy to some other place in your body that you don't associate with sexual feelings, such as your head, arms, or feet.

- **Distraction.** Intensely focus your awareness on something neutral in the environment, giving careful attention to the details. Involve as many senses as possible. Allow this distraction to crowd out your awareness of the arousal.

- **Split screen association.** Close your eyes and picture the man you're aroused by. Put his image on a TV screen in your mind and enhance the image until it's very clear. Then mentally turn off that screen. Now imagine another TV screen with the picture of a man you respect and love but for whom you have no sexual attraction. Enhance that picture until it's very clear. Then turn off that screen. Bring back up the image of the arousing man. Once you see it clearly, slowly bring up the image of the man you respect and love, beginning in the bottom left corner of the other screen. Gradually let it increase until it fills the entire screen. Repeat this several times. This often causes the feelings of arousal to shift. ✍ 7.14

THE GOAL OF MASCULINITY

Why should we work so hard to develop gender wholeness? Why go through the suffering and effort to intensify masculine sufficiency—to experience ourselves as men and to connect with the world of men? Why go beyond that to develop feminine comprehension—to experience the opposite sex as complementary to ourselves and to befriend our Animas? The reasons will be as varied as the individuals pursuing this path, and no one can say that one reason is valid and another is not. The majority of you who are reading this book might quickly respond that you're developing masculine sufficiency in order to diminish feelings of same–sex attraction. To me, that reason makes sense, but I also think it's incomplete.

I believe that when we focus our attention too narrowly on taking care of our own needs, we lose opportunities to experience the depth and breadth of the masculine and its interplay with the feminine. The Warrior serves the King or Transpersonal Other—the cause greater than himself. This seems to be an essential desire in mature men. It's observable all around us—highly developed men want to serve and give. That's our mission. The quote that I used to open Chapter Five on the Warrior I'll now use to close this chapter on masculinity. This is from *The Warrior Within* by Moore and Gillette:

> Mature masculine functioning…requires that a man have a mission that is beyond the merely private and self–preserving agenda—one that serves the most worthy authority and ideals that he recognizes…. Anything less is in fact a bastardization of an instinctual potential that contains the code for much of the nobility of our species.

When we focus our attention too narrowly on taking care of our own needs, we lose opportunities to experience the depth and breadth of the masculine and its interplay with the feminine.

Your service to mankind must begin with healing your own life and creating in yourself the strength, wisdom, and skills you will use to serve others. And your own healing process may even open a pathway for your ultimate mission. A final quote makes this point eloquently. This is from *Iron John* by Robert Bly:

> …where a man's wound is, that is where his genius will be. Wherever the wound appears in our psyches, whether from an alcoholic father, shaming mother, shaming father, abusing mother, whether it stems from isolation, disability, or disease, that is precisely the place from which we will give our major gift to the community. ✍ 7.15

---

[1] Neurons are the nerve cells that exist in our brains and nervous systems. They are responsible for all of our thinking and for conveying information from our sensory organs to our brains and from our brains to all parts of our bodies. They convey information by "firing" electrical impulses from one neuron to another, somewhat like a signal that's sent through a telephone wire or fiber–optic cable. The brain is a vast network of neurons. When we put things together in our minds—such as the letters c–a–t and the image of a fuzzy four–legged animal—the brain makes a link through this network allowing us to spell "cat" and know what it means. This is what enables us to learn new information. It's highly likely that everything we learn—including sexual attraction—happens through similar processes.

CHAPTER 8

THE MAGIAN

In order to find our own individual centers we need to be able to access the inner Magician. When we allow ourselves to be guided by his wisdom and his technological expertise, we can each find our way to the center of our own inner realm.

Moore and Gillette, *The Magician Within*

ppproximately three thousand five hundred years ago in ancient Persia, a man named Zarathustra is said to have received a heavenly vision in which a being of light led him to the presence of six Holy Immortals. One of those Immortals, called *Ahura Mazda*, was said to be God himself. This vision was followed by many other revelations in which Zarathustra, known in English as Zoroaster, asked God many questions and received many answers. The wisdom learned from these communications with God became the tenets of a new faith, called Zoroastrianism,[1] in which Zarathustra is considered a great prophet.

Among the most fundamental teachings of this faith, which still exists today, is the ongoing conflict between good, created by God, and evil, in the form of a destructive spirit known as *Angra Mainyu*.[2] Central to that battle between good and evil is the struggle between truth, called *asha*, and deceit, called *druj*. The purpose of humanity is to avoid deceit and sustain truth.[3] "Truth is the best [of all that is] good," Zarathustra wrote in one of his seventeen sacred hymns, known as the Gathas.[4]

Zoroastrian priests, known as *maguš* in Old Persian or *Magians* in English, were known anciently for wisdom, revelation, and devotion to truth. They gained a

Zarathustra

Zoroastrian priests were known anciently for wisdom, revelation, and devotion to truth.

reputation for having knowledge of astrology, which was considered an important science during that age.[5] Zoroastrianism, also called *Magianism*, gradually became known throughout the old world from Greece[6] to China.[7] Magians are mentioned in the Quran[8] as well as in the Gospel of Matthew's well-known account of "wise men from the east"—called "magi" in the original Greek—who came to visit the infant Christ.[9]

By the fifth century BC, Greeks had come to see Magians as sorcerers, conjurers, tricksters, and charlatans.

Perhaps more than any other culture, the Greeks both elevated and misunderstood the Magians. Pythagoras, the sixth century BC Greek mathematician, philosopher, and mystic, was said to have been instructed by Magians on principles of religion and how to conduct one's life. Some believe it was they who taught him to speak the truth in all situations.[10] By the fifth century BC, however, Greeks had come to see Magians as sorcerers, conjurers, tricksters, and charlatans. *Magike* became the term for the use of supernatural powers and for trickery and sleight of hand. This is the root of the modern English terms *magic* and *magician*.

In their writings, Robert Moore and Douglas Gillette use the image of Magician for the archetype of knowledge, wisdom, revelation, transformation, and initiation. In my view, the persona of Magician barely covers the active shadow of this archetype and lends very little understanding to the archetype in its wholeness. This is why I've used the much older and broader term, Magian, as the archetype label. Over the many centuries since Zarathustra first beheld the Holy Immortals, he and those who have been called by some derivative of the Old Persian term *maguš*—from magi to magicians—have personified every nuance of the whole archetype and his active shadow, in legend at least if not also in reality. Their reputation spans the entire realm from prophet to priest, to scientist, sorcerer, trickster, and imposter. And by illuminating the wholeness and active shadow of this archetype, they show the outline of the passive shadow as well.

When we discussed the King archetype in Chapter Two, we considered that archetype's function as our axis mundi, by which he creates and holds our Center. That function includes a psychic connection with our Self—the unmoving, unchanging core that guides the rest of our psyche, providing harmony and balance. It also includes a spiritual connection with our Higher Power—God or some other external power or principle—which helps to provide personal stability and spiritual sustenance. These connections to Self and Higher Power create clarity about our needs, values, priorities, and boundaries. It provides vision—

perspective, motivation, and an idea of where we're going in life. And it confirms a sense of validity, worth, and purpose. It's the King's job to hold the Center. But it's the Magian's job to *know* our Center. Without the wisdom of the Magian, the King would have no axis mundi.

The ability to know our Center is the foundation for authenticity, the second principle of growth out of same–sex attraction, and the subject of Chapter Nine. Without a clear awareness of what's at our core, how can we know who we are? And how can we share ourselves authentically with those around us? Moreover, without knowing ourselves well and relating authentically with others, how can we heal our lives? And how can we experience healing relationships? If we're to experience true wholeness, we must learn to live authentically. We must develop our Magian capacities.

> If we're to experience true wholeness, we must learn to live authentically. We must develop our Magian capacities.

But the Magian knows more than just our Self. It's through the Magian capacities that we apprehend and use knowledge of all kinds—whether we use that knowledge in beneficial or destructive ways. In this chapter we'll look at the attributes and functions of the Whole Magian and at his bipolar shadow. Then we'll review the synergistic potential that can be had by balancing his active and passive sides. Next we'll consider the healing power of the Magian, which comes to us through initiation processes and by using his power to steward our friendships. And finally, we'll consider a few suggestions for advancing Magian energy in our lives.

THE WHOLE MAGIAN

The essential mission of the Magian archetype is to help, heal, and transform—first ourselves and then the world—through our use of knowledge. As described by authors Moore and Gillette, the Magian accomplishes this mission through two main functions. First, he's the "Possessor of Knowledge," especially hidden or rare knowledge. And second, he's the "Master of Transformation,"[11] which means that he understands how to apply his knowledge to transform our lives through better ways of being.

> The Whole Magian
> - Possessor of knowledge
> - Detector of corruption
> - Master of transformation
> - Steward of sacred space
> - Initiator

Related to these main functions, he has some additional roles. His function as the Possessor of Knowledge brings with it a significant role of detecting corruption in his own life and the lives of those around him. His function as the Master of Transformation brings with it two additional responsibilities. The first is to create situations where his transforming work can be done. These situations are sometimes called "sacred space." The second is to initiate others, which means to teach and mentor them so that they can develop their own Magian abilities.

Key Magian Attributes

Before we address these functions of the Magian, let's first consider the attributes that characterize this archetype. 8.1

Exclusively Cognitive: The Magian is pure thought. He fulfills every aspect of his work within the confines of his mind, free of any connection to, or dependency on, his body. But he's connected to his body through other archetypal powers, which enables him to bring his thoughts into action in the real world. Because he understands well the principles of balance and moderation, he consciously evokes these other archetypes, as needed, to keep the body healthy and to satisfy the body's physical needs and desires.

> The Magian is pure thought. He fulfills every aspect of his work within the confines of his mind.

Introverted: His work is largely free of human relationships. The exceptions to this rule are the transforming relationships where he receives and gives healing and mentoring through thought and introspection. Beyond these relationships he seeks time alone, away from distractions by people in the outside world. In that solitude he becomes acquainted with his Self—his authentic core—and finds the truths hiding there. This is how he knows his Center, which knowledge is so vital to the function of the King. But he understands the significance of relationships to the whole self. So he limits his isolation and allows the Lover time to enjoy the company of others.

On a Quest: The Magian is always searching and will spend his entire life on his quest for understanding. His search follows an insatiable hunger for wisdom, growth, and transformation. He greets life with curiosity, openness, and a desire for more knowledge. In his search, he is not distracted by things that lack transformative power. He recognizes the counterfeit adventures and intellectual pursuits that may stimulate his interest, pique his curiosity, and provide "useful information," but which don't empower him. On some level he understands that his search is actually a quest to ever more deeply experience his own axis mundi— his Self and his spiritual connection with a Higher Power.

> The Magian is always searching and will spend his entire life on his quest for understanding.

Committed to Truth: His intention is always to see things as they really are at their deepest level. He is not beguiled by "the cold, hard facts," since these can distort more profound realities too subtle to be captured or conveyed by data. He understands well the poignant observation made by Robert Stoller: "Artists lie to tell the truth, and scientists tell the truth to lie." He properly appreciates the role of both fact and fiction in conveying what's real. He's capable of metaphor and symbolism and often uses them to bring awareness to levels of understanding far deeper than simple reason and logic can describe. His devotion to truth extends to an absolute commitment to using the truth only in ways that bless, help, and heal.

Self–Sacrificing: His commitment to truth and to helping and healing others sometimes places him in situations where he must make sacrifices or take on additional responsibilities. His quest for transformation and higher ways of being often means letting go of parts of himself that are contrary to his growth toward wholeness. But he must be alert to differentiate between legitimate and necessary acts of sacrifice and convenient abdication.

Conscious: Most significantly, the Magian is conscious. He's clear thinking, reflective, and introspective. He discerns and distinguishes, differentiating one thing from another and comprehending the significance of these distinctions. He's fully aware of his own thoughts, feelings, intentions, and impulses. He's equally aware of others in all of their complexity—he has learned to read them well. And he's conscious of every circumstance in which he finds himself. His choices are clear to him—both those that led him to where he is today as well as the options from which he may yet choose. In his most advanced state, he's aware of the future through the gift of intuition or prophecy. He can sense or predict the eventual consequences of present things, including his own actions. With such consciousness comes tremendous responsibility, which he willingly bears.

> The Magian is conscious. He's clear thinking, reflective, and introspective.

The Possessor of Knowledge

The special knowledge that the Magian possesses isn't the mere data and information that's so abundant in our age. It isn't statistics or factoids. Nor is it even "common sense" or "common knowledge" as understood by the general public. There is nothing special or archetypal about these kinds of knowledge, despite the fact that a large segment of our modern economy is driven by the selling and acquisition of such information.

The Magian's special knowledge is of things far deeper—more essential, fundamental, and foundational. His knowledge is of unchanging principles,

Albert Einstein

patterns, and universal laws, which are the basis of all that exists—although they are hiding from us in plain sight, obscured by everyday life. The Magian's knowledge is secret knowledge possessed only by those who have searched deeply or who have been taught or initiated.

This special knowledge can be obtained through a variety of methods and in diverse fields. Scientists and prophets are both accessing such knowledge, though they do so through different means. Truly, everyone who looks for and acquires understanding of underlying truths is exercising their inner Magian, whether their search leads them into the spiritual realm or into the physical world around them, whether they pursue understanding out in the universe or deep in their own mind and heart. For ease in discussion, let's divide the whole field of knowledge into two categories: external and internal.

The Magian's external field of inquiry is truly vast. It includes the temporal realm through such disciplines as agriculture, engineering, physics, biology, medicine, and all other physical sciences. It includes the realm of the human psyche and the understanding of why we behave as we do through such disciplines as psychology, sociology, and anthropology. It includes the disciplines of the mind such as language, literature, law, and information technology. It includes the understanding of art and self–expression. And it includes the spiritual realm and knowledge of the divine.

In contrast with the vastness of the external field, the range of the Magian's internal inquiry—which is merely our thoughts and feelings—may seem small. But consider that it's our thoughts and feelings that give rise to our behaviors, characterize our relationships, form our cultures, and establish our societies. Ultimately, it's what happens in our minds and hearts that determines whether we're happy, dissatisfied, or even miserable.

In fulfilling his mission to help, heal, and transform us, our Magian is seeking the patterns, principles, and laws that underlie our thoughts and emotions and the impulses they give rise to. He wants to understand what motivates our desires and intentions. Ultimately, he's searching for the truth of our potential as humans. Understanding of these things comes from mindfulness and self–observation.

The Magian's knowledge is of unchanging principles, patterns, and universal laws.

Our Magian is seeking the patterns, principles, and laws that underlie our thoughts and emotions and the impulses they give rise to.

Dr. Louis Ormont created the term "observing ego" to describe the part of us that simply witnesses what's happening inside and around us without judgment and without feeling. The observing ego could be called the inner eye of the Magian. It watches life. And it observes the other archetypal energies. Some men have described the observing ego as a sense of watching themselves, almost like being both inside their body and at the same time outside their body observing their actions. Some men experience this when they are doing intense healing work.

As you can see, the Magian archetype in his fullness knows all laws, patterns, and principles. Whether those are within himself or in his external world, he completely understands their significance and interrelationship. Of particular importance to our discussion, he comprehends the principles related to opposites, such as the opposing forces within the archetypal energies, the distinction of the two genders, and the Law of Polarity discussed in Chapter Two. As we have seen already in this book, the universe abounds with these opposites. Developing a Magian's understanding of opposition is especially helpful for our growth because it promotes the capacity for moderation and balance. And it increases tolerance and understanding of seeming contradictions, enabling far greater acceptance of the world as it is. This encourages us to be more flexible in our approach to life and can help us avoid falling into the immature dissatisfactions that can otherwise plague us. ✎ 8.2

> Developing a Magian's understanding of opposition is especially helpful for our growth because it promotes the capacity for moderation and balance.

Detector of Corruption

The depth and breadth of the Magian's knowledge provides him with a very keen awareness of illogic, pretense, contradictions, and other flaws in ourselves and others, as well as in the systems, organizations, and societies around us. This gives us the ability to perceive when the facts don't line up or the stories don't match. It tells us when someone is lying. And it spots faulty practices and foresees where foolish choices are leading. This awareness is sometimes referred to as a "bullshit detector," and it's foundational to the principle of authenticity that we'll discuss in Chapter Nine. The Magian uses this capacity in benevolent ways for the benefit of himself and his world.

Nowhere is this Magian capacity more blatant than in the perspective that some men with same–sex attraction have on the flaws that abound in male society. Sometimes we see these flaws with crystal clarity. Other times we just sense them but can't quite put our finger on the exact problem. But something within us is keenly aware of the problems with men. We can detect the shallow cultural rituals, the illogic, and the bull–headedness. We recognize the selfishness and relational ineptitude. We can see the emotional immaturity—when men are disconnected from their feelings and when they are being driven by them. In short, we're very quick to spot their shadows. We are particularly sensitive to their Tyrant and Sadist shadows—especially when those shadows are aimed at us.

> Nowhere are we more susceptible to being twisted by any of our shadows than in the proximity of our wounds.

But in our criticism of their shadows, we must be cautious not to slip into shadows of our own. As you will learn further on, the Manipulator shadow of the Magian can lead us to ruin with just the slightest twist of our perception and understanding. And nowhere are we more susceptible to being twisted by any of our shadows than in the proximity of our wounds. Those of us who have been wounded by men would do well to think twice before assuming that our "bullshit detector" is functioning with one–hundred–percent accuracy as it observes the corruption in the male world. ✍ 8.3

The Master of Transformation

The second main function of the Magian is to apply his knowledge of essential patterns, principles, and laws in order to bring about transformation, whether this transformation manifests as technology that enhances our practical lives or as growth that lifts our inner being. The invention of the airplane provides a simple example of a substantial technological transformation. Through years of experience with motors and printing presses, the Wright brothers learned essential principles of mechanics. Working with bicycles taught them about motion and balance. Extensive tests using wind tunnels clarified the essential laws of aerodynamics. Then it was through the combination and application of these and other laws and principles that they were able to transform the world through the technology that they called the "flying machine."

> The Magian's work is to tell us how we can combine and manipulate forces and energies to transform our lives and the world.

The Magian's mastery of transformation is still an entirely mental function—he's not a manufacturer of new gadgets. In order for his technological advancements to take form in reality, we must access other archetypes within ourselves. The Magian's work is simply to tell us how we can combine and manipulate forces and energies to transform our lives and the world. But it's also his job to help us avoid being destroyed by violating unchangeable laws, like those that govern our physical safety. And it's his job to show us how to apply in our daily lives the principles on which our peace and joy rely.

Key to his role as the Master of Transformation is the Magian's ability to channel power. The Magian's knowledge of things in the internal realm and in the outside world gives him the ability to, in the words of authors Moore and Gillette, "contain and channel" the powers existing in each of those realms. A few examples might help you understand what this means. Imagine a nuclear reactor containing the force of atomic power and then channeling that force through turbines, transformers, and a power grid until finally the electricity reaches your toaster. Or imagine a therapist helping a man to contain the intense urges in his body and then to channel those urges toward a safe and transforming expression of feeling. Finally, imagine your own observing ego making you aware of strong emotions arising from a painful childhood memory, which you then contain—perhaps with the help of a few phone calls or a well thought–out relapse prevention plan—until you can channel these feelings into an opportunity to heal.

One of the ways in which the Magian channels power is by controlling what is known and what is not known. Just like a stage magician, he can cause things to seem or appear the way he wants them to by controlling what is revealed and what is withheld, what he accentuates and what he hides. A magician can use this ability to affect our perceptions, our beliefs, and our feelings. The creation of appearance through what is revealed and what is withheld is a central focus for the Magian and for both of his shadow poles.

> The creation of appearance through what is revealed and what is withheld is a central focus for the Magian and for both of his shadow poles.

The Whole Magian uses this gift to intensify our perception of reality and to reveal new and healthier perspectives. He can give us a vision of our highest potential. He can show us how even the most difficult circumstances or crises are opportunities for transformation and growth. His authentic intention is to benefit others and enrich their lives, and he possesses the genuine capacities to accomplish that end. But when a Magian begins to control appearances for self–focused ends—or when he attempts to do so without having the real abilities—he has begun to go into shadow.

Film and television exemplify this well because through these media the world can be made to look any way the producer and director please. The best filmmakers use their Magian gifts to make us aware of the world in ways we may never have perceived before. They can transform our views, open us to new perspectives, and reveal from within us deeper emotions than we knew we had. When used benevolently, this is truly a great gift. It can also be used for tremendous evil. ✎ 8.4

Steward of Sacred Space

There are certain places, times, and states of mind where extraordinary things happen that bring about regeneration, growth, and transformation. These places are called "sacred space." Sacred ceremonies, the birth of a child, and rites of passage and initiation all might be considered sacred space, if they are transformative. So might be the deep healing work that takes place in psychotherapy. Laboratories and think tanks where breakthroughs advance humankind might also be considered sacred space. Experiential weekends succeed—when they are successful—because they effectively create sacred space.

The Magian is the steward of sacred space. If we're to experience regeneration, growth, and transformation, he must be active in our lives. One of the sad truths of modern human existence may be that only a few of us consciously experience sacred space or comprehend the significance of the sacred moments that do occur in our lives. In a sense, there is a certain "worthiness" that must be achieved and maintained if we're to experience sacred space. I'm not speaking of worthiness merely as a simple code of values or morality, but as an expansive spiritual attunement and a willingness to conform ourselves to the principles that govern sacred space.

Sacred space must be stewarded, but it can't be controlled. It's governed by powers far greater than those of any novice Magian, which includes most of humankind. So the work of our inner Magian is to learn those factors that foster it and then foster those factors. Boundaries that govern and protect sacred space—and the people in it—will always be one of those factors.

We can create sacred space for ourselves. This may involve an actual physical location, such as a church, temple, or mosque, a special room, or a place in nature. But it must also be an internal location, or a frame of mind, that we create within ourselves. The attributes of the Magian archetype are crucial here. They will help us to both prepare for and create sacred space as well as to discern those sacred moments when they unfold. ✎ 8.5

There are certain places, times, and states of mind where extraordinary things happen. These places are called "sacred space."

Sacred space must be stewarded, but it can't be controlled. It's governed by powers far greater than those of any novice Magian.

The Initiator

An additional significant aspect of the Magian's transforming work is his responsibility to initiate others into his knowledge and abilities, thus raising them to higher and more mature levels and forms of being. This could be referred to as the technology of Magian–making. It's through this initiatory role of the Magian that all wisdom is passed from one generation to the next. Without this passing along of knowledge, civilization would come to a halt in just a few generations. I fear that we are, in fact, witnessing exactly what I'm describing—a long and gradual decline of civilization as fewer and fewer men receive any type of initiation into mature manhood by their fathers and other mentors. Stemming this tide is one of my main hopes in writing this book.

One of the Magian's simplest yet most powerful tools of initiation is "beholding others," to quote Moore and Gillette. To "behold" means to examine closely, to fully see, and appreciate. Through this, the Magian recognizes, honors, and validates the Magian capacities in other men and in women. This is very similar to the King function of blessing his people, which we discussed in Chapter Three.

My experience with men who are working on resolving their homosexuality is that most of us never had the experience of being beheld by a mentor in the way I'm describing here. Or perhaps we were recognized and validated for certain of our attributes—perhaps even our Magian capacities—but were not honored in a *whole way* as boys and men. This can leave lasting wounds and the hunger to be seen by other men. I'll describe the process of initiation in much greater detail later in this chapter. ✎ 8.6

THE SHADOWS OF THE MAGIAN

Like all archetypes, the Magian has both an active and a passive shadow. Both shadow poles seek control—one through active manipulation, the other through passive false innocence. The active "Manipulator" is conscious, aware, and intentionally powerful. The passive "Innocent" is unconscious, unaware, and unintentionally powerless. The value of understanding these shadows is to help you recognize them in yourself. This understanding may increase your awareness of the nature of your specific wounds. Understanding these shadows may also be of value if it helps you recognize the shadowy traits of others who have affected your life, or who might affect your life. So let's look more deeply at the two extremes.

> Without this passing along of knowledge, civilization would come to a halt in just a few generations.

> Both shadow poles seek control—one through active manipulation, the other through passive false innocence.

Both poles of the Shadow Magian lack the vision of wholeness and an awareness of the Self. Both lack trust in others and in the providence of a Higher Power. And both are afraid and ashamed. The reaction of the active Manipulator pole to this dilemma is to forcefully manage his circumstances, including the people around him. The reaction of the passive Innocent pole to that dilemma is to make himself dumb and dependent. The active shadow pole tends to be blatant and aggressive while the passive pole is more reclusive and hidden.

The Manipulator

> The Manipulator's mission is to protect and advance only himself by controlling his world through information slight–of–hand.

The Manipulator knows that he possesses special knowledge, and he uses it selectively for his own gain. Like the Whole Magian, the Manipulator is fully conscious. But rather than using his consciousness to benefit others, he uses it to benefit himself at the expense of others. Whereas the purpose of the Whole Magian is to help, heal, and transform himself and the world through the use of knowledge, the Manipulator's mission is to protect and advance only himself by controlling his world through information slight–of–hand. He's disconnected from others and absorbed with his own wellbeing.

Charles Ponzi

Consider the character of notorious scammer Charles Ponzi, born Carlo Pietro Giovanni Guglielmo Tebaldo Ponzi in Lugan, Italy. Ponzi immigrated to America in 1903, arriving with just a few dollars in his pocket, and settled in Boston. For the next seventeen years, Ponzi took odd jobs in the Northeastern U.S. and Canada, committing a series of small crimes, including forgery and smuggling immigrants, for which he served prison time.

In 1920, Ponzi discovered a way to make money by purchasing internationally recognized postal coupons inexpensively in Italy then exchanging them in the United States for more expensive U.S. stamps, which could then be sold for a profit. Although this practice is legal, the overhead required to carry out such a business on a large scale makes earning a profit impossible.

But Ponzi convinced several friends to invest in his plan, promising them he could easily double their investment due to high profits he could make from the postal coupon exchange. Ponzi did pay these initial investors back with substantial interest. This encouraged others to invest and in a very short period of time he had formed a booming business, which he called Securities Exchange Company. But he never developed the actual postal coupon exchange business. Rather, he paid investors using the investment money of later investors.

From February to August of 1920, Ponzi's business grew with frenzied intensity. He hired agents all over New England, paying them large commissions, to find investors and collect their funds. As his reputation for quick and large returns spread, more investors poured in. At the height of the scheme he was taking in $250,000 each day. This allowed him to create a luxurious lifestyle for himself. He made some promises of philanthropic giving and even hired a publicity agent.

Ponzi's fantastic success began to arouse suspicion. His publicity agent found documents indicating that Ponzi's business was nothing more than a financial bubble. The publicity agent took this information to a prominent Boston newspaper, the *Post*, which printed an article showing Ponzi was insolvent and millions of dollars in debt. Within days, the Massachusetts Bank Commissioner launched an investigation, which prompted state officials to also investigate. Two days later, the *Post* ran another article about Ponzi's criminal past. And the next day, August 12, 1920, Ponzi turned himself in to federal authorities. News of the scandal caused the failure of six banks, and Ponzi's investors lost a total of about $20 million dollars, which at today's value would be approximately $225 million.[12] Scams of this type are called "Ponzi schemes" to this day.

In an interview near the end of his life, Ponzi told a reporter, "Even if they never got anything for it, it was cheap at that price. Without malice aforethought I had given them the best show that was ever staged in their territory since the landing of the Pilgrims! It was easily worth fifteen million bucks to watch me put the thing over."

Let's consider the traits of the Manipulator shadow in detail. As you read the descriptions below for each trait, take time to consider how strongly you experience each trait within yourself. Also consider whether you're triggered by any of these traits in other people. That may give you an idea of whether you're projecting aspects of the Manipulator onto those around you. ✍ 8.7

The Manipulator

- Detached
- Narcissistic
- Aggressively distorting
- Obsessive
- Withholding

Detached: Where the Magian in his fullness may be temporarily introverted and non–relational in order to fulfill his functions, the Manipulator is "schizoid," which means that he's simply incapable of, and disinterested in, relationships with other people. He lacks a healthy perspective of the needs of his Self, which prevents him from understanding the value of relationships. As a result, he prefers to keep to himself, engaged in his solitary mental pursuits. Men who are stuck in this shadow pole tend to feel very disconnected from the world they can see going on around them, but for some reason can never seem to take part in. This is similar to the type of detachment that's common among men with same–sex attraction.

A more extreme manifestation of the Manipulator shadow takes the trait of non–relationality to a more destructive level. Here a man may become entirely unconcerned with the feelings, needs, and wellbeing of others and disconnected from how his actions may affect them. This type of detachment is a more cruel and active lack of caring.

Narcissistic: This trait of the Manipulator is perhaps summarized best by the declaration *"It's all about me."* His detachment from others enables him to do what he wants and take what he wants without regard for the way his actions impact others. He considers himself to be entitled and sees others as simply a means to an end. "Of course my parents will give me the money I want." "Of course my wife will accept my acting out." "Of course everyone has to make me feel good about myself!" He's identified with the power of axis mundi—he *is* the turning point of the world.

The narcissist might find himself doing whatever is necessary to promote and protect his self–image, including things that are dishonest, unethical, or even illegal. His entitlement will prevent him from detecting the wrongness of his actions or how preoccupied he truly is with himself. But those around him are rarely fooled. They see his arrogance and ego–preoccupation and may often feel humiliated by his boundary violations.

The narcissist has never come to see that his place in the world isn't at the center of all things. But this grandiosity hides an even deeper shadow. Any experienced psychotherapist will tell you that narcissism is based on an underlying—and usually unconscious—sense of shame.

Men with same–sex attraction typically have a streak—or sometimes a swath—of narcissism, so this is an important point to understand. For us it often manifests

The Manipulator is incapable of, and disinterested in, relationships with other people.

The Manipulator considers himself to be entitled and sees others as simply a means to an end.

as an over–concern with how we feel about ourselves—particularly about our masculinity. We can be preoccupied with how we appear or come across to others. We tend to be especially concerned about our physical appearance—how we look and how we're dressed. In our relationships, we sometimes tend to pull others into the job of making us feel good about ourselves, and we may lose sight of their needs.

Aggressively Distorting: The Magian is a Master of Transformation. In his wholeness, he transforms his internal and external worlds into better places to live. The Manipulator's agenda is quite different. He uses his understanding of essential patterns, principles, and laws to transform his inner and outer worlds in ways that suit his shortsighted wants. This is how we get inventions that provide hours of fun, make great profits, or win wars, but destroy our world in the process. This is also how we get the destructive belief systems and false "common knowledge" that constantly sweep through our society. The Manipulator's world is one of distorted values, perspectives, and beliefs.

> The Manipulator uses his understanding to transform his world in ways that suit his shortsighted wants.

Part of the Magian's capacity to transform, you will recall, is his ability to control the way things appear. In his Manipulator shadow form, he uses this ability to distort the truth. Like the scientist referred to earlier, he tells the truth to lie—an all too common reality in our day where data and facts are so easily bent to support the favored hypothesis. As an artist, the Manipulator doesn't use the fabrications of his craft to show us deeper truths. He uses them to distort reality and promote his agenda. Moore and Gillette refer to this shadow pole alternatively as "The Trickster," pointing out the essence of his aim, which is to fool everyone around him in order to get what he wants. In this way, he may be mentally invasive and controlling.

The Trickster within us can be just as dishonest as a lying scientist or an agenda–driven artist. If we're not conscious and vigilant, this shadow can aggressively distort how we perceive ourselves, our lives, and our relationships. For example, we may find ourselves believing our addiction is no big deal. We might excuse our defensive walls as being a necessary protection. We might start assuming that our wives are the whole problem. We might confuse our need for friendship with a lust for sex. We might convince ourselves that other men will always reject us. Or we might view our bodies as inferior and disgusting.

> If we're not conscious and vigilant, the Trickster can aggressively distort how we perceive ourselves, our lives, and our relationships.

We might develop a toxic way of thinking that focuses exclusively on negative potentials. For example, we may focus our thoughts exclusively on pessimistic assumptions and expectations. We may come to prefer cynicism because it feels safer than optimism. We may assume the worst or even find ourselves unable to conceive of a positive outcome. Or we may see the world in black and white terms, expecting either perfectionism or complete failure.

Men with same–sex attraction distort a lot of things in our lives. But the appearance that many of us are best at transforming is that of our own personality. In his book, *Reparative Therapy of Male Homosexuality*, Joseph Nicolosi described a trait he had noticed among many men with same–sex attraction, which he called "the false self." This is a persona that some of us create to please the world around us and to avoid experiencing our own shame. The false self is usually very agreeable and "nice." It's a collection of traits we think others will accept, and it covers our deep insecurity and low self–esteem. We'll talk about the false self in much greater detail in the next chapter.

The Manipulator draws us into over-thinking, over-analyzing, and ruminating.

Obsessive: As a Master of Transformation, a Magian can cause things to appear as he pleases by controlling what he accentuates and what he hides. The Manipulator shadow sometimes uses that capacity to accentuate certain of our thoughts, drawing us into over–thinking, over–analyzing, and ruminating about certain things while ignoring other thoughts or activities.

We talked about obsessive thinking in Chapter Four as one aspect of obsessive–compulsive disorder (OCD) and obsessive–compulsive personality disorder (OCPD). The perspective I wish to share about it here is the way in which it can distort reality for the man or woman who suffers from it. In this sense, it's the Manipulator playing a trick on our own minds, diverting our attention with great urgency to things that are of far less importance than we are giving them.

For men with same–sex attraction, obsessive thinking may increase our sense of gender incongruity by focusing our attention so tightly on the differences we perceive between ourselves and the masculine norm that we become blind to our overall gender congruity. This is psychological slight–of–hand by which we can be tricked out of knowing the authentic masculine Self that truly exists within us.

Our Manipulator can also distort the reality of our relationships with other men by diverting our full attention to—and then sometimes exaggerating—every offense and rejection we receive from them. Such distortions can make normal male brusqueness and teasing seem like bullying and rejection. It can make bullying and rejection feel like substantial abuse. And it can make substantial abuse a debilitating wound.

Withholding: The Whole Magian is benevolent and generous, actively initiating others into his higher levels of understanding in order to empower the next generation. In contrast, the Manipulator is jealous and greedy. He withholds his knowledge and technological ability from those around him in order to protect himself from his own fear and shame. In doing so, he blocks others from progressing and advancing themselves.

> The Manipulator is jealous and greedy. He withholds his knowledge and technological ability from those around him in order to protect himself from his own fear and shame.

The fear he's avoiding is of his failure as a Magian. He fears that by giving to others, his wisdom may ultimately become irrelevant or that a greater Magian will eventually surpass him. In the outside world, his behavior may be to disregard or act with contempt toward the Magian capacities in others. He may engage in a "battle of the Magians" as he tries to outsmart them. His unspoken vow is to never empower another to become greater than he.

When he is active inside us, this shadow may withhold from us the knowledge and encouragement that we need in order to succeed in our own lives. Fear is at the bottom of this withholding as well. It's often expressed through statements like "I'm afraid that if I try, I will fail."

If he actually has failed, the Manipulator must cover up those failures by withholding information. This is standard practice in the world of politics and business as well as in our interpersonal relationships. Internally, our Manipulator may withhold from us the truth about our own failures and weaknesses by minimizing our problems and our mistakes. He also hides from us the existence or severity of our split–off shadows. This is particularly true of the Addict shadow of the Lover archetype, which we'll discuss in Chapter Ten.

The shame that the Manipulator is avoiding arises from the same underlying belief as his fear—that at his core he is nothing. In the outside world, narcissism is the Manipulator's shield against shame, and by withholding information and then cleverly dispensing it in bits and pieces, he supports the appearance of being truly magical. He believes this provides him with stature, superiority, and power. And, of course, he's careful to never dispense enough knowledge to fully educate and empower anyone else.

The Manipulator's internal withholding creates the denial that leads to the naïveté of the Innocent, as we will soon see.

The Innocent

The purpose of the Whole Magian is to help, heal, and transform himself and the world through his use of knowledge. The Manipulator's mission is to protect and promote himself through the manipulation of others with information. In contrast, the Innocent's mission is to get through life passively by denying his knowledge, pretending to be ignorant, rejecting his power, and making himself dependent on others.

The 1967 film version of Lerner and Loewe's musical, *Camelot*, portrays King Arthur in just such a light. In brief, the story depicts Arthur's denial of an affair between his queen, Guinevere, and his most beloved knight, Lancelot. The affair, which lasts for several years, leads to many deaths and an inevitable rift between Arthur and Lancelot, concluding in a battle between their forces. This is where the film begins—just before dawn on the day of the battle. In this opening scene, Arthur's face shows childish perplexity as he asks the memory of his long–departed mentor:

> "Merlin, why is [Guinevere] in that castle behind walls I cannot enter? How did I blunder into this agonizing absurdity? When did I stumble? When did I go wrong? …. Oh Merlin, how did it happen? I haven't got much time. A thin inch of sunlight and the arrows begin to fly. Merlin, if I am to die in battle, please, please do not let me die bewildered."

Though laced with other archetypal elements—mostly shadow but occasionally whole—Arthur demonstrates with chilling clarity the traits of the Innocent. From this pre–battle scene, we next review in flashback the long history of Arthur's denial of reality, naïve high mindedness, and intellectual dependence on the absent

The Innocent's mission is to get through life passively by denying his knowledge.

Merlin warns Arthur of Camelot's ruin.

240

wizard, Merlin. Sequence by sequence, we watch as he brings the downfall of his ideals and kingdom.

In a pivotal scene just after recognizing, for the first time, the attraction between Lancelot and Guinevere, Arthur's initial anger softens. He asks himself, "Did they ask for this torment? Can passion be selected?" It seems he would prefer to believe that this *ménage à trois* can't be helped, that the trio are victims of fate. Nevertheless, he exultantly resolves that, "we shall live through this together!" While his compassion and vision might be seen as a brief flash of true Kingship, Arthur soon shows that he has no real plan for resolving the dire situation, other than to collude with the lovers to hide their affair.

Arthur uses his newly created laws and court to accomplish this end. Devised as a plan to "civilize" his people, the laws require evidence for an accusation to be made. But Arthur is careful to see that no evidence of the affair exists. This passive–aggressive manipulation of circumstances actually crosses into the active pole of the Magian. The ploy fools only some of the knights. Accusations multiply, contention is stirred, and open disputes erupt. Arthur's only response is to banish the accusing knights, sowing the seeds of his own destruction.

Eventually, Lancelot and Guinevere are caught. Lancelot escapes but Guinevere is taken into custody, charged with treason, and sentenced to death by fire. Arthur again undermines his own legal system—this time to allow Lancelot an opportunity to rescue the unfaithful queen, whom Arthur still adores. The rescue costs many lives and demands a military response, leading us back to the morning of the battle on which the film opens. As the movie ends, Arthur is left entirely empty. His beloved Round Table has been destroyed both figuratively and literally. The ideals for which he strived have been lost. His only hope resides in a young stowaway whom he charges with the task of telling only the honorable parts of the story to succeeding generations.[14]

Now, as we look at the Magian's passive shadow traits, pay attention to the close relationship between the two Magian shadows. As with all archetypes, they are opposite sides of the same coin. And, as we saw in the vignette on King Arthur, those who are in these shadows sometimes cross back and forth between them. Carefully read the descriptions below, keeping an open mind about how these traits

> Arthur soon shows that he has no real plan for resolving the dire situation, other than to collude with the lovers to hide their affair.

> Arthur is left entirely empty. The ideals for which he strived have been lost.

may show up in your own personality and behavior. Also think about how you may be projecting these traits onto other people. ✍ 8.8

The Innocent

- Denying
- Naïve
- Victim
- Dependent
- Empty and passive–aggressive

Denying: The Innocent is not conscious. But his lack of consciousness isn't caused by a deficit in mental capacity. It comes from his refusal to see things as they truly are and his refusal to be taught. He doesn't want to know and he doesn't want to learn. He refuses to pursue or receive wisdom from external sources like teachers and mentors. In a classroom or a group, he might refuse to learn anything at all. Or he may learn only those things that endorse what he already believes are true.

He also refuses to learn anything from internal sources. His memory may be short. He likely has little or no insight or intuition. And his emotions teach him nothing— if he feels them at all. He's ignorant of his problems and weaknesses as well as of his strengths and potential abilities. The Innocent's denial is actually a product of the Manipulator's withholding, as we discussed previously. While on the surface the Innocent man looks naïve and unwilling to see reality as it truly is, deep inside him, his Manipulator is hiding the truth from him. As a team, these two shadows create an unconscious pretense of not knowing.

So in this shadow pole, men refuse to recognize the truth. They also refuse to speak the truth. Whether because they lack internal awareness or because they fear rejection, men often deny anything in them that isn't "innocent." They may deny that they have any motives other than the purest, or those they believe are the most appropriate for the situation. They may deny any "bad" feelings, particularly anger, but also fear, envy, sexual desire, and sometimes even guilt and sadness. And they often deny that they are having any problems or need any help.

Denial is a key component of the false self that so many men with same–sex attraction create. I referred to the false self a few pages back as one of the ways in which the Manipulator distorts appearances. A false self is actually a co–creation of both of the Magian's shadow poles. The Manipulator's active distortions manufacture the favorable appearance, while the denial of the Innocent serves to hide the faults.

Naïve: innocently ignorant and unlearned

Naïve: While the Manipulator may obsessively over–think, the Innocent tends to under–think. He can't seem to figure life out. He may feel dull and is often confused. In this state he doesn't know *himself*—and truthfully he doesn't want to. With very little tolerance for discomfort or pain, he won't endure the distress that comes with gaining knowledge. So he can't understand his own behavior or why others respond to him as they do. He can't comprehend consequences or why things happen the way they do in the world, in his work, or in his relationships. He can't speak up for himself because he doesn't know what to say. If he ever does speak up, it will be through the voice of the Manipulator, and then he won't understand the negative reactions he receives.

As with the Innocent's denial, this ignorance is not caused by a deficit in the man's mental capacity. This is *pretend* ignorance, although sometimes the pretense is happening so deeply in the man's unconscious that even he believes the lie. He will frequently say "I don't know" or "I just don't get it." And as the Innocent, he really thinks he doesn't.

> This is pretend ignorance, although sometimes the pretence is happening so deeply in the man's unconscious that even he believes the lie.

Nor is his lack of understanding excusable because he has not had the opportunity to learn. His naïveté is about things that the man should know. Being uninformed about the political situation in Congo isn't naïveté, it's just a lack of information—unless of course you're the ambassador to Congo. But being completely baffled as to why you continue acting out or why your wife has been angry with you for the past two years *is* naïve. Such a man may be of average or better intelligence. But for some reason he just can't figure out a few crucial things. His friends may wonder why such a smart guy can't get his life together.

This naïveté may contribute to a man's gender incongruity by telling him that he doesn't know how to be a man—that "I just don't get it." From that naïve place he may see other men as members of some mysterious club to which he is not invited—a club with special jargon, secret handshakes, and insider jokes. Consciously or unconsciously, he may believe that the knowledge that would make him masculine is unavailable to him. Or maybe, in his completely passive "innocence," he may lack the curiosity to find out. And so he becomes content to stay passively on the outside.

> This naïveté may contribute to a man's gender incongruity by telling him that he doesn't know how to be a man.

These beliefs and behaviors prevent him from getting close enough to other men to ever figure them out. He may be friendly, personable, and even "nice," but he struggles to grasp relational essentials, including intimacy, attachment, self–assertion, empathy, honesty, and forgiveness. So he doesn't *show up* in relationships.

As a result, he rejects the opportunity for initiation when other men offer it. This may be the most destructive of all the Shadow Magian's mistakes.

Victim: As a victim, the Innocent manifests the mirror opposite of the Manipulator's narcissist. Whereas the narcissist sees *himself* as the turning point of the world, the victim has no axis mundi. Lacking a Center and a connection to forces beyond his own, he can't figure out how to access power in his life. Unlike the Whole Magian who understands how to channel and use power, the Innocent is bewildered by it. He has projected the power and control that come from knowledge and understanding onto those around him, seeing everyone else as being "in the know." Everyone else has control and they are manipulating him with it. He's their innocent victim. The legitimate use of power by those around him leaves him endlessly confused, and he tends to react to it with fear and hurt.

He's also confused by boundaries. The boundaries that others set often seem cruel and imposing. He may feel manipulated, rejected, alienated, or even attacked— once again he's the victim. He may be too afraid to set his own boundaries, but if he does they will tend to be either too little or too much. Either way, they will ultimately be ineffective.

Consequences are another point of confusion for the victim. Because he has such poor insight into his own motivations and behaviors, he's often perplexed by the way others respond to him. He will likely see the consequences that befall him as more punishing and unfair than those that others receive. Everyone else gets off easy, but nothing ever goes right for him.

When this part of the Innocent shadow falls on a man with same–sex attraction, he will see himself as the victim of other men, and sometimes of women, too. His defensive reaction may be to detach from them, leading to the host of problems discussed in Chapter Seven. This isn't the cold disinterest in relationships that's typical of the Manipulator shadow. Rather, it's a withdrawal from pain and fear.

The victim's overall problem is that he doesn't understand where he stands in relation to other people. In opposition to the narcissist, he assumes he stands below them, and this is his constant preoccupation. So curiously, like the narcissist, it's still all about him.

The Innocent has projected the power and control that come from knowledge and understanding onto those around him.

The victim's overall problem is that he doesn't understand where he stands in relation to other people.

Dependent: Because he's naïve, the Innocent can't figure life out or make it work for him. Because he's a victim, he has no power to get what he needs. His own axis mundi resides in someone else, and he must depend on that person for his wellbeing, if not for his very existence. This may be one reason why he must maintain such an "innocent" false self. Since he is dependent on others for his life, he must retain their approval at all costs. He has to remain in their favor by being the best little boy he can.

Dependency doesn't mean that the person has any real relationships with others. Dependent relationships are not healthy friendships. They tend to lack all of the elements of community outlined in Chapters Three and Six. Rather than true commonality, these relationships are brought together by the dependent one's desperate needs. Instead of trust, the dependent one over–relies and simultaneously fears losing the other. A false self takes the place of authenticity. Rather than reciprocity, the dependent one only takes. Boundaries are really just a tug–of–war between the dependent one's attempts at enmeshment and the other person's ever–increasing resistance. And while the giver in the dependent relationship may feel genuine love and compassion, the dependent receiver can rarely believe that it's anything more than pity.

Among some of us with same–sex attraction, particularly younger men, I've noticed an additional dependent tendency. Some of us express a sense that we can't live up to the demands of life. Taking on the role of responsibility for a wife and family seems daunting. Sometimes it's even too much to be responsible for anything more than our basic needs. Sometimes we'll live with our parents or others for a protracted span of our lives.

Empty and Passive–Aggressive: The Innocent has no power to help, heal, or transform himself or anyone else. In his weakest and most passive state, he has no Magian capacity at all. He has no vision, and his creativity is dead. He can't even conjure up a false self. He's an empty vessel—unable to channel any power. This is the furthest extreme of the passive pole of the Magian shadow. Some men may live in this state for many years, while others may only occasionally fall into this extreme. To go any further in this direction will bring about a swing toward the active shadow, usually through aggression. Even to commit suicide from this empty place requires a shift into aggression. Suicide is a passive–aggressive disappearing act—the ultimate transformation of self into total shadow.

> Since the Innocent is dependent on others for his life, he must retain their approval at all costs.

> This is the furthest extreme of the passive pole of the Magian shadow. To go any further in this direction will bring about a swing toward the active shadow.

Passive–aggressiveness: actions that, on the surface, seem to have no obvious harmful or disruptive intent, but which actually are unconsciously intended to undermine, frustrate, or interfere with others.

Moore and Gillette describe a common dynamic that takes place at this transition point from the passive to the active poles of the Shadow Magian. Referred to as passive–aggressiveness, this dynamic consists of actions that, on the surface, seem to have no obvious harmful or disruptive intent, but which actually are unconsciously intended to undermine, frustrate, or interfere with others. Coming late, failing to follow through on assignments, and forgetting commitments can all be passive–aggressive behaviors. In the therapeutic setting, some men resist help after they've reached out for it or create chaos in the session by their lack of focus. Or they may complain about everything the therapist does—no intervention is quite right, and he never understands them perfectly. The most skilled passive–aggressive people can turn the tables on others instantly and with no warning, leaving those around them groping to try to understand what suddenly went so wrong.

Very often the man caught in this dynamic doesn't realize the chaos and aggravation he's causing. He may recognize that others often seem frustrated with him, but in his naïveté he simply believes he's being victimized yet again. For some men, passive–aggressiveness is a central part of their personality. Others resort to such behavior only when their people–pleasing fails or when it's insufficient to get them what they want.

THE SYNERGISTIC MAGIAN

We have examined the Magian in his wholeness and in his shadows. Let's take a few minutes now to review all of this together—to get a full view of the Magian's range of capacities and to see the synergistic potential among those capacities. As I explained in Chapter One, synergy comes from having a transcendent perspective of the archetypal energies and from balance, moderation, and integration of those energies.

Spend some time now familiarizing yourself with the table on the next page so that you can get the lay of the total Magian landscape. Use the same method you used when you reviewed the King and Warrior Trait Scales. First review the *Manipulator* column, then the *Innocent* column. Next review both of the *Moderation* columns together. After you've done that, review the table horizontally one trait scale at a time, considering the full range of the attributes associated with that trait.

Once again, there are numbered paragraphs below the table to help you understand the details of each scale. And take time to consider how each trait may be manifested in your life. Find your tendencies on each scale, remembering that we often have a range and may slide back and forth from one side to another, depending on our circumstances. ✍ 8.9

Magian Trait Scales

		Manipulator	Moderation	Innocent	
Traits	1. Relationships	Schizoid	Able to detach	Able to connect	Dependent
	2. Self-esteem	Narcissistic	Self-valuing	Humble	Victim
	3. Use of Power	Distorting	Transforming	Unadorned	Empty
	4. Thinking	Obsessive	Focused	Relaxed mind	Naïve
	5. Knowledge	Withholding	Giving	Receptive	Denying

1. Relationships

This scale describes the range of ways in which the Magian might respond in relationships with others. The Manipulator is *schizoid*, meaning that he has no desire or ability to connect. In moderation, this side of the Magian is *able to detach* from relationships at times when it's needed without being cold or unfeeling. The Innocent is *dependent* on others for his sense of wellbeing and perhaps even for his physical wellbeing. In moderation, he's *able to connect* with others in meaningful ways and under appropriate circumstances.

2. Self–Esteem

This scale depicts how the Magian might value himself in relation to others. The Manipulator is *narcissistic*, seeing himself as more important than others and treating them poorly. In moderation, he's *self–valuing*. He esteems himself highly but doesn't place himself above others. The Innocent sees himself as a *victim* of others who have greater knowledge and power than he. Accessing this trait in moderation, he's authentically *humble* and capable of understanding and accepting his true place in the world.

3. Use of Power

This scale looks at the Magian's use of his ability to transform things. The Manipulator uses his knowledge and power in an aggressively *distorting* way, twisting the truth and transforming his world to serve his own ends. A moderate active Magian uses his capacities in beneficially *transforming* ways, making his world a better place for all. The Innocent is completely *empty* of any transforming capacity. He has no power to do anything other than to exist in the bleakest reality. In moderation, this passive Magian attribute is an ability to live an *unadorned* life, free of any guise or pretense, and to show that unadorned self to others. He's also able to experience the world as it really is and to show the real world to others.

4. Thinking

This scale considers the possible nature and manner of the Magian's mental activity—in other words the nature of his thinking. On the far end of the active shadow, the Manipulator's thinking style may be *obsessive* or ruminative—he thinks far too much. But his excessive mental activity is not productive nor does it bring him to the truth. Instead, it leaves him confused, doubtful, and anxious. In moderation, the active Magian's thinking is *focused*, meaning that he's able to sustain clear, meaningful, and productive thought. The Innocent under–thinks, leaving him *naïve*. There isn't a lot going on in his mind. And his under–thinking may put him in pretty much the same place as the over–thinking Manipulator— confused, doubtful, and anxious. As a moderate passive quality, this trait allows the Magian to be *clear minded*—to free his thoughts of clutter, to meditate, and to leave himself open to inspiration from a higher source.

5. Knowledge

This scale has to do with the flow or transfer of knowledge and wisdom between the Magian and others. It's different from the other scales in that within its polarity it actually contains not just one set of opposites, but two: withholding versus giving of knowledge to others and denying versus receptive of knowledge from others. The Manipulator doesn't impart his knowledge to others—he's *withholding* except as it suits his selfish purposes to give. In contrast, the Whole Magian is *giving* and enjoys blessing others with his knowledge and wisdom. One of his key purposes is to help initiate and transform others by sharing what he knows. The Innocent rejects knowledge that comes from within himself or from others by *denying* the truth. In contrast, the Whole Magian is open and *receptive* of new understanding, whether it comes from within himself or from others.

THE HEALING POWER OF THE MAGIAN

We have reviewed at length the intensely destructive powers of the Magian's shadows. But equally powerful are his capacities to heal.

The Magian functions of possessing secret knowledge and mastering transformation are the energies of self–exploration and self–understanding. The inner Magian knows our unmapped internal terrain. By accessing that wisdom, we learn about our inner kingdom. The Magian is introverted and thoughtful. His introspection connects him with our deep inner truths. As the Detector of Corruption, he sees through the lies of our narcissistic illusions and shame–based distortions, bringing a more focused awareness of self. And he deflates the arrogant defenses that block our authentic self–expression.

As our observing ego, the Magian shows us our emotions from a place of helpful detachment. As the creator of sacred space, he helps us contain and channel those feelings. As the Master of Transformation, he brings the ability to navigate our mysterious, ephemeral feelings and to use our emotions to bring us to more whole places, like a mariner uses winds and tides to sail across a body of water. Under his guidance, our capacity to handle deep and conflicting feelings expands. The quest of our inner Magian leads us deep inside ourselves to places where he initiates us into higher ways of being a man.

> The quest of our inner Magian leads us deep inside ourselves to places where he initiates us into higher ways of being a man.

But there is only so far that our inner Magian can take us on our own. At some point, we must accept the leadership of outer Magians, or "ritual elders," who can guide us, support us, and challenge us. We must be willing to move through our terror, lean into our pain, and follow trustworthy mortal magians in search of our shadows.

Two aspects of the Magian's healing capacities warrant more in–depth discussion. The first is the Magian's ability to create powerful initiatory experiences that transform our lives. The second is the capacities he provides to steward conscious friendships so they too can transform us. We'll discuss these in the sections that follow. ✍ 8.10

INITIATION

Active connection to the Magian archetype brings powerful initiatory experiences. In the book *The Magician Within*, authors Moore and Gillette describe the initiation process as proceeding in three stages. Borrowing terms from Joseph Campbell, they refer to these stages as *the call, the belly of the whale,* and *the return.* The structure of these three stages is typical of all adventure stories and many performing arts genres, including movies, plays, and operas. If you have participated in any experiential weekends, you may notice that these stages are typically the broad structural framework of those weekends as well.

But this three–stage initiation process isn't something that people made up to tell stories and organize weekends. It's a process so innate to us as humans that we take it for granted. In our lives, we go through these stages repeatedly. Most particularly we go through this process at times of substantial change, such as adolescence, middle age, and retirement. But most applicable to our consideration here is the understanding these stages provide regarding the process of growth beyond same–sex attraction. In the sections that follow, I've paraphrased Moore and Gillette's concepts and applied them to our healing journey.

As you read about these stages, look for them in your own life. Keep in mind that you have the power to start this initiation process on your own. You don't have to wait for life experiences to bring it to your door. Moore and Gillette assure us that our inner Magian innately knows the "blueprint for the self," and he works to bring us into the fullness of our potential through initiation.

Stage One: The Call and Entry into Sacred Space

The call is essentially any life circumstance—internal or external—that brings us to the threshold of an opportunity for change. In the story of *Jack and the Beanstalk,* the call is represented by Jack's mother giving him the responsibility to go and sell the cow. At first, Jack's call seems like a simple afternoon journey into town and a small step toward greater responsibility.

But what begins as a simple journey toward responsibility quickly escalates into a much greater call when Jack finds the massive beanstalk growing outside his window. The discovery of the beanstalk is the first in a long series of drastic turns Jack's journey takes. The unexpectedness of this and so many other events in the story represents the unpredictability of the initiatory process with its many calls. It's never possible to tell what will happen next or where the journey will lead. This is likewise true of therapy and every other substantial growth process.

Initiation
- The call and entry into sacred space
- The belly of the whale
- The return

The call is essentially any life circumstance that brings us to the threshold of an opportunity for change.

If we heed the calls as they come, we're ushered into sacred space, which is any place where transforming initiatory experiences happen. Religious initiations have occurred for millennia in temples and sanctuaries, on mountains and in deserts. The kind of sacred space needed for the transformation you're seeking can be created in life–changing friendships, on a basketball court, in the space between the open door of an airplane and the ground below, in a therapist's office, and in countless other places.

Essential to a man's call and entry into sacred space are the feelings of "wonder and terror." This has led some to call fear the "gateway emotion" to the Magian. This is true in part because the man being initiated senses that he's entering unfamiliar and dangerous territory—he's embarking on an adventure with no guarantee of return. Something in him knows that the old self will be broken down, and he will never be the same again. He knows on some level that this will be a death. So fear and anxiety arise in anticipation of the process.

Let's take a moment here to become clear about the various feelings that may be grouped together under the heading of fear. These include fear, terror, anxiety, panic, and wonder. Fear itself is an emotional response to a specific threat that's known and immediate. Specific changes occur in our bodies when we feel fear. These include increased heart rate and quickened breathing, widening of the eyes, perspiration, and muscle tension. The observing ego becomes hyper–aware and external sensory perception is heightened. These states enable quick and powerful reactions. Responses to fear include fighting, fleeing, or playing dead. The word "terror" is used to denote unusually intense fear.

Fear: emotional response to a specific threat that's known and immediate

Terror: unusually intense fear

Unlike fear, anxiety is not a response to an immediate threat. Anxiety is a more generalized mood of worry and negative anticipation about problems or situations that aren't immediate threats. Usually the dreaded situation seems uncontrollable and inescapable to the person, and sometimes the source of the anxiety may be unclear or completely unknown. Very often, anxiety is caused by irrational thoughts like those created by our inner Manipulator's toxic thinking.

Anxiety: mood of worry and negative anticipation about problems or situations that aren't immediate threats

Most of the bodily responses that are typical of fear also occur when we experience anxiety. In addition to these, we may experience fatigue, nausea, headaches, or stomachaches. Our bodies are preparing us to fight or flee, but since the anxiety–causing situation is not immediate, not controllable, or not understandable, we can't respond in a way that brings resolution. This tends to result in a behavioral debilitation that's similar to playing dead. Responses are inhibited and capabilities are reduced.

The term "panic" refers to intense and sudden anxiety. And "wonder" is the emotion experienced in the presence of something unusual and unexpected. It's like surprise except that the feelings are positive, engaging, and can be lasting.

Panic: intense and sudden anxiety

Wonder: positive feeling toward something unusual and unexpected

In *The Magician Within*, Moore and Gillette describe the "wonder and terror" experienced by individuals entering into sacred space, or what they also call the "extraordinary world." In sacred space, wonder comes with terror—and the terror must be endured if the wonder is to be enjoyed. Terror often precedes a journey into the self. In one type of psychotherapy, fear and anxiety are considered "signal feelings"—in other words, markers of deeper feeling to follow. In my therapy office, and on many experiential weekends, I've often seen men show fear or anxiety at the beginning of a process and then drop through those feelings into the more powerful emotions of anger or grief that lay beneath them.

Many men are kept from the extraordinary and wonderful transforming power of sacred space by their anxiety and fear.

Many men are kept from the extraordinary and wonderful transforming power of sacred space—and from a true initiation process—by their anxiety and fear. Therapy is too frightening, so they avoid going—or they quit. Their men's group causes too much anxiety, so they sit quietly hoping not to be singled out. Speaking up for themselves terrifies them, so they ignore their emotional charges rather than risk hurting someone's feelings or looking stupid. The men at work intimidate them, so they interact with them only through their false self.

But fear is essential to the initiation process because fear itself is transforming—it stretches us and makes us capable of handling things for which our previous coping abilities were not sufficient. It calls up from within us a deeper set of capacities for handling the stress of the initiatory experience. Perhaps most of all, fear brings about the capacity for humility by reminding us of our own smallness and vulnerability.

If the fear is strong enough, it tears open the sophistry and illusion of the Manipulator and punctures the false naïveté of the Innocent. It also rouses the Warrior for battle. When the fear has passed, the King within may have a new Center, a new order, and a new law. Things that seemed impossible before are doable now. The experience of fear is like dying and rebirth—things take on a different significance and value, and life is experienced in a new way. Moore and Gillette make the point that "human beings need to die to their old selves before they can be born anew."

The worst mistake a man can make at the moment when he hears the call to initiation is to run from his fear. In doing so, he will derail the initiatory experience and stop his growth dead in its tracks. 🖊 8.11

Stage Two: The Belly of the Whale

The term "belly of the whale" comes from an incident that's recorded in the Christian *Old Testament*, the Jewish *Torah*, and the Muslim *Qur'an*. A prophet named Jonah (Yonah in the Torah and Yunus in the Qur'an) is invited into an initiatory experience by a call from God to preach to the wicked inhabitants of the city of Ninevah. Jonah runs from the call by boarding a ship heading in a different direction. But like Jack, his process takes a series of drastic turns by way of a terrible storm and a very large fish (often referred to as a whale).

Jonah is swallowed by the sea creature and spends three days in its belly.

Jonah is swallowed by the sea creature and spends three days in its belly. This is a transitional time for Jonah, who emerges from the fish more flexible and receptive, ready to fulfill his responsibility.

Jonah was lucky. God didn't allow him to escape his own initiation experience, but sent powers much bigger than Jonah to get him back on track. When we run from the things that call us into initiation, we're often not so fortunate. We often find a life of beguiling ease and comfort when we run away from the psychological and emotional distress involved in major change processes.

Crisis is a great inducer of change because by definition it overwhelms our old capacities. It forces us beyond our existing ways of responding to life. A crisis brings a certain type of death. Our old perspective of the world dies. Sometimes our innocence dies along with it. Old and inadequate parts of ourselves die as well. Sometimes following a crisis, when remembering back to our lives before, we don't recognize ourselves then. A quantum shift has happened, and we can never go back to the old self any more than a moth can go back to being a caterpillar. But this only works if we're flexible. A rigid response to a crisis will just reinforce and further harden our old, inadequate ways of coping.

In *Jack and the Beanstalk*, Jack heeds his call with enthusiasm. (Sometimes a little bit of genuine innocence isn't a bad thing.) Following where the beanstalk leads, Jack climbs his way into the belly of his whale—the castle of the Giant. But what this story dramatizes in just a few pages is actually a painful and grueling process that can span years. In real life, there is far more running from the shadow and wrestling with the giant than there are golden geese and magic harps.

To clarify, we are in the belly of the whale anytime we're in a life–transforming initiatory process. The term might be applied to the years of our overall recovery process or to any specific threshold–crossing experience within it. As referred to earlier, these are times when our old view of ourselves is broken down and a new self–concept emerges. Even after our main recovery is complete, we'll continue to have initiatory processes every time life invites us into a more mature way of being.

We are in the belly of the whale we meet our shadows and character flaws. We're invited to re–experience our past. This is the heart of our change process where the slow bucketing–out of painful and frightening repressed feelings takes place. This can be—and perhaps should be—a painful experience. St. John of the Cross referred to such times in our lives as "the dark night of the soul." Just as fear causes the breakdown of our immature and ineffective coping capacities, so too pain can be a powerful force for organic growth and maturation, if it doesn't kill us. The Magian within us—often assisted by magians around us—helps us transform our pain into growth and new strength over the course of months and years. Often this is where the greatest wonder is experienced.

If this time of initiation is to be growth–producing rather than merely terrorizing, certain things are required. In addition to "ritual elders," we need *containment* during our time in the belly of the whale. Literally, we need something to hold us together and help us to deal with the intense feelings and impulses that come up in the process. Sometimes our innate abilities to contain our own emotions and impulses can become overwhelmed, and we find ourselves wanting to act out sexually or with anger, manipulation, or withdrawal. Containment may come in the form of therapy, trustworthy friends, twelve–step meetings, men's groups, and positive daily rituals including meditation and prayer.

We are in the belly of the whale anytime we're in a life–transforming initiatory process.

Ritual elders: a term Moore and Gillette use for men who are mentors and guides for those in an initiation process

254

In addition to containment, we also need something stable in our lives to hold on to and to keep us in reality. This might be a therapist or the therapeutic process. It could include a religious community or healing fellowship of supportive friends. It can be a strong belief, which for men in the process of shifting their sexual attractions is often the secure belief that homosexuality isn't what they want for their life. The stable point can also be a connection to God or some other higher power. Our own observing ego can create a sense of stability by providing awareness that we're *in a process*—this is not real life. That can give a helpful bit of distance from the intensity of it all. ✎ 8.12

Stage Three: The Return

Sacred space must eventually be left behind. We have to return to the conventional world. Experiential weekends are joyful and satisfying, but they are not real life. Therapy sessions can be transforming, but when they end we have to go back home. The overall change process can feel distracting and urgent, but it's a time outside of real life, and the time comes when real life—whatever that means—should be resumed.

If all goes well, there will come a time when the main parts of your healing and growth process will have been concluded and you will find yourself getting back to "the real world." Only the real world won't seem to be what it was before the journey began. You will experience it differently because you will be different.

> The real world won't seem to be what it was before the journey began. You will experience it differently because you will be different.

This return to real life is something to be looked forward to. But we must take care to neither rush it or to avoid it—both are mistakes that happen too frequently among men going through this process. Often this has to do with how men handle their belly–of–the–whale time. The man who is attending his twentieth ex–gay conference because he needs a "boost" has probably not ever really gone into the darkest night of his soul. He has probably avoided his terror and just skimmed the surface of his wounds, perhaps barely even glancing at his shadows. Such men will have also missed the wonder of finding their wholeness. Conversely, the man who is "all done" in just a few months is most likely in the grips of the Innocent. If he's lucky, a fish will swallow him.

Initiation isn't accomplished until the return is successfully made. The change from same–sex attraction isn't complete until a new life without same–sex attraction as a central awareness has been established. If you can develop and maintain a strong connection to your inner Magian, you will know when you're there. ✐ 8.13

Stewarding Conscious Friendships

I've already emphasized in this book the importance of close male friendships to the process of healing the issues that lie beneath unwanted same–sex attraction. For many of us with same–sex attraction, having fulfilling same–sex affiliation is one of our non–negotiable core needs. In addition, friendships with other men can be a tremendous help in improving our sense of gender congruity.

But intimate friendships can be tricky for us, or even perilous. This is especially true when the friendship is between two men who experience attractions toward each other. In order for friendships to be beneficial, they must be stewarded by the wisdom of the Magian. We need to understand the risks and benefits entailed in various types of relationships. We also need to understand the diverse feelings we might encounter in our friendships. And we must know how to create and maintain consciousness in our friendships.

Understanding Risks and Benefits

The risks and benefits of male–male friendships differ depending on whether the men we choose as our friends are same– or opposite–sex attracted and whether or not we're attracted to them. Let's consider a few scenarios.

First let's discuss friendships with men to whom we're *not* sexually attracted. These are the safest and least complicated in terms of avoiding sexual missteps and painful emotional reactions such as anxiety, jealousy, abandonment, and hurt. If the friend is heterosexual, an additional layer of safety exists because the likelihood of a sexual slip is minimized. Key benefits in friendships with non–attractive heterosexual men may include fulfillment of same–sex affiliation needs and gaining a stronger sense of gender congruity, particularly if our friend seems masculine to us. These friendships can provide a bridge for us into the male world.

If the friend is same–sex attracted and we're not sexually attracted to him, we're still relatively safe from the possibility of a sexual misstep, although it's possible for sexual attractions to develop later in the friendship. The benefits of these friendships often include a strong sense of being understood, ease in sharing our life experiences, powerful feelings of compassion, and receiving meaningful support, encouragement, and advice. If our friend is same–sex attracted and gay–identified, meaning that he's not working toward changing his sexual orientation, these benefits may be diminished by differences in outlook and goals.

Now let's consider friendships with men to whom we *are* sexually attracted. These are less safe in both sexual and emotional terms. If the friend is heterosexual, there is usually little risk of a sexual slip. But we may still be at risk for developing feelings of anxiety, dependency, jealousy, vulnerability, and hurt in reaction to the underlying issues that are activated in conjunction with the attraction. We may experience unrealistic desires and expectations. And we may be prone to eroticizing the friendship through fantasy. But if we can avoid the risks, the benefits of these friendships can be tremendous. They can provide powerful fulfillment of same–sex affiliation needs and can foster profound growth in gender congruity. These friendships may provide the strongest bridge for us into the male world.

> Friendships with men to whom we are sexually attracted are less safe in both sexual and emotional terms. But if we can avoid the risks, the benefits of these friendships can be tremendous.

If the friend to whom we're attracted is also same–sex attracted, we stand the greatest risk of experiencing any or all of the sexual and emotional problems mentioned above. This is intensified further if the attraction is mutual and still further if the friend isn't actively involved in his own healing process. When attraction is involved, friendships between two same–sex attracted men tend to be unstable, even volatile, and require great consciousness and external accountability so they don't set us back in our progress. This can be true even if we maintain good sexual boundaries. In terms of benefits, these friendships can provide intense fulfillment of our needs for same–sex affiliation. They can also be a source of increased gender congruity although they tend to provide less of a bridge into the male world.

Both the risks and the benefits are greater in friendships with men to whom we're attracted, whether the friend is heterosexual or same–sex attracted. A certain amount of the risk can actually turn into a benefit if we're willing to submit our thoughts and feelings to close scrutiny and accountability. If we process the feelings that emerge with someone outside the friendship, we can experience tremendous growth. This will usually require a therapist with the skills and experience necessary to help us understand and resolve the underlying issues causing the feelings. At a certain level, however, the risks overwhelm the benefits and it may be most wise to discontinue the friendship. 🖋 8.14

> If we process the feelings that emerge with someone outside the friendship, we can experience tremendous growth.

Understanding Our Feelings and Desires

If we're to be conscious stewards of our friendships, we need to understand the nature and source of the feelings our friendships bring up.

In not enough simply to understand the risks and benefits associated with our friendships. If we're to be conscious stewards of our friendships, we also need to understand the nature and source of the feelings our friendships bring up. To increase that understanding, let's first remind ourselves of what we discussed in Chapter Seven on two key issues: gender incongruity and same–sex disaffiliation. Gender incongruity leads to feeling at odds or out–of–sync with what we believe a man is supposed to be. Same–sex disaffiliation leads to feeling alienated from, and incapable of connecting with, male community. These two issues underlie the attractions of most same–sex attracted men.

Now let me add that these two issues seem to create different types of attractions toward other men. The attractions created by gender incongruity seem to be more focused on a desire to gain access to another man's masculinity through seeing him, touching him, or having sex with him. The attractions created by same–sex disaffiliation seem to be more focused on a desire for intimate attachment and bonding with another man through closeness with him, whether or not that closeness is sexual.

Understanding how our underlying gender incongruity or same–sex disaffiliation can affect our feelings toward other men can shed light on how our friendships are impacting us.

Understanding how our underlying gender incongruity or same–sex disaffiliation can affect our feelings toward other men can shed light on how our friendships are impacting us. Shifts in the way we feel about our masculinity or male attributes may indicate that our friendships are creating changes related to gender incongruity. On the positive side this can look like feeling more masculine, more confident around other men, more capable as a man, or less interested in the masculine traits of other men. We tend to experience other men as less mysterious. On the negative side, this can look like feeling more intimidated by men, less confident about our maleness or our body, less willing to engage in masculine activities with other men, and more attracted to the masculinity of other men.

Shifts in our sense of connection with other men probably indicate that our male friendships are affecting our same–sex disaffiliation. On the positive side, this can include feeling more cared for and included by other men, loved and supported by them, and less lonely, needy of male attention, hungry for closeness, and attracted to the idea of being intimately bonded with another man. On the negative side, this can mean feeling the exact opposite of the above: not cared for or included, unloved and unsupported, and more lonely, needy, hungry, and attracted to the idea of intimacy with a man. Often, this negative state will be accompanied by feelings of anxiety, insecurity, and a desire to pull away.

Understanding the course of our attractions in a friendship can also shed light on how our friendships are impacting us. Typically, men with same–sex attraction notice that our attractions toward other men decrease as we get to know them. When we first encounter or meet another man whom we find attractive, his masculine mystery may tap into our gender incongruity. Or he may bring up our unmet need for affiliation. Either possibility can create sexual attraction. But by getting to know him, we may experience familiarity, thus dispelling his mystery and potentially lessening our sense of incongruity. Getting to know him may also provide affiliation, potentially fulfilling our hunger for closeness. Both of these can lessen our attraction to him.

But sometimes the opposite occurs—attractions actually increase as we become closer to another man. I believe this phenomenon results from what could be called a "desire/fulfillment gap." When there is a difference between the level of desire for closeness in a specific relationship and the level of fulfillment of that desire, attraction may occur in direct proportion with the difference, or gap, between the two. Let me explain. When we're barely acquainted with a man we're likely to have lower hopes and expectations for intimacy. But as the friendship develops, our hopes and expectations may rise, especially if we have strong same–sex affiliation needs. The increase in our desires for intimacy may outpace the development of our friend's feelings. Or perhaps our needs are simply beyond our friend's capacity to fulfill.

> When there is a difference between the level of desire for closeness in a specific relationship and the level of fulfillment of that desire, attraction may occur in direct proportion with the difference, or gap, between the two.

The difference between the level of desire for closeness and the level of fulfillment of that desire creates the gap. Our unconscious mind experiences the gap as a painful longing or urge for something to fulfill our unmet needs for same–sex affiliation. Since the unconscious is amoral, without boundaries, and closely connected with bodily impulses, it proposes the most direct and physical way of filling that gap, which may be through sexual intimacy with our friend. ✍ 8.15

Creating Consciousness

The foundation of consciousness is openness and honesty. Addicts in recovery often say, "You're only as sick as your secrets." If we apply that logic to

Friendships are only as healing as they are honest.

It's a principle of friendship that when one friend reveals himself, the other will reciprocate.

Take on yourself the responsibility to steward your friendships and invite your friends into that process.

friendships, we find the inverse is true: friendships are only as healing as they are honest. This doesn't mean every friendship you have has to be a totally authentic healing relationship. It's okay to have acquaintances and less intimate friendships. And it doesn't mean that you need to rush into deep honesty with your friends. It's better to take your time and move gradually. Just remember that the friendships that will heal and transform you the most will likely be those in which you're the most honest.

It's a principle of friendship that when one friend reveals himself, the other will reciprocate. So as you start opening up, expect that your friends will probably do the same with you. Their willingness to share with you is also vital for keeping the friendship conscious because that's how you will understand the strengths and weaknesses they bring to your interactions. It also has the added benefit of lessening any mystery that may exist around your male friends, which could otherwise contribute to attractions. And it will be beneficial for your friends as well—they also need someone to confide in. If you have a friend who doesn't reciprocate—who stays closed even after you've started sharing openly with him—it may be an indication that he's not ready to go deeper. After a few tries, if he doesn't respond, back off and allow that friendship to stay at the level that seems comfortable to him.

Bring into your friendships the knowledge you're gaining about friendships and what makes them work. We've discussed friendship in Chapters Three and Six, and I'll provide more specific information on the characteristics of healthy friendships in Chapter Ten. Rather than expecting your friends to understand how friendships should work, take on yourself the responsibility to steward your friendships and invite your friends into that process. Consciously and actively apply the principles you're learning in your friendships and talk openly with your friends about it. Of course, you need to keep that in moderation so that the topic doesn't become annoying or overbearing.

Push the envelope in your friendships by consciously attempting to make them mutually transforming, rather than just remaining unconscious and "getting along" with your friends. But remember that gradual movement toward intimacy is more comfortable for most men, and it's more sustainable long term because it allows relationships to comfortably find their optimal intimacy level. Avoid making abrupt moves toward greater honesty or closeness. Push progress along at a moderate pace, allowing your friends to catch on and adjust to the idea of the increase in closeness. Many men will be open to greater intimacy, but some men will be freaked out by it, especially if you move fast. Allow those men the freedom to run the other way without taking it personally.

Apply the Magian's role as detector of corruption to your friendships. This should mostly be applied to watching for your own issues to surface: your detachment, doubt, suspicions, falseness, and pretensions. Watch for the games you play and the ways in which you hide. Ask yourself questions like "What am I really after?" "What shadow might be behind my feelings, thoughts, or behaviors?" "How am I contributing to this problem we're having?" Again, be open about all of this with your friends. Secondarily, watch for your friends' issues to surface and, in compassionate ways, tell them what you see, owning your own stories and feelings around it.

> Apply the Magian's role as detector of corruption to your friendships. This should mostly be applied to watching for your own issues to surface.

In the case of intense friendships, which would include relationships where there is mutual attraction, it's wise to have a third person to process the friendship with. This could be someone close to you who has some experience in maintaining healthy friendships. But it may need to be a therapist if your relationship is bringing up strong feelings in you. If you have lots of wounding around your relationships with other males from earlier in your life, you will most likely need therapy to resolve that. Without help, the programming created by that wounding could continue to sabotage your friendships with current male friends.

Friendships with other men are not a panacea. They are not a replacement for emotional and psychological healing. Underlying issues must still be processed and healed. We still have to own and resolve our gender incongruity. We can't import masculinity from another man no matter how close we get to him. And we still have to heal the issues that lie beneath our same–sex disaffiliation. At the same time, the significance to the overall healing process of having healthy male friendships should never be underestimated. ✎ 8.16

> Friendships with other men are not a replacement for emotional and psychological healing.

ADVANCING YOUR MAGIAN

In the final pages of *The Magician Within*, Moore and Gillette suggest several tasks that are part of initiation into Whole Magian. I won't try to paraphrase them all here, but I'll focus on a few concepts that seem particularly relevant to the journey we're on. I offer them as suggestions for advancing your Magian.

Claim Your Intellectual Birthright

You have a right to use the full capacity of your mind. So allow yourself to learn. Some men have been discouraged from learning or have been told that they are intellectually inadequate. These men may need to push through some internal barriers to fostering their Magian. Some men may even need help from another person who can assist them in breaking their negative belief about their ability to obtain and use knowledge.

Don't compare the capacity of someone else's mind with your own. Don't compare their intellectual achievements or apparent wisdom with yours. This is an insult to your own Magian and may precipitate a fall into the Innocent shadow. Rather, spend your energy and time trying to find your own Magian gifts. Find your own ways of learning, processing, retaining, and applying knowledge. Some people are visual learners while others learn better through hearing, and still others learn best through physical interaction. If you want more information on this topic, search online for "learning styles" or "aptitudes."

As part of claiming your full intelligence, don't let yourself be deceived into believing societal and cultural myths that are false and destructive. We live in an age of run–amok Manipulator energy. These days it's often the person with the loudest microphone and the biggest name who gets to decide what the "truth" is going to be. The idea that homosexuality is natural, inborn, and unchangeable is one of these culturally fabricated "truths." This belief persists despite the lack of supporting data and the mountain of evidence to the contrary. If you find yourself ever wondering about the truth of an idea, research it out so you don't leave yourself vulnerable to the "Oprah–fication" of reality.

Seek Self–Understanding and Growth

Invest in understanding and mastering your mental and emotional life.

Your thoughts and emotions are the main tools you use in living life and engaging in relationships with others. So invest in understanding and mastering your mental and emotional life. As the Possessor of Knowledge, work to understand how you think, what causes you to feel the emotions you feel, and what motivates your actions. Investigate the patterns that occur in your life by first taking responsibility for these patterns as something that *you* are creating.

Of particular importance are the patterns that have prevented you from meeting your needs, that have frustrated the accomplishment of your goals, or that have created conflict in your relationships over the years. Once you have owned a pattern as your own creation, you can begin to discern the feelings and beliefs that are contributing to it and, searching more deeply, you may recognize the life experiences that are giving rise to those beliefs and feelings. Then, as the Master of Transformation, you can apply what you're learning through finding or creating processes that can bring about growth.

In pursuing this step, it's very wise to obtain the help of a Magian with greater wisdom, or at least a different perspective. Often it takes someone who isn't under the influence of our inner shadows to help us see them. In addition to accessing the help of others, you can find or create sacred space and involve yourself in initiatory experiences. This might include therapy, twelve–step work, deeper study of the archetypes, engaging in a group, or in meaningful and searching conversations with trusted friends or with your spouse.

Balance Your Magian With the Other Archetypes

When our traits and attributes are not balanced by contrasting aspects of our personalities, we tend to slip into shadow. One of the best ways to bring balance to archetypal shadows is to develop or intensify aspects of the other archetypes. You can bring any shadowy Magian tendencies you've identified in this chapter into balance through accessing energies of the King, the Warrior, and the Lover.

> You can bring any shadowy Magian tendencies into balance through accessing energies of the King, the Warrior, and the Lover.

For example, if you tend to gravitate toward the active Magian shadow of detachment from others, you can access the Lover's desire for union and connection as a source of balance. If you find yourself narcissistically making everything about you, consider developing a Warrior's transpersonal commitment or the King's function of beholding others. If withholding from those around you is a tendency, you might put effort into developing your King's desire to bless others. Or if obsessive thinking is a challenge, you may need to bring up your Warrior's discipline and establish firmer mental boundaries by cutting off thoughts that threaten your wellbeing.

On the other hand, if you lean toward the passive Magian shadows of denial and naïveté, the Warrior's courage and fearless authenticity might be necessary in order for you to begin seeing things as they really are. If you experience yourself as a victim or as dependent in your relationships, the Warrior's boundaries, aggression, and discipline might free and empower you. Or if you find yourself to be empty, it may be the King's vision and the Lover's libido you need to access.

Prepare Yourself to Help Heal Corruption

The accumulation of the many efforts described in this chapter is a preparation toward becoming a "ritual elder" who possesses the capacities that are necessary to bring others into mature masculinity. Part of this role is to serve as an example in your community.

One of the Magian capacities I described earlier in this chapter is the ability to detect corruption. I remarked in that section that a lot of men with same–sex attraction have a particularly strong ability to detect corruption in the larger world of men. We can be pretty rough on other men and on male culture as a whole. Sometimes it's well deserved. But a mature Magian doesn't stand back and idly watch the world burn. Only a Manipulator withholds his knowledge and skills when they are needed. Only an Innocent chooses to remain a victim of his circumstances. Remember, as men on the path of initiation into mature Magian capacities, it's our responsibility to help initiate other men into higher ways of being.

As soon as you're ready, I encourage you to begin finding ways of reaching out to other men who you think might be receptive. Share with them the things you're learning. Invite them into more mature ways of relating by relating with them in mature ways. Create male community with them through trust, authenticity, reciprocity, boundaries, and unconditional love and compassion. Exemplify the archetypal capacities as well as you can, and let them know the ways in which you're trying to develop yourself.

> As soon as you're ready, I encourage you to begin finding ways of reaching out to other men who you think might be receptive.

With every gift we receive comes a responsibility. The things you're learning through your own initiation process are a tremendous gift, and it's your duty as a man to use them in ways that help, heal, and transform yourself first and then others. But here's the miraculous part. With a gift like this, it's impossible to ever give away more than you receive. I can personally attest to the reality that the more I give away the gifts of knowledge, leadership, and love, the more those abilities are amplified in me and the more those blessings are returned to me in ways that bring tremendous joy. Give yourself the gift of giving. ✍ 8.17

INITIATION BRINGS AUTHENTICITY

Initiation is the route to authenticity. It brings a wholeness of self without shame or split–off parts. It brings mastery of self, including the ability to experience our full range of emotions. We come to know ourselves and experience the wonder of our lives and our own gifts.

From this place we can reveal our true selves to others authentically, without anxiety. We see them for who they really are without the distortions of our projections and transferences. We can relate to them directly without manipulation, understanding them with compassion and greater clarity. And we can forgive. This all brings a sense of greater mastery in our ability to relate.

With boundaries and assertion provided by the Warrior, we can practice the art of friendship and intimacy, causing our relationships to deepen. This, of course, opens the way for greater fulfillment of our same–sex affiliation needs. Our sense of gender congruity becomes more solid as we experience ourselves as deeply, authentically masculine.

As our inner Magian grows stronger, his energy enriches our other inner archetypes. To our Lover he gives knowledge for the practical expression of our libido and emotions, uniting us with those to whom we express ourselves. To our Warrior, the Magian brings discernment and mindfulness. And to our King he provides the wisdom, insight, and skills needed to bless ourselves and those around us.

Initiation is the route to authenticity. It brings a wholeness of self without shame or split–off parts.

---

[1] http://www.bbc.co.uk/religion/religions/zoroastrian/beliefs/god.shtml

[2] http://www.bbc.co.uk/religion/religions/zoroastrian/beliefs/dualism.shtml

[3] http://en.wikipedia.org/wiki/Zoroaster

[4] http://en.wikipedia.org/wiki/Gathas

[5] http://en.wikipedia.org/wiki/Biblical_magi

[6] Zaehner, Robert Charles (1961), *The Dawn and Twilight of Zoroastrianism*, New York: MacMillan, p. 163.

[7] Mair, Victor H. (1990), "Old Sinitic *Myag, Old Persian Magus, and English Magician," *Early China* 15: 27–47. http://www.dartmouth.edu/~earlychina/docs/earlychinajournal/ec15frntuni.pdf

[8] The Quran 22:17

[9] Matthew 2:1–12

[10] http://en.wikipedia.org/wiki/Pythagoras

[11] Moore and Gillette use the term "Master of Technology" to label this function. I've used the term "transformation" because I think it avoids confusion and gets more directly to the underlying purpose of this aspect of the Magician's role.

[12] http://en.wikipedia.org/wiki/Charles_Ponzi

[13] Ogunjobi, Timi (2012), *SCAMS – and how to protect yourself from them*, Tee Publishing, p. 175

[14] *Camelot* is a trove of archetypal characters. The Magian is fully displayed through Merlin as a Whole Magian, Arthur as Innocent, and Mordred as Manipulator. Arthur also shows Weakling Abdicator and Mordred demonstrates much of the Tyrant King archetype. Lancelot displays alternately Whole Warrior, Addict, and Impotent One. And Guinevere provides an interesting sketch on Anima, particularly a warning about Anima possession. The Whole King archetype is present only in the concepts Arthur espouses but which he is too weak to carry out.

CHAPTER 9

AUTHENTICITY

γνῶθι σεαυτόν – Know thyself.
Socrates

To thine own self be true.
Shakespeare, *Hamlet*

o be authentic means to live out of the core of who we truly are, undistorted by our shadows, wounds, or symptoms. It means being the real thing—being genuine or pure. It's something more than blunt honesty. Rudeness is sometimes honest. Rage can be honest. So can hatred, lust, and selfishness. But authenticity represents the highest and most mature level of ego consciousness of which we're capable.

Authenticity springs from the guiding Self that exists at our Center. It conforms itself to unchanging principles, patterns, and universal laws that govern its existence. Authenticity requires the joyful, gracious, and confident acceptance of our whole self in the present, exactly as we are—works in progress. We're able to openly acknowledge our flaws of character, without shame, as we work on them. This description makes it clear that we'll always be *becoming* authentic. We'll never arrive there.

The Magian's dual role as the Possessor of Knowledge and the Master of Transformation makes that archetype essential to the process of becoming authentic. As the Possessor of Knowledge, he continually brings us to deeper awareness of our shadows and our potential wholeness. As the Master of Transformation, he continually initiates us into higher ways of being and doing. The Magian is on a quest to find our deepest authenticity. Ever conscious, he's committed to revealing our core truth, and he's willing to sacrifice whatever is necessary to manifest that in our lives.

Authenticity is of two types: internal and interpersonal. In this chapter we'll explore the roles of both types of authenticity in the pathway out of unwanted same-sex attraction. We'll use our understanding of the Magian archetype to help us comprehend what authenticity entails, how we obscure and hide our own authenticity, and what we can do to uncover and further develop it. First, let's review the essential meanings of authenticity.

Internal authenticity means being whole within ourselves and accepting ourselves totally, rather than splitting off, repressing, or denying parts of ourselves. This requires an understanding of who we are on a deeper level than our job description, sexual feelings, or the labels given to us by our family, friends, or society. It requires the capacity to feel and tolerate the full range of our own emotions and impulses, which can sometimes seem confusing, conflicting, and painful. Internal authenticity includes clarity about where we fit in the world and in our relationships with others. And it depends on an ability to integrate all of this into a whole individual who can meet the challenges of life and relationships.

> Internal authenticity means being whole within ourselves and accepting ourselves totally, rather than splitting off, repressing, or denying parts of ourselves.

The second type of authenticity—interpersonal authenticity—means being true to our Center[1] in our interactions with others. It's the ability to be fully present and assertive in our relationships to whatever degree is appropriate and to respond out of our Center at all times. Interpersonal authenticity depends foremost on being internally authentic. We must know ourselves before we can behave in a genuine way.

> Interpersonal authenticity means being true to our Center in our interactions with others.

Interpersonal authenticity does not imply that we must reveal all that we are to everyone around us. Nor does it imply being raw in our expressions or inflicting our every emotion on those around us. Usually our raw emotions—particularly anger—are not the product of an integrated and authentic man. Rather, they are usually outbursts of shadow. This is not to say that we may not need to find safe and appropriate places to express many such outbursts in the process of healing ourselves, integrating our shadows, and becoming authentic. But the sharing of our information and emotions with others should be done with discernment.

Ultimately, I believe that authenticity is far more an internal way of life than an interpersonal practice. In other words, authenticity comes from knowing and accepting our Selves. What we show to others and what they understand about us is secondary and of lesser importance. We can live authentically within ourselves even if we consciously choose to hold back details about our truth that others don't have the capacity, or don't choose, to understand.

For men who are trying to resolve homosexuality, understanding the shadow aspects of the Magian may be particularly important in the process of developing authenticity. These two shadow poles—the Manipulator and the Innocent—can block our authenticity in a variety of ways. The Innocent encourages passivity and denial, while the Manipulator distracts us from what's really important. The Manipulator can also obscure our true identity with a false self and distort our perceptions of others through transferences and projection. These last three shadow effects—false selves, transferences, and projections—create a world of fragments. We are not whole, and we can't see the wholeness of the people around us. All of these shadowy tricks contribute to gender disruption in some insidious ways.

This chapter is mostly a "heads up" of the various ways we can lose or become alienated from our authenticity. It's somewhat like the black half of the yin–yang symbol, which by its outline shows us the definition of its opposite—the white side of the symbol. In other words, this chapter will show you much of what authenticity is *not*. The last several pages, however, are devoted to describing a process that can lead us back to our authenticity.

PASSIVITY AND DENIAL

The mission of the Innocent is to get through life passively by denying his knowledge, keeping himself ignorant, rejecting his power, and making himself dependent on others. The Innocent within us might undermine our internal authenticity by refusing to engage the subject of our sexuality and identity. His denial may keep us totally uninformed and naïve. In *The Magician Within*, Moore and Gillette suggest that the man in this shadow "doesn't want to know himself, and he certainly doesn't want to make the great effort necessary to become skilled at containing and channeling power in constructive ways."

The passivity and denial of the Innocent can make us susceptible to many self–sabotaging mindsets and behaviors. For example, we may believe we don't know what we need to do to change our lives, and we may have little drive to find out. We may not understand why we're attracted to certain men or what those attractions mean. We may not have a sense of what the needs are beneath our attractions. We may not be able to comprehend how our unmet needs lead to unhealthy patterns

> For men who are trying to resolve homosexuality, understanding the shadow aspects of the Magian may be particularly important in the process of developing authenticity.

> The mission of the Innocent is to get through life passively by denying his knowledge, keeping himself ignorant, rejecting his power, and making himself dependent on others.

and cycles of behavior. Being so consumed by our own emptiness and victim mentality, we may be unable to reach out to other men. Being unaware of how we contribute to the unhealthiness and failures in our relationships with women, we may choose to either just avoid women or to remain in comfortable or dependent relationships with them. Or we may be completely clear about the problems in our relationships with women but we just passively tolerate them.

When we're naïve, we don't understand consequences, and we refuse to take responsibility for our actions and inaction. For example, we can be seduced into believing that we can continue our homosexual behavior and, at the same time, somehow change our same–sex attraction. We can beguile ourselves into thinking that we can overcome our body shame issues without doing anything to take care of our bodies. And we can trick ourselves into shifting the responsibility for meeting our same–sex affiliation needs onto the men around us.

Passivity and denial can create a pious innocence—both internally and with others—to avoid touching any of our inner pain or power. On a deeper level, we may fear that we can neither contain nor channel the intensity of our emotional and psychological forces, and so, unconsciously, we determine that remaining ignorant of them is the most prudent course. We may stay active in worthy pursuits, using those activities to avoid anything that feels too real. Having resolutely shied away from discomfort and pain, we will develop little or no tolerance for either.

The passive Magian pole readily joins forces with the passive poles of the other three archetypes: the Weakling Abdicator, the Masochist, and the Impotent Lover. Together these passive inner forces keep us pure and clean, but also dull and lifeless. With them in the lead we're left anxious, empty, and unable to access our native masculinity in any meaningful way. ✍ 9.1

DISTRACTION

In a magic show, one of the magician's main ploys is to keep the audience's attention on some irrelevant action while he works the trick in a place where they aren't looking. Our personal Manipulator does the same thing when he distracts us internally from our own healing process using the problems, concerns, comforts—and most convincing of all, the necessities—of daily life. The Manipulator in our own minds can keep our attention so focused on our job, the demands of family,

> When we're naïve, we don't understand consequences, and we refuse to take responsibility for our actions and inaction.

> Passive inner forces keep us pure and clean, but also dull and lifeless.

our travel schedule, worries about money, or putting others first, that we never get around to doing the therapeutic work and being in the healing relationships with either males or females that will bring about change. Of particular concern is the way we can distract ourselves from every opportunity to connect with other men, which tends to greatly intensify our same–sex disaffiliation.

The Manipulator can also focus our attention away from authentic healing programs by suggesting to our minds that the easier, faster, cheaper, or more comfortable route is all we need. He can blind us to the necessity of going through the discomfort that accompanies any deep initiatory process. One of the most debilitating ways he may accomplish this is by supporting the Addict shadow pole of the Lover through what has been called "addictive thinking." More will be said about the Addict in Chapter Ten. ✍ 9.2

> The Manipulator can focus our attention away from authentic healing programs by suggesting to our minds that the easier, faster, cheaper, or more comfortable route is all we need.

PROTECTIVE SELVES

The personalities of psychologically healthy men and women are a unique expression of their individual intrinsic traits. Their interests, feelings, desires, impulses, preferences, and typical behaviors all combine in a coherent and cohesive ego, which may be comprised of many varied and complementary ego states. And that ego is pretty much the same from one circumstance to another.

But children who grow up in shame–bound families split off and hide the parts of themselves that they believe are bad or unacceptable. We discussed this at length in Chapter Four. This blocks them from developing a single, cohesive, internally authentic personality. Instead, they develop a protective false self,[2] with their real traits—or authentic selves[3]—hidden somewhere underneath.

Children create protective selves in reaction to the people around them. It may be that the loss of the authentic self (through splitting and hiding) leaves a void, and in order to fill that void—to give them someone to *be*—children unconsciously construct the protective self. Moore and Gillette offer a slightly different perspective in *The Warrior Within*. "A man develops a false self early in life after his true self is attacked or ridiculed," they say. To them, the false self is a kind of mask these shamed children wear in order to get along with those whose acceptance and care they require. By conforming to other's expectations, these children hope to get some of their needs met. In *Healing the Shame that Binds You*, John Bradshaw puts it more simply. There he describes the false self as an escape from the painfully shamed true self.

Regardless of what exact psychological mechanisms lead to its creation, protective selves show up in a wide variety of forms. Bradshaw writes that, "[t]he false self is always more or less than human," meaning that they are either too good or too bad to be real. For example, the upstanding overachiever and the derelict dropout may both be protective selves. Likewise, the perfect church–going husband and the out–and–loud queer man may both be hiding their authentic selves. Also, it's important to understand that a person can have more than one protective self. For example, a man could have a primary protective self that looks really good to society, while also having a contradictory "bad boy" protective self that he manifests only when he's acting out.

There are certain factors that all types of protective selves seem to have in common. In general, the protective self can be characterized as being inauthentic, unaware, disempowered, and defined by others. Conversely, the authentic self can be characterized as real, aware, empowered, and self–defined. The table on the facing page provides lists of words further characterizing these differences.

The protective self in archetypal terms is a Shadow Magian's trick indeed. It's a disappearing act where the eyes of our personal audience are kept firmly fixed on our public face so that our shadows, insecurities, and fears can creep off the stage. This can create some serious problems. For example, when we relate to other men through our protective selves, our inner Manipulator can get us to believe that "no one really knows me." And because our protective selves exist to cover our shame, we'll typically assume that if others *did* know our "shameful" authentic selves, they would reject us. This blocks one of our most core needs, which is to be known and loved by other men.

When we relate to women, many men with same–sex attraction are particularly good at using protective selves to cover our insecurities, fears, and other distressing feelings. We may play nice–nice with women so they won't detect how much we actually mistrust or loathe them. We may pretend to be calm and confident so they won't realize how much they scare us. We might act like one of the girls to mask the grief we feel from depriving ourselves of close bonds with other men. Our relationship with the feminine within us—our Anima—can also bring on a

---

The false self is an escape from the painfully shamed true self.

The protective self can be characterized as being inauthentic, unaware, disempowered, and defined by others.

The authentic self can be characterized as real, aware, empowered, and self–defined.

Signs of the
Authentic and Protective Selves

Authentic Self | Protective Self

Within Self

Authentic Self	Protective Self
Masculine	Unmasculine
Adequate, on par	Inferior, inadequate
Secure, confident, capable	Insecure, unconfident, incapable
Experiencing authentic emotions	Emotionally dead or over-emotional
Energized	Lonely, bored, angry, depressed
At home in body	Body is an object
Physical confidence	Anxious clumsiness
Feeling empowered, autonomous	Feeling controlled by others
Accept imperfections	Perfectionistic
Active, decisive	Passive
Creative	Stagnant

With Others

Authentic Self	Protective Self
Attached	Detached
Outgoing	Withdrawn
Spontaneous	Over-controlled
Forgiving, accepting	Retaliatory, Resentful
Genuine, authentic	False, role playing
Seek out others	Avoidant
Animated	Frozen
Aware of others	Constricted awareness
Assertive, expressive	Nonassertive, inhibited
Mature in relationships	Immature in relationships
Respectful of others' power	Resentful of others' power
Trusting	Distrustful
Empowered	A victim
Integritous; open	Double life; secretive
Rapport with oposite gender	Misunderstanding of opposite gender
See other men as like self	Pulled by mystique of other men

protective self when we let her possess us through exaggerated effeminacy. This cloak of disguise is probably a comfortable hiding place for a gender–shamed or double–bound boy. But rarely does it fool the onlookers.

Many of us are very confused about our authentic and protective selves. We tend to show the world a "good boy" self, which we believe is false and protective, while covering up a "bad boy" self, which we believe is authentic. I think we make this assumption because the "good boy" self is a persona we use to please society and to cover up feelings and impulses that we see as unacceptable. Remember that the rules of shame–bound families require that every imperfection must be hidden and covered with a perfect–looking lie. After living that way for many years, we come to see *truth* as synonymous with *hiding*. Therefore, we assume that whatever we're hiding must be the truth and whatever we're showing in public must be a lie. The Shadow Magian is working overtime.

> We come to see *truth* as synonymous with *hiding*. Therefore, we assume that whatever we're hiding must be the truth and whatever we're showing in public must be a lie.

But both the "good" and the "bad" selves are false protection—and both contain the truth, also. The "good boy" may contain our authentic kindness, generosity, sensitivity, and spirituality. The "bad boy" may contain our autonomy, power, assertion, passion, and sensuality. The tragic mistake we often make is to live in this false dichotomy with such intensity for so long that we eventually feel drained by the contradiction and cover–up. Finally, we run out of patience and energy and go with whichever ego state brings the quickest relief.

A final note about the effects of protective selves may be useful. If we lose contact with our authentic self, we may be susceptible to getting our sense of who we "really" are confused with our sexual attractions and the social label of "gay." This confusion arises from the belief that we created our protective self to cover up our homosexuality and that the remedy for this is to come out as gay. Lacking clarity about the chronology of our own histories, we don't realize that the protective self came first *followed by* the attractions and the labels. Confused about the *cause*, we may mistake the *symptom* for the *cure*. The most dangerous magical trick is the one that fools the magician himself. As Moore and Gillette wisely observed about men gripped by protective false selves, "A man may forget who he really started out to be."

> The most dangerous magical trick is the one that fools the magician himself.

Outgrowing our protective selves is core to living authentically, which is essential to resolving homosexuality. Only by experiencing ourselves fully—free of repression and denial—can we feel internally masculine and enjoy satisfying and authentic relationships with other men and with women. But after so many years of living through protective selves, how can we escape those patterns and learn to live fully from our authentic core? The main process for relinquishing our protective selves is by healing toxic shame, which we discussed in Chapter Four. As we pursue that healing, we must be on the lookout for the pieces of our authentic selves that are scattered throughout our various protective selves. We do this by noticing our heartfelt values, our sincere emotions, and our truest desires and impulses. Understanding the nature and background of our protective selves can be very helpful in this process.

The main process for relinquishing our protective selves is by healing toxic shame.

One of the most powerful tools for empowering and growing our authentic self is to join or create safe situations for experimenting with and expressing our authentic self. This can be done in individual friendships, experiential weekends, or in ongoing groups where full expression of feelings and impulses is welcomed and safely handled.

When a pattern of living through false selves is deeply entrenched, help from a therapist, life coach, or someone else with strong Magian energy might be necessary to heal the underlying trauma that led to the creation of these false selves. ✍ 9.3

TRANSFERENCES

As very young children, we're subjected to the relationships created by our parents and the other significant people around us. Those relationships may be cruel and abusive or nurturing and supportive. From these relationships we begin to learn important dynamics, like how people interact, what to expect from others, and what our role is in society. These dynamics, and the beliefs we learn from them, are reinforced by additional events that occur as we grow up. This may be because our minds are more receptive to experiences that confirm what we already believe than to experiences that disprove what we think we know. When we reach adulthood, we may still be living out those same childhood relationships—whether cruel, abusive, nurturing, or supportive. But now we're probably engaging in them with a whole different crowd of people. Why does this happen?

When we reach adulthood, we may still be living out childhood relationships—whether cruel, abusive, nurturing, or supportive.

It happens because our foundational paradigm of the world is built by the experiences of our early childhood. Once we're taught by the circumstances that surround us to accept the given patterns, dynamics, roles, expectations, and outcomes, we'll tend to accept those—and only those—throughout our lives, unless we grow truly weary of them and change them. So if our close childhood relationships were with selfish people, or cruel people, or loving people, we'll tend to see selfishness or cruelty or love in the people around us—even if it's not really there. This leads us to unconsciously recreate patterns from *past* relationships in our *current* relationships.

This tendency is both internally and interpersonally inauthentic. Freud created a name for this tendency—he called it "transference." To put it in practical terms, transference is when your boss reminds you of your father or your wife brings up the same old feelings your mother used to trigger. Some additional examples might be helpful. We might transfer our father's authoritarianism onto a boss, a religious leader, or even God—and respond to them with the same resentment and anger we had toward our father. We might transfer our mother's neediness onto a significant woman in our life and fear being close to her. Or we might transfer the schoolyard bully's penetrating will to shame us onto the man that fixes our car and go into anxiety and dread whenever we have to talk to the repairman.

Sometimes these current–life people just happen to really be like our parents, bullies, or abusers. And sometimes we actually turn them into those people with the power of our expectations. Our transferences can repel us, attract us, or both. Transferences block us from becoming more fully authentic by keeping us stuck in outmoded roles and relationships from childhood. Transference is the Manipulator using stories from the past to blind us to the reality of the present.

Transferences can contribute to every aspect of gender disruption. First, the distortions caused by transference—whether unrealistically positive or negative—tinge our interactions with other men with inauthenticity. Inauthentic relationships tend to be poor sources of attachment, resonance, approval, and support. Such relationships can foster same–sex disaffiliation. And since disaffiliation prevents us from really getting to know other men, it supports and maintains our sense of gender incongruity.

Likewise, the distortions caused by our transferences may color our interactions with the women in our lives today. The patterns, dynamics, roles, expectations, and outcomes we experienced with the females in our youth will tend to show up in our

> Transference is when your boss reminds you of your father or your wife brings up the same old feelings your mother used to trigger.

> Transferences can contribute to every aspect of gender disruption.

adult relationships with the opposite sex. Our transferences can be cross–gender as well, like when your father's personality gradually emerges in your wife or when every one of your boyfriends ends up being just like your mother.

A very good way of spotting your transferences is to be on the lookout for bad relationships that you stay in because they feel strangely comfortable and familiar. Or watch for moments when you find yourself thinking, "I'm so sick of people treating me this way!" And be sure to keep your eyes open for the most blatant transference–based thought: "That person is just like my _____ (fill in the blank from your past)!"

Transferences are not bad or good. They are just unconscious echoes from the past. Sometimes they provide accurate warnings of danger. But they can also be false alarms that distract us from seeing the truth of another person. Awareness of our transferences allows us to manage them wisely and to learn about the effects of our past relationships. ✍ 9.4

PROJECTIONS

Simply defined, projection is the act of seeing in someone else a feeling, impulse, desire, or personality trait that we hide, repress, or deny in ourselves. Speaking archetypally, projection is the Manipulator hiding our self from ourselves, then making pieces of us appear in the faces, bodies, and actions of other people. As Carl Jung said, as quoted in *The Portable Jung*, "Projections change the world into the replica of one's own unknown face." In terms of their impact on authenticity, we could say that projections begin as an unconscious internal lie and become an equally unconscious interpersonal fabrication. This is psychological slight–of–hand, like when a carnival magician makes a coin disappear from his hand then pulls it out of your ear. To help you understand this concept fully, we need to review a few principles you've already learned.

Throughout this book we've discussed how aspects of ourselves may become split off and pushed into shadow by painful and shaming life experiences. In our infancy and childhood we're able to experience all of the divergent energies and traits of the boyhood archetypes. That's why babies can cry one moment and laugh the next, or why little children can be very strong willed and self–centered one minute and then hand their toy to another child ten minutes later. In *A Little Book on the Human Shadow*, Robert Bly describes this as "360 degree personality," meaning

> Projection is the act of seeing in someone else a feeling, impulse, desire, or personality trait that we hide, repress, or deny in ourselves.

that nothing has yet been cut off and hidden in our unconscious, which he calls "the long bag we drag behind us." In other words, children have no shadow.

But painful and shaming life experiences split the archetypal energies apart by making it unsafe to exhibit certain energies or traits. So we cut off those traits in ourselves that seem unwanted or unsafe and we stuff them in "the long bag" of our unconscious shadow. On the other hand, we amplify those traits that keep us safe or get us the things we want. We come to experience these safe parts of ourselves as "*who I am.*" They become our identity. The energies or traits that we've pushed into shadow become experienced as "*who I am not.*"

But our split–off parts can't simply be jettisoned, *because we need them.* They are parts of ourselves—just like our body parts—and we can't live healthy lives without them. Our feelings are meant to be felt. Our impulses need to be recognized and learned from. Our needs must be fulfilled. And our opposing archetypal energies are meant to be held together in a compound wholeness.

Much damage can be done in our lives by splitting or fragmenting ourselves.

Much damage can be done in our lives by splitting or fragmenting ourselves. In fact, many of the problems we've discussed in the past chapters are the result of fragmenting ourselves. Without the help of effective reintegration processes— which we'll discuss later in this chapter—humans seem to respond to fragmentation or splitting in two different ways. The first is through dysfunctional emotional states, which could include feelings of emptiness, anxiety, and depression. These are reactions to *not* being whole and *not* having our emotional needs met. They are counter–emotions and don't bring resolution or heal the splits. The second response to self–fragmentation is through various kinds of pseudo–integration, which could be defined as ineffective attempts to become whole. Projection is a type of pseudo–integration, as are co–dependency, addiction, and same–sex attraction. Let me explain this further.

Projection resolves the conflict between our normal need to own all aspects of ourselves and our unhealthy compulsion to disown the parts we've come to see as bad. Experiencing those parts in another person allows us to hold a repressed or denied trait at a distance from ourselves, but still connect to its energy in our life. In a sense, we live that energy *through another person.* In their book, *The Warrior Within*, Moore and Gillette put it this way: "When we project, we make others bear our own shadows."

For example, imagine that your Warrior energies have been fragmented—you're identified with your Masochistic side and your Sadistic side has been repressed deep into your unconscious. These energies must remain balanced—every Sadist has a Masochist to exploit and every Masochist has a Sadist to keep him in his place. Your repressed Sadistic energy must show up somewhere in your life. So perhaps you project your Sadist capacities onto people around you—in fact you attract these people to you—and then you find yourself being bullied, treated unfairly, and feeling like a victim. Through this relationship you experience both poles of the shadow Warrior.

We may project many different traits onto others. But all of our potential projections fall into three categories: we might project what we are, what we wish we were, and what we fear we might be or become. I'll explain these further.

Projecting what we are refers to traits that are present in our bodies or personalities but that we have blocked ourselves from recognizing and expressing. These may be desirable or undesirable traits. Often, gender imperatives are in this category of projection. The masculine man who sees himself as weak and effeminate but is drawn to the masculinity of other men exemplifies this. So does the man with underlying rage who won't admit his own anger but thinks everyone around him is mad.

Projecting what we wish we were refers to traits we haven't developed in ourselves, but which we believe are desirable or necessary. Gender imperatives are often in this category, too. The timid man who has never allowed himself to be powerful exemplifies this when he idealizes the aggressive, confident man. So does the man who has no heterosexual feelings but is attracted to men who can have sex with women.

Projecting what we fear we might be or become refers to traits we see as undesirable, that we've repressed in ourselves, but that we need to own in order to balance an opposite trait. This takes us back to the concept of synergy and the archetype trait scale tables. Any of the extreme traits on those scales could be in this category. For example, the man who projects arrogance onto other men may need a dose or two of that arrogance to counterbalance his tendency to abandon and fear his own power.

> We might project what we are, what we wish we were, and what we fear we might be or become.

Just like transferences, projections are neither bad nor good. They are our unconscious trying to show us ourselves. Sometimes they provide accurate information about the feelings and intentions of other people. Other times they are just mirrors in which we see our own split–off ego states. As such, they blind us to the other person's reality. When we are aware of our projections, we can manage them wisely, and they can help us learn about ourselves.

Now let's connect the concept of projection to the issue of same–sex attraction. There are some extremely important links. Like transferences, projections can foster both same–sex disaffiliation and gender incongruity because of the distortions they create in our relationships with other men. By disowning onto them our split–off negative and positive traits and potentials, we create an illusion for ourselves of being very different from them. We make them into what we refuse to see in ourselves. Usually, that includes core aspects of our manhood. The result of this illusion is that they are the men, we're something else—and we just can't relate.

The distortions caused by our projections also impact our relationships with the opposite sex through the same process I've been describing, but with different outcomes. The shadows we make women bear may simply increase either the opposition, avoidance, enmeshment, or comfort we already feel regarding them. If we see women as dangerous, troublesome, weak, or manipulative, they can become easy targets for our darkest projections. If we see women as powerful, cheeky, and fabulous, we may be making them carry our strength, assertion, and coolness. Either way, we can't relate to them in a healthy, authentic, and gendered way.

We can project both negative and positive traits onto others. It's easy to understand why we might split off and project some of our negative traits because of the shame and insecurity they create—not to mention the negative responses they get from other people. The negative traits that men with same–sex attraction most commonly project onto other men—especially straight men—relate to:

- The Tyrant shadow of the King (authoritarian and dominating)

- The Sadist shadow of the Warrior (insensitivity, anger, and aggression)

Projections can foster both same–sex disaffiliation and gender incongruity.

The distortions caused by our projections also impact our relationships with the opposite sex.

- The Innocent shadow of the boy Magian (stupidity and naïveté)

- The Addict pole of the Lover ("men only want one thing…")

It may be more difficult to understand why we would disown and project our positive traits. Gender shaming and gender double binding experiences in childhood can make us blind to—or even afraid of—our admirable masculine qualities, such as power, aggression, strength, confidence, and independence. This may be why we disown them. But since these traits are core to our beings as men, they are—like core needs—non–negotiable. This means that we will connect to them one way or another. We will experience these traits—either as native within ourselves or as traits that we project onto other men. Men with same–sex attraction often project some of their most positive potentials onto other men. These positive traits typically relate to:

- The Whole Warrior (strength, power, courage, discipline, and assertion)

- The Whole King (leadership and having it all together)

- The Whole Lover (sensuality, sexual freedom, and being uninhibited)

When we project, we often "physicalize" the trait we're projecting. To physicalize a trait means to associate physical attributes with personality traits. This is a common thing that most people do. This is one way stereotypes are created. For example, it would be common to associate a large bald–headed muscular man with personality traits like fierceness, rebelliousness, and fearlessness. Beautiful women with blonde hair are often associated with sexuality and stupidity.

When we physicalize a projection, we associate another man's bodily traits with our disowned personality traits. For example, if we've split off our own strength, power, and courage, we may find ourselves noticing men whose bodies and demeanor *look* strong, powerful, or courageous. Or, if we've split off our own vulnerability and insecurity, we may find ourselves noticing men whose stature and mannerisms look vulnerable and insecure. Those men's bodies become the screens onto which we project our own strength, power, and courage or our vulnerability and insecurity.

> Gender shaming and gender double binding experiences in childhood can make us blind to—or even afraid of—our admirable masculine qualities.

> When we physicalize a projection, we associate another man's bodily traits with our disowned personality traits.

As we watch the "movies" of our disowned fragments, we often experience emotional reactions to what we see. There are at least two conditions that can cause such reactions, and each brings with it different sorts of emotional responses. The first condition is created when we deeply and fully disown a trait, while the second condition is caused when we admit to ourselves, on some level, the *prospect* of actually owning the trait. These two concepts can be a bit tricky to understand, so bring your Magian online, take your time, and read carefully.

First, let's explore the condition that's created by completely disowning a projected trait. If the split–off trait you see in the other man is *desirable*, your emotional reaction may include feelings of anger, sadness, or shame. The message trying to come up from your unconscious mind may be something like "I *have* to be that, but I can't." But your emotional reaction to a desirable projected trait might include feelings of curiosity, envy, desire, or longing. The unconscious message here may be more like "I wish *I* felt like *he* looks" or "I wish *I* could experience what I believe *he* is experiencing." On the other hand, if the disowned projected trait you see in the other man is *undesirable*, your emotional reaction might include feelings of superiority and contempt. The unconscious message beneath this reaction may be something along the lines of "Thank goodness I'm not *that* bad."

Owning a desirable projected trait you see in another man may bring feelings of wellbeing, excitement, or confidence.

Now let's take the second condition, which is created by admitting to ourselves—perhaps only on a somewhat subconscious level—the prospect of actually owning a projected trait. If the projected trait you see in the other man is desirable, you might feel a sense of wellbeing, excitement, or confidence as you imagine yourself owning it. I believe many heterosexual men experience this type of physicalized projection when they see other men with admirable physical traits and athletic skills. This may be one reason why superhero movies and video games are so popular among young men today—they can't connect fully with their own power internally, so they take it in through Batman. Their unconscious mind may be trying to say something like "That's what I *really* am." But if the projected trait you see in the other guy is undesirable, you might feel disgust and hatred. Here the unconscious message trying to make its way to your conscious awareness may be "I hate the *me* I see in *him*."

Of course, any of these feelings can become sexualized, whether as an anesthetic to cover our pain, a weapon to act out our anger, or as a portal for re–integrating what's already rightly ours.

The projection of our disowned positive traits is part of what creates our gender imperatives. You may remember from Chapter Seven that gender imperatives are attributes that a man considers necessary in order to be truly masculine or to be seen as attractive, desirable, good, valuable, lovable, or complete as a man. When we're attracted to our gender imperatives, we're being drawn to missing parts of ourselves. The reason these traits feel so imperative is because they are what we believe we lack. We think that if we just had these traits, *we* would be sufficiently masculine—attractive, desirable, good, valuable, lovable, and complete as men. Joseph Nicolosi refers to this phenomenon as the "projected idealized self." This is essentially living life through someone else's power. What a waste of a life! Think about that the next time you want to lose yourself in some porn.

> When we're attracted to our gender imperatives, we're being drawn to missing parts of ourselves.

Many of us who have lost the connection with our own power settle for just looking at it. That's why some of us are drawn to men with confidence, muscular bodies, and athletic abilities—we're hungry for power and we've projected ours onto them. We do this because, early in our lives, our own power was split off from us somehow. And since core needs are non–negotiable, we search for a way to experience power without facing true risk. Sometimes that's through lust. ✎ 9.5

FRAGMENTATION VS. WHOLENESS

Painful and shaming life experiences cause us to split off parts of ourselves. Projection is a kind of "pseudo–integration," or an ineffective attempt to maintain connection with our missing parts. It's an internal and interpersonal falsehood. But with all of our projections, we litter the people of our world with the cast–off fragments of ourselves. Many—or perhaps even most—of our relationships become like little shards of a broken mirror, reflecting back to us bits and pieces of our disowned best and worst potentials. The people that reflect our darkest possibilities repel or frighten us. Those who show our most ideal potentials attract us. This is simple. And it's universal among humankind. Same–sex attraction just takes it a few steps further.

> Painful and shaming life experiences cause us to split off parts of ourselves.

But this isn't the whole story on fragmentation. When we transfer childhood relationships onto people in the present, we make them hold up for us fragments of the mirror of our past—perhaps the fragment of some bully or icon. Then, as these things typically go, we relate to just the fragment of their total self that draws our transference—maybe the scowl that looks like the bully or the prowess of the icon. Next, we probably detach from the scowl and we may fantasize about the prowess.

But still the story is not complete. The distant man whose closeness we crave for the affection, approval, and support we hope it will give—he's also a mere fragment. As in the other cases, it's usually just a piece of him that gets our attention—his smile or his warm eyes. It's that desirable slice of him that draws forth our longing to attach and resonate. We don't apprehend anything close to his entire self, which is always a complex mix of whole and shadowy traits offset by an otherwise pretty average personality. That wholeness is obscured by the flash of what we want him to be *for us*.

Tincture: to have a trace, a touch, or a smattering of something

From another perspective, we're naturally drawn to archetypal wholeness when we see it. The traits of the archetypes are so vast and encompassing that every man reflects some aspect of them. When we encounter men with particularly well–developed archetypal traits, or with archetypal capacities we're particularly in need of, we may fixate, reducing these men to just that trait. But as you may have already suspected, their traits are no more than fragments. They are not the whole of that man, nor are they in any way the whole of the archetype. Even the most magnificent man is just a tincture of the full–strength archetypal potentials. He's still just a fragment—no more.

But so far I've ignored the other dark side of fragmentation, which is the way we divide *ourselves* up into pieces. As you've already seen, we split off our disowned traits as projections, we make our past a broken mirror through transference, and in our cravings for closeness with other men we accentuate a single emotional need for special consideration. So singly can we focus on those cravings that in their strongest moments we are that need and nothing more. But reality would remind us that any need is just one of many—non–negotiable though it may be.

How selfish our attractions are when we relate to only that slice of a man that has personal meaning for us.

These scenarios show us the roots of most of our sexual attractions to other men. They also make clear how selfish our attractions are when we relate to only that slice of a man that has personal meaning for us. And they give us a hint of the damage we do to ourselves through all the dividing, disowning, splitting, breaking, and need accentuation. It's no wonder that we need therapy! But most importantly, these scenarios show us an antidote to our self–injury and unwanted attractions, which is to abstain from fragmenting and always look for wholeness.

The problem with this antidote is that fragmenting things is *so* much simpler than seeing their wholeness. And fragmenting has become a habit—both personally and

284

culturally. We quickly size other men up and shove them into categorical boxes. Gay culture would be notorious for this if it weren't so politically incorrect to criticize it. But think about the fragmenting labels gay men slap on others of their gender: Gay, Straight, Bi, Transgender, Queer, Breeder, Fag, Hottie, Bear, Queen, Twinkie, Top, Bottom—and that's just what I could think of off the top of my head. The more one considers such a list, the creepier it becomes. But we each have our own private–label lists. Some are more complex than others. The simplest ones boil down to just two categories: *hot guys* and *men I ignore.*

To me it's clear that fragmentation is one of the most pressing problems we need to overcome if we're to live our lives authentically—and if we're to move away from unwanted sexual attractions toward other men. If we're to cure ourselves of fragmentation's insanity, we'll first have to accept the average and even the ugly as essential parts of masculinity. We tend to be spoiled rotten in our myopic focus on male perfection, as if maleness is a box of man–candy from which we're entitled to snitch only the flavors we like best. Our worship of the tasty pieces is like psychological idolatry where a part is given the power of the whole. We can't continue that practice *and* heal our lives.

But what *is* the whole we're looking for? In this context, I would define the concept of wholeness as *the manifestation of every potential.* Billions of men and boys have lived on this planet, and each one is a multifaceted manifestation of male traits. The masculine whole can be defined by the summation of those billions. Together we all are the authentic whole. And within that universal wholeness, each individual can also be an authentic whole within himself by developing his every potential. One way to pursue this is by developing and balancing what we've been calling the archetypal traits.

None of us will ever become truly whole because we can never manifest every masculine potential. But it's apparent by nature's design that this is what is intended. A few lines from the movie, *The Last Samurai,* written by John Logan, illustrates this eloquently. At one point in the movie the character Katsumoto, who is the last samurai, stands observing blossoms on a flowering tree. He remarks to the American Captain Algren, who is becoming a disciple of samurai ways: "The perfect blossom is a rare thing. You could spend your life looking for one and it would not be a wasted life." Near the end of the film, as Katsumoto lies dying

> Fragmentation is one of the most pressing problems we need to overcome if we're to live our lives authentically.

> Billions of men and boys have lived on this planet, and each one is a multifaceted manifestation of male traits. The masculine whole can be defined by the summation of those billions.

on the battlefield where he has led his noble class of warriors in their final act of service to the king, he utters his final words: "They are all perfect."

None of us will ever be a perfect archetypal whole. Only the archetypes are perfect. The archetypes are really just a representation of God's perfection. But if we are indeed made in God's image, then we must have the potential for perfection. Do you hear the contradiction? This is the nature of wholeness. By necessity any true whole must contain every opposite and therefore every contradiction. We have the potential of perfection, but in an imperfect world we will never manifest it. But that, it seems, is not the purpose. The purpose is to try.

For me, serenity comes from knowing that within myself I carry the essentials of the whole male gender. But I am not the whole gender. I'm just one manifestation of it. But I am a *whole* manifestation. The perfection in our individual design is the way that our imperfections teach us. The perfection is in the way our shadows lead us to our wholeness. Allow me to adjust Katsumoto's lines to complete my point: You could spend your life looking for perfection within yourself and it would not be a wasted life. All that you are is perfect. ✐ 9.6

INTEGRATING THE SHADOW: BECOMING AUTHENTIC

In his book, *A Little Book on the Human Shadow,* Robert Bly outlines a process to help us look for wholeness. He describes the process as consisting of "five stages of reintegration" of our projections. Here I apply it also to owning our transferences and integrating all fragments. Bly explains that we don't progress through these stages in an orderly fashion, but rather we may be in several stages at the same time in different parts of ourselves. A stage may show up as an event, a moment, or a set of experiences rather than as an extended period of time. The benefit of understanding this process is that by our awareness of it, we can foster it and encourage it. For our discussion, I've expanded on these stages a bit and applied them to the situation of men with same–sex attraction.

The First Stage: Disowning

In our most unaware stage, which is where we all start, our projections are placed out onto individuals, groups, and institutions in the world. We're entirely unconscious of the way we transfer relationships from childhood onto people in our present life. We experience our past and present selves, as well as the people around us, only in fragmented ways. In this state we're fully unconscious of our shadows. We

---

Integrating the Shadow

- Disowning
- "Something starts to rattle"
- Denial
- Feeling diminished
- Retrieving the shadow

Our projections are placed out onto individuals, groups, and institutions in the world.

maintain connection to our disowned parts only through our emotional reactions to other people, groups, or institutions that show them to us.

For the man with same–sex attraction, this is the stage of seeing the men around him as having what he needs. In this stage, the mans with same–sex attraction experiences the locus of masculinity as being outside of himself. His connection to his own masculinity is maintained through his emotional reaction to the maleness of the guy *over there*. He experiences his self–love and self–acceptance only through receiving the "love" of another man. "If that guy *over there* thinks I'm attractive, I must be worth something."

This is also the stage where the man with same–sex attraction transfers his father, brother, and perpetrators onto the men in his present life. His mother and sisters and female perpetrators may also be transferred onto women in the present time. In this stage, people conform to our expectations. Women will always behave as we expect. Men will always fulfill our stereotypes. And there will always be a line of attractive guys for us to react to. Our lives are completely fragmented. We've unconsciously traded wholeness for pleasant predictability. ✍ 9.7

The Second Stage: "Something Starts to Rattle"

This stage of integrating a shadow begins when we start to see past our projections and transferences. The masks we've placed on those around us start to "rattle" and may even slip off momentarily. We see something gray in our otherwise black and white world. Maybe the tyrant in our life shows a sign of weakness. Maybe a racial or cultural stereotype gets challenged. Perhaps we meet a dignified black girl, a smart Mexican, a generous Jew, or a Mormon who seems truly Christian. Or perhaps our trust in our own group gets shaken a bit—a guru or leader makes a mistake or we see some faults in our cultural doctrine. One way or another, our prejudices have come into question. Bly describes this as a time of "troubling inconsistency." In the second stage, these moments will be too disturbing to pursue beyond a momentary uncomfortable awareness.

For the man with same–sex attraction, this stage may appear as a conflicting perspective on other men. It may start with the realization that our gender imperative is imperfect. It could begin with noticing love from a man we've always thought was stern and uncaring or feeling accepted by a group of "straight guys." Or this stage might appear as a change in perspective of

> We start to see past our projections and transferences. The masks we've placed on those around us start to "rattle."

ourselves. It could begin with recognizing masculine traits in ourselves that we've previously only seen in other men, whether we see these traits as desirable or disgusting. ✍ 9.8

The Third Stage: Denial

We fix the rattle—we slap the masks of projection and transference back onto those around us.

The only intelligent way to handle the troubling inconsistency of the second stage is to retreat back into the security of what we "know" is right. So in the third stage we fix the rattle—we slap the masks of projection and transference back onto those around us before we have a chance to experience the upsetting reality behind them. Something in us reminds us of "the way things really are" and assures us that it's best to not monkey with it. We prefer to see the world through our projections and transferences because that's the world that makes sense to us. It's the world we grew up with and, therefore, the one that's most comfortable.

Bly suggests that we misuse our "moral intelligence" when we do this. Moral intelligence is the awareness we have of *what* and *who* are right and wrong. It's the ability to be morally opposed to certain individuals, groups, or ideologies. It's the awareness of them and us. This can be a very good and socially–constructive ability when it galvanizes us against a truly dangerous outside force. It's the wisdom of the Magian, axis mundi of the King, and the strength of the Warrior setting and enforcing boundaries. But when our moral intelligence is merely an extension of our projections and transferences, it enforces self–righteousness, racism, and every other form of prejudice. It helps us settle back into our comfortable assumptions that black girls really are sluts, Mexicans are dumb, Jews are greedy, and Mormons really aren't Christian.

I've seen men with same–sex attraction pass through this third stage quickly and with little notice. We discard the imperfect gender imperative and replace him with a new object. We tune back into the stern and uncaring side of the man who surprised us with his tenderness. We retreat into anticipating rejection by the group. And we immediately discount or ignore the male qualities we saw so clearly in ourselves only moments before. Even the most eye–opening Stage Two experiences can be forgotten in a week or two. We tend to have a very resilient sense of "them and us." We can be quite confident that, "men are just jerks," that "women are like that," or that "he's a dumb jock." ✍ 9.9

The Fourth Stage: Feeling Diminished

This is the stage when we truly begin to be aware that inauthenticity in all its forms—passivity, distraction, false selves, transferences, and projections—leave us feeling *less*. We start to feel diminished—empty, soft, powerless, and unmasculine. And we admit this diminishment to ourselves. I believe that until we've experienced and acknowledged this diminishment, we'll have no true motivation to continue into the fifth stage. Most people never make it to this stage.

This stage may hit those of us with same-sex attraction when we're no longer soothed by our attraction—the porn feels empty, the hook-up loses its power, relationships leave us disappointed. We may admit to ourselves that the gay lifestyle just isn't delivering what it promised. Or it may hit with the dawning realization that we feel devoid of masculinity or that we really hate ourselves. For some, this stage may not start until the maturity of middle age has stripped away enough of our illusions that the world starts to look like our own hair—shades of gray. This is a wonderful and terrible stage full of potential for destruction and growth. This is the stage in which men sometimes give up. But it's also the stage we must pass through in order to create a new life for ourselves. ✍ 9.10

The Fifth Stage: Retrieving the Shadow

The final stage, which Bly also refers to as "eating the shadow," is an active phase of consciously searching for and integrating our projections and transferences. This is a process that can stretch on for years. In fact, some would say that it will continue in some form for the rest of our lives. There are many ways of going about this process. If you can establish a firm intention to find and own your projections and transferences, you will certainly succeed. Below are a few suggestions to consider as you move forward.

Journaling: You might start a "projection and transference journal" where you list and describe what you find through the processes described below. You can organize the journal any way that works for you, but try *not* to be too perfectionistic—that will stifle your progress. Just write down what you notice and learn about yourself.

Observe Relational Conflicts: A valuable method for discovering projections and transferences is to notice the kinds of people you've tended, over time, to have negative relationships with and describe those relationships in your journal. Those relationships may be characterized by feelings like fear, anger, resentment,

We truly begin to be aware that inauthenticity in all its forms leaves us feeling *less*.

We consciously search for and integrate our projections and transferences.

detachment, and disgust—or they may be characterized by obsession, longing, dependency, envy, and lust. Try to identify the specific traits these people possess or the things these people do that trigger your reactions toward them.

As you journal, describe the dynamics of the relationship. Consider the other person's archetypal qualities and how those might relate to your own archetypal qualities. Consider whether the other person reminds you of someone from your past. Consider whether the dynamic happening between you feels familiar, like something you've experienced before. And challenge yourself to own the very traits you are reacting to in the other person. Write all of this down in detail.

Observe Your Attractions: Notice the men you have strong attractions or obsessions toward. Try to identify what it is about these men that causes you to be attracted or obsessed with them. Push yourself to *be specific*. For example, you may notice that you have a common pattern of attraction toward men with a certain physical feature or body type.

Spend time contemplating the stories you tell about the attractive traits.

Now get even more specific. Spend time contemplating the stories you tell about the attractive traits. Ask yourself questions like, what does that trait *mean* about that man? How does that trait affect his life? What advantages does it give him? How does it impact his relationships with other men or with women? How does he feel about himself because of it? What would it feel like to be that man's friend? And be sure to ask yourself whether the traits that attract you to him remind you of anyone from your past.

This is a very good method for uncovering gender imperatives that have been projected onto other men. It can also reveal transferences and unmet same–sex affiliation needs.

You may find it very helpful to discuss your findings with a trusted confidant.

Ask For Insight: As you begin making discoveries about possible projections and transferences, you may find it very helpful to discuss your findings with a trusted confidant who has the capacity to understand these concepts. That might be a friend who knows you well, a fellow member of a self–help or support group you attend, or a therapist or life coach who understands projections and transferences.

Describe to your confidant the discoveries you're making about yourself and your reactions to other people. If you think you're projecting, tell him whether you think you might be projecting something you *are*, something you *wish you were*, or something you *fear being or becoming*. If you think you're transferring a past relationship dynamic onto a current one, describe to him the pattern you're observing. And of course, ask your confidant for his candid input. Often, just the process of describing what you're thinking and feeling is enough to clarify what's really going on.

Clearings: A process that originated within the Mankind Project (MKP) community can be very helpful in identifying and owning projections and transferences. Called a "clearing," this process assists men in getting "clear" on how their own issues are impacting their feelings and reactions toward others. There are two types of clearings: In–Person Clearings, which are done as a formal process within a group, and Mental Clearings, which are done individually in your own mind. Many men have found Mental Clearings to be very helpful in diminishing attractions to other men. The clearing process described below has been modified somewhat from the way it is typically practiced in MKP circles.

> This process assists men in getting "clear" on how their own issues are impacting their feelings and reactions toward others.

There are always at least two men involved in both types of clearings: the "Clearer," who is feeling an emotional charge toward another man, who is the "Clearee." A facilitator always guides an In–Person Clearing. The Clearer asks the Clearee if he is willing to assist him in getting clear of an emotional charge. The Clearee may accept or decline. If he declines, another man may be asked to stand in as a proxy for him. If the Clearer knows that intense negative feelings are likely to be expressed, he has a responsibility to warn the Clearee so that the Clearee can decide whether to ask for a proxy or perhaps even to leave the room during the clearing. Clearings can also be performed with an inanimate object such as a chair or a mirror in the place of the Clearee.

With an In–Person Clearing, the next step is to place a tall staff between the Clearer and the Clearee. The two men hold the staff with one hand, with the Clearer's hand below the Clearee's hand. The staff represents a mirror for the Clearer to see himself in and a shield to protect the Clearee. It also represents a conduit that will channel the Clearer's emotional energy into the ground. This is why his hand is placed below the Clearee's hand.

The next step in an In–Person Clearing is for the Clearer to take ownership of whatever personal issues may emerge through the clearing. A simple statement like the following may be recited to the Clearee:

"I take full responsibility for my beliefs and feelings. They are mine. My intention is to gain greater clarity and peace—within myself, and in relationship to you—not to try to change you."

With a Mental Clearing, none of these initial steps are performed and no facilitation is required. Rather, you simply imagine that the other man is acting as a mirror in which to see your projected parts or transferred relationships. The following six steps are performed in both In–Person and Mental Clearings. With In–Person Clearings, the facilitator guides the process. In a Mental Clearing, you are the Clearer.

Clearing Outline
- Data
- Story
- Feelings
- Wants
- Ownership
- Closure

1. **Data**: The Clearer states the facts as he experiences them. Facts are a list of details or events relevant to the emotional charge. Facts are free of judgments or opinions. For example, the statement "You have shoulder–length black hair" may be a fact. But the statement, "You have gorgeous hair" is not a fact, it is an opinion. The statement, "You said you would arrive at 8 o'clock and you entered the room at 8:05" may be a fact. But the statement, "You are always late" is an opinion. The statement, "Your muscles are larger than mine" may be a fact. But the statement, "You are dangerous" is a story.

2. **Story**: The Clearer states the meaning he gives the data. Now it's time to state the opinions you so carefully omitted from the data. This may include your beliefs regarding what the data means about the other man and how the data impacts you. "You have gorgeous hair," "You are always late," and "You are dangerous" are stories.

   Differentiating the data from the stories helps us to get more clear on how we interpret reality, which in turn leads us toward our projections and transferences. For example, we learn that shoulder–length black hair is "gorgeous" to us, that we have issues related to tardiness, and that we equate muscular men with danger.

   But try to go much deeper than this, looking for the story under the story. For example, "You have gorgeous hair" may have a deeper story like, "My hair has always been so thin and short. Thick, long hair looks wild and masculine to me." Also, "You are always late" may have a deeper story like, "Your lateness disrupts the group." And, "You are dangerous" may have a deeper story like, "You could easily beat me up."

3. **Feelings**: The Clearer expresses any emotions, counter–emotions, and associated bodily sensations that arise from the stories he tells about the data. For example, "I feel jealous when I think your hair is gorgeous," "I feel nervous and angry when I tell myself the story that you are always late," and "I feel afraid when I think that you could beat me up."

4. **Wants**: The Clearer verbalizes what he wants from the Clearee. The Clearee just listens without responding. Recognizing our wants can provide additional information about our projections and transferences. Again, try to go deep here, looking for the wants that may be deeply hidden. For example: "I want hair like yours. I want to be free and wild like your hair looks." Or, "I want this group to be punctual. I want things organized and not chaotic." And, "I want you to either be my friend or to stay far away from me."

5. **Ownership:** The Clearer owns the projections or transferences that are becoming clear. Be aware that clearings can also bring up unmet needs. If the projections, transferences, or unmet needs are not yet clear, the Clearer may need to go back through the stories, feelings, and wants with a deeper level of introspection. Eventually, the true issues will emerge. For example, the Clearer may own that he's projected all his wild masculine energy onto other men. He may own that he's transferring the chaos of his childhood household onto the tardy Clearee. Or he may own that he's transferring a childhood bully onto the man with big muscles.

6. **Closure:** The Clearer assesses whether he is now "clear," which means that he understands the cause of his trigger. Usually by now the Clearer will also feel a diminishing of the charge. If the charge is still strong, the Clearer may need to do additional work on the projection, transference, or unmet need that was revealed.

Question Your Transferences: Once you have discovered a transference and have traced it back to the original relationship, you might want to consider the questions below. These questions all relate to the original relationship that's being transferred onto people today. You might discuss these with your confidant or simply journal about them.

- What emotions am I still carrying about this person? Sometimes these emotions can be buried so deep that we no longer feel them. You may need help from a professional to access such feelings.

- What prevents me from releasing the negative emotions I'm carrying about this person and moving on? What will I lose if I let go of this person? What will I gain?

- What work do I need to do *before* I can forgive and move on? Sometimes we need to process through deep anger or grief before we are genuinely able to forgive. Sometimes we need to be assured that forgiveness doesn't make an abuser's actions okay.

> Transferences can be healed by feeling and fully clearing the emotions we still carry toward the person who is the source of the transference.

Transferences can be healed by feeling and fully clearing the emotions we still carry toward the person who is the source of the transference. When an emotion is fully felt, it naturally shifts into another emotion. By feeling and shifting through the layers of emotion we have toward those who hurt us, we can very naturally arrive at a place of resolution and even forgiveness. Sometimes this process can be done without help. But often we may require the help of a trained professional to safely access and resolve deep wounds, especially when abuse was involved.

Question Your Projections: Once you have discovered a projection, you might want to consider the questions below. Again, you might discuss these with your confidant or simply journal about them.

- Why did I reject this part of me in the first place? What made it unsafe or undesirable for me to openly possess this trait?

- What has prevented me from integrating this trait in the past? In other words, why have I kept it at a distance?

- What will integrating this part mean for me now? What do I fear about owning it? And what good could it bring into my life?

- Am I ready now to integrate this projection into myself, or do I choose instead to continue living life with it disowned?

If you decide that now is the time to own this projection, below are some suggestions for how you might do this.

Become Your Projection: If the projected trait is something that you wish you were, you might simply challenge yourself to develop the trait. Projected traits like spontaneity, strength, assertion, confidence, physical fitness, and self–control can all be developed with consistent effort. But consider the following two cautions. First, check your motivation for wanting to develop the trait. Are you trying to conform to a standard or definition of masculinity that is not authentic for you? Are you doing it in order to make other men attracted to you sexually? Or are you doing it to avoid facing underlying wounds and issues? Second, consider whether the trait you want to develop is possible for you to attain. For example, if you are five–and–a–half feet tall you are not going to develop the trait of being six foot four. Rather than be discouraged by that impossibility, consider other ways of being "tall." Consider what being tall means to you, for example, being respected, being noticed, or being confident. Those are traits you can develop.

> If the projected trait is something that you wish you were, you might simply challenge yourself to develop the trait.

Internalize Your Projection: Projections of traits that you wish you had and traits that you already have but don't recognize in yourself can be internalized through a process involving vivid imagination. Before attempting this process, be aware that individuals with a strong tendency toward obsessive–compulsive disorder (OCD) or obsessive–compulsive personality disorder (OCPD) may find this process somewhat less effective. Also be aware that the effectiveness of this process depends on your ability to imagine the presence of your Higher Power, which can be any power that you believe has the capacity to assist your growth and healing.

> Projections of traits can be internalized through a process involving vivid imagination.

Doing this process alone will require substantial preparation in order to learn the steps involved. You might consider having a friend or therapist do it with you so they can guide you through the steps.

This process is best done in a relaxed and meditative state with eyes closed. It is important that the conscious mind—which analyzes, reasons, and plans—is quiet so that the spontaneous imaginative unconscious self can do its work.

Begin by inviting your Higher Power to be present with you and ask for his help in developing or integrating a positive new trait. As you proceed through the process of developing the Ideal Self, seek the approval of your Higher Power and imagine him guiding the process.

Now, imagine a version of yourself who fully possesses the trait you want to internalize standing out in front of your Actual Self that is sitting in the chair. This is the Ideal Self. Picture the Ideal Self exhibiting the desired trait as intensely and vividly as possible. Notice your body and the way you stand and move as the Ideal Self. Look at your face and particularly look deeply into your eyes, imagining that you can see right into your soul as the Ideal Self. Notice every possible way in which your Ideal Self exudes this desired trait. Imagine seeing the Ideal Self responding to everyday situations in the future as though you are strong in the desired trait. You might envision yourself at work, with friends, with family, and so on.

Add the sense of touch to your experience of the Ideal Self. What kinds of tactile experiences would be new to you as the Ideal Self? This might include objects that are unique to your environment, such as equipment in a gym where you work out, a desk in your new office, clothing on your in–shape body, or a microphone in your hand as you speak or perform.

Add the sense of hearing to your experience of the Ideal Self. Imagine hearing any sounds that are associated with the Ideal Self. If there are activities you engage in as the Ideal Self, what sounds are associated with those activities? Hear your voice as the Ideal Self. Specifically, imagine that you can hear yourself describing to some friends how grateful you are now that you have developed or accepted the desired trait. Hear the emotion in your voice. And imagine hearing the voices of the friends affirming you truly are strong in the desired trait.

Add the emotions you experience as the Ideal Self. Imagine how you feel about yourself, your life, your career, your body, or anything else that has changed for you as the Ideal Self. Imagine how you feel toward your Higher Power for helping you develop or accept the desired trait. The more fully and vividly you can experience it, the better. And give yourself plenty of time to enjoy all of this.

Now, as you take in the whole Ideal Self, imagine that you can see a color of the Ideal Self. It may be a color you exude, a color you see in your eyes, or a color that surrounds you like an aura. Take a moment to notice and enjoy that color. Then imagine the Ideal Self standing there in the future, waiting for you.

Next, tune into your Actual Self, who is sitting in the chair, and who does not possess or own the desired trait. Specifically, imagine all of the attributes in your Actual Self that conflict with, contradict, or prevent you from living as the Ideal Self. This might include beliefs, attitudes, behaviors, emotions, counter–emotions, and physical issues that are within your power to modify. It might include relationships and career or living situations that are in opposition to living as the Ideal Self. Imagine all of these as vividly as possible, accessing as many of your senses as possible, just as you did when you imagined the Ideal Self.

Now, imagine that you can look into the past and see your entire history stretched out behind you as if you were looking at a time line of your life. Imagine that you can see yourself at every age. In each of your Younger Selves, imagine that you can see or perceive the experiences that occurred, the traits you developed, the decisions you made, and the beliefs you adopted that got in your way, or were not in harmony with you becoming the Ideal Self.

You must make a decision. Are you ready and willing to release each aspect of the Present Self that prevents you from being the Ideal Self? If the answer is "No," you are not ready to live as the Ideal Self and the process is over. In this case, you may want to take some time reassessing what you really want. If the answer is "Yes," continue to the next step.

Imagine the presence of your Higher Power, as if he is right there with you. Then visualize him going to each of your Younger Selves and healing or cleansing them of the feelings and beliefs that are in opposition to becoming the Ideal Self. Watch as he sends intense, healing beams of light through them. Imagine him changing all situations that need to be changed in order for you to grow up as the Ideal Self. And imagine him forgiving everything that needs to be forgiven in order for you to grow up as the Ideal Self. Be as specific and vivid as possible.

Next, imagine your Higher Power doing the same with your Actual Self. Allow him access to all parts of your conscious and nonconscious mind, your body, your heart, and your soul so that he can completely remove from your Actual Self everything that conflicts with, contradicts, or prevents you from being the Ideal Self. Imagine your Higher Power sending intense beams of healing white light into every part of you to complete this process.

Sidebar notes:

Tune into your Actual Self.

Imagine your Younger Selves.

You must make a decision.

Imagine the presence of your Higher Power cleansing your Younger Selves.

Imagine your Higher Power cleansing your Actual Self.

Imagine your Younger
Selves growing up into
you.

Now imagine the Younger Selves growing up into each other from the youngest to the oldest. Then imagine the oldest Younger Self growing up into you. Notice how different their lives are as they grow up, now that they have been changed by your Higher Power.

Integrate your Ideal Self.

Once all of the Younger Selves have merged into you, invite your Ideal Self to come and stand in front of you. Then imagine the presence of your Higher Power standing beside you and the Ideal Self, forming a triangle with you. Visualize beams of intense white light coming out of your Higher Power and connecting your Ideal Self to you. Specifically, imagine the beams of light connecting your minds, hearts, bodies, and souls together. Now just watch what happens and allow plenty of time for the Ideal Self to integrate or merge with you. Then take a moment and express gratitude to your Higher Power for helping you complete this process.

Integrating and Balancing a Projection: Negative projected traits that you fear you might be or become are probably aspects of yourself that need to be integrated into a balanced and moderated whole. This can be accomplished using a process of vivid imagination similar to the one just described. And as I mentioned previously, this method of processing tends not to be effective for men with strong symptoms of OCD and OCPD. Also, consider asking a friend or therapist to guide you through it.

Begin by getting into a relaxed and meditative state with your eyes closed. It is important that the conscious mind—which analyzes, reasons, and plans—is quiet so that the spontaneous imaginative nonconscious self can do its work.

Imagine the Projected
Self possessed by the
unwanted trait.

Now imagine a separate version of yourself standing out in front of your Actual Self that is sitting in the chair. This version of you is completely possessed by the projected trait that you fear being or becoming. We will call these the Projected Self and the unwanted trait. Picture the Projected Self exhibiting the unwanted trait as intensely and vividly as possible. Notice your body and the way you stand and move as the Projected Self. Look at your face and particularly at your eyes. Imagine that you can see right inside the body and brain of the Projected Self. Where does this trait reside inside you? What does this trait look like in the body and brain of the Projected Self?

Now try to experience the unwanted trait in the Projected Self through as many of your other five senses as possible. Hear the voice or the sounds of the Projected Self.

Try to associate a smell and taste to the unwanted trait in the Projected Self. Imagine the feelings of the Projected Self. The more fully and vividly you can experience it the better.

Next, imagine that the Projected Self is like a magnet, pulling out of your Actual Self (you sitting in the chair) every feeling, thought, and trait that supports or resonates with the unwanted trait. Notice that the magnet pulls it out of every part of your body and every level of your conscious and nonconscious mind. Experience this until it feels as though your body and mind are completely empty of the unwanted trait and it's all inside the Projected Self.

Empty yourself of the unwanted trait.

Now, imagine another separate self standing out in front of you next to the Projected Self. We will call this the Opposite Self. Imagine that this Opposite Self contains exactly the opposite traits of the Projected Self. For example, if the Projected Self is angry and aggressive, the Opposite Self might be depressed and passive. Imagine a vertical line separating the Projected Self and the Opposite Self. Follow the same process as above to create a fully formed Opposite Self: experience it with the five senses and let it become magnetic and pull out of you everything that supports or resonates with it.

Imagine the Opposite Self, which contains exactly the opposite traits of the Projected Self.

When the Opposite Self is fully formed, imagine the presence of your Higher Power above and between the two selves in front of you, forming a triangle with them. Visualize beams of intense white light coming out of your Higher Power and connecting the two selves. Specifically, imagine the beams of light connecting the minds, hearts, bodies, and souls of the two selves. Now just watch what happens and allow plenty of time. Typically, the two selves will integrate or merge in some way.

Allow them to merge.

If they merge together on one side of the line, this means there is still another opposite that needs to be integrated. Invite that other opposite out of you using the same method as before. You may not know what that opposite is, so just relax your mind and watch what comes out. Then allow your Higher Power to connect these opposites with beams of light in the same four places and watch for them to merge.

If the opposites merge in the middle, replacing the line, then you know the process of integration is complete. So now imagine beams of light coming from your Higher Power and connecting this newly Merged Self into your Actual Self's mind, heart, body, and soul. Imagine that the Merged Self is being integrated into every part of

Use the five senses to experience the unwanted trait.

your Actual Self using as many of your senses as possible. Once you feel the Merged Self is fully integrated into your Actual Self, the process is complete.

Healing Relationships: Shadow integration is often a natural result of involvement in twelve–step work, experiential weekends, participating in support and therapy groups, and engaging in good psychotherapy, counseling, or coaching. These processes facilitate integration when they make it safe for us to explore and express all of our thoughts, feelings, impulses, and desires.

> Of particular value are relationships and processes that help us heal emotional pain and revise the mental programming that creates such pain.

Of particular value are relationships and processes that help us heal emotional pain and revise the mental programming that creates such pain. Often these processes lead us to hidden, repressed, and denied parts of ourselves, which can then be healed and integrated. If you find that you have difficulty doing the work or completing the processes described in this chapter, you should seek the help of a mental health professional. 9.11

LIGHT FROM YOUR SHADOW

Find and own your shadows. You need them if you're to become whole. And the world needs whole men.

> The darkness of your shame can be turned into a light for the world.

The Magian uses his capacities to help, heal, and transform—first himself and then the world. He goes deep within himself, into his darkest shadows. Then, like an alchemist, he transforms that shadow into gold. By doing this he learns that the shadow has been a gift all along because of the opportunities it has brought him. Through transforming the shadow, what was poison becomes a source of abundance, what was bitter now grows nourishing fruit, and what looked like death now feels like morning. The darkness of your shame can be turned into a light for the world.

Can you see now that your journey is far, far greater than merely being gay? Your quest is to transcend your shadow and use the breadth of authenticity that process gives you to bless the world. A mission that big surely dwarfs the miniscule trouble of unwanted sexual attractions.

In *The Lord of the Rings: Fellowship of the Ring*, the Magician Gandalf the Gray confronts the monstrous Balrog on the bridge of Khazad–dûm deep inside the mines of Moria. In doing so, he protects Frodo and his fellows from destruction.

But he must sacrifice his own life. He falls with the Balrog and battles with him to his own death—and beyond death. The Magician is transformed and returns as Gandalf the White, thereafter possessing far greater powers. His new–found powers are ultimately crucial in turning the tide of the war against the evil forces of Saruman—in a moment of extreme need he appears as a light in the East, turning the tide of the battle. ✍ 9.12

---

[1] As a reminder, I defined *Center* in Chapter Two as the Self in connection with a Higher Power.

[2] A British pediatrician named Donald Winnicott is credited with developing this concept, which he labeled the "false self." To translate that into the terminology I've been using in his book, the false, or protective, self is an ego state that's used to mask shameful core feelings and temperaments, and more authentic ego states.

[3] The term "authentic self" refers to a personality that's authentic as described in this chapter.

CHAPTER 10

THE LOVER

When we begin appropriately accessing the Lover we feel more alive
than ever before. The world seems to take on new color. ... A deep
sense of authentic meaning fills our being. We feel our masculine joy
and potency.

Moore and Gillette, *The Lover Within*

magine an archetypal Little League game. The Magian coaches
the junior Warriors on how to hit and where to run while the King
officiates and inspires the players from the sidelines. But over in left
field, the Lover is staring off into the trees watching a strange bug
flit among the leaves. Whether this image makes you laugh or cry, it
depicts well the bliss and plight of the most misunderstood archetype. The Lover is
off in his own world—a place with no schedule, no structure, and no demands. The
time is always *now*. And the purpose is always *joy*.

In this chapter we'll pursue the mysterious and primal capacities and desires that
we call the Lover archetype. We'll consider where these traits come from and how
they show up and affect our lives. We'll consider the connection between the Lover
and the core emotion of sadness. Then we'll delve into the complex and interwoven
shadows of the Lover—the Addict and the Impotent One. All of this will prepare us
to view the entire structure of the archetype, with his shadows, to gain a perspective
on the synergy that can be experienced when his diverse traits are held in balance.

At the end of the chapter we'll consider some ways to channel Lover energy in
healthful ways. Specifically, I'll discuss some important principles related to
friendship, which is one of the most important avenues for channeling Lover energy.

THE WHOLE LOVER

The Lover holds the power of our passion, urges, and desires. He's internally driven and centered in the body. He's our ability and urge to sense the endless variety in the world outside us, and the awareness of all physical and emotional feelings from the world within. He doesn't know boundaries and isn't goal focused—other than the goal of satisfying his urges. The Lover's activities all culminate in pleasure, fulfillment, and joyful expression through creativity. He seeks union and wholeness, bringing together all opposites through the ordering function of the King archetype. He assists the King and Magian in their vital functions of creating axis mundi. The King *holds* the Center. The Magian *knows* our Center. And the Lover *feels* our Center.

The Lover is also unifying within relationships. He's the power at work when a little boy holds his father's hand, an adolescent boy hangs out with his friends, and a young man makes out with a girl. He's active in the adult male making love to his wife, holding their newborn child, and sacrificing for his family. He's present in the older man looking lovingly into his wife's eyes at their fiftieth anniversary and doting on their grandchildren. He fills the leader with compassion for those who follow him as he tries to make a better world. And he's alive in a man feeling the Spirit as he kneels before God. Lover is empathy, compassion, and the source of our deepest spirituality.

The energies and capacities included in what we call the Lover are distinctly different from those of the other archetypes.

The energies and capacities included in what we call the Lover are distinctly different from those of the other archetypes as a group. The other three archetypes—King, Warrior, and Magian—tend toward non–relatedness, separation from their feelings, a greater focus on external goals and mission, a more mind–driven approach, and a propensity to organize, separate, classify, and distinguish things in the world. It's the energy of the Lover that unifies and balances all of these traits within our psyches.

The Lover is also distinct from Anima, although sometimes those distinctions can be a bit blurry. Whereas Lover is masculine and comes from inside us, Anima is feminine and feels like it comes from the outside. Lover is experienced in very physical ways through our five senses, while Anima is experienced more spiritually and mentally as inspiration, intuition, and impressions. And while Lover energy moves toward contact, connection, completion, and incarnation, Anima seems more ethereal and abstract.

However, Anima may often cooperate with the Lover in ways that can blur the thin line between them. For example, Anima may bring inspiration or vision to an artist. This inspiration may awaken an emotional reaction in the Lover, urging the man to embody his vision in a work of art. Or Anima may inspire strong humanitarian impulses in a man, arousing the compassion and generativity of his Lover and awakening within him a desire to serve.[1] Ultimately, dissecting these traits much further than this becomes purely an academic pursuit, so we'll stop here.

Let's explore the complex set of energies, traits, and attributes that we call the Lover in greater depth. First, we'll review concepts about where Lover energy comes from. Next, we'll consider the three essential aspects of Lover energy: sensation, libido, and union. Then we'll consider how Lover energy is manifested in relationships.

The Birth of Lover

The Lover in his fullness exists in what Moore and Gillette call "the garden of delight." This garden image has been firmly etched into our psyches for countless generations. It's the Garden of Eden that we remember from the Bible where all things were perfect and all needs were supplied without effort. It's also the age–old idea of a social and environmental utopia like Camelot or Shangri–La where all things live in perfect peace and harmony. And it's the concept of heaven—a place of peace, rest, reward, and reunion with God following death.

> The Lover in his fullness exists in "the garden of delight."

But we know this "garden" in a more personal way, too, as an unconscious memory of the warm and peaceful union in the womb, where all our needs were supplied to us without our having to do anything and without us even being aware that the needs existed. The separation at birth and the weaning from our mother gradually brings this utopian existence to an end. We experience less and less attachment and attunement with our mothers. As we discussed in Chapter Five, in order to enter the Father's world, we must sacrifice and deny ourselves of the Mother's world. Some boys do this easily. Some do it with ambivalence. And some refuse to do it at all.

Whether this loss of union and attunement with mother happens early or late, gently or severely, it will happen. Mother is never perfect, and even the experience of the most normal and gentle misattunement will break that union. This is the birth of the Lover. As Moore and Gillette write in *The Lover Within*, Lover energy arises out of the boy's "deep yearning for the infinitely nurturing, infinitely good, infinitely beautiful Mother." A sense of yearning can only exist in the absence of the thing yearned for. And so the "garden" relationship with mother must be lost in order for Lover to emerge. Just as separation from mother is essential for Warrior energy to develop, the desire to reunite with mother is essential for Lover energy to form. Likewise, separation from mother is essential for genderedness and the urge to return to the mother's "garden" is essential for complementarity.

There may be another "garden" for which we long. I'm one who believes in the existence of a soul that preceded birth and will continue after death. That belief makes me wonder whether some of the yearning we feel in our lives may not be a longing for a blissful union we knew before but have forgotten, except through the universal human desire for nirvana, utopia, or heaven. Although these ideas exist in many religious traditions, they can't be proven. But as I've said before, when a belief shows up in so many cultures and religions across time, I consider it very unwise to ignore it.

But in hypothesizing about the loss of mother and longings for heaven, let's not forget something much closer to home for which the Lover longs—his own lost self. As I've amply described in previous chapters, painful and shaming early life experiences cause children to cut off, repress, or deny aspects of their ego that seem unwanted or make them unsafe. But with the loss of those parts, their ego becomes diminished, and they lose their connection to their Center. This self–alienation leaves them naturally longing for their lost child parts. This is why we project our split–off traits onto others—so that we can still experience ourselves through someone else. But it leaves us forever longing for wholeness.

We learn from all of this that life sets us up for longing—we are *supposed* to yearn. It's an inevitable part of our makeup. But our culture perpetuates a terrible lie about such desires. With its emphasis on fulfilling every craving, modern culture teaches us *not* to yearn. It teaches that we have a *right* to get everything we want right now. Even worse, it teaches us that the fulfillment of every craving is to be had from things in the world. This mentality feeds the shadows of the Lover, which

---

Mother is never perfect, and even the experience of the most normal and gentle misattunement will break that union.

This is the birth of the Lover.

Life sets us up for longing —we are *supposed* to yearn.

are essentially diverse unhealthy reactions against healthy and normal yearning. Modern culture fosters and facilitates the shadows of the Lover.

So the Lover is always wounded—always seeking to recover the love of his parents, his heavenly beginnings, and his whole self. Lover must be wounded to exist. But each man differs in the depth of the wounds to his Lover and in how he responds to these wounds throughout his life. These variables can make a tremendous difference in the type and extent of the shadows his wounds will create. We'll discuss the shadows created by these wounds a bit later.

Lover must be wounded to exist.

But there is more to the story. Lover energy is not simply a reaction to separation and loss. Knowing so many men who exhibit strong Lover energy, it's apparent to me that they are rich in traits that are likely to be innate. Certain men seem to have more gentle or expressive temperaments that connect them easily to Lover energy. Some men have traits that fill them with Lover capacities, such as aptitudes for perception of sound, color, form, and spatial relationships. And some men show a strong propensity for feeling emotions and relating with others, which may be due to brain structure. I believe that these innate traits exist separate from any wounding a boy receives from his mother.

As we discuss the three core aspects of Lover energy, see if you recognize how family dynamics and inborn traits might combine in each of these areas. Also, consider how each of these traits is manifested in your life. ✎ 10.1

Lover as Sensation

Lover is the experience of every type of sensation, including feelings of pain, pleasure, and every nuance in between. He's our vivid awareness and sensitivity. He delights in the endless variety of things in the world—in multiplicity or diversity. The Lover wants to sample every chocolate in the box, and he savors the subtle and strong differences in the flavors of each one. He feels the urge to wander through the rainforest indulging himself in the experience of every animal, bird, insect, flower, and tree. The more diverse his experience is, the better. This is why heterosexual men constantly check out women—the Lover wants to experience every beautiful thing.

Multiplicity: having a great number of forms; variety

This aspect of Lover involves the *passive* experience of stimuli from *without and within*: sights, sounds, tastes, and smells as well as tactile, spiritual, and emotional sensations. Primary among all of these is the Lover's connection to his own emotional states—as he experiences the world, he's acutely aware of the feelings that arise inside himself. He's equally aware of the self–generated emotions that occur—joy, peacefulness, agitation, fear, anger, sadness, love, and many other nuanced feelings.

This kind of emotional awareness is like a gauge the Lover uses to stay in tune with his world. Being in tune with our environment is essential so that we can respond appropriately to it. Being attuned to our inner environment is important for the same reasons. Our emotions give us essential information about our wellbeing and our needs. In order to maintain accurate emotional awareness and attunement, the Lover must be able to shift from one sensation and feeling state to another. Without this ability, the Lover will carry feelings from one situation to another where they don't fit, thus compromising his ability to experience the feelings from the new situation.

An example may help you understand this concept better. Imagine a man sitting in a very tense and angry meeting. His inner Lover takes in and experiences all of those feelings strongly. Then he leaves the meeting and goes to a party where the atmosphere is entirely different. If he can't shift emotionally and experience new feelings at the party, he will stay emotionally at the tense meeting and entirely miss the relaxation of the party. ✍ 10.2

Lover as Libido

As you may remember from your reading on the King archetype in Chapter Two, libido refers to life energy, life instincts, or "lust for life." It's all the energies of being awake, alive, and passionate. This aspect of Lover is *internally generated* and is active. Libido is the experience of appetite, urge, and drive—it's the physical appetite for food and drink, the urge for action and rest, and the drive for self–preservation and sex.

This same energy is the feeling of wanting more—more wealth, more freedom, more experience, more pleasure, more friends, and more power. It's the longing, motivation, and enthusiasm for growth and expansion, expression, advancement, movement, and reproduction. It's aroused by everything that feels urgent to us, whether that urgency feels alarming, painful, or pleasurable. It's the feeling of "I *want*…" It is hunger of every type.

Libido is all the energies of being awake, alive, and passionate.

Another aspect to this libidinal energy is the urge to express feelings and impulses. This is the basis for expressions of fondness, love, and sexual desire. It's the primal urge that causes men to create art of every kind. It's also the vision and drive behind expressive architecture, journalism, design, and political movements. Anywhere that the creative urge is manifested, the Lover is at work in the background.

The urges and desires of libido seek *incarnation*, which means they look for ways to come into physical form. The simplest and most frank example of this is the way that libido is incarnated when blood fills the *corpus spongiosum* within the penis, creating an erection—desire becomes physical, and an urge can be expressed. But sexuality is just one of the almost endless ways in which Lover can be expressed. Feelings of fondness may be incarnated through gentle physical touch or a soft voice. Love of green things may be incarnated through tending a garden or walking in the woods. Passion for color might be incarnated through painting, photography, or interior design. The urge for movement may be incarnated through dance, running a marathon, or creating a motion picture. The possibilities are truly endless!

In bringing itself into physical form, the Lover must often rely on the capacities of other archetypes. For example, the urge to erect a skyscraper is pure libido. But it takes a lot of the Magian's secret knowledge of engineering, the Warrior's discipline and focus on goals, and the King's capacity to regulate and organize in order to actually erect the structure. A look at all other complex Lover endeavors will reveal similar joint ventures.

Conversely, the other archetypes must also rely on certain capacities of the Lover if they are to fulfill their highest potential. An active and Whole Lover keeps our King, Warrior, and Magian connected to feelings of love and compassion, desires for unity, and the joys of relationships. The Lover's influence pulls these archetypes away from shadow and moves them toward their most whole potential. Lacking that influence, feelings like fear, anger, and disgust can cause the King to ossify into absolutism and tyranny, the Warrior to drift into rigid discipline and sadistic fierceness, and the Magian to slip into self–serving manipulation.

The Whole Lover experiences and expresses his libidinal life forces in gentle, compassionate, nurturing, and creative ways. It's only when the Lover has slipped

Another aspect to this libidinal energy is the urge to express feelings and impulses.

In bringing itself into physical form, the Lover must often rely on the capacities of other archetypes.

into Addict and is perhaps under some influence by the Sadist that libido becomes gluttonous or otherwise destructive.  10.3

Lover as Union

Even as he enjoys the multiplicity of the world and the nuance of every feeling, the Lover also seeks union and connection with all things. This aspect of Lover is once again *internally generated* and *active* and it seeks incarnation. He doesn't want to merely sense the taste of the cake—he wants to make it part of himself by taking it into his body. And even as he's sensing the tree, the canyon, and the stars as things outside himself, the Lover somehow feels a connection with them as well, bringing them into himself.

Lover is the energy that makes a whole out of the parts and searches for meaning. He not only senses his connection to the tree, the canyon, and the stars, he also senses the connections, relationships, and interactions *among them* as well. For him the starry night is a complex interweaving of disparate and complementary sensations, and the whole of it has deep personal meaning for him. This awareness may exist on a conscious level or only on the level of mysterious intuition and feeling, but it is there.

This unifying energy brings together the opposites and all conflicting energies. It's the principle of yin–yang: opposing qualities of the same phenomena held in union. For example, summer and winter are opposite qualities of the phenomenon of season, joy and grief are opposite qualities of the phenomenon of emotion, and blue and yellow are opposite qualities of the phenomenon of color. Lover energy understands these opposites as a whole phenomenon because he can bring into harmony divergent qualities, concepts, principles, and points of view.

This is the energy of reconciliation, reunion, and solidarity that instills in some men's hearts a desire to bring people together. This is one of the reasons men form teams. It's one of the forces behind the civil rights movement. It prompts détente. It's the impulse that brings an apology and creates the willingness to ask for and extend forgiveness.

It is this same capacity that unifies and harmonizes the four archetypal energies, bringing us to our most whole potential. For example, Lover embraces the Warrior's discipline and mission so that they serve only the King. Lover unifies the Magian's

The Lover seeks union and connection with all things.

wisdom with the King's impulse to bless his people, resulting in initiation of the next generation. And Lover causes the King to yearn for deeper connection with his Higher Power, fostering a powerful axis mundi.

The unifying capacity of the Lover can create a sense of connection with others of our own sex, which may be incarnated through friendship and male community. This connection is a key aspect of gender wholeness as we discussed in Chapter Six. As we relate authentically in community with other men, the attachment and resonance we feel with them may open a new and perhaps mysterious understanding of the union between us. Even with a clear recognition and appreciation of another man's individuality and differences from us, we may come to experience the other man as also being very *like* us. On a deeper level, we may even sense that the other *is* us. Gender wholeness on the grand scale is the Lover experiencing all men as one. The Lover's understanding of masculinity is that it is defined, not by certain outstanding men, but by the summation of *all* men.

> The Lover's understanding of masculinity is that it is defined by the summation of *all* men.

Perhaps most mysterious of all, Lover harmonizes the opposite qualities of gender—male and female. He does so on a deeply–felt level of acceptance, appreciation, and respect. This unifying capacity of the Lover is what I referred to in Chapters Three and Six as *complementarity* with the opposite sex. In those chapters, I explained that complementarity refers to a favorable relationship between the two sexes where each fulfills, balances, and perfects the other. Together they make a complete unit. It takes these two energies together to be truly whole. 🖎 10.4

Lover in Relationships

As mentioned earlier in this chapter, Lover is created by the separation that occurs in the relationship with mother. Moore and Gillette believe that an essential aspect of mature Lover energy is the impulse to return to mother's perfect embrace and the "garden of delight" that she represents. They would say that it's out of this impulse that the Lover's quest for union emerges. As boys grow, this quest for relationships is turned toward father and male peers. Then, eventually, it turns back toward females, leading the man to a wife or lover, at which point the man has made a full circle back to loving a mother.

> As boys grow, this quest for relationships is turned toward father and male peers.

I believe that more basic than any impact of the loss of connection with mother, humans have an innate need for relationships. Connections with others are necessary for our survival and essential for our happiness. Through our Lover capacities, we can experience a variety of relational feelings, which are discussed in Moore and Gillette's books *King Warrior Magician Lover* and *The Lover Within* using the names *amor, eros, storge, philia,* and *agape.* These are Greek words that have been used over millennia to designate different types of love and friendship. These concepts are presented in a variety of ways by various writers, defying any simple understanding of them. For our purposes, a simple explanation of each is sufficient.

Storge

Storge (pronounced *stor–jee*) refers to love for family members, and this is likely the first type of love for others that a child experiences beyond the union with mother. This includes the love of children for their parents, parents for their children, and the love among siblings. This love may extend to known relatives outside the immediate family unit, such as grandparents, aunts, uncles, and cousins.

Philia

Philia is friendship, whether between close acquaintances or lifelong intimate friends. This can include business contacts, neighbors, members of a religious community, or other people whom we know at least reasonably well. *Philia* implies fondness, affection, and reciprocity. This may be the second type of love experienced in a child's life when he feels it for his young friends. *Philia* can also be very close and intimate, and this is the type of love that is most healing for men who wish to fulfill unmet needs for same–sex affiliation.

Eros

Eros is an ecstatic connection with another person and is usually sexual. It's the experience of being carried away or transported by the relationship to a place and time outside of reality and the present. This is the love that drives toward orgasmic moments with another. This type of love emerges in late adolescence or young adulthood and can be very promiscuous. It's interesting to observe how boys who previously showed little or no Lover energy seem to suddenly gush with it when this type of love emerges in their lives.

Amor

Amor refers to a whole union with another that is both sexual and spiritual. In *amor*, the other is fully recognized and appreciated with all her beauties and flaws. A boundary of individuality exists, but is also transcended through the deep connection. This is the deepest romantic love celebrated throughout the history of literature and art. It exists only within pairs. As children come into the lives of such a couple, their capacity for *storge* increases. One can observe men in this period of their lives emanating an even stronger Lover energy. As they grow older still and grandchildren enter the picture, these men reach the peak of their Lover capacities.

Agape, simply put, is brotherly love. Moore and Gillette also refer to it as a "fellow feeling." It's unconditional and non–sexual love for others. The concept of charity in Christian traditions matches this type of love. One could say that it's Lover energy channeled through the King. It's a more mature form of interpersonal love. ✍ 10.5

Agape

In addition to these human relationships, some men experience a union with God. Lover energy brings with it the capacity for transcending the mundane world and connecting to "the mystery" of the divine forces of the Universe. Each religion has its own ways of facilitating such connections. In the Jewish Talmud, the revelation of God to Moses on Mount Sinai is referred to as the marriage ceremony between God, as the groom, and the Jewish people, as the bride. The lifelong goal of a religious Jew is to cling to God as a bride to her husband. The devout Muslim asks forgiveness from Allah the Most Merciful, Most Compassionate through daily prayers, fasting during Ramadan, and making the pilgrimage to Mecca. And for Christians, the atonement of Jesus Christ reconciles the believer with the Father.

Union with God

For some, this divine association may be a vague longing for connection with a Higher Power or higher purpose. For some it is a connection with a benevolent spirit that operates in our lives. Some experience it as a personal though distant God whom they feel obliged to serve. And some experience this in an ecstatic and very physical way as a divine union that, similar to *eros*, transports them to a place outside of earthly bounds. ✍ 10.6

Finally, in addition to all of these external relationships, I also have a relationship with myself. We discussed this at length in the previous chapter on authenticity. I believe that to have a satisfying and joyful relationship with myself, I must be living from the core of who I really am—from my Self or Center. I have to experience myself without the distortions caused by my shadows, wounds, or symptoms. I have to understand myself on a deep level. And I need the capacity to feel and tolerate the full range of my own emotions and impulses. Then I have to extend compassion to all aspects of myself, including the shadows I intend to surrender. Having a relationship with myself that is less than this will always be

Relationship with self

less than fully satisfying. And having a relationship with only my false self can be downright painful.  10.7

SADNESS AND THE LOVER

One might expect that the core emotion connected with the Lover would be joy, since that feeling state is his constant aim. But it is sadness that we connect with the Lover because it's through that emotion—caused by separation and loss—that the Lover comes into being. This is consistent with the other archetypes: it's joy that brings a man into his highest King energy and the desire to bless others, anger that brings a man into his Warrior capacities, and fear that is the gateway into the Magian's domain.

This point is illustrated beautifully in the 1939 movie classic, *The Wizard of Oz*. In the closing scenes, Dorothy has found a way to get back to Kansas and must leave her troop of followers, including the Tin Man. You may remember that the Tin Man didn't have a heart. In archetypal terms, he was an impotent Lover. But as he hugs Dorothy, he begins to weep and then blubbers his most classic line: "Now I know I have a heart… 'cause it's breaking." His Lover has awakened.[2]

When it isn't blocked by defenses, sadness is a full Lover experience—it involves each of his three core aspects: sensation, libido, and union. The Lover's desire for union gives rise to the sadness. Sadness is always precipitated by loss, whether the loss is a close relationship, a prized belonging, an opportunity, or our self–esteem. The loss leaves the Lover feeling fragmented, and sadness is his reaction. Sadness can't be fully experienced without sensation. Often that sensation is described as heaviness somewhere in the upper body and pressure behind the eyes. When these sensations are sufficiently strong, they come into physical form as sobs or a flood of tears. In those moments, our life energy, or libido, becomes entirely focused on expressing and releasing the passion of our sadness.

Through our sadness we gain a more clear and poignant understanding of our relationship to the thing we've lost. In a mysterious way, the sadness more deeply unites us with what we've lost, then helps us transition into acceptance that it's no longer with us. The sadness heals our fragmentation and brings a new wholeness, often in a new configuration that is stronger and more resilient. And the sadness imbues the experience with meaning, resolving those difficult questions that always begin with "Why…?"

All of us are wounded by our separation from mother. If we indeed did exist before this life, we may bear unconscious wounds due to our separation from that joyful state. Most of us are also wounded by the splitting–off of our unwanted traits in childhood. And many of us are wounded by mistreatment from others as we grow up. So there is a broad range, in degree and depth, of sadness that people may have, depending on our life experience and the extent of our wounds. Some of us have very little underlying sadness and may experience it only occasionally when a present loss brings it on. On the other extreme, some of us may experience it as a constant companion due to severe injuries we've sustained over the course of our lives.

Some of us respond to our sadness with great authenticity, allowing ourselves to feel it fully until it brings us through the pain to the emotions beyond. Others deny the existence of our sadness and repress its sensations. And some are taken prisoner by our sadness, living in what we call depression for many years.

The relationship we have with our sadness—whether we allow ourselves to feel it healthfully, avoid it, or become imprisoned by it—may have a lot to do with how our sadness was treated in our formative years. Children who grow up in families where sadness is appreciated and respected may be more likely to develop the ability to feel and express sadness in healthy and healing ways. On the other hand, children who grow up in families that ignore sadness or punish them for expressing it may have difficulties dealing with sadness in adulthood. If we're to heal our lives and maintain a healthy relationship with our Lover energies, we need the ability to feel and express our sadness. ✍ 10.8

> The relationship we have with our sadness may have a lot to do with how our sadness was treated in our formative years.

LOVER IN THE MODERN WORLD

Before going further, let's spend a little time considering how Lover energy is responded to in modern society and culture. This may provide a helpful context for understanding how we personally experience this most misunderstood archetype. Men today seem to have difficulty relating to the full spectrum of Lover traits and capacities that we've been exploring. I believe three social and cultural tendencies contribute to this.

> Men today seem to have difficulty relating to the full spectrum of Lover traits and capacities.

First, the driving forces of modern society—which are business, politics, and government—favor the capacities, both shadowy and whole, of the Warrior, Magian, and King. Today's expectations of men call for the rational, logistical, and disciplined traits of these other archetypes. Most predominantly it's the Warrior's dedication to getting the job done and the Magian's scientific and technological mind that are valued. So the demands on us as men favor the development of everything but Lover.

Traces of Lover energy do show up in society, but we generally find them channeled into furthering the goals of the other archetypes in the pursuit of influence, power, or financial gain. For example, the Lover's libido—his lust for life and wanting for more—is channeled into financial and business acquisitions. His drive for union and relationship are parlayed into "getting in bed" with a business partner or forming a union of workers or employees. And his appreciation of diversity generally has distinct political motivations, rather than arising from the sheer enjoyment of multiplicity.

Second, modern culture typically represents the Lover in stripped–down and over–simplified terms, devoid of the real richness of the Whole Lover. This means that if we, as men, want to fit in and seem masculine, we have to experience and express Lover within a pretty narrow range. Essentially, we have cultural permission to connect with sensation, libido, and union as long as we do it in ways that are recreational, which means through sex, drugs, sports, entertainment, and casual friendship. Usually these ways of experiencing Lover are also self–serving, extreme, and addictive, as opposed to being transcendent, balanced, and moderate.

The culture industry—which includes movies and television, the commercial news media, and advertising—seems to be more limiting of Lover than does real culture. In real culture—which is the sum of what real people actually believe and do—men are given somewhat greater latitude to experience and express Lover traits. But the culture industry has a vested interest in cultivating the addict in each of us, because the addict's insatiable craving for "more" results in reliable sales and higher profits. So sensation, libido, and union have been recruited, or hijacked, to drive us to consumption. The culture industry has turned the Lover into something of a sophisticated pimp—a purveyor of sensual pleasure.

There are some notable exceptions to what I've just described. The culture industry these days does include portrayals of the family man, the heroic husband, and the patriot who loves his country or his people. But usually these portrayals

> Traces of Lover energy do show up in society, but we generally find them channeled into furthering the goals of the other archetypes.

> The culture industry seems to be more limiting of Lover than does real culture.

of the Lover are heavily laced with the Warrior's commitment to fight and die for what he loves.

And then there are chick flicks and romance novels. These are the closest the culture industry comes to portraying and celebrating the Whole Lover. The perennial story in these genres centers on hunky, Warrior–type males becoming so smitten with *amor* for a girl that they sacrifice everything to be with her. But, besides being shallow and idealized, these stories are for "chicks." And their standard for masculinity is only valid in "chick culture." So they're doing little, if anything, to broaden the perspective of the Lover archetype among men.

Third, many of the traits that belong to the Lover tend to be viewed in our culture as feminine, particularly his functions of sensation and union. Being sensitive to our physical surroundings, the physical sensations within our bodies, and our emotions isn't viewed as being particularly manly these days. These impractical, "touchy–feely" capacities are usually viewed as being more typical of women. The same is true of the ability to nurture, to relate lovingly with others, and to connect spiritually.

Many Lover traits are viewed in our culture as feminine.

If Lover capacities are not viewed as feminine, they may be viewed as gay, causing men to back away from them. For example, there is substantial evidence that mainstream culture has grown far less comfortable over the past hundred years with the expression of Lover energy between men. Photographs of groups of men taken a century ago and earlier show men touching each other in more close and intimate ways than would typically be seen in a modern male group photograph.[3] Also, letters from men to other men from that same period are extremely expressive of feelings of fondness and intimacy. Some speculate that the loss of this type of closeness among men is due to the rise of gay culture, which they hypothesize has caused men to pull back their fond expressions out of fear of being or seeming gay.

Photo postcard from early 1900s
(Collection of Bob Young)

As a result of these societal and cultural onslaughts, the Whole Lover tends to be experienced as an enigma at best and viewed with suspicion or even disdain at worst. The societal and cultural void of healthy Lover energy this creates is a sad and dangerous occurrence, if it's true. It's sad because it leaves us devoid of a level of richness we would otherwise experience. It's dangerous because that energy is being forced into shadow. Authors Moore and Gillette make the point that Lover energy can't be repressed. Attempts to do so will merely drive it out of its appropriate channels and it will invade other parts of life, emerging in destructive ways. We sometimes refer to this as "coming out sideways." I see plenty of evidence these days of Lover energy coming out sideways. The most blatant example may be the burgeoning addiction to online pornography. ✍ 10.9

SHADOWS OF THE LOVER

Very young children need their parents to provide close attachment, adequate attunement, and acceptance of their true self. Later, the child trades much of his attachment for autonomy. He forsakes attunement to gain individuation. And rather than acceptance, he prefers respect.

This separation process doesn't need to go perfectly to be healthy. In fact, some imperfections in a child's relationship with his parents are important to help the child learn to tolerate and repair misattunement later in life. These are essential skills for having relationships. But children can only tolerate so much imperfection before damage to the child begins to be done. Certain parenting flaws can be particularly damaging to children, including:

- Failure to bond with the child, which means that the parents' natural impulses to love and nurture the child are weak or don't develop at all. This can result in the child losing his attachment to his parents.

- Misattunement with mother and typically thereafter with father. Misattunement means that the parents are emotionally out of sync with the boy. If mother is distracted by stress, marital problems, ill health, chemical dependency, or depression, she may not be able to attune with her child. If father isn't in touch with his own Lover capacities, or if he's absent or addicted, he may also be out of tune.

- Invasion of the child's boundaries through verbal, physical, emotional, and sexual abuse as well as manipulation. Mothers may invade when they cling too tightly or too long to their boys or use them as surrogate husbands, pulling them too deeply into their own issues. This is an attack on the child's independence and innocence.

- Shaming the child. While always damaging, shame is particularly destructive to a boy's Lover energy if it's aimed at his Lover qualities, such

> Children can only tolerate so much imperfection before damage to the child begins to be done.

as emotionality, sensitivity, creativity, and expressiveness. We discussed shame at length in Chapter Four.

- Failure to recognize and respect the child's true self. This is especially problematic when the mother fails to recognize and affirm the boy's budding maleness. Equally damaging is when fathers fail to respect a boy's unique personality when it is different from the father's personality or from the personalities of the boy's brothers.

At a certain level of exposure to these flaws—which level is different for each individual—a boy can begin to develop any of a number of problems. He may develop deep and chronic feelings of shame, fear, and insecurity, which leave him feeling unsafe to express his authentic feelings and needs because he sees them as unwanted, dangerous, or bad. He may become very depressed, anxious, and detached from his emotions. He may experience difficulty sensing, establishing, or holding boundaries. He may develop lasting insecurity in all or most relationships and may have difficulty forming or maintaining relationships. Problems like these are common in the childhoods of men with same–sex attraction.

A core problem for boys who experience misattunement and loss of attachment with their mothers can be the development of a dynamic marked by conflicting impulses of detachment and dependency. On one hand, these boys may feel compulsions to reject their mother and withdraw from her in hurt or anger. On the other hand, these impulses may be opposed by equally strong compulsions to cling to their mother out of a deep insecurity and unmet needs for attachment.

> A core problem for boys can be the development of a dynamic marked by conflicting impulses of detachment and dependency.

The detached side of this dynamic can show up in adulthood as avoidance (passive withdrawal from others based on hurt and vulnerability) or estrangement (aggressively alienating others to escape the demands of connection). The dependent side of this dynamic can show up in adulthood as clinginess (passive over–reliance on others for identity, approval, support, and care) or abusiveness (aggressive pursuit of other people to further an addiction).

As you may already sense, both sides of this dynamic tend to be reactionary and compulsive due to the underlying pain and fear caused by misattunement and attachment loss with mother. A boy's relationship to his mother sets the tone for all subsequent relationships in his life, so each succeeding relationship will likely be tinged with the issues that arose in the bond with her. Thus, the detached–dependent dynamic may be transferred into the relationship with father and then into relationships with other people—both male and female. In adulthood, this can lead to same–sex disaffiliation, which we discussed in Chapter Seven, and to reactionary and compulsive desires for union with a man to whom we can dependently cling. This dynamic can also be transferred onto the relationship with a Higher Power with equally unhealthy results.

The detached–dependent dynamic manifests itself in the relational tendencies of both shadow poles of the Lover, as illustrated by the graphic in the sidebar. The Impotent shadow pole manifests it in passive, internal, and powerless ways, while the Addict shadow pole manifests this dynamic in active, external, and aggressive ways. Men may tend toward one pole or the other. But, as with all the shadows, these opposing energies seek wholeness *through* one another. So men will shift back and forth between detachment and dependency and between addiction and impotence. We will discuss this dynamic in greater detail later on in this chapter.

Problems originating in the mother–son relationship are not the only influences that can push Lover into shadow. Moore and Gillette make the point in *The Lover Within* that "the primary reason adult men get stuck in the Shadow Lover is that they never had older men who 'held them in their hearts,'" quoting that last phrase from Robert Bly. Boys need mature men to help "them to find nurturing, sensitivity, relatedness, and spirituality in the context of masculine identity." Lover energy needs to be modeled for boys by adult men with whom they feel a solid connection. This gives boys not only an example, but also permission to feel and express their Lover impulses. Without this bridge, boys can languish for much of their lives in various shadow poles, including those of the Lover.

The situations I've described can affect boys in many different ways. As you read about the Lover's two shadow poles, realize that some or all of the concepts may apply to you—or perhaps none of it will apply to you. Your challenge is to think about it carefully and see what you resonate with.

Because of the complex nature of the Lover's shadow poles, I've broken them down a bit more than in previous chapters in order to make them more comprehensible. Each shadow pole is presented below in two sections: first, the *characteristics*

The detached–dependent dynamic may be transferred into the relationship with father and other people.

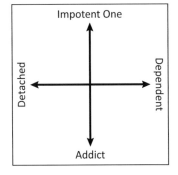

of the shadow, and second, the ways in which each shadow may manifest in *relationships*. The material below is extensive. I encourage you to absorb what you can now without worrying about whether you comprehend every paragraph. Perhaps on your first reading you might look for the overall themes that are present. Then on later readings you may dig deeper into the finer points of each concept.

The Impotent One

The Impotent One is shut down and holding on. The wounds of childhood have left him not knowing how to feel. His shame has left him with what Fossum and Mason describe in *Facing Shame* as "an inner sense of being completely diminished or insufficient as a person." He has built defensive walls against his feelings, leaving him empty and depressed. From this position, he can't bring Lover energy into the world. If the wounds of childhood also left him insecure, the Impotent One may manifest as compulsiveness or a sense of need for control.

Men caught in the Impotent shadow may experience either or both sides of the detached–dependent dynamic. The detached side may manifest as a lack of energy or courage to engage in relationships, leading to avoidance and withdrawal from other people. The dependent side of the dynamic may manifest as a lack of individual identity and compulsive needs for approval, support, and care from others, leading to clingy and dependent behavior.

The 2009 musical film, *Nine*, tells the story of Guido Contini, a fictitious 1960s Italian filmmaker whose superstar career is now in free–fall.[4] The film provides many windows into the development of the Lover and his two shadows. Particularly, it amply illustrates the impact of the mother–son relationship on Lover and the interrelationship between the Addict and Impotent One—Guido inhabits both shadows, almost at the same time. Let's consider what this film teaches about the Lover more generally and then we'll zero in on what it reveals about the Impotent shadow specifically.

As I've already described, Lover is borne from imperfections in the mother–son bond, particularly those imperfections that leave a boy longing for a lost attunement. Guido's relationship with his mother strongly suggests such loss and longing. Though she is dead, his mother is one of his most significant female relationships. We see that relationship through Guido's haunting memories of past events and through his fantasies, in which past and present often blur together. In fantasy,

NINE

The 2009 musical film, *Nine*, tells the story of Guido Contini, a fictitious 1960s Italian filmmaker whose superstar career is now in free–fall.

his mother is almost an angel of comfort and a shield from distress. In the fantasy follies that open the film, she appears with all the flourish of a celebrity. Guido runs to her, gushing, with his hand over his heart. In a later musical fantasy, in which Guido imagines her walking with his nine–year–old self, she sings these lyrics:

> How the moon glows when it smiles over you…
> And when you're a man, pray that I'm there to guide you…
> You will always be mine, yes, mine…
> This one good night kiss will keep all your life perfect like this.

Then we hear adult Guido's voice say, "Hold onto me, Mamma. Don't let me wake from this." Guido's dependency on his mother is clear.

Guido's dependency on his mother is clear.

A very different side of his mother is revealed in Guido's flashbacks of actual childhood memories. There she is shaming and abandoning. In one memory, again from age nine, Guido has escaped his Catholic boarding school with some other boys to visit a prostitute who lives in an abandoned war bunker on the beach. Priests from the school soon arrive and drag young Guido, from what seems to have been a relatively innocent adventure, back to the school where his mother is waiting. "I'm ashamed of you," she scolds. Then she turns her back as the priest beats Guido with a rod. With that beating, the mother–son bond and Guido's sexuality are wounded.

Guido's detachment from his mother is also clear.

A few scenes later, we see a brief clip of young Guido, again at the beach, running. And we hear his mother's voice calling after him: "Guido, where are you running to?" Guido's detachment from his mother is also clear. But this brief scene suggests more than just detachment from mother; it also suggests running toward the prostitute. It reveals the full detached–dependent dynamic. This is Guido's life–long race—flight from mother's shaming and the chase after a perfectly nurturing attachment, which he seeks in a multiplicity of other women.

Men occupy only peripheral roles in Guido's life. His father is never once mentioned. The only males who appear in his childhood flashbacks are the stern priests at his boarding school. As an adult his only significant male relationship is with his producer, who mostly enables Guido's addiction. Given his over–enmeshment with the feminine and his lack of masculine connection, it's not surprising that Guido would have such little tolerance for the reality principle, which we discussed in Chapter Five. Guido's typical response to demands of the real–life world is to run—and sometimes he literally sprints.

The fictitious life of Guido Contini illustrates the setup for a dangerously out–of–balance Lover. Overall, Guido is an addict. But the arc of the movie is his increasing impotence—this story is about his descent into paralysis, depression, avoidance, and clinging dependency.

His impotence is most obviously illustrated by his inability to write the script for his new movie. We also learn that his two previous movies were "flops." In one scene, a reporter confronts him at a press conference and asks him point blank, "Have you run out of things to say?" Though he tries repeatedly to create, no amount of time alone or inspiration from his beautiful muses can unblock his creative flow. His cinematic libido is paralyzed.

> His impotence is most obviously illustrated by his inability to write the script for his new movie.

But his career difficulties are just the surface of his problems. He is palpably unhappy and his addiction no longer keeps him above his misery. In one scene, he laments to a Catholic cardinal he has met, "I'm not happy. I'm searching for something. I feel a sense of misery and despair…" Several times he uses the word "lost" to describe himself. On one occasion he indirectly refers to himself as "dying" and "bleeding to death." He also shows signs of sexual impotence. During a sequence where he is in bed with his mistress we see him suddenly gasping for air, which ends their foreplay.

In his relationship with his wife, Luisa, he is both avoidant and dependent. He keeps her at a considerable distance in order to facilitate the affair with his mistress. But he depends on Luisa creatively, having lost connection with his own creative source. Late in the film, Luisa leaves Guido due to his blatant sexual impropriety. Still he calls her on the phone and pleads with her to attend a screening of "dailies," or footage shot during the day. He clearly needs her there. "Otherwise, I won't know where to start," Guido whines. "I won't know what I'm thinking."

> "Otherwise, I won't know where to start. I won't know what I'm thinking."

This dependence extends to other women as well. He runs to his mistress for relief from distress; he relies on an older woman, Lilly, as his confidant; he uses Claudia, the female lead of his films, as a primary source of inspiration. But Guido has nothing to offer these women in return. He can't provide, protect, or even love them genuinely. Ultimately, he is left alone. Near the end of the film, as everything is unraveling, Guido cries out in pain, "Help me Luisa, help me Mamma, help me someone!" Later in the same sequence, he bemoans, "I destroyed everything, Mamma! I destroyed everything! You make one wrong turn and because of it all the turns after it are wrong." His fantasies wind to their conclusion with a final response from his mother: "No one can help you find your way. It's up to you, Guido. Up to you. Nobody else."

Characteristics of the Impotent One

The Impotent One is like a man hanging from the edge of a cliff in the freezing cold. He's paralyzed with fear, numb from the cold, and has little energy remaining. Without the power to climb up to safety, he can't do anything but hold on for dear life.

Think carefully about the character traits of the Impotent One described below. Consider whether you experience any of these traits within yourself. And consider whether you might project any of these traits onto other people. ✍ 10.10

Paralyzed: The parenting flaws described at the beginning of the section "Shadows of the Lover" can overwhelm a young person's emotional capacity. Moore and Gillette speak of parents crossing boundaries, of psychological and emotional abuse, and of parenting that's confusing and lacking consistency. I would add "critical" and "shaming" to their list of parenting flaws. They also speak of the chronic distrust and fear that can result from such parenting. This leads to the emotional paralysis of the Impotent One, which is an inability to know what his emotions are, what they "should be," or what they mean. Chronic fear may also lead to an inability to respond to the emotions of others. Sometimes this may be accompanied by a lack of emotion. At other times he may feel intense emotion and yet be incapacitated in his efforts to comprehend or respond to it.

Numb: The Impotent One may also lack the capacity to experience much physical sensation. This symptom is probably not due to issues with his central nervous system. Rather it's likely a consequence of having numbed himself from pain for many years, whether its original source was emotional or physical. Or he may have numbed his physical sensations as a means of coping with the confusing feelings and emotions that come from sexual abuse. At its most extreme, the Impotent shadow is entirely devoid of sensation. But it's more likely that a man may be able to feel certain sensations but not others, or that his overall experience of, or responsiveness to, physical sensation may be diminished.

Depressed: Along with the symptoms described previously, the Impotent One may experience a lack of energy toward life. He's without libido and lacks any appetite. He doesn't feel any drive to make things happen. Even activities or pursuits that he may have found pleasurable and meaningful earlier in his life are forsaken. There are many types of depression with many different causes. The depression of which Moore and Gillette are speaking is a "self–administered anesthetic that keeps the *ego* from experiencing underlying passion, fear, and rage."

Impotent: The term "impotence" refers to the inability to achieve an erection or to procreate. In the larger context we're discussing here, impotence extends to the incapacity to bring any Lover energy into the world, which is undoubtedly why Moore and Gillette chose this trait as the name for the Lover's passive shadow. The Impotent One can't "incarnate" himself, or bring his energy into living flesh. In this shadow, a man is without vigor, strength, or power and is thus unable to create a life with any color, interest, or joy in it.

Controlling: Like the man hanging from the cliff, the Impotent One may feel an intense impulse to keep a strong grip on things. His desire for control may be compulsive and might manifest as obsessive–compulsive behaviors and personality traits like those described in Chapter Four. His behavior may be highly constrained, and he may spend a lot of time in his head ruminating. The Impotent One may compel a man to maintain control in his living situation, job, environment, daily activities, or sexual behavior. Extended or total abstinence from sexual activity may be a manifestation of this control. In Chapter Four we discussed the control–release cycle. The Impotent One is the control side of that cycle.

The Impotent One in Relationships

People have relationships with other people, but we also have relationships with ourselves, with God, and with things. In this section we'll consider how the shadow of impotence may affect each of these categories of relationships. We'll also consider the impact of the detached–dependent dynamic on the Impotent One's relationships with other people and with his Higher Power. Consider how the tendencies described below might be manifested in your relationships and how

> The Impotent One may experience a lack of energy toward life. He's without libido and lacks any appetite.

> We have relationships with other people, with ourselves, with God, and with things.

you may project them onto others. Keep in mind that you may manifest a few, all, or none of these tendencies. ✍ 10.11

Unaware: In his relationship to himself, the Impotent One may be unaware of who he is or what he wants from life. Moore and Gillette sub–title their chapter on the Impotent One "Lost in the Wasteland," which is an apt description of how he experiences his own inner life—there isn't much there, and yet he's very lost within it. Since he's not substantially differentiated from other people, he may lack a sense of himself as a unique individual. He may be unsure of his opinions, wants, or needs. If his boundaries were repeatedly violated, he may spend much of his time feeling vulnerable and afraid. Since his mind and heart have been unwelcoming places to explore—and because he has never felt the courage to venture there—he may remain unacquainted with himself as a person. In this state, whether temporary or life–long, he can't sense his personal capacity, and so his own potency is cut off from him.

Avoidant: The abuse, neglect, misattunement, shame, and crossing of boundaries that create emotional paralysis in young children can leave the Impotent One feeling so hurt or vulnerable that he may fully detach from others, passively avoiding all but the most necessary interaction. This is a manifestation of the detached side of the detached–dependent dynamic. He might tend to avoid any situations where he could be criticized or rejected. He may be overly sensitive and might perceive disapproval and rejection where none is intended. Avoidance of relationships may seem a necessary price to pay for freedom from emotions and impulses he finds overwhelming or disturbing. His boundaries may be high protective walls that are held in place by a very rigid and compulsive mindset of distrust of people and fear of feeling.

Without the strength and support that comes from interdependent bonds of friendship and intimacy, the Impotent One would likely experience a magnification of his paralysis, numbness, depression, and impotence. Any interpersonal challenges he experiences may feel too big to deal with, so he exerts even greater control over his world by backing further away. As a result, he never develops a sense of capacity for handling relationships or facing the world.

Clingy: Lacking a sense of individuality, devoid of connection to his own power, and unable to form true strengthening bonds with others, the Impotent One may

---

The Impotent One in Relationships

- Unaware
- Avoidant
- Clingy
- Non–believing
- Fanatical
- Disinterested

The Impotent One may fully detach from others, passively avoiding all but the most necessary interaction.

326

unconsciously determine that he must cling to others for support and nurture. In doing so, he is enacting the dependent side of the detached–dependent dynamic in a passive and powerless way. He may project the strengths of his King, Warrior, and Magian onto people who he sees as having all the power. He may sacrifice his autonomy and submit to these people—perhaps masochistically—formatting his behavior and personality to suit them in exchange for their approval, support, and care. As a result, his identity would fail to develop properly. The others to whom he clings for dear life may be entirely unaware of this aspect of the relationship.

This kind of clinginess reflects an unresolved psychic dependence on mother for direction and identity, which is often unconsciously transferred onto other women and men. Sometimes the dependence on mother is very literal and conscious in the actual current relationship with mother. The Impotent One may live with his mother long after the age when it would have been appropriate to leave her side. He may depend on her for some of his basic necessities. If he does live on his own, he may visit or speak with her often. Sometimes the dependency is disguised by a veneer of reciprocity in which the man cares for his needy mother who, in return, provides him with a sense of connection, safety, and approval.

> This kind of clinginess reflects an unresolved psychic dependence on mother for direction and identity.

Non–Believing: The Impotent One may avoid faith in a Higher Power or transcendent cause in much the same way that he avoids relationships with people, and for many of the same reasons. This is a manifestation of the detached side of the detached–dependent dynamic. The Impotent One may be too paralyzed and numb to generate an interest in God or a Higher Power. He may be too depressed to exert the energy necessary to consider his beliefs or to act on what he believes. Or he may ignore his latent faith in order to avoid feelings of shame and anger about the eternal damnation he's certain God has in store for him. This detachment from a Higher Power is not explicit atheism, which results from careful and rational thought. Rather, it is the product of passive withdrawal from the effort of belief.

Fanatical: On the opposite extreme, the Impotent One may tend toward fanaticism, which I'm defining here as compulsive dependence on a divine being or a transcendent cause. This is a manifestation of the dependent side of the detached–dependent dynamic. Whether his Higher Power or transcendent cause is a divine being or an institution or movement, the Impotent One is likely to pursue it compulsively rather than as a result of feelings of love, devotion, or faith. He

> *Fanaticism:* compulsive dependence on a divine being or a transcendent cause

would be driven by vulnerability, fear, and a deep need to feel safe, contained, and worthy. So his beliefs may tend toward dogmatism, his service may be forced, and worship may be highly ritualized.

Things don't have much significance to the Impotent One.

Disinterested: His relationship to *things* is likely to be one of disinterest. "Things" might include his home and car, his clothing and personal objects, and "toys" such as entertainment equipment, recreational vehicles, and hobby items. I would also include in the category of "things" activities such as work, recreation, entertainment, and other pleasurable pursuits. Without the ability to derive pleasure from his interactions with objects and experiences, things don't have much significance to the Impotent One. For him, only the most life–sustaining things are valued.

The Addict

If the Impotent One is *shut down* and *holding on*, the Addict is *turned on* and *throwing off* all personal constraint. The wounds of childhood have created a deeply shamed personality, covered by an inflated character with big feelings, high energy, and out–of–control behavior. The wounds and conflicts that create the Addict are the same ones that create the Impotent One. And as I've already explained, both poles of the shadow Lover share the detached–dependent dynamic. Rather than the Impotent One's passive, avoidant detachment, the Addict tends to detach by actively pushing others away. And rather than the Impotent One's powerless clinging, the Addict's dependency tends to manifest in abusive and rebellious behaviors. Whereas the Impotent One implodes, the Addict explodes. Where the Impotent One shrivels under shame, the Addict covers his shame by inflating into narcissism. While the Impotent One becomes avoidant, the Addict relentlessly pursues. And where the Impotent One tends toward control, the Addict is all about release.

The Lord of the Rings contains an elegant allegory for addiction.

J.R.R. Tolkien's classic trilogy, *The Lord of the Rings*, contains an elegant allegory for addiction. The allegory is expressed through the behaviors and interactions of several characters and their relationship to a simple but powerful object—a ring.

It begins with the character of Gollum, or Sméagol as he is originally called. Sméagol is a Hobbit, which is a race of small people known for their simple lives and enjoyment of comfort, eating, and socializing. A close relative and friend of Sméagol's discovers a ring at the bottom of a river while the two are fishing on

Sméagol's birthday. Sméagol is fascinated with the ring from the moment he sees it and asks his friend to give it to him as a birthday present. The friend refuses and Sméagol becomes insistent. A struggle ensues, ending in Sméagol murdering his friend and taking possession of the ring.

The ring for which he has killed is no small trinket. It's the Great Ring of Power—created by Sauron, an evil sorcerer—which gave Sauron the ability to rule the world. Many ages earlier, the ring had been taken from Sauron in a great battle and was later lost in a river, where it remained for two thousand years, until it came into the possession of Sméagol. But the ring has an intelligence of its own and serves only its creator. The dark magic in the ring is treacherous and manipulative. Its power causes those who are susceptible to its enchantment to desire it to the point of insanity. It brings about the eventual corruption and deterioration of those who possess it.

Such is the fate of Sméagol. Physical deterioration comes first in the form of a cough, the sound of which earns him the name "Gollum." Corruption of his character begins with the murder of his friend and soon results in banishment from his homeland. His lifestyle deteriorates to the point of living alone in caves, eating raw fish and goblins, devoid of all relationships except that with the ring, which he calls "the Precious." For over 500 years, Gollum lives a life of enthrallment by the ring—possessing and being possessed by it.

But the ring can't be controlled. It abandons Gollum in a cave and is taken by Bilbo Baggins, another Hobbit. Gollum is inconsolable. He vows his hatred of Baggins and begins a long and tormenting quest to recover his Precious. His quest takes him into Mordor, the most evil place in Middle–earth, where he is tortured by the servants of Sauron. Gollum eventually catches up with the ring, now in the possession of yet another Hobbit, Frodo Baggins, who is on a quest of his own to destroy the ring. The two form a strange alliance because of their relationship to the ring—both of them affected by differing degrees of hatred and love for it, and by conflicting feelings for each other.

The power of the ring can't be overcome simply. Over the course of the trilogy, we learn that it can't be kept safe even by those with the best intentions. It can't be hidden because it has a mind and will of its own. And it can't be used in any positive way because its will is bent on sheer destruction. To be free of the ring,

> The ring is no small trinket. It's the Great Ring of Power which gave Sauron the ability to rule the world.

> But the ring can't be controlled.

Overcome by the ecstatic reunion with his Precious, Gollum loses his balance and falls into the lava, taking the ring with him to his death.

one must face great fear and personal struggle in order to return to the place where the ring was created. Only there can its power be overcome. For Gollum and Frodo, this means traveling into the very heart of Mordor to the volcano known as Mount Doom—the very spot where Sauron forged the ring. On a precipice above a river of molten lava another struggle ensues, much like the one in which Gollum originally acquired the ring. Gollum prevails again, taking the ring from Frodo by biting off his finger. Then, overcome by the ecstatic reunion with his Precious, Gollum loses his balance and falls into the lava, taking the ring with him to his death. Frodo survives his encounter with the ring, but his life is forever changed.

Characteristics of the Addict

Characteristics of the Addict

- Histrionic
- Ecstatic
- Manic
- Promiscuous
- Indulgent

As you read the descriptions below, take time to consider how you exhibit any of these character traits in your own personality. Also be aware of traits that you may commonly project onto others. ✍ 10.12

Histrionic: This term refers to a psychiatric condition that's characterized by "excessive emotionality and attention seeking."[5] The emotions of the Addict shadow tend to be shallow, fleeting, and overly dramatic. These theatrical displays of emotion are not authentic expressions of feeling but conscious or unconscious attempts to bring attention to the Addict and to meet his needs for attention, connection, and love. This behavior may also be used as a tool for the Manipulator shadow of the Magian to further his agenda of creating appearances and beguiling others.

Ecstacy: beyond reason and self–control through intense emotional excitement, pain, or other sensation

Ecstatic: Within his body, the Addict's experience of physical and emotional sensation may take him "beyond reason and self–control through intense emotional excitement, pain, or other sensation."[6] He may be high on drugs, sex, gambling, caffeine, or nicotine. He may be sedated by alcohol, marijuana, or food. Or he may be tripped out in fantasyland by a psychedelic drug, a sexual escapade, or a never–ending game of D&D. In all these cases, he experiences the out–of–body sensuality that's typical of addictive behavior. He is lost in feeling. And he has lost control. Moore and Gillette believe that the Addict is searching for the "paradise lost" of his blissful union with mother—a paradise that was probably lost too soon or in too painful a manner.

Manic: The Addict's libido is overactive—he has too much "life energy." He may feel an internal frenzy or madness with extreme levels of energy as if he's ready to take on the whole world. He may need little sleep and can pursue his addiction for long periods of time. His mind may be full of ideas, which sometimes gives rise to unusual levels of creativity. He may involve himself excessively in pleasurable activities of all kinds. His outlook may be expansive and grandiose. When mania is part of bipolar disorder, the highs are limited to periods of a week or more and often alternate with periods of depression. When it's an aspect of addiction, the mania may continue indefinitely.

Promiscuous: The Addict brings Lover energy into the world in careless, indiscriminate, and haphazard ways, acting without forethought or planning. Unmitigated by the Magian's wisdom, without commitment or boundaries from the Warrior's discipline, and lacking moderation from the King, he may engage in random sexual acts, create works of art that are ill conceived, or eat impulsively. He may get involved in a random or poorly planned creative project or indiscriminately pursue an unwise relationship with another person.

> The Addict brings Lover energy into the world in careless, indiscriminate, and haphazard ways.

Indulgent: Behaviorally, the Addict binges. Whether as an anesthetic for his pain or a reward for good behavior, he "acts out" with a mood altering substance like alcohol, drugs, caffeine, or food, or with a behavior like sex or gambling. Free of any inhibitions and lacking any of the Impotent One's compulsive control, he satisfies every urge. This is the most blatant act of release in the control–release cycle. Although the chemical pathways in the body differ depending on the type of addiction, the ultimate pay off is the same: enhancement of pleasure and reduction of pain.

The Addict in Relationships

Now let's consider how the shadow of addiction can impact our relationships with ourselves, other people, our Higher Power, and things. We'll also look at how the detached–dependent dynamic impacts the Addict's relationships with others and with God. As always, consider how these tendencies show up in your relationships and how you may project them onto others. ✎ 10.13

> The Addict in Relationships
> - Lost
> - Estranged
> - Abusive
> - Idolatrous
> - Rebellious
> - Over–attached

Lost: In his relationship to himself, the Addict is lost in many ways. Like a wallet that is lost, he doesn't have possession of himself. Like a ship that has been lost, he has brought himself to destruction. Like a leg that has been lost, he's deprived of himself. Like time that has been lost, he's unable to make proper use of himself. And like a temper that has been lost, he's unable to maintain or control himself.

Whereas the Impotent Shadow pole is lost in the wasteland of his inner life, the Addict pole is "lost in the world."[7] His Self has become entirely obscured through his over–involvement in sensual things and behaviors that feed his addiction. He has given away his heart to those things. Several Greek mythologies tell of the Sirens who were bird–women that lured unwary seamen toward the rocky coast of their island by their singing. Enchanted by the irresistible sound of the siren's voices, the sailors sailed their ships right into the rocks and lost their lives. Most men caught in the shadows of the Lover are lost on both shadow poles—in an inner wasteland and in the outer world.

> The Self of the Impotent One has become entirely obscured through his over–involvement in sensual things and behaviors that feed his addiction.

Estranged: The Addict may alienate other people through his behaviors and attitudes. He is manifesting the detached side of the detached–dependent dynamic in an active, aggressive, and external way. Rather than passively avoiding relationships like the Impotent One, he may push people away in order to separate himself and avoid being subject to their beliefs, expectations, and needs. To accomplish this, he may be cold and angry or withdraw his love. He may make hurtful comments that degrade or insult. He may turn the blame onto those around him. He may lie in ways that hurt or manipulate others or cause them to doubt themselves. He may refuse to meet his obligations or ignore the expectations and needs of intimate partners or dependents. He may instill fear and dread through sadistic, detached cruelty. All of this behavior has the unconscious intention of distancing others so that the Addict can pursue his promiscuous and indulgent behavior unimpeded by connections with other people. The implicit message in his behavior may be "I am my own man. I can do what I want!"

> The Addict may push people away in order to separate himself and avoid being subject to their beliefs, expectations, and needs.

Abusive: On the other hand, the Addict may actively pursue other people as tools or objects for the furtherance of his addiction. This is a manifestation of the dependent side of the detached–dependent dynamic in that he depends on others to give him what he wants. He may relate to others without compassion or empathy and he may have little or no compunction about violating boundaries. People tend to be something for him to use, manage, or ignore—depending on the immediate expediency.

The Addict may use other people to supply him with money, drugs, or alcohol. He may use them to support his narcissism by setting them up to envy and praise him. He may even use others as part of his addiction, as is the case with love addiction and is often the case with sexual addiction as well. In these relationships, the other person is only an object used to drive the addiction forward. Deceit, betrayal, and abandonment are classic abusive Addict behaviors. They are also common among married men with same–sex attraction in the treatment of their wives, especially when they lie and cover up their true feelings, intentions, and behaviors.

From the perspective of authors Moore and Gillette in *The Lover Within*, addiction is demanding mother's love, or the "garden of delight," outside the bonds of any real relationship. By this they mean that the Addict tries to recover the lost love of his mother in forceful ways through the pleasures of his addiction. The Addict can only relate to other people in fragmented ways; he connects with that fragment of a person that can help him access the fragment of his mother that should have loved him better. This helps explain why the Addict can be so hurtful in his relationships. It is because he isn't actually having a relationship with the people in his life. His only relationship is with his addiction—his compulsive need for "mother's love"—which relationship he fosters at the expense of all others.

Idolatrous: Recovering addicts speak of a "God–shaped hole" within them. They are referring to the idea that the wounds lying beneath addiction include alienation from God, which leaves a hole in the shape of God that only He can fill. They need God's presence in their lives and hearts, but rather than seek Him, they try to fill the hole with *things* and with sensuality. This is a manifestation of the detached side of the detached–dependent dynamic. The Addict is disconnected from his Higher Power and actively seeks to replace Him with idols in the form of objects, substances, or processes. This prevents spiritual development and the ability to experience or appreciate anything transcendent.

Rebellious: To review, the idolatrous Addict detaches from God and actively replaces Him with physical things or experiences. The non–believing Addict simply avoids a relationship with faith and Higher Power. In contrast, the rebellious Addict compulsively clings to an angry, resentful, and defiant relationship with his Higher Power. This is a manifestation of the dependent side of the detached–dependent dynamic. As with the abusive Addict, he may demand

> The other person is only an object used to drive the addiction forward.

> The rebellious Addict compulsively clings to an angry, resentful, and defiant relationship with his Higher Power.

that the "garden of delight" be provided to him on his own terms and according to his own timeline. He probably wants to feel God's comfort and love. He probably wants his prayers to be answered. But he lacks the patience and faith necessary to invite those blessings into his life. As a result, he has probably experienced little of the divine and may have never felt God's presence. This may mirror the relationship with his mother in which attunement and attachment were wanted but never realized.

The rebellious Addict may be active in a religion and secretly fighting with God. He may be disenfranchised from his faith and afraid to venture back in. Or he may be outside any religion and actively opposed to all faiths. He may have many ostensible reasons for his quarrel with God—prayers don't get answered, religious people are hypocrites, God hates him, or he doesn't fit into God's plan. But on a deeper level his resistance may grow out of a shadow of guilt over his addictive behavior. Or perhaps his anger provides the permission he needs to act out his addiction without considering the consequences.

Addiction "is the idolatrous attachment to a finite thing."

Moore and Gillette, *The Lover Within*

Over–attached: Moore and Gillette point out in *The Lover Within* that addiction "is the idolatrous attachment to a finite thing. Within such an attachment a finite thing is made to bear the significance and power that only 'God' can legitimately carry." We've already discussed idolatry in terms of its impact on the Addict's relationship with his Higher Power and the development of his spirituality. In this section we're considering the way in which an "idolatrous attachment to a finite thing" impacts the Addict's relationship to the physical world. The "finite thing" to which Moore and Gillette are referring is the object of addiction—the drug of choice—whether that thing is a substance like drugs or alcohol, or a process like sex or gambling. What they are saying, most simply, is that the Addict is over–attached to things.

In addition to substances and processes, the Addict within us can also become over–attached to things that, while not addictive in the classic sense, nevertheless may take the place of a Higher Power in our lives. I'm speaking here of the same sorts of things I mentioned previously when discussing the Impotent One's disinterest in things—possessions like home, car, clothing, jewelry, collectibles, and "toys," plus activities such as work, recreation, entertainment, and other pleasurable pursuits.

The Addict may pursue his high, his compulsion, his lust, or his possessions and activities as if they will redeem him or save him from his pain. This is again a fragmented connection wherein a bit of pleasure, release, or relief is taken from a thing rather than a fullness of joy, redemption, and healing being sought from a Higher Power. The Addict worships a part in place of the whole. This can only lead to eventual disappointment and despair.

THE SYNERGISTIC LOVER

We have examined the Lover in his fullness and in his shadows. Let's take time now to review all of this as a whole. The Lover is the most complex of the archetypes, so it will take a bit more work to get a full view of his range of capacities and traits in order to see the synergistic potential among them. As with the foregoing sections on the Lover's shadows, I've divided the trait scales on the following pages into two sections. The first illustrates the *characteristics* of the Lover, and the second depicts the traits of the Lover in *relationships*.

The Lover is the most complex of the archetypes.

My hope in presenting such a complex paradigm is to help you create a clear and useful sense of your inner structure and a language through which you can describe and discuss it with others. I hope to inform your Magian by creating tremendous self–awareness, which in turn empowers your King to keep your life centered, balanced, and moderated.

Spend some time familiarizing yourself with the two tables using the same method you've used with the other trait scales. Complete your study of the first table before moving on to the second table. On each table, review the *Addict* column first, then the *Impotent One* column. Next review both of the *Moderation* columns together. After you've done that, review the table horizontally one trait scale at a time, considering the full range of the attributes associated with that trait. Use the numbered paragraphs below each table to help you understand the details of each scale. And take time to consider how each trait may be manifested in your life. The shadows of the Lover are more interwoven than those of the other archetypes, and men caught in these shadows tend to move back and forth among them with regularity. See if you can discover your own tendencies.

Characteristics of the Lover

The table on the next page depicts the trait structure of the essential characteristics of the Lover. 10.14

Lover Characteristics Trait Scales

Traits	Addict		Moderation	Impotent One
1. Emotion	Histrionic	Feeling	Calm	Paralyzed
2. Sensation	Ecstatic	Sensuous	Nonphysical	Numb
3. Libido	Manic	Desiring	Satisfied	Depressed
4. Incarnation	Promiscuous	Generative	Realistic	Impotent
5. Behavior	Indulgent	Uninhibited	Self-controlled	Controlling

1. Emotion

The Addict's experience and expression of emotion is *histrionic*, or excessively emotional. In moderation, this becomes the trait of being an emotionally connected and *feeling* person. The Impotent One is emotionally *paralyzed*. A more moderate trait is to be emotionally *calm* and able to enjoy states of peace and tranquility.

2. Sensation

The Addict's choices and tendencies regarding his inner experience of feeling tend to be *ecstatic*, whether this means high, sedated, or lost in fantasy. In a more moderate form, he's *sensuous*, which implies delighting in the senses and being body–focused. The Impotent One is *numb* to his inner sensations. In moderation, this becomes the ability to be *nonphysical* or undisturbed by sensations. It also implies an ability to disconnect from the body and become spirit–focused.

3. Libido

For the Addict, the life force behind his actions is *manic*. His libido is out of control. In a moderate form, his life energy is *desiring* of life, sensation, and experience. He's vigorous, alive, and blissful. The Impotent One is *depressed*, lacking any energy or drive toward life. The moderate form of this trait is to be *satiated*, though this will always be temporary. In this state, he's restful and grounded. This is like the refractory period following sexual release.

4. Incarnation

The Addict's approach to bringing his libidinous urges into physical form is *promiscuous*, meaning careless, haphazard, and without discrimination. The moderate form of this trait is to be *generative*, which implies being creative and productive in ways that are mediated, boundaried, and moderated by the other three archetypes. The passive shadow is incapable of bringing any Lover energy into the world. Hence he is called *impotent*. A moderate version of this holding back of life energy is to be *realistic* and unmoved by emotion or flimsy visions of the "garden of delight."

5. Behavior

The Addict is *indulgent* behaviorally. He refuses to hold himself back. A more moderate version of this trait is to be *uninhibited* by internal repressions or emotional blocks—to be free and unrestrained. The Impotent One is behaviorally *controlling*—constantly governed by internal compulsions. A moderate version of this trait is to be *self–controlled*, which implies that the act of control is a conscious and willing decision.

The Lover in Relationships

The table below depicts the structure of the Lover's traits as they are manifested in relationships with himself, other people, God, and things. Notice that the Lover's shadows can manifest in very different, and even contradictory, ways in relationships with other people and God. You'll notice this in the *Individuation* and *Relationships* scales (scales 2 and 3) and in the *Spirituality* and *Faith* scales (scales 4 and 5). This complexity has to do with the diverse ways in which men may respond to the detached–dependent dynamic. ✍ 10.15

Lover in Relationships Trait Scales

	← **Addict**	**Moderation**		**Impotent One** →
1. Self	Lost	Suprapersonal	Authentic	Unaware
2. Individuation	Estranged	Individuated	Affiliated	Clingy
3. Relationships	Abusive	Interactive	Boundaried	Avoidant
4. Spirituality	Idolatrous	Secular	Spiritual	Fanatical
5. Faith	Rebellious	Religious	Believing	Non-Believing
6. Things	Over-attached	Multiplicity	Simplicity	Disinterested

Traits

1. Self

The Addict has *lost* himself in the world of sensual things. A more moderate form of this is the ability to transcend the self by being *suprapersonal*. This implies an ability to step outside yourself so that you can connect with others and with things beyond you. The Impotent One is *unaware* of who he is and what he wants from life, as if he has no self. Here the moderate trait is nearly the opposite—to be actively searching for your *authentic* Self. This means to be gaining self–awareness and developing a deep inner connection to your masculine soul and your Anima.

2. Individuation

In order to separate himself from others, the Addict may actively detach from people by pushing them away through cruelty and mistreatment. This leaves him *estranged* from his significant relationships. A moderate trait is to be *individuated* from others—to have emotional, mental, relational, temporal, and physical independence while still engaging in loving attachments. Genderedness depends on this moderate trait in that it requires a deep psychic individuation from the opposite sex. The Impotent One is *clingy* in his relationships with others. With little sense of his individuality or personal power, he depends on other people for support and nurture. Moderation is found in being *affiliated* with other people in a variety of relationships. These may include intimate relationships, acquaintances and friends, or community or religious groups.

3. Relationships

The Addict may be *abusive* and narcissistic in his connections with other people. He may aggressively pursue relationships with others, treating them as extensions of himself and using them as objects or tools for the furtherance of his addiction. A moderate version of this tendency is to be *interactive*—engaging others through permeable boundaries in open and receptive ways. The Impotent One may feel so hurt or vulnerable that he becomes *avoidant* of all but the most necessary interactions with others. A moderate version of this trait is to be *boundaried* in a healthy way, with the ability to access the Warrior's capacity to set limits and to separate from others when needed.

4. Spirituality

This scale considers how an individual handles his need for spiritual sustenance. The Addict may be *idolatrous*, filling his "God–shaped hole" with things instead of God. A more moderate approach would be the ability to have a *secular* focus in order to pursue needs and desires in the physical world without shutting God out. The Impotent One is spiritually *fanatical*. Driven by his vulnerability and fear, he may pursue religion or spirituality with compulsive dependence. A more moderate version of this is to be truly *spiritual*, relying on God in ways that are deeply felt but not compulsive.

5. Faith

This scale considers the nature of an individual's belief in God and how he engages with Him. Angry engagement characterizes the Addict extreme of the scale. Apathetic disengagement characterizes the Impotent extreme. Faith, which is a synergy of belief and action, characterizes the center. The wholeness in the middle of this scale is not the result of moderation as it is with all the other scales we've considered. Rather, wholeness on the faith scale is brought about by the experience of love for and from a Higher Power. This scale is easier to understand when considered in reverse, beginning with the Impotent extreme.

The Impotent One may feel apathy toward the idea of a Higher Power and disengage from belief and religion. His passive *non–believing* response to God comes from detachment, paralysis, numbness, and depression rather than from rational consideration and rejection of the idea of God. Experiencing love for or from God would breathe life into his dormant faith, enabling him to be *believing*. An Addict may be *rebellious* toward God, engaging him with resentment and defiance. He lacks love for God and faith in His goodness. Love would change the nature of the intense engagement with God, allowing the man to be truly *religious*, meaning to put his belief into action out of love.

6. Things

The Addict's relationship to things is *over–attached*. Fragmentary objects and experiences are given all the power and significance of the whole or the Higher Power. A more moderate version of this would be to enjoy the *multiplicity* of things in the world. The Impotent One is *disinterested* in the world of things. Things don't matter to him—the fewer varieties and options the better. A moderate version of this would be to enjoy *simplicity*, to be able to detach from things and to find satisfaction in the basics. Moderation of this trait would also be to experience the harmony and connection among all of the diversity in the world.

CHANNELING THE LOVER

Lover energy can't be repressed. When we try to repress it, we eventually find it coming out sideways, often in damaging ways. It's far better instead to channel it in productive ways that are in keeping with our values. Below are some ways you might consider for experiencing and enjoying Lover energy while also keeping it channeled in a positive direction.

Find ways to express your thoughts, feelings, impulses, and creative impressions.

- **Deep spirituality**. Develop a deeper involvement in spiritual practice and strengthen your relationship to the Divine. This may include organized religion or individual practice. For developing Lover, it's important that you allow these experiences to be sensuous, meaning that you focus yourself on the feeling of the spiritual experience. It's also important that you engage in some kind of service that bonds you with others.

- **Sensual appreciation**. Expose yourself to art, music, cuisine, yoga, nature, and other experiences that involve and enhance your five senses. As you do this, consciously try to experience things in a different way than you have before. Look and listen for the things you've never noticed. Notice opposites by doing things like imagining the forest as red instead of green or seeing the shape of the empty space between the trees or buildings. Or mix up your senses by imagining the taste of a color, the texture of a sound, or the color of a smell.

- **Self–expression**. Find ways to express your thoughts, feelings, impulses, and creative impressions. The options here are nearly endless: conversation, performing, writing, singing in the shower, remodeling your house, making art, playing sports, engaging in therapy, and many more.

- **Conscious giving**. Giving is an act that unifies the giver with the one receiving. Consider giving in a way that brings you closer to a person you want to bless. This implies spending time gaining an understanding of his or her desires, preferences, and needs, carefully determining the impact you wish your gift to have, and then deciding on an act that will have that positive impact. This will also help connect you with King energy.

- **Full acceptance of self**. This is a form of giving to yourself. You may do this a little at a time or through a single major decision. Just as in giving to others, you might start with seeking an understanding of your own desires, preferences, and needs, determine the impact on yourself that you want your gift to have, and then find the act that will provide that impact. May I suggest that accepting your shadows might be one of the greatest gifts you could ever give yourself.

- **Mentoring other men**. This is also a form of giving and can be profoundly connective. It tends to build a sense of mastery and meaning when you notice that your life experience is a true blessing to someone else.

- **Appreciating the dynamic opposites of gender**. Experiencing gender is central to the process of transcending the limits of homosexuality. You might want to make an informal study of gender by noticing the differences between males and females or perhaps reading literature on the subject. Be careful not to try to push yourself into attractions to the opposite sex if they're not yet developing. Begin by just observing, noticing, and appreciating.

For many of us, channeling the energy of our Lover is a challenging process. This can be so for any number of reasons, including problems with addiction, having uncontrollable emotions, or seeing our Lover qualities as feminine or gay. Those of us with active addictions will need help to free ourselves from the grip of the addiction. We discussed this in Chapter Four. There I suggested two valuable resources for sexual addiction: the LifeStar program and Sexaholics Anonymous. Check http://becomingawholeman.com for links to these and other resources.

Those of us who experience feelings that are so strong they are difficult to control may also need outside help to learn containment of our emotions. We may feel "possessed" by emotions or counter–emotions, including anxiety, worry, depression, sadness, jealousy, longing, love, or mania. We may need the help of a well–trained therapist to move beyond these difficulties.

Those of us who have internalized the perspective that our Lover qualities make us feminine or gay need to disconnect those associations and learn to experience our Lover traits as being fully masculine. It may be helpful to look for other men with these same Lover traits who manifest them in masculine ways. These men can provide a new perspective and role modeling for us to follow. In some cases, we may need to relinquish certain of our Lover tendencies that leave us feeling distinctly non–masculine. ✍ 10.16

> For many of us, channeling the energy of our Lover is a challenging process.

UNDERSTANDING FRIENDSHIP

Experiencing deep and lasting friendships with other men is one of the most important ways of channeling Lover energy for men who are moving their lives away from homosexuality. Although you may already believe this concept, you may not understand what makes some friendships work while other friendships dwindle—or crash and burn. Most of the homosexual men that I've known have difficulty with some aspect of their relationships with other men. This section is intended to help you with that difficulty by clarifying the underlying characteristics that make or break friendships.

When thinking about a genuine friendship, it's easy to wishfully envision an intimate "soul mate" connection of two tightly intertwined lives. But in reality, many of our friendships tend to be distant and superficial. In the world of "straight" men, most male–male friendships tend to fall somewhere between these two extremes. Consider this description of a hypothetical "average" relationship between Dan and Josh.

The Story of Dan and Josh

They met in a student study group for a university computer science class. As a result of casual conversations, they realized that in addition to computer science, they both had an interest in movies and racquetball. They began playing racquetball on Saturday mornings, taking dates to films, and meeting for lunch on Tuesday afternoons between classes just to hang out. Over time, they shared personal information and became acquainted with each other's weaknesses as well as strengths. Their personalities were quite different: Josh was conservative and reserved in many ways while Dan tended to be more liberal and spontaneous. Occasionally a few weeks would pass without them seeing each other, and they would occasionally disagree. But, generally, there was a connection and total acceptance and support for each other.

Their mutual understanding and friendship allowed them to encourage, support, compliment, and challenge each other in their studies and in their attempts to be better men. When either of them had a special need for support, they always knew they could count on the other. After graduation, the time they spent together decreased somewhat. Dan took a job in a different town, and Josh remained with the local company where he interned during graduate school. However, when they did get a chance to speak or spend time together—playing racquetball or just talking—it was like no time had passed. The mutual interest and caring were still apparent and fulfilling.

Genuine friendships like Dan and Josh's are very common among men. They form and deepen over time through the sharing of interests and experiences. The more we share with a friend, the more rewarding the relationship becomes. Building friendships requires patience and a willingness to invest. But not every friendship will develop into a deep emotional bond. Life circumstances, individual needs, and personality traits influence the potential of every friendship. Some friendships may remain less intimate, even after many years. Yet these relationships may still be genuine and can be valuable. I encourage you not to discount them.

Characteristics of Friendships

Genuine friendships have certain positive characteristics that can be described and even subjectively measured. The sections that follow describe nine such traits. They also describe the opposites of these positive traits. As you read, think about friendships you've experienced that manifested the positive and negative sides of these characteristics. You'll notice that this list repeats some of the "Elements of Community" that we discussed in Chapters Three and Six. But here we'll break things down a bit further. You may want to go through this with a specific relationship in mind or give thought to your tendencies across a series of friendships.

Well–matched vs. Mismatched. Well–matched friendships are characterized by similarities that bring two individuals together. This is comparable to commonality, the first element of community. These similarities may be in such areas as vocation, recreational interests, values, temperament, maturity level, and sense of humor. Similarities tend to create a sense of resonance between two people. Strong friendships can be developed when you have a reasonably close match in a few areas. A degree of diversity in other areas may add quality or interest and scope to your friendship. On the other hand, when there is little that brings the two of you together, a relationship may simply feel too strained and foreign for you to honestly connect or feel peaceful in the friendship. Such a relationship is mismatched.

Mutual vs. One–Sided. Mutuality refers to a shared interest and investment in a relationship. This is comparable to reciprocity, the fourth element of community. In a balanced friendship, there is a mutual interest in each other—in wanting to spend time together and maintain the friendship. Both of you take responsibility for making the friendship work by putting in time, effort, and other resources. And both initiate interaction, creating a reciprocal relationship. When the interest and investment in the relationship are not shared, the relationship is one–sided.

Characteristics of Friendships

- Well–matched vs. Mismatched
- Mutual vs. One–sided
- Balanced Power vs. Power Imbalance
- Open vs. Closed
- Accepting vs. Rejecting
- Validating vs. Invalidating
- Boundaries vs. Enmeshment
- Encouraging Growth vs. Discouraging Growth
- Encouraging Masculinity vs. Discouraging Masculinity

Balanced Power vs. Power Imbalance. Balanced power in a friendship comes from both of you having similar personality strength. Balance implies that each has influence in decision making and that there is equality in the give and take of the relationship. Balance enables equal expression and valuing of attitudes and opinions and a balance of talking and listening. A pattern of domination by one partner over the other in the friendship creates a power imbalance.

Open vs. Closed. Openness in friendships includes sharing of thoughts, experiences, and feelings. Openness in relationships is based on trust, which is the second element of community. Disclosures may be deeply intimate, covering many facets of your personal lives. Or you may communicate less deeply, talking mostly about a few shared interests. Either way, there is a sense of being understood. There is a comfortable trust that what's disclosed won't be used to embarrass or harm either of you. When such trust is lacking, you're hesitant to disclose. You may fear sharing even superficial information. In such relationships, men tend to remain closed.

> Openness in relationships is based on trust.

Accepting vs. Rejecting. Acceptance of each other in a friendship is manifested by approval of one another in such areas as how each of you looks, talks, and acts, how smart each of you seems to be, how you dress, what you listen to, and what your political views are. This is an aspect of unconditional love and compassion, the sixth element of community. Approval may be openly spoken or simply implied through tone of voice, facial expressions, and other elements of body language. Accepting friendships are characterized by kindness and respect for one another. A lack of acceptance might show up as a feeling that the friend doesn't measure up to what's desired or expected. You may criticize each other directly or to other friends. You may feel embarrassed by each other. Or you may make cutting or sarcastic remarks about each other. Such relationships are rejecting.

Validating vs. Invalidating. Validation of one another in a friendship suggests a valuing and affirmation of each other's "true self" qualities. This is another aspect of unconditional love and compassion. Good traits eclipse personal flaws in your view of one another. And it's primarily through these good traits that the two of you relate to each other. Interactions in your friendship leave both of you feeling good about yourselves. When friends don't see one another's good qualities or don't value those qualities, they can't validate each other. Such friends may regard each other with cynicism and may try to change each other. Relationships like

> Validation of one another in a friendship suggests a valuing and affirmation of each other's "true self" qualities.

these slowly erode self–confidence and self–worth. You become less sure of who you are. Such relationships are invalidating.

Boundaries vs. Enmeshment. Healthy emotional boundaries are an essential part of genuine friendships and are the fifth element of community. Boundaries are limits on such things as time, energy, interaction, disclosure, intimacy, and physical space. Respect for each other's time might mean being punctual and not staying too long. Boundaries on intimacy may include sharing and asking about only what's appropriate given the degree of openness in the relationship. Physical space boundaries could include standing at an appropriate distance, touching only in ways that are comfortable for both, and respecting the privacy of each other's home and work environments.

> Boundaries are limits on such things as time, energy, interaction, disclosure, intimacy, and physical space.

Boundaries in a relationship enable individuals to maintain privacy, retreat when necessary, and say "No" when it's appropriate. Feeling invaded, smothered, or controlled are signs of boundary problems. Having obsessive thoughts about the other person, feeling trapped in intimacy, and feeling compelled to spend inordinate amounts of time together may indicate enmeshment.

Encouraging Growth vs. Discouraging Growth. Encouragement of growth and personal development in a relationship makes moving forward in life seem desirable and more possible. Such relationships encourage working toward individual or shared positive goals or aspirations. You support each other's personal values and encourage each other to be better people.

> You support each other's personal values and encourage each other to be better people.

But some friendships go in the opposite direction. Such friendships may discourage adherence to a person's values or thwart attempts to set and reach goals. This effect may come through direct messages, such as making fun of one another's goals or aspirations. Or discouragement may be indirect, as when efforts required for growth are interfered with. Or there may be mixed messages. This type of relationship discourages growth.

Encouraging Masculinity vs. Discouraging Masculinity. Support of masculinity occurs in friendships where there is acceptance of each other's male characteristics and encouragement to be manly in the best ways possible for each of you. But such friendships avoid becoming preoccupied with conformity to societal gender stereotypes or pushing each other into or out of specific gender roles. Remarks about gender are encouraging and supportive. These supportive relationships reinforce confidence about being male and about manifesting masculine characteristics.

Opposite effects occur when a specific and narrow set of male traits are overvalued or expected, while the actual male traits of either person in the relationship are overlooked or criticized. Distrust of other men and detachment from them is likely to increase under these circumstances. Friendships like these discourage masculinity. Also, friendships that focus predominantly on the shared experience of homosexuality are likely to become less beneficial over time and may eventually discourage masculine development. This may also be true of friendships with men whom you perceive as "gay" or non–masculine. ✐ 10.17

Union Beyond Affiliation

> "Any project or therapeutic process that offers us the hope of embodying bliss completely within the context of our personal relationships is holding out a false promise."
>
> Moore and Gillette, *The Lover Within*

A final caveat is important here. Our friendships with other men are not the entire solution to our pain and longing. Moore and Gillette wisely warn in *The Lover Within* that "Any project or therapeutic process that offers us the hope of embodying bliss completely within the context of our personal relationships is holding out a false promise." Remember, it isn't just with others that the Lover seeks relationship. It is also with his own true self and with the transcendent power that weaves the universe together. To aim your libido lower than that is to ensure continued dissatisfaction.

STEWARDING THE LOVER

In Chapter Eight, I talked about how the Magian is the steward of sacred space. I suggest that like sacred space, the Lover needs to be stewarded. He needs our Warrior to protect him through strong, clear, and flexible boundaries, and to provide the focus, discipline, and courage that are necessary in order to incarnate him. He needs the intelligence and wisdom of our Magian to channel his libidinous urges into a transformative quest. He also needs the Magian to detect any corruption that might arise within him. And he needs our King to organize him, to provide him with balance and moderation, and to give him a spiritual center. He also needs the King to praise and bless him.

Let's end this chapter where we began—with the archetypal Little League game. That game is going on inside us all the time. Our Magian's role is to busily think, teach, and initiate us. Our Warrior's job is to dutifully run the bases. And our King must impose the rules while also cheering us on. But, whether the other folks like it or not, it is the Lover's very purpose to follow the little bug off into the forest. Our work is to create space in our lives for him to do just that.

---

[1] Though it is beyond the scope of this chapter, it's interesting to note that other archetypal traits may be involved in complex processes such as art and humanitarianism. For example, the governance and desire to bless associated with the King, the knowledge of the Magian, and the discipline of the Warrior may all be required to bring such ventures to successful completion.

[2] This film portrays the archetypes with surprising clarity. The Tin Man, as I've said, is a Lover. The protective Scarecrow is a Warrior, though he combines qualities of the Magian in his search for his brains. The Cowardly Lion is the King of the Forest. And the Wizard of Oz is full Magian. Dorothy, who rescues these archetypes from their shadows and then in turn is rescued by them, is an Anima. Glinda, the good witch, and the Wicked Witch of the West add a representation of wholeness and shadow.

[3] For examples, see *Picturing Men: A Century of Male Relationships in Everyday American Photography* by John Ibson.

[4] *Nine* was based on a stage musical of the same title by Arthur Kopit and Maury Yeston. Directed by Rob Marshall. Cast includes Daniel Day–Lewis, Penelope Cruz, Nicole Kidman, Marion Cotillard, Judi Dench, Kate Hudson, Fergie, and Sophia Loren.

[5] *DSM–V*, page 667.

[6] *Merriam–Webster's Third New International Dictionary*, "ecstasy."

[7] This quote is from a heading in the chapter on the Addict in Moore and Gillette's *The Lover Within*.

Chapter 11

Surrender

Today I accept that the life I have known is over.

I am entering a new and blessed phase of my time here.

I accept pain as my teacher and problems as the key to a new existence for me.

I let the Spirit melt the hardness of my heart.

Patrick Carnes, *A Gentle Path Through the Twelve Steps*

ears of civil war have left the kingdom in ruins. Famine and plagues have been a constant threat. The losses have been great and suffering is everywhere. The country is gripped by fear and hatred. Those loyal to the king despise the warlords in the outlying provinces, whom they blame for this desolating insurrection. These warlords are said to be dark and evil—a shame to their country.

But in the provinces, the people cling to the warlords for protection from a king they've grown to hate and from his soldiers who, on occasions when the king is unaware, commit atrocities among the people—pillaging and raping for sustenance and pleasure. Common provincial folk say the king is a tyrant who demands loyalty with the sword. Some say that being captured by his men means sure death. They hear the king's pleas for unity as a trick to enslave them. Most believe that, as bad as things are now, they would be much worse if they gave up their rebellion and rejoined the empire.

Years of civil war have left the kingdom in ruins.

But the king is not the only threat to those in the provinces. The warlords have begun to feud among themselves. Their soldiers also commit atrocities among the citizens of their own land, as well as in neighboring countries. No one is safe. The situation is truly dire.

Few remember the start of the rebellion. Most of the people never understood the circumstances in the first place except that it began when the warlords were banished by the king. There are stories of how a foreigner instigated it, but the stories differ greatly depending on which faction is telling it. Only the king himself and the chief warlords know how it all began, and they won't speak of it.

Those who are old enough can remember that the kingdom was once a beautiful place known for its peace and prosperity—a true garden of delight. Now it is locked in an impasse. The war is unwinnable by any faction. If the future follows history, the war will grind on for decades until the entire kingdom is destitute or dead.

Surrender consists of two opposing and complementary aspects—*letting go* and *letting in.*

This story will provide an allegory for the process of surrender. It's called "The King's Vow." Like most of the principles I've surveyed in this book, surrender consists of two opposing and complementary aspects. It's both *letting go* and *letting in.*

Letting go implies releasing and turning away from what was—the old ways of thinking and behaving, the old hopes, the old intentions. We accept that our old lives are over, and we leave them behind. This involves changing our minds about the course we've been on by accepting that it isn't working. It's the "white flag" part of surrender—the admission that we're done fighting. Letting go also involves putting down our weapons, which includes all those things that we've been using to keep our battle going—everything we use to fight against change or to inhibit growth.

The *letting in* aspect of surrender involves choosing to follow, or letting in, a new commander. Whether that commander is an idea, a person, or a Higher Power, we submit ourselves to its superior force and trust in its goodness. Reciprocally, the new commander accepts our surrender and receives us. Then surrender involves uniting our lives with that power and becoming part of it, which implies integration.

In the sections below, we'll look at four distinct phases of surrender represented by four commands. The first two of these commands have to do with letting go. They are *"change your mind"* and *"drop your weapons."* The other two commands have to do with letting in. They are "*follow the king*" and "*unify the kingdom.*" Each phase is related to the functions of a specific archetype. The Magian enables us to change our minds (phase one) through his capacity to transform our thinking. It takes the Warrior's courage, discipline, and ability to detach in order to drop our weapons (phase two). The King represents the pattern of wholeness that we'll follow (phase three). And the passion of the Lover's libido and desire for union is the power that will unify our inner kingdom (phase four).

These four phases don't necessarily represent a sequential path of surrender, although it is more common that the first phase will precede the others and the last phase will more often follow the first three. But rather than seeing them as linear, think of these phases as being more like components or even principles that might occur in a variety of sequences. As we go through the process of surrendering a major issue in our lives, we may go back and forth among these phases. And we'll likely cycle through them again and again as we work our way toward greater wholeness. Once you know these phases, you will find that the process of surrender is active—or needs to be activated—in many aspects of your life.

CHANGE YOUR MIND

There is a Sage in the kingdom who is renowned for his wisdom and fairness. This one man alone has the trust of the king as well as the warlords—although that trust has never yet been sufficient to convince them to end the war. His pleas have fallen on the deaf ears of men with too much pride—and too much fear of their own shame.

But now something is different. The king and the warlords are listening to the Sage. Maybe it is the utter hopelessness of the situation. Maybe age and experience have brought new wisdom. Maybe they are longing for a return to the beautiful days of the past. Or maybe they've finally caught a vision of something better. Whatever the case may be, their minds have changed. The warlords are accepting that they can't win this war, their insurrection is a failure, and the situation is unmanageable.

With rigorous and painful honesty, the warlords have considered all aspects of their condition: the physical, spiritual, and emotional toll on the people and the failure of all their previous attempts to destroy the king. They've considered the future and have realized that what didn't work yesterday probably won't work tomorrow. Now they are willing to admit that they lack the ability to govern the

Four phases of surrender:

- Change your mind
- Drop your weapons
- Follow the king
- Unify the kingdom

There is a Sage in the kingdom who is renowned for his wisdom and fairness.

351

kingdom. And most important of all, they are ready to humble themselves before the king and admit their wrongdoing. They are ready to fully let go and rely on the mercy of the king.

The king too has recognized the futility of trying to beat the warlords. Despite his disdain for these outlaws, he admits now that the kingdom will only survive if he makes peace with them, whatever the cost. He is willing to set aside his pride, prestige, and even his power, if necessary, to restore safety and serenity to the nation.

A change of mind is an act of volition—willfully deciding and shifting from one way of thinking to another. For some of us, this shift will only happen after our current way of thinking has completely failed. Alcoholics in recovery have understood this concept for decades. Step One of the Alcoholics Anonymous Twelve–Step program is, "We admitted we were powerless over alcohol—that our lives had become unmanageable." We often speak of addicts hitting "rock bottom" before they begin authentic recovery. Rock bottom is usually when the addict has lost everything, and so he's forced into making changes in his thinking. Jonah's heart changed in the belly of the whale—it's easy to imagine how being swallowed by a huge fish might have been a rock bottom experience for him.

> A change of mind is an act of volition—willfully deciding and shifting from one way of thinking to another.

Some of us start to think about resolving our homosexuality only when we're at rock bottom—after realizing that our hopelessness, depression, shame, sexual behavior, or the gay lifestyle are threatening our very lives. But I've met many men who became motivated to change long before their homosexuality took them to the depths.

The desire to resolve your homosexuality can be motivated by many factors, and every man's story is unique. One of the common factors is having personal goals that can't be fulfilled through homosexuality, for example, the desire to father children in a traditional family or to keep the family you've already created intact. Some of us have heterosexual desires that conflict with our homosexuality, and we decide that the heterosexual desires will bring us the greatest joy.

Another factor that may motivate us to change our minds about homosexuality is our dislike of the gay lifestyle. Some of us who are pursuing change have been in that lifestyle and found it to be anything but "gay" and not at all what we wanted. Other men simply view the lifestyle from the outside and know that it doesn't have what we're after in life.

A third motivating factor that's common among us is the sense that homosexuality doesn't reflect our true nature. Many of us are clear that our same–sex attraction is strictly the result of problems that occurred in childhood, like gender incongruity, same–sex disaffiliation, or sexual abuse. We don't want to pursue a lifestyle that we know is just compensating for our wounds and perceived deficits.

For those among us who are religious, the love shared between us and God is often a powerful mind–changing factor. Although many modern religions are beginning to accept the gay lifestyle, a lot of us who experience homosexual desires find them to be incompatible with our sense of God's purpose for us.

Whatever the motivating factors may be, there are just two requirements for a change of mind. The first is recognizing that your life isn't what you want it to be and that the old ways don't work and never did—they can't make you whole. The second requirement is a willingness to turn yourself in a new direction. ✍ 11.1

> There are just two requirements for a change of mind. The first is recognizing that your life isn't what you want it to be. The second is a willingness to turn yourself in a new direction.

I see this phase of surrender as being primarily driven by Magian energy. This phase happens mostly in the mind, although a secondary *emotional* shift is often required as well. We awaken our observing ego to see the unvarnished truth about our lives and to detect the corruption in our former way of thinking. We adopt an unwavering commitment to rigorous honesty and to the development of greater authenticity. We subscribe to this affirmation by Patrick Carnes: "I commit to reality at all costs knowing that is where I will find ultimate serenity." This change of mind is a *call* into initiation, and it starts us on a new quest of life transformation.

Sometimes early in the process we can't really see the truth of our situation, and so we may need to rely on the wisdom of other Magians—ritual elders who have already walked this road, whether those are wise friends, a sponsor, a therapist, or facilitators of groups or weekend experiences. Often they may invite us into this phase by asking us, "How's that working for ya'?"

The Magian's consciousness is essential to this phase. We have to make choices. The path will be far longer and costlier if we try to passively let change happen without conscious, proactive choice. Some of us try to change our sexuality without having made a conscious change of mind. Eventually, those men will either make a choice or they will gradually and unconsciously meander back to where they were.

Some of us are able to make a major change of mind in one powerful act of faith. Others have to make incremental choices that lead us gradually in a new direction. If you find yourself unable to choose, or if you make choices and then find yourself questioning them or turning back on them, it probably means that you're making choices on a level that's too advanced for where you are at the time. You can only make choices about things that you are ready to make choices about. Let me explain this absurdly blatant statement with an example.

Some people know exactly what car they want to buy before they even decide to get a new car. Maybe they've read a lot about cars and have a strong opinion, or their friend had a certain model that they really liked. One way or another, the choice is clear to them right from the outset.

But other people don't have a clue what kind of car is right for them. So they have to go through a process involving many small choices before they can make the big choice. First they have to decide that the car they're driving isn't working for them anymore. Sometimes that choice is made for them because of a crash or a breakdown. Then they have to make a choice to start looking for another car. That will be followed by a variety of choices about *where* to look. As they research and test different cars, they have to make choices about what they like and don't like. They have to decide the make, model, and year they want. Eventually they have to decide on a dealership they want to work with. And finally they have to choose the specific car they are going to buy.

So it is with people who are dissatisfied with their sexuality. Some of us already know exactly what we want to do. Those men often have an advantage because many of their toughest decisions are already made. If that's you, just keep plowing

---

We have to make choices. The path will be far longer and costlier if we try to passively let change happen without conscious, proactive choice.

---

ahead. But many of us come to the process knowing only that our car is broken down or that our life has crashed. We know we need to change something, but we're not quite ready to make a determination of what we want the final outcome to be. I'll be honest with you—this is a harder road.

But if this is where you are, this is where you are. Introspection and meditation can help. You might weigh the options in your life, considering what you would lose by making a change and what you're losing by staying where you are. If you pray, you might ask God for guidance. But ultimately you need to just start making the choices you can make right now. For example:

Do I want to continue the direction I'm going? *No!*

Am I ready to change something? *Yes.*

Do I want to change my sexuality? *I don't know yet.* Okay, so back up to a more basic choice.

Do I want to feel better about being a man? *Yes.* Do I want to learn how to relate to men in more healthy ways? *Absolutely.* Do I want to stop being addicted to porn? *No question.*

Start with the decisions you *can* make and work your way from there. Making choices about a few basic things and then following through on those decisions may coax your Innocent shadow Magian out of his naïveté. This might help you make more difficult choices down the road. Your Magian is probably in that "I don't know" shadow because he doesn't believe your Warrior will enforce his choices. Without a Warrior's disciplined action, your Magian is no more than wishful thinking. 🖊 11.2

DROP YOUR WEAPONS

The king promises clemency to any warlord who is willing to stand down. He longs to have his people back together again as one nation, so he is willing to extend forgiveness. At first the warlords hesitate. Then, with unparalleled courage, they comply. Not knowing the true heart of the king, they fear retaliation and revenge. But the warlords are compelled by a need that has become greater to them than their own safety—the good of their people.

> Many of us come to the process knowing only that our car is broken down or that our life has crashed.

> Making choices about a few basic things and then following through on those decisions may coax your Innocent shadow Magian out of his naïveté.

White flags fly from the battlements. It is a tense time of great uncertainty.

So they command their troops to stop fighting and to open their fortresses. White flags fly from the battlements. It is a tense time of great uncertainty. Anxious common folk watch from behind their shutters as the rule of the king gradually extends into every province. But along with the fear there is relief as well. A horrible war has come to an end. Hope for a better future is now imaginable.

The king's command to his troops has been clear: exercise restraint and show mercy. The atrocities must stop. But this is difficult for the common soldiers. They don't trust the people in the provinces who have fought and killed them for years. The situation is also difficult for the loyalists—those who have stood behind the king throughout this rebellion. They don't want the province–dwellers welcomed back into the kingdom. They consider them an embarrassment and blight—dirty, wrong, and unpredictable. They want to see them punished—banished, imprisoned, or killed. Though hostilities have officially ceased, the problems in the kingdom are far from over.

The commoners in the far provinces continue for awhile to wage skirmishes against the king's forces. And atrocities by rebel soldiers continue as well. Communication is slow in the dense forests of the far provinces. And even when orders do arrive, the people are slow to follow. These people have been disenfranchised and felt the shame of banishment for years. They are hardly willing to simply hand control of their territory over to the king. They swore to never risk exposure to the cruelty they've been taught to expect from him. These are stubborn folk. It takes time, and they have to be shown that the king has treated other provinces well. But gradually, one village at a time, they are convinced to end their resistance. Eventually, each man must accept that to experience the help and mercy of the king, he must drop his weapons.

Insidious: something destructive that gradually and subtly entraps or ensnares

In the allegory, this phase seems obvious and intuitive: put down your weapons and the war is over. But in real life, this may be the most difficult stage. It can stretch on throughout our lives because the inner conflicts are so ingrained and because the weapons are so insidious.

Like the warlords and the people in the provinces, our split–off and alienated parts have been disowned and shamed for most of our lives. These parts of us don't want to be exposed for fear that they'll be attacked again. They don't trust the King in us anymore. They may not trust any power or ideal that requires any more of them than to hide in their cellars—and they'll put a knife in anyone who gets too close. Like the warlords, we may decide to stop fighting, but the common folk of our far provinces may continue to resist until they feel completely safe.

So we keep our defenses up and keep fighting against wholeness even though the bigger part of us really wants it.

But our benevolent King wants our inner conflict to end. He wants to extend the blessings and protection of his realm into the rebel provinces of our lives. He wants us to experience the serenity that comes from wholeness, and so he yearns for our missing parts. But at the same time, our conscious mind, like the armies of the king, may not trust these parts because they have been a problem in the past. Consciously we don't want our split–off parts back any more than they want to be exposed. Like the king's people, we tend to see these parts as dirty, wrong, and unpredictable. So the conflict continues.

> Our benevolent King wants our inner conflict to end.

I opened Chapter Nine with the statement that authenticity means to live out of the core of who we truly are, undistorted by our shadows, wounds, or symptoms. Here I would add that persisting in anything other than that is doing battle against our inner King, because his mission is to conform our lives to the blueprint of our Self, which he holds. When we engage in our shadows, wounds, and symptoms, we thwart his purpose. Speaking metaphorically, we usurp his throne.

The weapons we use in our battle against wholeness are what might be called our "symptoms" because they are reactions to our underlying hurt and shame. They are thoughts, feelings, and behavior that are defensive, self–defeating, compensatory, and self–soothing. Some of these are aggressive weapons that push others away, like detachment and anger, or that push our self–understanding off track, like projections and gender incongruity. Others are feelings that prevent us from progressing toward wholeness, like shame and counter–emotions. And still others are compensations for what we're missing inside, like homosexual thoughts and behavior. Through such compensations we are trying to fix what's wrong inside us with outside things.

> The weapons we use in our battle against wholeness are what might be called our "symptoms."

So the phase of *dropping your weapons* entails ceasing—or determining to cease—the thoughts, feelings, and behaviors that are propelling you in the direction of continued inner conflict. It's a phase of knowing and doing the work that has to be done in order to let go of the past.

I see this phase as being primarily driven by Warrior energy because it involves both sides of the Warrior—his capacity for determination, aggression, courage, and discipline, as well as his ability to change his strategy when a foe is too great. This duality of the Warrior is often overlooked, but it's essential to understand that the Warrior is the part of us that must fight our battles, but it's also the part of us that must drop our weapons. In the second phase of surrender, the Warrior does both: he fights for our dignity and freedom, but he does so primarily by surrendering and letting go.

Before our inner Warrior can do that, we must first get him turned in the right direction. Like the soldiers among the loyalist and rebel forces, parts of us may continue to pursue the destruction of our own kingdom with a Warrior's aggression and determination (not to mention an Addict's passion, a Manipulator's deceit, and a Tyrant's entitlement). We must redirect that energy so that rather than fighting against wholeness, it begins to fight for it.

In the sections that follow we'll revisit a number of issues we've already discussed in this book, this time to show how they may be weapons against your inner King. I don't go into specifics here about how to overcome the issues—I've written about that in other chapters. This discussion is divided into three sections: weapons of feeling, weapons of thought, and weapons of behavior. It should provide a nice review and summary of the major issues we've discussed over the previous ten chapters, this time from a slightly different perspective.

Pace yourself as you go through this section. If you tend to get overwhelmed, just scan the headings and look for topics that seem relevant to where you are now and read those in depth. Then review this section again in a few weeks or months looking for what's relevant at that time. You'll have this book for a long time, so don't think you have to squeeze everything out of it right now. These issues are best worked on a little at a time.

Before proceeding, let's borrow another hopeful affirmation from Patrick Carnes' book, *A Gentle Path Through the Twelve Steps*: "I accept that life is difficult and that leaning into the struggle adds to my balance."

The Warrior is the part of us that must fight our battles, but it's also the part of us that must drop our weapons.

Weapons against wholeness:

- Weapons of feeling
- Weapons of thought
- Weapons of behavior

Weapons of Feeling ✍ 11.3

Shame: Shame is a weapon against wholeness because it turns us against ourselves. It causes us to split off and cover up the parts of ourselves that we've been taught are unacceptable, thereby fragmenting us. Archetypally, the feeling of shame overloads the sensations of the Lover. The Magian, in a manipulative act of mercy, makes the shame–causing trait disappear. In Chapter Four, I quoted from the book *Facing Shame*, by Merle Fossum and Marilyn Mason. They describe shame as "an inner sense of being completely diminished or insufficient as a person. It is the self judging the self." Shame is an ongoing sense of fundamental badness, inadequacy, defectiveness, or unworthiness. It can cripple our innate capacities for intimacy, self–esteem, and assertion, and block our ability to experience authentic emotions or to feel peace and contentment. Once shame has been evoked in this way, it tends to become a long–term weapon against our inner King. It's the nuclear bomb in the war on wholeness.

> Shame is an ongoing sense of fundamental badness, inadequacy, defectiveness, or unworthiness.

Anxiety and Depression: Anxiety and depression fight against wholeness by preventing us from feeling authentic emotions and physical sensations and by diminishing the libido of the Lover and the King. These counter–emotions also blunt the consciousness of the Magian and weaken the courage of the Warrior. They hurt our relationships with other people and get in the way of fulfilling our needs, particularly the needs for mission and adventure.

Chronic Anger: Handled properly and in appropriate doses, anger is a healthy boundary–setting emotion. It wakes up the Warrior, moves him into action, and then it's surrendered. But anger can become a weapon against wholeness when it lingers as underlying feelings of disgruntlement, resentment, or misanthropy. These feelings lock us into the Sadist shadow of the Warrior and prevent us from enjoying the unifying and relational urges of the Lover. When these feelings are specifically aimed at the male gender as a whole, they also contribute to the fragmenting effects of same–sex disaffiliation, which I'll discuss later.

> *Misanthropy:* a hatred or distrust of humankind

Weapons of Thought ✍ 11.4

Negative Core Beliefs and Thinking Errors: In Chapter Four, I described how children sometimes form negatively distorted beliefs about themselves based on painful and shaming life experiences. These beliefs may include assumptions that the child is responsible for the bad things that were done to him, that he deserved the abuse, or that he's still unsafe. If such beliefs are not corrected, they may remain present in the person's psyche throughout life, forming a pessimistic, shaming, and doubtful underlying core perspective on life.

Thinking errors[1] are similar to negative core beliefs. Simply put, thinking errors are ways of thinking that are incorrect and damaging to our hope and self–esteem. We can think of them as the Manipulator aggressively distorting reality. They include such cognitive tendencies as:

- Mind reading: believing we know that others are thinking negative things about us.

- Pessimism: focusing on the negatives in life and making negative assumptions.

- Black–and–White Thinking: seeing life in absolute terms—things are all one way or the other.

- Unchangeabililty: seeing our negative feelings, personality traits, and life situations as fixed.

- Magnification: blowing things out of proportion, making problems severe.

- Perfectionism: expecting unrealistically high abilities or performance from ourselves or others.

> Negative core beliefs and thinking errors are weapons against wholeness because they are lies.

Negative core beliefs and thinking errors are weapons against wholeness because they are lies. They distort the truth about who we really are, and they support feelings of shame. They minimize our strengths and growth, and they undermine joy. These false beliefs can become ingrained to the point where we lose the ability to see ourselves in an accurate way, even when our positive traits are directly pointed out by others. I see this as a major stumbling block for many men who are trying to overcome unwanted same–sex attraction.

Obsessive Thinking: We've discussed obsessive–compulsiveness in Chapters Three and Eight. Over–thinking, over–analyzing, and ruminating distort reality by accentuating certain perspectives, beliefs, and concerns. Obsessive thinking also distracts us from thoughts and activities that are truly important, from meeting our real needs, and from recognizing our authentic traits and abilities. This is a shadow Magian's weapon against wholeness because it stops us from seeing things as they truly are and from fully engaging in life and relationships. It can also undermine gender wholeness by focusing our attention so tightly on the differences we perceive between ourselves and the masculine norm that we become blind to our overall gender congruity. When we're obsessed with another man, we thwart wholeness by continuing to look outside ourselves for affirmation, love, and the fulfillment of our needs.

Passivity and Denial: Each archetype has a passive pole. The King has the Weakling, the Warrior has the Masochist, the Magian has the Innocent, and the Lover has the Impotent One. When caught in these passive shadows, we tend toward being self–abandoning, disempowered, cowardly, naïve, and impotent. These passive traits fight against wholeness by preventing us from becoming self–magnifying, assertive, courageous, focused, and generative. For those of us with same–sex attraction, these passive traits also compromise masculine sufficiency by undermining gender congruity and making it very difficult to find our way into male community.

Denial is a key trait of the Innocent shadow of the Magian. He refuses to see things as they really are. He's also naïvely incapable of understanding himself or figuring out how life works—traits that he shares with the passive Weakling shadow of the King. The Magian's active Manipulator shadow also contributes to denial by twisting and distorting our perceptions of ourselves and the world. The unawareness of the Lover's Impotent shadow contributes to denial by preventing us from seeing who we really are or what we want from life. Denial saps all energy from the process of growth toward wholeness because we don't perceive the need for growth. It disables the capacity for authenticity because we can't understand ourselves. And it prevents us from fulfilling our needs because we don't know what they are.

Gender Incongruity: Gender shame, gender double binds, and gender imperatives can cause us to see ourselves as being at odds or out–of–sync with what we believe a man is supposed to be. In Chapter Seven, I described these factors in detail and explained how they contribute to gender incongruity. I'll review them briefly here to point out how each is a weapon against wholeness.

Obsessive thinking is a weapon against wholeness because it stops us from seeing things as they truly are.

Denial saps all energy from the process of growth toward wholeness because we don't perceive the need for growth.

Gender shame is an ongoing sense of being fundamentally bad, inadequate, defective, or unworthy as a male. In all of its many forms, it's a weapon against wholeness because it disrupts the natural connection that we should have with our own masculinity and thereby contributes to gender incongruity.

Gender double binds are contradictory messages about males and being male that we have no way to resolve. The contradictory impulses and feelings they create lead to stifling ambivalence. They leave us craving and rejecting our own gender, yearning for and fearing connection with other males, and longing to express our masculinity but deeply insecure about doing so. It's not the double binds themselves that destroy gender wholeness, but the seeming insolvability of those binds. Sadly, the only resolution that most of us found was to split off the masculine aspects of ourselves. This led many of us to experience a mix of lust and loathing for other men.

Gender imperatives are attributes that a man believes are necessary in order to be truly masculine or to be considered attractive, desirable, good, valuable, loveable, or complete as a man. Often those of us with same–sex attraction tell ourselves the story that we don't possess these traits, that we're incapable of obtaining these traits, and that this makes us inferior. Gender imperatives are weapons against wholeness because they fragment our perceptions of other men, leaving us looking at only their most admirable traits. They also undermine our appreciation of our own masculine wholeness.

Gender incongruity can lead to another weapon against wholeness. Because feeling congruent with our own gender seems to be a basic and essential human need, gender incongruity creates a psychologically unstable situation. Since we can't find enough masculinity inside ourselves, we try to absorb it from the idealized men around us. The locus of masculinity goes outside our own bodies and resides with other men, increasing our belief that we're incomplete within ourselves.

Sexuality Labels: The male gender is multifaceted and diverse. There truly is an endless spectrum of all traits such as race, nationality, ethnicity, religion, physical size, intelligence, and athleticism. Labels abound for different kinds of men in each of those categories. The traits of sexuality and gender identity also exist on a broad spectrum that ranges from stereotypically masculine, to intersex, to

Gender shame is a sense of being bad, inadequate, defective, or unworthy as a male.

Gender double binds are contradictory messages about males and being male that we have no way to resolve.

Gender imperatives are attributes that a man believes are necessary in order to be truly masculine.

hermaphroditic—having both male and female sexual characteristics. The term "gay" is a label that distinguishes a certain type of man on the spectrum of sexuality and gender identity.

Labels are tricky things. On one hand, they can be divisive and fragmenting. They can separate us in ways that are inauthentic, limit our potential, and narrow our self–perception to a single defining trait. On the other hand, labels are merely linguistic symbols for distinctions that our minds naturally make. They are a simple way of communicating about diversity that's natural and desirable. They can be a way of affirming who we are, where we belong, and what we value.

Those of us who are trying to move away from same–sex attraction would be well advised to think carefully about how we use terms like gay, ex–gay, homosexual, SSA, and "struggler" as labels for ourselves. These labels may be weapons against gender wholeness if they over–emphasize one facet of our total self and if they separate us from the whole male gender to which we rightfully belong. I believe that same–sex attraction can't be changed without a conscious choice to stop defining and labeling ourselves as gay or homosexual. As I've said before, if you want to stop being homosexual, you have to stop being homosexual. This includes, above all, shifting your self–perception.

Distorted Views of Women: As we discussed in Chapters Six and Seven, experiencing gender wholeness requires both masculine sufficiency and feminine comprehension. To review briefly, masculine sufficiency entails both seeing ourselves as gender congruent and being involved in male community. In short, it means having masculinity inside us and around us.

Feminine comprehension means that we grasp the nature, significance, and meaning of femininity, and that we include, involve, and embrace it in a way that brings completeness. Feminine comprehension is based on two components. The first component is genderedness, or an awareness of the differences between the two sexes. The second component is complementarity, which is an appreciation of the way the two sexes complete and balance each other. In short, feminine comprehension means that we experience the distinctions between the genders and the wholeness of the two genders together—the *complementarity* of the feminine with the masculine.

> Labels are tricky things. On one hand, they can be divisive and fragmenting. On the other hand, labels are merely linguistic symbols for distinctions that our minds naturally make.

Negative views of women can create feelings of hatred, disgust, distrust, and fear toward the opposite sex. Idealization of women creates unrealistically positive feelings toward the other gender. These are weapons against gender wholeness because they prevent us from seeing the true nature of the opposite sex in a whole and balanced way, thus undermining an authentic sense of complementarity. Identification and over–familiarity with women contribute to gender incongruity and obscure awareness of genderedness by blurring the distinctions between your masculine and her feminine. This again undermines complementarity.

Anima Possession: Anima is the feminine within the male psyche. In Chapter Six, I said that the feminine part of our male minds and emotions helps us mitigate the intensity of our masculine energies, creating balance and bringing wholeness. Without it, we risk being overwhelmed by the severity of our own Warrior. But I also warned that, while we need to be close to our Anima, we must never be seduced or overcome by it. Though we may love it, we must maintain a boundary with it.

> We must never be seduced or overcome by our Anima. Though we may love it, we must maintain a boundary with it.

Feeling over–connected with the feminine part of us is a weapon against gender wholeness if it diminishes our sense of maleness and creates gender incongruity. It can also be a weapon if it undermines genderedness and complementarity by weakening our sense of the opposite sex as distinct from us.

Projections: As I described in Chapter Nine, projections are the act of looking for ourselves in other people. They are the Manipulator hiding our Selves from ourselves, then making pieces of us appear on the faces, bodies, and actions of other people. We might be looking for our banished archetypal shadows, our repressed emotions, our unmet needs, our compromised wellbeing, or our own self–love. Those of us with same–sex attraction are also looking for our disowned masculinity, which is what creates gender imperatives. And we're looking for community with other men, which we have lost or perhaps never experienced. Simply put, projections are weapons in the war against wholeness because they sustain and reinforce fragmentation.

> Projections are the Manipulator hiding our Selves from ourselves, then making pieces of us appear on the faces, bodies, and actions of other people.

Projections are reinforced by powerful emotions like the fear or anger we feel toward someone we've projected our Sadist onto or the intense desire or lust we feel towards someone we've projected our masculine self onto. We engage our projections when we allow ourselves to act out of the beliefs or feelings that our projections bring to our minds and bodies. We can't help feeling the emotions themselves, but we can choose to stop believing that they are worthy of a response.

Transference: Also in Chapter Nine, I described transferences, which are unconscious recreations of past relationship patterns in current relationships. This distorts our view of our present selves by keeping us stuck in the roles and relationships we had in childhood. It also distorts our perspectives of the people in our lives today. Sometimes the current–life people just happen to really be like the significant people from our past—our parents, bullies, or abusers. But other times we turn them into those people with the power of our expectations. Transference is the Manipulator using stories from the past to blind us to the reality of the present.

> Transferences keep us stuck in the roles and relationships we had in childhood.

Transferences are weapons against gender wholeness because they contribute to every aspect of gender disruption. First, the distortions caused by transference make our interactions with other men less authentic, limiting our ability to experience attachment, resonance, approval, and support in those relationships. Not only can this situation foster same–sex disaffiliation, it can also prevent us from really getting to know other men, thus supporting and maintaining our sense of gender incongruity.

Likewise in our relationships with females, the distortions caused by our transferences can color our interactions with the women in our lives today. The patterns, dynamics, roles, expectations, and outcomes we experienced with the females in our youth will tend to show up in our adult relationships with the opposite sex.

Weapons of Behavior ✎ 11.5

Same–sex Disaffiliation: Affiliations are connections or associations with others that include close contact, cooperation, companionship, bonding, and love. Affiliation is about being united with or adopted into a relationship or community. By all observations, affiliation with others of our own sex is a core human need and therefore is essential for wholeness. In Chapter Seven, we discussed how defensive detachment, negative male stereotypes, and gender incongruity can break or prevent normal same–sex affiliations, alienating us from our male peers.

> Defensive detachment, negative male stereotypes, and gender incongruity can break or prevent normal same–sex affiliation.

Like gender incongruity, which we already discussed, defensive detachment and stereotyping of men are weapons against gender wholeness because they prevent the natural affiliation that should tie us to the male community. The natural needs for connection, affection, affirmation, and resonance with other males are not fulfilled and instead become longings and cravings.

Repetition Compulsions: Some of us tend to re–create painful interpersonal dynamics from our childhood in our present–day relationships. These so–called "repetition compulsions" are attempts to fix conflicts or challenges that we felt unable to "get right" when we were small.

But these situations merely create more painful—though familiar—feelings and end up working as more of a punishment and distraction from moving on with life. If we're involved in this kind of compulsive relationship, we never really allow ourselves to "get it right." Such behavior is common, and some would argue typical, among homosexual men. The best way to spot this tendency in yourself is by observing whether you seem to always end up in the same situation over and over again, even when you try to avoid repeating past destructive relationships.

Repetition compulsions are weapons against wholeness because they keep us engaged in painful, destructive, and futile behavior. And like transferences, they distort our relationships with other people and keep us stuck in roles and relationships we had in childhood.

Homosexual Thoughts and Behavior: Homosexual thoughts and behavior are weapons against gender wholeness in a surprising number of ways. First of all, keep in mind that any pleasurable sexual thought or behavior will reinforce an attraction because "neurons that fire together wire together." The more we do it, the more we want it. This means that the effects of these weapons are multiplied by engaging in them again and again.

Engaging in homosexual behavior can increase our sense of gender incongruity by making us feel different from our heterosexual male peers. It can also increase same–sex disaffiliation when comrades are turned into sexual objects or when we consider our sexual orientation to be a big secret that we have to keep hidden from everyone else.

When used to compensate for our perceived lack of masculinity, homosexual thoughts and behaviors may simply perpetuate our sense of inadequacy as men. If

> "Repetition compulsions" are attempts to fix conflicts or challenges that we felt unable to "get right" when we were small.

> The effects of homosexual thoughts and behavior are multiplied by engaging in them again and again.

366

we can't find masculinity within ourselves, we may try to import it from someone else. But this is like a trade deficit that keeps us always in debt to other men for our sense of gender congruity. It diverts our attention away from the reality that we have to develop an internal masculine self–concept if we are ever to feel truly adequate. Since we can't gain our masculinity from someone else, if we fail to develop it within ourselves we'll always come up short.

> We may try to import masculinity from someone else. But this is like a trade deficit that keeps us always in debt to other men.

Many of us with same–sex attraction feel a void or hollowness within ourselves, which is usually caused by a need for love and acceptance of our core selves. Homosexual fantasies and behaviors may be attempts to fill that empty place. Wholesome friendships with other men and with women can lessen that sense of hollowness, but the void can only be completely filled by receiving the love and acceptance of our Higher Power and developing full acceptance and love for ourselves.

Addictions: We discussed addiction at length in Chapters Four and Ten. Addictions are weapons against wholeness because they are based in self–alienation and shame, and they create more self–alienation and shame. Addictions also thwart meaningful relationships with other people, which isolates us from the rest of the world. And they undermine any real relationship with ourselves by blunting our feelings and creating over–focus on the addictive behavior or substance.

> Addictions are based on self–alienation and shame, and they create more self–alienation and shame.

Addictions also undermine wholeness because they make it impossible to fulfill our real needs. In the addiction, all time, money, and energy are channeled into accessing the drug of choice. Finally, the control–release cycle that's behind addiction creates an unhealthy emotional and behavioral equilibrium that prevents growth and maintains secrecy and shame.

Distraction: In Chapter Nine, we discussed how the Manipulator can keep our attention so focused on our job, the demands of family, our travel schedule, worries about money, or putting others first, that we never get around to doing the therapeutic work and developing the healing relationships with either males or females that will bring about change. Distraction can become a lifestyle, and it blocks wholeness by preventing growth and stopping the fulfillment of needs.

> Distraction blocks wholeness by preventing growth and stopping the fulfillment of needs.

Protective Self: A protective self can be characterized as inauthentic, unaware, disempowered, and defined by others. In Chapter Nine I detailed how protective selves develop as an escape from the painfully shamed authentic self, which has been fragmented and dissociated. Shame–bound families block children from developing a single, cohesive, internally–authentic personality. So the children in those families learn to wear a mask in order to get along with those whose acceptance and care they require. The protective self also gives them someone to *be*, since they can't be who they truly are.

Protective selves are one big shadow Magian's trick. And they are weapons against wholeness because they separate us from the men and women around us. Protective selves are a primary component of same–sex disaffiliation. They allow us to interact with the world of men while keeping the more authentic aspects of our ego—not to mention our core Self—safely protected behind a sort of "Invisibility Cloak." When we're among women, they allow us to hide our fear, and perhaps loathing, while looking perfectly calm and even charming. On a far more dangerous level, protective selves undermine wholeness by deeply fragmenting us and then creating chronic self–alienation by confusing us about who we really are.

Camp: One manifestation of false selves that deserves special mention is the exaggerated effeminate behavior that's commonly referred to as "camp." Think of this as the Anima gone wild. This and other gender atypical behavior can be fun, amusing, and even fulfilling in some way. But that amusement may come at a cost. Camp may be a weapon against your gender wholeness when it reinforces to you, or to those around you, that you are unmasculine, effeminate, or gay.

FOLLOW THE KING

Before the rebellion, when the kingdom was young, the warlords had been knights of the young sovereign. In fact, they were his inner–circle of most loved, trusted, and influential servants, until a man, known only as the Foreigner, came to visit from a distant and powerful nation. Through a guileful combination of bluster and subtle belittlement, the proud Foreigner undermined the confidence of the unlearned king and his court. Out of insecurity, they chose to trust whatever he told them. The Foreigner used that power to create sedition through a series of terrible lies.

He filled the king's mind with lies about his most trusted knights, turning him against them and sowing in him feelings of distrust, hate, and disgust toward those he had once prized as his most favored subjects. The Foreigner warned the king

---

A protective self can be characterized as inauthentic, unaware, disempowered, and defined by others.

Camp is exaggerated effeminate behavior. Think of this as the Anima gone wild.

A man, known only as the Foreigner, came to visit from a distant and powerful nation.

that unless he banished them immediately, he risked losing his kingdom. Among the knights, he spread a rumor that the king secretly feared their power and intended to execute them very soon. He warned that the king was hungry for absolute control, and he urged them to flee to the outer provinces and hide themselves there.

All of the lies soon became true. The king accused the knights of treason and the knights fled to the outer provinces. Banding together and spurred on by the Foreigner, the knights determined that any king who would turn against his most loyal friends was not fit to rule. Knowing the true deficits of the young king, they believed he could not properly manage the kingdom without their help. So they agreed on a strategy to free the people from their tyrant leader and reestablish peace in the land. But with inferior forces, they were obliged to resort to guerilla warfare, always attacking the king's soldiers from the shadows when they least expected.

But the Foreigner's nasty work was not complete. He next spread lies among the banished knights, turning them against each other until the kingdom was fragmented into numerous factions. Year after year the Foreigner continued his profusion of lies. With the desperate kind of trust that grows out of paranoia, the king and the knights—now known as warlords—continued to believe everything this great manipulator told them, never knowing he was playing both sides. Everyone looked to him as the voice of sanity and reason.

But the Foreigner's nasty work was not complete.

But now, in their desperate circumstances, the warlords are ready to accept what the Sage has tried to tell them for years: that the Foreigner is the most dangerous of liars, that they were fools to trust him, and that they were wrong to mistrust their king. The king is also ready to accept the Sage's sincere rebuke: he was foolish to believe the Foreigner's shameful distortions and rash to banish his friends. Now the king and the warlords must take responsibility for the destruction of their kingdom, which they themselves caused by trusting the wrong man.

Next, they must learn to have faith in each other. So the Sage teaches them how to have real trust. First, he urges the king to set an example by pardoning the warlords and receiving them back as his old friends and as new partners in rebuilding the kingdom. Then the Sage teaches the king and his knights how to be entirely truthful and transparent with one another. It begins with introspection—each man searching himself for the flaws in his character that allowed him to place his trust in such shadowy stories. Then they confess these flaws and gracefully forgive each other. Above all, the Sage teaches them to trust in the transcendent vision they have of a unified and peaceful nation. He teaches that it is the intention of the Supreme Power of the universe for men and women to live in that way.

These changes are not easy after decades of living by the sword. But for the good of the whole, they persist. As for the Foreigner, the king orders the knights to hunt him down, the Sage tries him for his crimes, and he is hanged in the most public square. His is the one crime that cannot be tolerated.

Still this is not enough to heal the kingdom. Too much internal conflict and mistrust remain among the people to rule them by decree. And the king has not yet earned the respect or trust of his people—either loyalist or rebel. The wise Sage understands this. He knows that, in order for the nation to be saved, the king and his people must combine their faith in a shared intention that is higher than the rule of a mortal king. The king must point his people toward something greater than himself.

For God and the whole

The Sage suggests that the king publicly commit himself to a vow of trust in a transcendent ideal.

So the Sage suggests that the king publicly commit himself to a vow of trust in a transcendent ideal and that he invite—but not compel—his people to commit themselves to the same oath. "For God and the whole" is the vow the Sage suggests. This vow represents a primary commitment to the wellbeing of the whole nation, as designed by God, rather than pursuing the wellbeing of any faction. And it ensures those who take the vow that their commitment is to something more stable and trustworthy than a human authority. Recognizing the necessity of such a vow, the king publicly commits himself to it. Many follow his lead. And this is the turning point of the nation's recovery.

The Sage also suggests that the king add a new law to protect the kingdom from future civil war. This new law makes punishable by death the perpetuation of any lie that undermines the integrity of the nation. The king proposes the law, the knights sustain it, and it is obeyed.

Still, the recovery is long and difficult. At times, the king and his knights lapse into their old mistrust. Sometimes they return to believing the Foreigner's lies—occasionally even talking of returning to the rebellion. But ultimately, the former warlords maintain their faith in the king, who in turn follows God's design for the kingdom.

Having changed our minds by deciding that our old ways don't work and having dropped our weapons of feeling, thinking, and behavior, surrender next invites us to change the object of our faith—from trusting in the old ways to trusting something new and untried. In this phase, we shift from being primarily in Magian or Warrior energy and we open ourselves to the power of the King.

Traits of the King archetype exist in multiple forms and on multiple levels both within us and in the world around us. Anywhere guidance and leadership happen, some of his traits can be found, whether in shadow or in wholeness. Earlier in the allegory, the king has represented the form of the King archetype that operates within our ego. On that level, the King is our governing mind or conscious principled self. This may be the lowest level of our inner King. It's merely the part of us that runs our everyday life, holding us to our goals, priorities, and values, and making decisions—some of which are good for us and some of which hurt us. But in making his vow, which is aimed at unification of the kingdom, the king in the story comes to represent a deeper level of the King archetype within our psyche. He now represents our Self, which you will remember from Chapter Two is our central organizing structure. Also, the vow itself, "For God and the whole," invokes a third form or level of the King archetype, the Ultimate King or Higher Power.

So now two new levels of the King archetype are represented in the allegory—the King as our Self and the King as our Higher Power. The process of surrender calls on us to trust and follow the King on both of these levels. Let's look at these two levels of the King a bit more closely. Then we'll consider some vows or affirmations to help you trust in higher ways as you unify and heal your inner kingdom.

Trust Your Self

In our basic design as men, we have been endowed with a blueprint for wholeness. This blueprint resides in the central organizing structure that we have been referring to as our Self. As described in Chapter Two, our Self is the unmoving, unchanging core that guides and directs the rest of our psyche. We might see it as our core

Surrender invites us to change the object of our faith from trusting in the old ways to trusting something new and untried.

Follow the King
- Trust your Self
- Trust your Higher Power
- Trust in higher ways

intelligence, our spirit or soul, or as our conscience. It provides clarity and vision about our course through life, and it instills validity, worth, and purpose. It helps us to maintain balance and moderation and to integrate all aspects of ourselves into a unified and functional whole.

Trusting your Self means believing that, no matter how dysfunctional we feel, our Self is whole. The capacity to guide and heal our lives is part of that Self and will always be with us. Trusting our Self means believing that we can develop the capacity to hear the voice of our Self and to follow its promptings. It means trusting that pursuing wholeness will meet our needs better—and bring greater peace and joy—than pursuing our old relinquished thoughts and behaviors. And most importantly, trusting our Self means developing a vision of ourselves as already whole and then following that vision into reality no matter the cost.

> Trusting your Self means believing that, no matter how dysfunctional we feel, our Self is whole.

To accomplish this, we'll have to forgive ourselves for our history of dysfunctions and flaws. We have to let go of the past because dwelling on the past merely keeps it alive in the present. We may look at the past to learn the lessons it has to teach us about ourselves. Then we may use those lessons to make ourselves stronger. Otherwise, we keep our eyes looking steadfastly forward.

An incident from the Bible illustrates this principle well. Lot was told by two heavenly messengers to leave the city of Sodom. They told him to flee with his family and not to look back. As Lot fled with his wife and two daughters, the city was destroyed. The family left their old residence and way of life. In a sense, they accomplished the first two phases of surrender by accepting that staying in Sodom was no longer working and by letting go of their past in that city. But then Lot's wife made her infamous error. She failed in the third phase of surrender. She didn't trust the heavenly messengers—her faith in her new path wavered. She looked back and she paid for it with her life.

> So our attention must be focused on the King within us and the blueprint he provides of our whole, authentic Self.

So our attention must be focused beyond our dysfunctions—on the King within us and the blueprint he provides of our whole, authentic Self. But we don't stop there. A wise mortal king recognizes his place in the cosmos. He knows that in all his greatness he's nothing without the guidance of something more transcendent than himself. And so he seeks connection to a Higher Power or a higher way. If we'll listen, our inner King will urge us toward that Higher Power, drawing us upward toward the ultimate King archetype. The King within us feels a resonance with something that's eternal—a King of a higher order that exists somewhere in the universe. Our inner King seeks Him. And if we listen, the King in us will make us more like that King. ✎ 11.6

Trust Your Higher Power

To follow the King as Higher Power, we must be willing to act out of hope, having confidence in things that we can't prove. And we must be willing to rely on powers beyond our own capacities, letting the power of the King replace our meager attempts at control. Faith helps us overcome our fear of relinquishing control. We can do this if we believe that our Higher Power has control over all things and that he wants us to grow and develop—even if it's through hardship. So we can put ourselves in his hands and trust him. In this way, faith itself becomes an energy source.

For some of us, this kind of faith is a gift, and we can "follow the King" just as soon as we find out where he wants us to go. Others of us don't have that kind of trust. We have to surrender to a new object of faith a bit at a time as we gradually feel greater certainty through successful experiences with powers beyond our own. Whether done all at once or through many small decisions, spiritual surrender requires a recognition that we're a smaller force in the universe, and that there is some force greater than ourselves that wants our wellbeing. What I taught in Chapter Three about faith applies also to surrender: we must remember that, although we are kings, we are not *the* King.

How can you develop a connection of trust with a Higher Power if you don't already experience it? Or how can you increase or heal a connection that's less strong than you want it to be? Let's return to a concept from Chapter One for some ideas. There I mentioned the ancient theological doctrine of "synergism," which teaches that divine grace cooperates with human activity in the process of spiritual regeneration. The concept of synergism offers a model or pathway for learning to trust in a Higher Power.

Addicts in recovery have practiced the doctrine of synergism for decades through the Twelve–Step program. Let's refer to the Twelve Steps of Alcoholics Anonymous as a model to help us understand how practicing synergism can create or increase faith. If boiled down to their most essential elements, the Twelve Steps become just two steps: We trusted, we acted. Trust suggests reliance on the help

> We must act out of hope, and we must be willing to rely on powers beyond our own capacities.

> If boiled down to their most essential elements, the Twelve Steps become just two steps: We trusted, we acted.

of a Higher Power. And to act suggests both making choices and then following those choices with congruent behavior. There is no trust without action. Otherwise it's just talk. If I say I trust my friend, but I won't let him into my house, do I really trust him? If I say I trust my teacher, but I don't follow what he teaches, do I really believe him?

As we review the Twelve Steps, notice the combination of personal action with trust in a Higher Power. It begins with recognition that we need the help of a Higher Power. The first step, which I quoted earlier in this chapter, states that, "We admitted we were powerless…and that our lives had become unmanageable." This admission that our past willfulness has left us with no power to govern our lives is an essential act of humility and readiness to change.

It may be that this kind of action comes more readily to those of us who have hit rock bottom because the guise of *control* has already been stripped away from us. In that state, we're finally ready to humbly admit that we have no control. Most of us have just hidden that stark reality from ourselves through denial. This reality was brought home to me in a harsh way on Thanksgiving Day 2010, just two days prior to writing this section. A very close friend named Stuart was driving with his family to meet relatives for a Thanksgiving celebration. But instead of arriving at the celebration, the family was involved in a gruesome auto accident, which took his life and that of his daughter. We think we're managing our lives until an event like this rips away our denial and we realize that we control very little. We're in the hands of a benevolent, and sometimes stinging, Higher Power.

The second step states that we "[c]ame to believe that a Power greater than ourselves could restore us to sanity." This is an act of trust in our Higher Power. Belief, or perhaps even just a desire to believe, is the foundation of trust and the beginning of faith. Step Three adds that we "[m]ade a decision to turn our will and our lives over to the care of God *as we understood Him.*" This step is synergistic within itself since it combines personal action with trust in our Higher Power. The decision, which is a personal action, places us in the care of our Higher Power upon which we then must rely for help. This expresses what may be the most difficult and contradictory act of trust: to use our will to surrender our will to a Power beyond our own.

As we review the Twelve Steps, notice the combination of personal action with trust in a Higher Power.

Belief, or perhaps even just a desire to believe, is the foundation of trust and the beginning of faith.

This step is followed by several other personal action steps that support steps two and three. In Step Four a "searching and fearless moral inventory" is made. In Step Five, the recovering addict admits his wrongs to God, to himself, and to another person. Then in Step Six, the focus returns to trusting and seeking assistance from our Higher Power: we "[w]ere entirely ready to have God remove all of these defects of character." And in Step Seven, we "[h]umbly asked Him to remove our shortcomings." In the next two steps, the focus is back on the actions of the individual. Steps Eight and Nine are about making amends to others, and the tenth step calls on the person in recovery to continually "take personal inventory" and admit when he's wrong.

The Step Eleven, like Step Three, is synergistic within itself: we "[s]ought through prayer and meditation to improve our conscious contact with God *as we understood Him*, praying only for knowledge of His will for us and the power to carry that out." Here again, the personal actions of prayer and meditation bring us to trust in our Higher Power's will—another difficult step for most of us. And in Step Twelve, the focus moves back to individual action with the commitment to try "to carry this message to alcoholics, and to practice these principles in all our affairs."

To summarize, the Twelve Steps boil down to just two things: trusting in a Power greater than ourselves, and acting in ways that turn our lives over to that Power. Now, there is an aspect of synergism that isn't explicitly stated in these twelve steps, but which is observable in the lives of many successful recovering addicts. This phenomenon results from personal action and trust in our Higher Power, but goes a step beyond that. It's essential enough that it could have been an additional step. It might have been worded something like this: In return, our Higher Power lifted our burdens from us, raised us out of the wreckage of our past, and manifested His will for our lives. This step acknowledges God's reciprocal and real intervention in our lives, which comes as a result of our faith in him. This is the fullness of synergism. ✍ 11.7

> In return, our Higher Power lifted our burdens from us, raised us out of the wreckage of our past, and manifested His will for our lives.

In my own life, I've experienced the two–part synergistic process suggested by the Twelve Steps as well as the phenomenon of the additional step. Together, these three parts—trust, action, and God's intervention—have shaped my life and created an ever–deepening faith. To me, this is the single most hopeful and strengthening truth I've learned through my years of growth into more mature manhood. There *are* powers beyond our own psyches that cooperate with our efforts in creating personal wholeness. I know those powers exist because of the many times I've directly—and sometimes miraculously—experienced them. And I assure you that they are real and that you can access them by aligning your inner King with the Universal King. That faith has become a central aspect of my perspective on how men heal from unwanted sexual attractions.

This perspective was introduced to me many years ago while I was just beginning my own process of growth out of same–sex attraction. I climbed a mountainside to be alone and seek some kind of understanding of my situation. As I sat on the hillside meditating, I heard a voice in my mind say very distinctly, "Healing is from God." I hadn't really thought of that concept before then. But I've thought about it many times since. I've been all over the map regarding that idea. What is now becoming increasingly blatant to me is that every type of healing is the gift of a source greater than anything we understand. More specific to our discussion here, the resolution of unwanted same–sex attraction is mediated by a Higher Power, which I call God. I urge you to seek the help of that Power, regardless of what you call it.

For men who are part of a faith tradition or who have directly experienced God in some other way, I suggest that you seek a more profound relationship with God through your own faith. Surrender the things in your life that are incompatible with drawing closer to him. Apply what you've been taught about seeking God and receiving His help in your life.

> I heard a voice in my mind say very distinctly, "Healing is from God."

For those who have not experienced a Higher Power as an actual divine being, I suggest a different route. First, consider the fact that there are powers in the universe that caused us to exist. That isn't much of a stretch—we're here and we certainly didn't create ourselves. Therefore, there must be a transcendent power, even if it's nothing more than a long process like evolution. Next, notice that life on this planet is persistent—it always finds a way to continue. Species adapt, our bodies heal themselves when we become sick, and there is a strong will in most organisms to survive. This is also pretty easy to accept.

> For those who have not experienced a Higher Power as an actual divine being, I suggest a different route.

Here comes the act of faith: you may choose to believe that these powers are benevolent, which means that somehow there is an intention inherent in these powers to promote growth and happiness even while those powers also allow for, and even cause, pain and death. That choice is the beginning of trust in a Higher Power. From there, follow the three–part process I described previously and your trust will grow.

I've gained another perspective about God's role in the healing process. This one comes from years of working with men from a wide variety of faiths and with no faith. God's healing power works for everyone who seeks it. We call the source of that power many names—God, Christ, HaShem, Allah, nature, psychology, and so forth. Some of us try to claim exclusive rights to his power. But I've plainly seen that religious people and non–religious people both heal. Christians heal, Jews heal, and Muslims heal. So do Hindus, and Bahais. God himself seems big enough and gracious enough to bless everyone who lets him in—no matter what name they give him.

A Christian scripture from the twenty–fifth chapter of Matthew in *The New Testament* expresses this concept beautifully. Jesus has been instructing his followers to love and bless those that persecute them. Then he tells them that God "maketh his sun to rise on the evil and on the good, and sendeth rain on the just and on the unjust" (*KJV*).

The trouble I've seen with men trying to access the help of a Higher Power seems to come when the man is truly estranged from his concept of God. Sometimes this estrangement comes from the man's own anger toward God. Other times it's created by what might be called a "religious double bind," which is where he was taught that he must love God but all of the evidence he saw of God made God seem horrible and cruel. Another source of trouble I've observed with men trying to connect to a Higher Power is an obsessive–compulsive view of God as a maker of excessive and impossible demands. This is usually the result of transference or projection, and these can be owned and surrendered just like any other transferences or projections.

When God is felt in the heart, when there is a sense of strong reciprocal love, and even when there is nothing more than a simple choice to accept the idea of a power greater than ourselves, I've noticed that trust in a Higher Power creates a strong positive force for change. 11.8

God himself seems big enough and gracious enough to bless everyone who lets him in—no matter what name they give him.

Trust in a Higher Power creates a strong positive force for change.

Trust in Higher Ways

Having now discussed the two levels of the King—as our Self and as the Ultimate King or Higher Power—let's next consider some affirmations which, like the King's vow in the allegory, may be able to help you focus your commitment on the healing of your inner kingdom. Each affirmation is stated as an expression of trust in something that can help to balance your life and bring greater joy and stability.

These seven affirmations are choices and commitments that I suggest for your consideration. They are commitments to a simple and real way of living.

These seven affirmations are choices and commitments that I suggest for your consideration. If your old methods have not been able to bring you authenticity, wholeness, and joy, try these. These affirmations are commitments to a simple and real way of living. While they don't deny the inevitability of difficulty or the potential of struggle in our lives, they unanimously affirm that there is a positive intention in our existence and they show a way to actualize it.

One: I trust that there is meaning and purpose in my existence. Rather than centering my faith on the concept that I am of no consequence, I choose to believe that a Higher Power designed and created me for a reason. Rather than believing that what I do doesn't matter, I choose to believe that my actions have both positive and negative consequences. Especially, I choose to believe that I have the power to make a positive impact in the world.

Two: I trust in the goodness of my authentic self. Rather than investing my faith in negative core beliefs and a sense of being bad, I chose to believe in the dominance of my goodness, even though I'm flawed. Rather than relying on repression, denial, and projection of my shadows, I choose to trust the synergistic potential that comes from balancing, moderating, and integrating the bipolar tendencies of my archetypal traits. I choose to believe that by living in this bipolar tension, I'll become my most whole self and will experience my greatest freedom, power, and joy.

Rather than believing the feelings and impulses that I have toward other people onto whom I've projected my split–off parts, I choose to trust that the things I react to in them actually belong to me and have nothing to do with the other person.

Rather than relying on my protective self to create secure and satisfying relationships, which it has so far failed to do, I trust instead that my authentic self has a place in the world. I choose to believe that authenticity is far more an internal way of life than an interpersonal practice. In other words, authenticity comes from knowing my Self. What I show to others and what they understand about me is secondary and of lesser importance. I can live authentically within myself even if I consciously choose to hold back details about my truth that others don't have the capacity to understand.

Rather than believing that I'm blocked from becoming authentic, I put my faith in the power of natural healing and growth processes. I trust that these will help me learn to live from the core of who I truly am. And rather than continuing to believe in the disproven notion that I can handle this on my own, I trust others who can help me to grow.

Three: I trust that I am intended to live with a serene heart and mind. Rather than believing that counter–emotions like shame, anxiety, depression, numbness, and chronic anger are acceptable feeling states, I commit myself to the belief that I'm intended to be free to experience my core emotions. I'm committed to allowing my core emotions to lead me to joy and serenity.

Rather than placing my confidence in thinking errors, which distort reality and damage my hope and self–esteem, I trust in sane and rational ways of seeing myself, others, and the world.

Rather than trusting in the power of obsessive thinking to fix my life, which it has so far failed to do, I trust that I'm safe, that I can relax and let go, and that only the Higher Power has total control.

Four: I trust that wholeness is founded on love of self and love from my Higher Power. Rather than believing that objects, experiences, and other people can supply me with the love that's essential for wholeness, I choose to believe that it's by loving myself that I'll become whole. And I trust that feeling the love and approval my Higher Power has for me will greatly increase my love and acceptance for myself.

Five: I trust in the goodness and intentionality of my maleness. Rather than doubting that I was designed to be a man, I trust that the power that created me intended for me to be male and masculine. Rather than trusting the notion that I'm inadequate as a man, I choose to believe that my Higher Power placed in me all the masculine characteristics that I need. I trust that I can access and develop those qualities. Rather than putting my faith in external standards or opinions about what a man is, or is supposed to be, I trust that my Higher Power designed me as part of the diverse male gender. And I trust that the design is good.

Rather than believing that sex, lust, touch, or even friendship with another man will cure my gender incongruity, I choose to experience, accept, and develop the fullness of my masculinity as defined and designed by my Higher Power. I choose to believe that friendships with other men who possess the masculine qualities I aspire to may help me in this process, but ultimately those friendships won't benefit me if I don't find masculinity from within. Rather than believing that the traits that trigger me so much in other men are about some special wholeness or shadow they contain, I accept that these are actually my own projections.

Rather than submitting myself to labels that limit me, fragment me, or insult my dignity or masculinity, I choose instead to trust that my true self is more expansive than those labels. I rely only on labels that affirm who I am, where I belong, and what I value. Rather than disregarding the dignity of my masculinity and entrusting myself to be possessed by my Anima, I choose to believe that it's better to honor maleness in all my actions.

Six: I trust that I can relate healthfully with other men. Rather than believing that I don't belong in male community and that I'm fine in isolation, I choose to believe that I can create safe and satisfying authentic friendships among men who are worthy of my trust. Rather than seeing myself as always needy and incapable of contributing to other men, I accept that I have gifts to offer, and I choose to believe that reciprocity is an essential part of male friendships.

Rather than trusting that my obsessions with certain men hold any value or that the other man has any power to heal me, I accept that what I'm demanding from him I can only find within myself. Rather than having faith in my stereotypes, I accept that even men who may seem simple are complex individuals with both strengths and weaknesses. Rather than trusting that the fear, anger, resentment, and mistrust that I transfer onto men are a healthy way of living, I chose to believe that most men are worthy of my trust, respect, and love.

Rather than relating to other men as sexual objects, I trust that I'll find a far deeper satisfaction from relating with them as whole and authentic individuals. Rather than putting my faith in sex, lust, or even in non–sexual physical contact as my primary source of male love, I choose to believe that the man whose love I most need is myself. Though they may be an important part of my journey, intimate friendships with other men, in the end, won't heal me. If I believe in a masculine God, I choose to believe that his love will also help to fill my empty spaces.

Seven: I trust that I am intended to appreciate women as my complimentary opposite. Rather than overlooking the significant distinctions between the two genders, I choose to accept that, according to the design of my Higher Power, we are different in essential ways. Rather than trusting that my resonance with women means that I'm somehow like them—or one of them—I choose to believe that on deep and mysterious levels they are my opposite. I believe that genderedness is intentional, and I trust that I'm part of that intention.

Rather than believing that the anger, fear, mistrust, and disgust that I transfer onto women are accurate, warranted, and beneficial, I trust that each woman is a unique individual and that my Higher Power created women and men to complement one another in beautiful and generative ways. ✐ 11.9

UNIFY THE KINGDOM

On a day that had long been anticipated, the warlords return to the capital city. This is the first time they have set foot in their former home in many years. Setting a powerful example of forgiveness, the king publicly welcomes them and receives them into his court. In fact, he restores them to their ranks as knights, and he appoints them to be his chief advisers in the process of restoring the kingdom. The king orders all levels of the military and civil government to follow his lead. They become one people and one nation again, all governed by the same laws and enjoying the same protections.

On a day that had long been anticipated, the warlords return to the capital city. The king publicly welcomes them.

Then the Sage teaches the king another vital lesson. "Idle people make good enemies," the Sage mutters. "You must give them something new to do." The end of the war has left a strange vacuum. The conflict had been the total focal point of everyone's activities, not to mention their energy and emotion, for many years. Many people had been making their living from the war, providing equipment and supplies or fighting as soldiers. Many others had used the war to support themselves in far less noble ways. The people needed a new mission—and new jobs. So the king put the people to work building a beautiful new kingdom.

As a young prince, the king had seen this beautiful kingdom in a vision, many years before he took the throne. He carried that vision in his mind for years. Upon becoming king, he tried to realize the vision and was beginning to achieve it, although in a rather naïve and haphazard way. But all of this was brought to a sudden halt when his kingdom was fragmented by the insurrection. Now, with greater wisdom and doubled resolve, the king and his trusted knights set about rebuilding the kingdom according to the king's original design. But this time, they build more wisely. Their design is more balanced. The provinces are better integrated. And their expenditures are more moderate. And they create an effective border patrol to defend against infiltration by designing foreigners.

As part of their new design, a system of roads is built to connect all of the provinces. The people now move freely from place to place. Trade and commerce resume between the capital city and the former rogue villages. The provinces, which once were a liability, become a great source of wealth. Everyone flourishes beyond any level of abundance they'd ever known before. The king also normalizes relations with neighboring countries. He realizes that a nation cannot support itself in isolation.

The king's vow becomes a national pledge. Both children and adults learn to recite it: "For God and the whole." Inspired by this vow, the people unanimously invest in the kingdom as one nation. The good of all is placed above personal interest or selfishness aims. It is a joyful time for all.

In this fourth phase of surrender, we do the work of unifying our lives. Within our psyche, as also in the allegory, this unification happens from two directions. From one direction, our "rebel" parts come home to us and are integrated back into the whole. From the other direction, our inner King receives back these parts and puts them to work in promoting our wellbeing. Our split–off parts and unmet needs never had gone away. They've been present all along, showing up in our cravings and projections. Now all these parts of us are welcomed home.

> As a young prince, the king had seen this beautiful kingdom in a vision, many years before he took the throne.

> In this fourth phase of surrender, we do the work of unifying our lives. This unification happens from two directions.

Like the system of roads the king constructs, we need to create conscious connection with our entire self. And, like the people of the allegorical kingdom, we'll likely find that our new wholeness creates a wealth of energy and emotional freedom. But we don't just unify within ourselves—we also connect with other people.

The allegory also is reminding us of a natural law we learned about in Chapter Two: Nature abhors a vacuum. If we let an old thing go, we must let a new thing in. Otherwise, the old thing will remain with us or will soon return. We might continue to experience the thing we've surrendered as an emotionally charged memory or longing. Or if we do enjoy a season of freedom from it, the old thing, or something like it, may simply return. This is why we so often see people trade one addiction for another.

> If we let an old thing go, we must let a new thing in. Otherwise, the old thing will remain with us or will soon return.

In the allegory, the warlords and their rebel forces dropped their weapons and ended the war. Letting go of the war created the vacuum. In our lives, behavioral change creates loss—loss of the old behaviors and ways of living. Dictionaries define the word "surrender" using synonyms like yield, resign, and abandon. All of these words suggest relinquishment and loss. The behavioral aspect of surrender leaves emptiness. In the form of a longing, lost things can remain with us energetically or emotionally forever. But if something of equal or greater value is put into that empty place, we can truly let go of the thing we lost.

The simplest way to understand this is to remember an experience when you lost a possession that you really liked. If you were able to fully replace its value in your life, you probably didn't long for what you lost. For example, if you lost your cell phone and you bought a new one that was the same or better, you probably forgot about the one you lost.

But surrendering old lifestyles and behaviors is more difficult than forgetting about a lost possession, especially if the behavior is addictive. Behaviors come from *inside* us as expressions of our feelings, needs, and beliefs—conscious and unconscious. And if the behavior is addictive, there are also powerful chemical and neurological factors reinforcing it. So we have to change behavior by choice. And what makes this harder still is that addictive behaviors are impossible to exactly replace with anything other than another addiction. We can take up new behaviors that genuinely fill the needs underlying the addiction, but the experience will never *feel* as high.

As the addict shifts from addiction to sobriety, he may experience a substantial loss. So he engages in many healthy behaviors on a daily basis to help fill the void. Twelve–step meetings, working with a sponsor, daily rituals of prayer, reading, and service, and "working the steps" replace the addictive behavior, restore wholeness, and provide meaning to his life.

But for the addict, and anyone else trying to recover from fragmentation, all of this behavioral modification—though important and necessary—is incomplete. The lifestyles and behaviors we've been discussing are attempts to reclaim lost parts of ourselves or to soothe the pain of our alienation from self. So surrendering old behaviors must be part of a larger process that includes integration of fragments. In other words, it's our lost and alienated parts of self that we need to put into the empty space. Our Higher Power also needs to go there.

Integratio: to renew or restore to the original untouched condition

Ultimately, this phase of surrender is one of restoring us to our original design with all of our diverse elements back together in their *original and untouched condition.* As I taught in Chapter One, the Latin word *integratio,* which is the root of "integration," means to renew or restore, as in restoring to the original untouched condition.

Wholeness is in our basic design, and we still carry the memory of that wholeness.

Wholeness is in our basic design, and we still carry the memory of that wholeness. So in this phase we're putting our kingdoms back the way they should be, with everything in its rightful place with its rightful importance. Our emotions are given their rightful importance, our needs are appropriately valued, and we connect ourselves with other people. We extend love to ourselves, invite back lost or dissociated parts of our personalities, own our projections, and integrate our archetypal shadows. Then, by living in the full self, new synergistic effects occur. New strengths and capacities emerge, new desires are felt, and new behaviors spontaneously occur.

This is Lover work. It's yearning for union, for which that archetype is known, that drives the synergistic power of the King. As I wrote in Chapter Ten, Lover is the energy that makes a whole out of the parts and searches for meaning. This is the energy of reconciliation, reunion, and solidarity that instills in some men's hearts a desire to bring people together. It also inspires men to bring *themselves* together. And through this reunion of self, the Lover becomes healed and whole so that his longing can turn toward his opposite and to his Higher Power. Rather than his love being narcissistic, he can now be Other directed.

Now let's look at this phase of surrender in more specific and practical ways. Let's consider seven different things that we may need to open ourselves to, let in, or own. This is an outline for how to unify the kingdom—to create wholeness by putting ourselves back together the way we were originally designed to be.

Welcome Our Feelings

One of the first things we need to *let in* is our own feelings, and particularly our core emotions. Some of us struggle with this more than others. Often we might be in touch with certain of our feelings, but find that we can't access other feelings. For some, anger is so guilt producing or scary that it's immediately shut down by strong defensive reactions. For others, sadness is the emotion their defenses prohibit. And I've also known men who couldn't tolerate feelings of joy and love.

This intolerance of our own emotions usually comes from painful or distressing childhood experiences. For example, some parents punish their children for having feelings: "I'll spank you if you don't stop crying!" Other parents contradict their children's emotions: "You don't really feel sad," or "You don't really want to wear that shirt." There are parents who use their children's feelings to manipulate them: "You love mommy, you don't want to hurt my feelings." And of course there are double–binding parents who cause children to see their feelings as futile: "You don't even appreciate me, you ungrateful kid!" In a double bind it doesn't matter what you feel—you are wrong for it and there is nothing you can do.

Surrendering to our own feelings is often an early and ongoing part of the process of healing and recovery. Some of us may be able to open to our feelings without help from others. But the majority of us who have closed down some aspect of our emotional life will need the help of a skilled therapist, coach, or group facilitator if we're to get past the well–structured defenses that have been blocking access to those feelings for so many years. Some experiential weekends can also be very helpful in getting past defenses and opening to emotion.

In determining which therapist or coach can best help you with this, you might question the prospective therapists about how they approach working with emotion. You want someone who will provide a safe place for you to open up those emotions,

---

Unify the Kingdom
- Welcome our feelings
- Meet our needs
- Let other people in
- Love ourselves
- Invite back split–off parts
- Own our projections
- Integrate our archetypal shadows

Surrendering to our own feelings is often an early and ongoing part of the process of healing and recovery.

feel them, and express them. Tell the therapist what you understand about your defenses, even if all you know is that you can't ever feel a certain emotion. Ask them how they would help you get past those defenses. ✍ 11.10

Meet Our Needs

We must also be willing to open ourselves to the fulfillment of our true needs. Like the people in the allegory who needed to be given things to do to build the kingdom, we need to engage in new behaviors that meet our needs in order to fill the vacuum and help us let go of our old ways of living. This is particularly true if homosexual behavior, including use of pornography, was a significant part of our past lifestyle.

In Chapter Six, I taught that much of the craving associated with same–sex attraction, for most of us who experience it, comes from failure to meet our core needs for connection with our own masculinity and connection to other men. Failure to meet these needs results in what I called *masculine insufficiency*, which I've found to be a major problem for almost every man with same–sex attraction I've ever worked with.

We need to integrate into our lives the kinds of habits that will meet our non–negotiable needs:

- A mission
- An adventure
- Comrades
- Spiritual connection
- Physical care
- Genderedness and complementarity

So we need to let in the awareness of our non–negotiable needs, and then we need to integrate into our lives the kinds of habits that will meet those needs. Some needs will be more important to us at certain times than other needs. The six needs I described in Chapter Three may not all be top drawer for you right now. For example, early in the change process the needs for comrades, adventure, and physical care tend to be very high. It's often not until later in the growth process that men tune into the need for genderedness and complementarity.

That said, I also want to give a warning about the danger of repressing our needs. Sometimes our willingness to fulfill a need—or even to admit that it is a need—can be blocked by negative feelings about that need or simply by unwillingness to do the work that it takes to fulfill it. We may think we're more comfortable ignoring it. Meanwhile, our self–esteem may be low and our depression high. Our same–sex attraction may be soaring and our growth process lagging. Our so–called comfort may come at a high price.

More than any other, the need for physical care is overlooked in this way. I've noticed that many men don't want to admit that they have a body with needs. They don't want to let in the reality that they must care for their physical self if they're going to feel a sense of power and self–mastery. The result of this is that they tend to project physical wellbeing, discipline, and strength onto other men whose bodies reflect these qualities. Rather than becoming unified with their whole self, they continue to live a fragmented life.

Let me add a few words about another need where some surrender may need to happen—the need for a mission. At some point, we need to shift the focus of our mission from being all about recovery and *not* being gay to being whole and serving others. If we keep our focus on the war, we'll just perpetuate the war. And if we keep the focus on ourselves, we'll never experience a complete sense of wholeness. To experience that, we must engage in service to something greater than ourselves.   🖊 11.11

Let Other People In

Returning again to the allegory, like the king, we can't live in isolation. So part of the letting in aspect of surrender is letting in other people. Relationships with others are essential for many reasons. We need the love, affection, and companionship that affiliation with others provides. We also need to experience resonance, affirmation, and approval from other people, especially from men. Since none of us is truly self–sufficient, we also need help and support. And if we're to grow as men, we need the mentoring, guidance, and insight that other men and women can offer.

> We need the love, affection, companionship, resonance, affirmation, approval, help, and support of other people.

In addition to the very favorable relationship dynamics described previously, we also need relationships with others who provide contrast, diversity, and even opposition. How else will we see our shadows? And how else can we really grow in wisdom and understanding? People who challenge us are vital to our development as men. Such relationships enable us to move beyond our previous comfort zones, and they are more likely to be found outside the community of same–sex attracted men, in the general population.

> People who challenge us are vital to our development as men.

At some point, we may also need to let in—or let *back* in—the opposite sex. I taught about this in Chapters Three and Six. I wrote that the second component of gender wholeness is having a healthy sense of completion with the opposite sex. Men need a healthy comprehension of the feminine. Feminine comprehension means that a man experiences the wholeness of the two genders together—the *complementarity* of the feminine with the masculine.

As we pursue the overall healing process, we start to see others more clearly without our projections, transferences, and unmet needs blinding us to their authentic selves. As we become more whole, we may be drawn to a whole different set of people. Rather than relating to others compulsively as lost parts of ourselves, we relate to them as individuals with boundaries. ✍ 11.12

Love Ourselves

While it's part of our original design to need other people—including their love and affirmation—we must eventually accept a truth of which authors Moore and Gillette remind us in *The Lover Within*. There they state that, in our surrender process, part of "the grieving that we must do involves the…recognition that the love we needed, in the way in which we needed it, will never be ours. We can never experience this love fully in the context of our human relationships."

For so many years in my own healing process I craved the love of other men. There were times when I felt deeply loved by a male friend. But there were also the inevitable losses of those intense connections. No relationship could possibly fulfill my needs fully on an ongoing basis. It was not that my friends were inadequate or that the friendships were faulty. It was just that we were human and that life is imperfect. Through painful experiences, I eventually came to accept that in starkest reality, I am my only lifelong male companion. I learned that the love that I need most from a man is the love of my masculine self for me.

> The love that I need most from a man is the love of my masculine self for me.

But so many of us with same–sex attraction hate ourselves. Since childhood, we've split off and covered up aspects of our personalities that were not welcome in our families of origin, leading to the self–alienation we discussed in Chapter Four. And in adulthood, most of us still carry a pervasive shame about our perceived inadequacies, especially about our attractions toward other men. The result is that much of who we are is either banished or rejected.

> On an unconscious level, we miss our split–off parts. We also long to embrace the known but rejected parts of ourselves.

This self–hatred can create an inner loneliness. On an unconscious level, we miss our split–off parts. We also long to embrace the known but rejected parts of ourselves. This inner loneliness may be matched and compounded by an outer loneliness. Because of our self–hatred, we often isolate ourselves from those around us since we're sure that, if they really knew us, they'd hate us as much as we hate ourselves. So we experience a double loneliness—lonely inside and lonely outside—leaving us feeling completely alone.

Hatred, shame, splitting, and rejection—these are the very conditions that fragmented our wholeness and created the problems we are trying to overcome. As Einstein said, "The significant problems we face in life cannot be solved at the same level of thinking we were at when we created them." Thus, if we are ever to heal our lives and live in a state of happiness, we have to raise ourselves to a higher level of thinking about ourselves. We must develop genuine self–love. But that love can't be fragmentary. It has to be whole and unconditional. So self–love requires that we unify our inner kingdom by owning and integrating all aspects of our true selves. In the next three sections I'll discuss ways of accomplishing this. ✍ 11.13

Invite Back Split–off Parts

The split–off parts that lie hidden behind our false selves become "sub–personalities" within us. Most of us are just vaguely aware of their existence, noticing them only when they intrude as sudden shifts of emotion, attitude, or behavior. These sub–personalities can operate beneath our awareness, pursuing agendas very different from that of our dominant personality. To become whole, we have to retrieve these split–off parts, welcoming them back into a complete, true self.

> Sub–personalities can operate beneath our awareness, pursuing agendas very different from that of our dominant personality. To become whole, we have to retrieve these split–off parts.

A variety of methods exist for reintegrating aspects of our personalities of which we're unaware. Voice dialog is a formal process of communicating with disowned selves as if you were speaking with another person. Originally developed by psychologists Hal Stone and Sidra Stone in the 1970s, voice dialog has become a relatively popular method. Their book, *Embracing Our Selves: the Voice Dialogue Manual*, provides ample instruction to help you do this process on your own.

Similarly, inner child work attempts to access the true self that was lost in childhood. This method assists in working through traumatic memories and reconnecting to the strengths, gifts, and perspectives that are innate to us but have been lost for many years. Many resources have become available on inner child work since Charles Whitfield, M.D., wrote the original book on this topic, *Healing the Child Within*. An internet search will quickly bring up a number of book titles.

Some individuals have split off parts of themselves in a more literal sense. In Chapter Four I discussed dissociation, which is a disruption in consciousness, or a separation of one part of the self from other parts. There are many different types of dissociation. The simplest and most common would be "zoning out." In more advanced forms of dissociation a person has aspects of himself that function or act differently from the rest of himself. This is commonly referred to as having a "split personality." Many people who struggle with addiction experience something like this through their "Dr. Jekyll and Mr. Hyde" behaviors. In the most advanced form of dissociation, an individual is partially or completely unaware of the existence of his sub–personalities. This is referred to as dissociative identity disorder. If you have a sense that you are dealing with parts of yourself that you can't fully account for and that cause you distress, I encourage you to speak with a licensed mental health professional as soon as possible. ✎ 11.14

Own Our Projections

In Chapter Nine we discussed Robert Bly's five–stage process of integrating the shadow. The fifth stage is called "retrieving the shadow." In *A Little Book on the Human Shadow*, Bly wrote that "this long process amounts to the state of mind in which we retrieve the giant, retrieve the hero, retrieve the witch, retrieve the wicked child…. Eating our shadow is a very slow process. It doesn't happen once but hundreds of times."

The process of retrieving our shadows isn't intended to return us to the innocent childhood state of having a "three–hundred–sixty degree personality," which Bly describes in his book. Nor would we want to return there. The original child personality has no boundaries at all, which is why he can straight out tell grandma that her purple hair looks funny and her perfume makes him sick. Rather, our aim is to integrate our native energies and capacities so they are available to us for conscious and intentional use according to the design of the King—in balance and moderation.

For specific suggestions on owning and integrating projections, return to the final pages of Chapter Nine. ✎ 11.15

Integrate Our Archetypal Shadows

The blueprint of your masculine psyche, which this book has tried to illustrate through the four archetypes, gives you a guide to find what's missing and what's out of balance. A study of the design of the archetypes, together with self–awareness and introspection, can help you understand what you've done with your archetypal capacities. This will enable you to find those that are missing and integrate them.

"This long process amounts to the state of mind in which we retrieve the giant, retrieve the hero, retrieve the witch, retrieve the wicked child."

Robert Bly

A study of the design of the archetypes can help you understand what you've done with your archetypal capacities.

Wholeness comes from understanding and developing each capacity and trait while also balancing and integrating them. I described this in Chapter One as being a compound wholeness. There I compared the balancing of archetypal energies to the perfect day where the breeze is cool but the sun is warm, or the twenty–four–hour cycle where the day enables action and the night enables rest. When balanced, these energies become something more than their constituent components—the perfect day isn't experienced as the bitterness of cold and the oppression of heat because together those opposing qualities balance and complement each other.

We really need the synergistic potential of each archetypal capacity. We need to be able to live in the synergistic bipolar tension that inevitably exists between the opposing tendencies of these traits. Once understood, and with a little practice, this isn't a difficult thing to do. It's something you can do on your own. And the freedom, capacity, and sense of mastery that come from developing this ability are tremendous. It's an essential route to the whole self. Truly it is a lifelong process and will never quite be finished. But much of the joy and interest in life comes through the journey itself. Below are two specific methods that may be useful for integrating archetypal shadows.

Active Imagination Dialogue: In the conclusion of their book, *King Warrior Magician Lover*, Moore and Gillette describe a method they call "Active Imagination Dialogue," which is very similar to Voice Dialogue. This is essentially a journaling technique where you give the shadow a voice and let him speak. And you speak back to him. For example, if you were trying to integrate an angry, sadistic shadow, you would write questions to him and then write his responses. Or perhaps you might be trying to integrate two opposing traits, such as a Tyrant and a Weakling. These two parts might write to one another.

This is essentially a journaling technique where you give the shadow a voice and let him speak.

The purpose is to create understanding of and between these parts, and perhaps to arrive at some concessions or agreements that might make our lives easier and more integrated. Some cautions are in order. Moore and Gillette warn about the possibility of running into hostile inner parts, which may require the help of a trained therapist to handle and integrate. I would add the caution that if Chapter Four revealed that you have issues with posttraumatic disturbance or dissociation, this process may not be wise for you to do on your own. Also, if Chapter Four showed you have a strong tendency toward obsessive–compulsive disorder (OCD) or obsessive–compulsive personality disorder (OCPD), you may find this process somewhat less effective.

Shadow Integration: Once a shadow has become clear in your mind, it can be integrated with its polar opposite using vivid imagination. The same cautions described previously apply to this process as well. Particularly, I have noticed that this method of processing tends not to be effective for men with strong symptoms of OCD or OCPD.

This process is best done in a relaxed and meditative state with eyes closed. It is important that the conscious mind—which analyzes, reasons, and plans—is quiet so that the spontaneous, imaginative unconscious self can do its work.

Imagine the Shadow, using the five senses.

Begin by picturing the shadow part of yourself standing out in front of you. We will call this part the Shadow. Picture it as clearly as possible. Notice its body and the way it stands and moves. Look at its face and particularly at its eyes. Now try to experience the Shadow through as many of your other five senses as possible. Hear its voice or the sounds it makes. Imagine what the Shadow is feeling. Imagine what it would feel like if you touched it. Try to associate a smell and taste to the Shadow if you can. The more fully and vividly you can experience it the better.

Next, imagine that the Shadow is like a magnet, pulling out of your body and mind every feeling, thought, and trait that supports or resonates with the Shadow. Experience that until it feels as though your body and mind are completely empty of traits belonging to the Shadow and the Shadow is fully formed.

Imagine the Opposite Shadow, using the five senses.

Now, imagine the Opposite Shadow standing out in front of you next to the Shadow. For example, if the Shadow you imagined was an addict, you might now imagine an impotent self as the Opposite Shadow. Imagine a vertical line separating the two. Follow the same process as previously to create a fully formed Opposite Shadow: experience it with the five senses and let it become magnetic and pull out of you everything that supports or resonates with it.

Invite your Higher Power and connect him to your Shadow and Opposite Shadow.

When that is complete, imagine the presence of your Higher Power above and between the Shadow and the Opposite Shadow, forming a triangle with them. Visualize beams of intense white light coming out of your Higher Power and connecting the two shadows together. Specifically, imagine the beams of light

392

connecting the minds, hearts, bodies, and souls of the two shadows. Now just watch what happens and allow plenty of time. Typically, the two shadows will integrate or merge in some way.

If they merge together on one side of the line, this means there is still another opposite that needs to be integrated. Invite that other opposite out of you using the same method as before. You may not know what that opposite is, so just relax your mind and watch what comes out. Then allow your Higher Power to connect these opposites with beams of light in the same four places and watch for them to integrate.

Allow them to merge.

If the opposites merge in the middle, replacing the line, then you know the process of integration is complete. Imagine beams of light coming from your Higher Power and connecting this newly integrated part into your own mind, heart, body, and soul. Imagine that the part is being integrated into every part of you using as many of your senses as possible. Once you feel the part is fully integrated, the process is complete. ✍ 11.16

THE KING'S VOW

Admitting that our old life doesn't work and accepting that it's over; relinquishing every weapon that we've used against our own wellbeing and wholeness; choosing, of our own free will, to change the object of our faith and trust in a new way of living; then working to restore our Self to its original design: this is the process of surrender.

Transcending this whole process is the power greater than our own to which we surrender. There are many levels of greater powers—the greater strength of my men's group, the greater experience of my therapist, the greater capacity of my psyche to heal itself, the greater force of my needs and emotions, the greater wisdom of my Self, and the omnipotence of my Higher Power. All of these are synergistic in that they may cooperate with our own activity in the process of our spiritual regeneration.

For God and the whole

In the allegory, the king's vow, "For God and the whole," was the turning point in restoring his nation. With this synergistic vow, the king acknowledged his continuing commitment to do his part in healing the kingdom. He also demonstrated his humility and recognition that he is dependent on the pattern of wholeness that can only be supplied by his Higher Power.

¹ The concept of thinking errors is articulated by David Burns in The Feeling Good Handbook.

CHAPTER 12

WHOLENESS

Seek him that maketh the seven stars and Orion, and turneth the
shadow of death into the morning and maketh the day dark with night:
that calleth for the waters of the sea, and poureth them out upon the
face of the earth: The Lord is his name.

Amos 5:8, *KJV*

n case I haven't sufficiently overemphasized this point—because
it's deserving of great overemphasis—it is in the King that all things
meet. This archetype represents the turning point of the world
where the synergism of all archetypes come together and which, as
axis mundi, connects us to the powers beyond our own. The four
archetypes—centered, balanced, moderated, and integrated by the King—are the
blueprint of who we're designed to be at our very best—the source of our whole
and unfragmented Self.

Why is this worthy of such overemphasis? To remind you that you have a King
within you whose purpose and ability it is to make you whole. In *The King Within*,
Moore and Gillette describe the King as the one who dances the four quarters.
"When he is dancing," they write, "he is accessing himself and the Warrior,
Magian, and Lover in a balanced and generative way. He is balancing the four into
one generative unity."

Metaphorically, they are describing a man "dancing" among the four chief aspects
of his psyche, accessing, balancing, moderating, integrating, and organizing all
parts of himself. One might also use the metaphor of weaving together strands of

various capacities into a whole self. Put succinctly, this dance creates, maintains, and expands synergy. Without this dance, a man gradually slides into his shadows.

The metaphor doesn't describe the King as *wrestling* the four quarters or *forcing* them, but rather *dancing* among them. And Moore and Gillette say that the dance is done "*playfully.*" "[T]he psyche that has reached this stage of maturity can't help but take pleasure in itself, and all the things of creation," they say. So it isn't through force or excessive energy that the King keeps his world in creation. It isn't through fear or shame that he balances, moderates, integrates, and organizes. Rather, he does his synergistic dance from the sheer joy of becoming a whole self. The process is one of liberation. If it feels like drudgery or a burden, it's being driven by a shadow.

> Humanity is one species with two genders. We can't experience true wholeness if we appreciate only one half.

But wholeness doesn't end with the self. It reaches out to the feminine as our opposite and embraces her as well—both as Anima and as living woman. Humanity is one species with two genders. We can't experience true wholeness if we appreciate only one half. This doesn't mean that every man must settle down and make a home with a woman in order to be whole. We may experience that "harmonic resonance" with the feminine in any number of ways outside of an intimate relationship. If we wish to fully appreciate our masculinity, it's necessary for us to experience it in contrast with a woman's femininity.

HEAR THE CALL

Traits of the King archetype exist in both shadow and wholeness on many levels. We have explored in depth how he exists as the governing principle within our own psyche. He also exists in the father's role as a provider and leader within his family. He exists in the business world on every level of management. He exists in organized crime as gang leaders, mafia bosses, and drug lords. He exists in governments and militaries as presidents, ministers, generals, commanders, and literal kings. And he exists in religions as clergy, rabbis, and imams. These all represent various levels of lower kings. Above all of these, the great and central archetype exists in the form of the Higher Power, whatever that Power may actually be.

On each of these levels, this King offers us a paradigm of governance, more or less clear and pure. The higher we look for a pattern by which to live our lives, the higher will be the pattern of our existence. Unfortunately, it's the lowest patterns that are most visible and accessible because it's those patterns that exist so abundantly in our world. Because of this, it's the lowest patterns that are most often lived.

If we're to attain anything higher or more transcendent than these ways, we'll have to look harder—and higher. We'll have to look with different eyes than those of the average man. Only by so doing can we ever manifest anything close to the fullness of our potential. And it's that full potential that our inner King wants us to become—and which our Highest King calls us to become. Our world has an overabundance of average men—men who are simply living out the patterns provided by the lower kings. Most of these men are essentially good, but we have enough of them. You are called to be something more.

> Our world has an overabundance of average men. You are called to be something more.

Some of you may be enlivened, inspired, and set on fire by reading those words. You already knew that you were called to something higher. You already felt the voice of a King beckoning you. Since you already hear the call, my only advice to you is to continue to listen and to follow.

Others reading this may be feeling fear. If it's fear you're feeling, it's undoubtedly because something in you knows that what I'm saying is true—that you indeed are called to become something more than the average man and something far beyond the way you're currently living. To you, I suggest that Chapter Eleven is of particular importance for your continued consideration. Your first task is to determine what you will choose to trust and make the object of your faith. Will it be your lower self? The easy self? The fear-based self? If you really listen to what your fear is telling you, you already know those choices will never do. Remember, fear is the gateway emotion to initiation: you have already been called. You will continue to feel the fear—and you will continue to resist that fear through your usual shadows—until you accept the king's vow and step through the fear.

> Your first task is to determine what you will choose to trust and make the object of your faith.

The rest of you reading this are probably feeling doubt. Doubt shows up in many ways, and we weave many stories around it in order to justify it. But if we undress the doubt, we'll see that it's really just avoidance of a truth that awaits us. We don't doubt things that our deepest consciousness knows are not true. We simply dismiss those things. For example, I don't doubt Santa Claus—I dismiss the concept altogether. We only doubt the things that some part of us believes are true. If you knew that what I've been saying throughout this book was completely false—like Santa Clause—you would never have persevered to this point and this sentence would be in the trash instead of in front of your eyes. So part of you knows that what I'm saying is true. But another part of you is avoiding that truth—and probably using various weapons against wholeness to help you avoid it.

What is the truth you're avoiding?

What is the truth you're avoiding? Your Magian knows what it is. Your King perceives it in his center. Your Lover feels it in his body. And your Warrior wants to fight for it. It probably has something to do with your highest potential and your Higher Power's intention for you to reach it. Like the men feeling fear, you will continue to be troubled by your doubt—and you will continue to react to it in shadowy ways—until you square yourself with the truth, surrender your doubt, and choose a new object of faith. Like Jonah, you can run but you can't hide. I have a simple invitation for you: this is your call. Your whale is waiting.

FOUR KEY TRAITS FOR GROWTH

Four Key Traits for Growth

- Desire
- Curious consciousness
- Love the self
- Discipline

I suggest that the King within us must access just four simple traits in order to dance successfully among the four quarters. These might be considered key traits that can, when accessed in combination with one another, unlock everything else we've been discussing in this book. The King accesses these traits from the other three archetypes: two from the Lover and one each from the Magian and Warrior.

The first and most basic trait is accessed from the Lover's libido. This is the trait of *desire*—specifically our sincere and strong interest in experiencing ourselves as whole and authentic men. It's essential that the focus of the desire be positively aimed at the good thing we're becoming. If our desire is focused on something negative, the power of that desire will simply reinforce the very negative results from which we're trying to escape. For example, if our strongest desire is to *not* be in pain, or to *not* be unworthy or to *not* be homosexual, the results will likely be that we'll continue to experience all three of these unwanted things. Instead, we need to turn ourselves around mentally and focus our Lover's libido on desiring the whole man we're becoming. This is in harmony with the law that Thought Becomes Reality, also called the Law of Attraction.

The second trait is accessed from the Magian. It's his trait of *curious consciousness*—being awake and aware of ourselves with an interest in knowing and understanding more. Curiosity demands openness and a welcoming attitude toward new discovery—in this case self-discovery. This is the opposite of the shaming reactions many of us tend to have when new information is revealed about our shadows. The shaming mind says, "I can't believe I did that, I'm such an idiot. Cover it up and forget about it!" The curiously conscious mind says, "Wow, that's really interesting that I reacted that way. I wonder what that was about?"

The third trait is accessed again from the Lover. It's his ability to unconditionally and uncompromisingly *love the self*. This self–love is always and only accomplished when we're free of manipulative and masochistic self–judgments and shame. Unconditional love of self can be confusing for men who sincerely want to change themselves because it may sound like acceptance of faults and shadows. The proper perspective on this type of love can be compared to the love that a mature parent has for a small child. We love them even when they throw up on us. We can continue to love them through several years of these kinds of inconveniences because we can separate the child from the behavior. Our love for them isn't permission for them to continue to throw up on us. Rather, we discipline and teach them as they grow into responsible adults.

The fourth trait is accessed from the Warrior. It's that archetype's *discipline*—his commitment to the rigors that are necessary in order to develop mastery over himself. Through this discipline, we keep ourselves focused on making choices that are increasingly more in keeping with our intentions and our hopes for a whole self. The Warrior's discipline is never compulsive, shaming, or hurtful to us. It's always done with great patience and compassion.

SERVANT LEADERSHIP

As conscious men we must not waste our new–found capacities on merely meeting our own needs. We haven't been given the gift of struggle so that we can indulge ourselves in a life of cure–seeking—or worse, a life of self–pity. We are the stewards of the gold behind our own shadows. If we're to ever truly be men, we must spend that gold in the service of our fellow brothers and sisters and of the planet as a whole.

All of the archetypes in their whole form have as their main aim to serve or seek something greater than themselves. The Warrior serves the transpersonal other, which is essentially the King himself. The Magian serves those he initiates into higher understanding. He also serves the King. The King in turn serves the people of his realm and the Higher Power for which he acts as axis mundi. Even the Lover seeks something outside himself through his desire for union and relationship with another. I believe that we can't fully escape the pull of our shadows until we put ourselves in service to something bigger than ourselves.

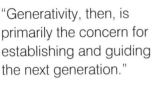

"Generativity, then, is primarily the concern for establishing and guiding the next generation."
Erik Erikson

The developmental psychologist Erik Erikson, in his book, *Identity: Youth and Crisis*, wrote of the developmental stages humans experience over their life span. During childhood, adolescence, and young adulthood, those stages are all oriented around the development of a solid self that can function in relationships with others. Once that self has emerged, the individual naturally moves into the next stage, called generativity. "*Generativity*, then, is primarily the concern for establishing and guiding the next generation." Moore and Gillette expand on this concept. In *The King Within* they write: "Generativity means primarily a concern for the future." They explain that there is a range of "degrees of generativity" from home and family, to community, to the world as a whole. Then they call us to action: "It is time we started to move away from being concerned only for the individual and move toward a more encompassing concern."

The wisdom of the *Tao* teaches these same principles. Consider the following from John Heider's book *The Tao of Leadership*, which is a modern adaptation of the ancient *Tao Te Ching* by Lao Tzu: "True self–interest teaches selflessness. Heaven and earth endure because they are not simply selfish but exist in behalf of all creation…. Enlightened leadership is service, not selfishness. The leader grows more and lasts longer by placing the well–being of all above the well–being of self alone."

Jesus washes Peter's feet

The life and teachings of Jesus exemplify this principle completely. He said, "For I came down from heaven, not to do mine own will, but the will of him that sent me" (John 6: 38). In *The New Testament* record of his life, he reiterates this same message many other times. His actions were constantly those of a servant leader. He spent his entire ministry teaching and serving others, he washed the feet of his disciples, and ultimately he suffered the pain of all to provide a universal atonement.

The book, *He*, by Robert Johnson makes these points eloquently. The book follows the ancient folktale of *Parsifal*, who begins life as a fool but becomes a great knight. I described Parsifal's relationship with Blanche Fleur—his Anima—in Chapter Six. The latter half of the story tells how Parsifal spends his adult life in service to King Arthur seeking the Holy Grail. The Grail is said to possess the power to

400

fulfill every want even before it's spoken. It's a source of tremendous healing and abundance. Earlier in Parsifal's quest, a wise mentor had taught him that when he finds the Grail Castle he must ask an all–important, though mysterious, question: "Whom does the Grail serve?" But the mentor doesn't explain the purpose or significance of the question.

Many years later, Parsifal finds and enters the Grail Castle and wisely asks the mysterious question. At this point in the story, Johnson interprets the significance of this question. He tells us that it "is the most profound question one can ask." This simple–sounding question is really asking, "Where is the center of gravity of a human personality; or where is the center of meaning in a human life?" He explains that it is the *asking* of the question that is so significant, because in the act of asking, a man demonstrates his awareness that the Grail—the great source of all gifts—does *not* serve him. Asking shows that the asker recognizes that the abundance of life is meant to be spent in pursuit of something beyond himself.

This is reminiscent of the Buddha's teaching on cravings, which we discussed in Chapter Two. Buddha taught that fulfilling our cravings through self–indulgence doesn't bring joy because cravings can only lead to suffering. In the language of *Parsifal*, asking the Grail to serve me will never result in true joy. Happiness, Buddha said, results from surrendering our cravings and thus eliminating our suffering.

Robert Johnson's interpretation of *Parsifal* takes this teaching a step further. Returning to the story: as soon as Parsifal asks the mysterious question, a voice echoes through the Grail Castle saying, "The Grail serves the Grail King." The Grail King is synonymous with the concepts of "Higher Power," "higher purpose," and "Self" as I've been using them throughout this book. Johnson is teaching us that the true and proper use of the Grail—the source of all good in our lives—is to use its abundance in the service of something greater than our own lower selves. He's reminding us that we're not the center of the universe. "The object of life is not happiness," Johnson says, "but to serve God or the Grail." And he follows that unconventional statement with an even harder wisdom: "If one understands this and drops his idiotic notion that the meaning of life is personal happiness, then one will find that elusive quality immediately at hand." Placing this in more conventional language, I would say that happiness will elude us if we try to pursue it directly. But it will be our immediate experience when we use the Grail in the service of things greater than ourselves.

Much of the growth I've personally experienced over the past twenty years since I began my journey out of same–sex attraction has come through the work I've done in my roles as a therapist, writer, and co–creator of healing experiences. In part, this has been because my service has been specifically related to the realm of healing—I've been healing myself through helping others. But much of my growth has been fueled by the awareness that others needed my strength and my example. So I've tried, in my own faltering way, to live up to those expectations. I encourage you to find a cause that needs *you*. Not just a cause that needs another "warm body," but a cause that needs *you* specifically—your gifts, your perspective, your life experience.

WHAT IS A WHOLE MAN?

I began this book with a question: "What *is* a whole man?" In truth, this is a question few males in our age can answer. To begin with, wholeness means living the fullness of our masculine potential. This implies that all of the essential traits represented by the four archetypes are online and active, integrated into a functioning and unified self. It also implies some type of connection with the feminine—our opposite and other half. And it implies alignment with, and service to, a power or purpose higher than ourselves.

As we learned from our study of the Magian, our mission is to first transform our own lives and then to initiate others. This book has been your call to that transformation. But none of what I've taught you will be of any real use if you don't make it active in your life. Change will only come as you move the knowledge that's in your head downward into your chest, your guts, and your limbs through action. You will have to put what you've learned here to work. I encourage you to choose to believe that *right now* is the perfect time to do that. So, what is a whole man? The journey of your life is to become the answer to that question. What's your next step? ✍ 12.1 - 6

BIBLIOGRAPHY

Allen, James. *As a Man Thinketh*. Cornerstone Books (Online), written in 1902.

American Psychiatric Association: Diagnostic and Statistical Manual of Mental Disorders, Fifth Edition. Arlington, VA: American Psychiatric Association, 2013.

Balfour, Patrick (Lord Kinross). *Love conquers all* in *Books and Bookmen*, vol. 20. Oxford, England. 1974.

Bly, Robert. *A Little Book on the Human Shadow*. San Francisco, CA: Harper San Francisco, 1988.

Bly, Robert. *Iron John: A Book About Men*. New York City, NY: Addison–Wesley Publishing Company, Inc., 1991.

Bradshaw, John. *Healing the Shame That Binds You*. Deerfield Beach, FL: Health Communications, Inc., 1988.

Buddha. *The Four Noble Truths*. Public domain.

Buddha. *The Noble Eightfold Path*. Public domain.

Buechner, Frederick. *Wishful Thinking*. New York City, NY: HarperCollins Publishers, 1973.

Burns, David. *The Feeling Good Handbook*. New York City, NY: Penguin Group, 1999.

Carnes, Patrick, J., PhD. *A Gentle Path Through the Twelve Steps*. Center City, MN: Hazelden, 1994.

Deida, David. *The Way of the Superior Man: A Spiritual Guide to Mastering the Challenges of Women, Work, and Sexual Desire*. Boulder, CO: Sounds True, Inc., 2004.

Eldridge, John. *Walking With God*. Nashville, TN: Thomas Nelson, Inc., 2008.

Eldridge, John. *Wild at Heart*. Nashville, TN: Thomas Nelson, Inc., 2001.

Epictetus. *Discourses of Epictetus, with the Enchiridion and Fragments.* Trans. by George Long, New York City, NY: A. L. Burt, 2004.

Erikson, Erik H. *Identity: Youth and Crisis.* New York City, NY: W. W. Norton & Company, Inc., 1968.

Fosha, Diana. *The Transforming Power of Affect: A Model for Accelerated Change.* New York City, NY: Basic Books, 2000.

Fossum, Merle A., and Marilyn J. Mason. *Facing Shame: Families in Recovery.* New York City, NY: W. W. Norton & Company, Inc., 1986.

Gurian, Michael. *The Wonder of Boys.* New York City, NY: Tarcher/Putnam, 1997.

Heider, John. *The Tao of Leadership.* Lake Worth, FL: Humanics New Age, 1985.

Householder, Leslie. *Hidden Treasures.* Mesa, AZ: ThoughtsAlive Books, 2005.

Ibson, John. *Picturing Men: A Century of Male Relationships in Everyday American Photography.* Chicago, IL: The University of Chicago Press, 2002.

Johnson, Robert A. *He: Understanding Masculine Psychology.* New York City, NY: Harper & Row, 1989.

Jung, Carl. *The Portable Jung.* New York City, NY: Penguin Books, 1971.

Konrad, Jeff. *You Don't Have to be Gay.* Newport Beach, CA: Pacific Publishing House, 1987.

Logan, John. *The Last Samurai.* Script, 2003.

Merriam–Webster's Third New International Dictionary, Unabridged, http://unabridged.merriam–webster.com.

Moberly, Elizabeth. *Homosexuality: A New Christian Ethic.* Cambridge, England: James Clarke & Co. Ltd, 1983.

Moore, Robert and Douglas Gillette. *King, Warrior, Magician, Lover: Rediscovering the Archetypes of the Mature Masculine.* New York City, NY: HarperCollins, 1991.

Moore, Robert and Douglas Gillette. *The King Within: Accessing the King in the Male Psyche.* New York City, NY: William Morrow and Company, Inc., 1992.

Moore, Robert and Douglas Gillette. *The Lover Within: Accessing the Lover in the Male Psyche.* New York City, NY: Avon Books, 1993.

Moore, Robert and Douglas Gillette. *The Magician Within: Accessing the Shaman in the Male Psyche*. New York City, NY: Avon Books, 1994.

Moore, Robert and Douglas Gillette. *The Warrior Within: Accessing the Knight in the Male Psyche*. New York City, NY: Avon Books, 1993.

Nicolosi, Joseph. *Reparative Therapy of Male Homosexuality: A New Clinical Approach*. Lanham, MD: Rowman and Littlefield Publishers, 1991.

Ortberg, John. *Overcoming Your Shadow Mission*. Grand Rapids, MI: Zondervan, 2008.

Pittman, Frank. *Man Enough*. New York City, NY: The Berkley Publishing Group, 1993.

Reber, Arthur S. *The Penguin Dictionary of Psychology*. London: Penguin Books, 2001.

Stoller, Robert J. *Presentations of Gender*. New Haven, CT: Yale University Press, 1992.

Stoller, Robert J. *Sexual Excitement: The Dynamics of Erotic Life*. New York City, NY: Pantheon Books, 1979.

Stone, Hal and Sidra L. Stone. *Embracing Our Selves: The Voice Dialogue Manual*. Novato, CA: Nataraj Publishing, 1989.

Trent, John and Gary Smalley. *The Blessing*. Nashville, TN: Thomas Nelson, Inc., 2004.

Twerski, Abraham. *Addictive Thinking: Understanding Self–Deception*. New York City, NY: HarperCollins Publishers, 1990.

Tzu, Lao. *Tao Te Ching*, Trans. by J. H. McDonald. Public Domain. Available at http://abuddhistlibrary.com/Buddhism.

Wattles, Wallace D. *The Science of Getting Rich*. Blacksburg, VA: Thrifty Books, 2009.

Whitfield, Charles, M.D., *Healing the Child Within*. Deerfield Beach, FL: Health Communications, Inc., 2006.

Picture Credits

Creative Commons: Page 143

GNU Free Documentation License: Page 39

iStockPhoto (Disclaimer: Individuals pictured are models and are used for illustrative purposes only): Pages 3, 4, 8, 13, 15, 19, 22, 64, 71, 77, 79, 82, 85, 87, 96, 98, 103, 127, 133, 140, 149, 174, 181, 191, 199, 202, 205, 208, 215, 256, 262, 267, 271, 278, 283, 303, 310, 328, 335, 340, 342, 356, 395, 401

Public Domain: Pages 75, 98, 223, 246, 253, 349, 351, 368, 381

Wikimedia Commons: Pages 2, 11, 29, 36, 39, 54, 59, 88, 154, 159, 166, 195, 227, 234, 240, 314, 400

Made in the USA
San Bernardino, CA
09 November 2013